Drive On

The Uncensored War of Bedouin Bob

and the All-Americans

Robert J. Dvorchak

TACTI6AL

Drive On
Copyright © 2016 by Robert J. Dvorchak

First Edition

Because of the dynamic nature of the internet, any web address or links contained in this book may have changed since publication and may no longer be valid.

Brand names, trademarks, and service marks appearing in this book are the intellectual property of their respective owners.

The views expressed in this work are solely those of the author and do not necessarily reflect the views of the publisher, and the publisher hereby disclaims any responsibility for them.

Published by Tactical 16, LLC
Colorado Springs, CO

eISBN: 978-1-943226-19-1
ISBN: 978-1-943226-20-7 (hc)
ISBN: 978-1-943226-21-4 (sc)

Printed in the United States of America

Dedicated to every American who has worn the uniform with honor, especially my Army brothers in the Falcon Brigade of the 82nd Airborne Division and The Nasty Boys of Bravo Company, for having crossed a line of departure onto a battlefield.

CONTENTS

PROLOGUE
Story of Stories

I tried to bury something a long time ago, but like an unexpressed secret that haunts the soul, it kept coming back in flashbacks and regrets until the only way to find peace was to exhume it and put it into words. Down the basement steps, through the door to the attached garage, in a file cabinet against the far wall was a bundle of dust-covered notebooks dating back a quarter of a century. Scribbled inside was an unpublished journal of a war waged in a place where the first civilization wrote things down with inscriptions on clay tablets, the same place where images of journalists having their throats slashed in unresolved conflicts are flashed instantaneously on the worldwide computer network. Failing to publish that journal would mean going to my grave as a voice in the desert, an unacceptable fate for one who made a living writing stories, especially since the heart of the experience is how I joined the 82nd Airborne Division, the motivated, dedicated Army organization that lives by the creed *Airborne All The Way*. Either get the job done or die trying.

The journal started out during the assignment of a lifetime, when going to war was a great adventure. In the heyday of print journalism, I had a prized job on the payroll of the world's largest news agency, headquartered in the media capital of New York City, on call to go anywhere at a moment's notice on the company's tab as a newshound whose purpose in life was to track down stories and bring them home. The job description of a national writer for The Associated Press usually meant going to places struck by disaster, like catching the first available flight to Charleston, South Carolina, after Hurricane Hugo or to San Francisco after an earthquake disrupted the 1989 World Series. My peers and I called it parachuting into a story. For me, it was a front row seat to history, and somebody actually paid me to do it.

As summer gave way to autumn in 1990, the biggest story in the world was the gathering of American and allied forces on the Arabian Peninsula to confront the marauding army of Iraq, which had lit the fuse of war by invading and swallowing up neighboring Kuwait.

The thought had crossed my mind about what it would be like to cover a war. On a big story, there are only two places to be — on the front lines or anywhere else. It's like the old joke about the difference between being involved or being committed. For a breakfast of eggs and bacon, the chicken was involved, but the pig was committed. In the early days of the crisis, I was merely involved. A disruption of the status quo in the tinderbox of the Middle East created an oil crisis that was like a gun pointed to America's head in the shape of a gas nozzle. World leaders condemned the aggression, and the American military was ordered to respond with the largest deployment of forces since the Vietnam War. Logisticians had moved the equivalent of the population of Richmond, Virginia, along with combat and support equipment, to makeshift camps in the Saudi Arabian desert. More reservists had been called to active duty than at any time since the Korean War. The national mood ranged from a hand-made sign hung on an overpass in Georgia that said "Kick Their Ass and Get The Gas" to the cadence of pacifists in Seattle chanting "Hell, no, we won't go, we won't die for Texaco." Mindful of the hostile treatment shown to those who served in Vietnam, everyday citizens created grass-roots drives such as Operation Something From Home to send necessities, such as lip balm and chewing gum to playing cards and moist towelettes, to troops hunkered down thousands of miles from home. "They'll perform a lot better knowing the country is behind them and that no rotten vegetables will be thrown at them when they return home," said organizer David Heard of Manassas, Virginia, a veteran of Korea and Vietnam who had two sons serving in the Persian Gulf.

Then everything changed on the first Monday of October. While working the phones at my desk and doing the grunt work journalists do, the boss walked by. A family emergency forced the recall of a veteran AP staffer who had been sent off to ground zero, and a replacement was needed. The AP's executive editor, who was a combination of top news authority and commander-in-chief, emerged from the morning news meeting and was on his way back to his corner office. Instead of stars on his uniform collar, he wore the dress-for-success fashions that were *de rigueur* for someone of his rank — leather suspenders, those starched blue shirts with the contrasting white collar and a power yellow necktie. He used to say things like, "If it ain't broke, break it." And those of us under his command whispered that once you got to know him, he had the heart of a little boy, which he kept in a jar on his desk. One noticeable thing about him was a stiff gait, the result of a back injury suffered in his second tour as an Army officer in Vietnam.

"Bob, I want you to go to Saudi Arabia," he said in his most matter-of-fact tone.

"For how long? Two weeks? Two months? Two years?" I asked.

"For as long as it takes," he replied, without breaking stride.

The AP's headquarters, then located at Rockefeller Center in Mid-Town Manhattan, consisted of a warren of international, national, financial, photo and sports departments. From around the world or around the block, four million words of copy a day came in from various bureaus to be edited and packaged by priority in New York, and four million words went out over the wires for use by newspapers, TV stations and broadcast outlets. The wires churned day and night, every day of the year. The inside joke was that if a neutron bomb wiped out everybody in the building, those wires would somehow still hum. At the moment, however, everything seemed to stop. Reporters are trained to operate at arm's-length detachment, and outwardly, I was as expressionless as any other time I was asked to catch the first available plane to begin an assignment. Inwardly, however, I pumped my fist and said, "Yessssssss!"

Go to war? In the insane world of journalism, stories are best when circumstances are worst, and what could be worse than a war. I didn't start it. I wouldn't fight it. But if someone was crazy enough to draw the sword, my job was to get as close to the action as possible. I had never left the States before, even during my service in the U.S. Army, but it made sense that one of the reasons the assignment landed on my shoulders was that my personnel file included a honorable discharge. Military service was part of my family history. My father battled Japanese suicide bombers known as kamikazes from his gun mount aboard the *USS Appalachian* during World War II, and he pulled shore patrol in the atomic ashes of Hiroshima. My oldest brother was a Vietnam combat veteran, receiving two Purple Hearts within ten days while serving with the Air Cavalry Troop of the Army's 11th Armored Cavalry Regiment. Now war beckoned again, and I could see it for myself.

Before he had taken another step, the boss said one last thing that defined this assignment as unique.

"Keep a journal," he said.

Like a good soldier, I followed orders, jotting down my own feelings and observations about heading off to a foreign land while recording the names and hometowns of those who battled the desert and confronted the Iraqi army. Even at its best, journalism is a rough first-draft of history. Because stories are reported piecemeal and often out of context, it's impossible to tell the story of a war while it's unfolding. In this war, only reporters who were assigned to media pools were authorized to be on the battlefield. Censorship imposed in the name of operational security, along with an unreliable delivery system, limited what news made it back from the front. The only way to communicate what really happened was to write when it was over.

One immutable truth is that war is a different experience for everybody, which means there are 700,000 versions of what happened in Desert Shield and Desert Storm. This one is mine. Journalists know better than anyone that nothing is older than yesterday's news, and war has a certain inevitability about it when the outcome is known. On the home front, viewers sat in front of their television sets to watch a sanitized version. My war wasn't on television. Scores of books have been written about it from the perspective of commanders and policy-makers, and in a better world, I wish nobody would ever have to write about war again. Nothing I've read, however, matched what I saw and felt while living with the privates, sergeants and combat officers who carried out the mission. If this helps in any way to understand what going to war is like, and if it helps to explain how America ultimately ended up in a war against religious radicals who kill in the name of God, it will have been worth the battle of going through it again. Still, the only thing tougher than going to war is writing about it.

Desert Storm wasn't the last war. It wasn't even the last war in Iraq. It's been called America's shortest war, but short or long is irrelevant. It was a single moment in time — a brief/long, shining/dark moment in time.

CHAPTER 1
Into The Unknown

When leaving home for a far-off land that few outsiders get to see, language and cultural barriers must be overcome. And that was just dealing with the foreign-born cabbie on the taxi ride to JFK International Airport. But seriously…It's Saturday, October 20, 1990, time to try out this one-man act on an overseas audience. Tourists, business people and assorted travelers are milling about an airport at the crossroads of the universe, but I'm the only one starting a journal. Departure time of 10 p.m. is four hours away. Hurry up and wait, just like in the Army. Travel papers include a visa to Saudi Arabia stamped inside my first-ever passport and a first-class ticket aboard KLM Airlines. The Associated Press has never been known for lavish spending. You can't spell cheap without AP. But the company had done all right by me, and it does book a first class seat on overseas flights, a much appreciated gesture for one bound for the unknown.

The circle of life never ceases to amaze. My first time aboard an airplane was to report for basic training at Fort Dix, New Jersey, as a raw recruit about to become the property of Uncle Sam. That was in 1973, almost 18 years ago. At least the regimented world of bad haircuts, olive drab uniforms and barking drill sergeants got me away from the farm I grew up on in southwestern Pennsylvania. The surge of power from the jet engines made an indelible impression and aroused a wanderlust that ultimately landed me in New York City for a career of jumping on and off planes to cover news stories. This time, I'm off to a military adventure as a P.F.C. — Proud Fucking Civilian.

What a time that was. Baby Boomers like to say that if you can remember the Sixties, you weren't really there. Yeah, and those ignorant of history are doomed to repeat it, and those who study history are doomed to watch everyone else repeat it. The enemy then was godless Communism, and my introduction to that Cold War began during the Cuban Missile Crisis when the nuns at St. Mary of the Nativity Roman Catholic Grade School in Uniontown, Pennsylvania, taught us to hide under our desks as the only defense against a nuclear attack. In other words, tuck your head between your legs and kiss your ass goodbye because the nuns dutifully said that none of us would survive a nuclear attack anyway. Coming of age in the years that followed meant keeping pace with a music revolution that ran the gamut from Doo-Wop to Motown to the British invasion to Woodstock, assassinations, race riots, the Great Society's war on poverty, a space race with a moon landing, free love, long-haired Hippy freaks, rejection of materialism, Earth Day, do your own thing, rebellion against authority, a generation gap and a credibility gap, in which the rule of thumb was don't trust anybody over 30. There was also that damned war in Vietnam. The law of the land required every male, upon reaching his 18th birthday, to register for the military draft. Not everyone was called by the Selective Service Administration, which came up with a lottery system that attached numbers to birthdays. We lucky bastards born on Christmas Eve in 1949 were assigned Number 95, the last number ever called in the last draft ever held during the transition to an all-volunteer force. It's the only lottery I've ever won. America's combat role in what was then its longest and most unpopular war had already ended when a draft notice from President Richard M. Nixon arrived in the mail. Uncle Sam still needed bodies in the ranks, and it was a young man's duty to serve if called, except for the draft-dodgers who burned their draft cards, or fled to Canada, or got phony medical excuses or strung out deferments that protected them from going because they had other priorities. Millions of other draftees did a lot more than me, but despite disagreement with the civilian masters who got us into that mess in the first place, I still believed in something bigger than myself and took the step forward.

Of the 250 trainees in Alpha Company, 4th Battalion, 2nd Combat Infantry Training Brigade, I was one of only two college grads in a hodge-podge of sad sacks and riff-raff who would have lasted mere minutes in combat. The fundamental lesson was to obey orders. Well, at least the lawful ones. Also taught was how to dress uniformly without violating the gig line and to step off smartly on the left foot in a proper military manner when ordered to march. Skills were acquired on how to put on a gas mask inside a gas chamber, fire an M-16 rifle and dig regulation foxholes. Every time we marched, we sang cadence. *"Ain't no use in going home. Jody's got your gal and gone...I wanna be an Airborne Ranger, live me a life of guts and dangers… If I die in a combat zone, box me up and ship me home."*

Drill sergeants gave up trying to pronounce my last name, opting instead to call me Alphabets or Eye-Chart. Helpful instruction included this gem: "Gentlemen, I do not piss in your ashtrays, so please do not throw your cigarette butts in my urinals. It makes them soggy and hard to light."

With no war to fight, I never fired a shot in anger or got farther from home than Fort Lee, Virginia, home of the Army's Quartermaster Corps, the supply command derisively known by the politically incorrect name as the Jewish infantry. TV sets in the day room of my barracks carried updates on the Watergate investigation that doomed Richard Nixon's presidency. Drug use in the Army, before testing became mandatory, may not have been as prevalent as it was on college campuses. But I hitched rides back home with a cook who dropped acid and fired up a joint before taking the wheel. To the grunts, I was a pogue, which rhymes with rogue and is Army slang for one on administrative duties who never faces the rigors of front-line duty. The basic rule in that Army was go along to get along, and never, under any circumstances, volunteer for anything. Still, a quote sometimes attributed to the Greek philosopher Socrates and sometimes to the 20th Century historian George Santayana notes that only the dead know the end of war. My drill sergeant, Willie E. Williams, phrased it this way: "Wars are like women, maggot. There's always another one coming along every couple of years." His preferred cadence song was *Check Out Your Mind* by The Impressions, the one thing I could relate to with the guys in the Smokey Bear hats. I did what I had to do to get an honorable discharge, no more, no less.

Anyway, almost three weeks have passed since the word came to go to Saudi Arabia, and everything is a blur. The first order of business was to get a passport, which meant I had to call my mom to get a copy of my birth certificate. She was less than thrilled to know why it was needed. I also called the ex and my two daughters living in Pittsburgh to say I loved them and to say I was leaving the country for an undetermined amount of time. Arrangements were made to mail my paychecks to them, with instructions on how to pay the rent on my apartment while I was away. A $10,000 cash advance from the company was what I would live on. The corporate credit card would cover big expenses. One comforting thought was that the AP doubled the indemnity on my life insurance policy to $100,000. The company nurse was upset with me, however. Southwest Asia is considered to be one of the unhealthiest regions in the world, and the State Department recommends a whole series of inoculations for U.S. citizens traveling there. Time restraints prevented me from getting them. Along with a scolding, the nurse shot me up with gamma globulin in my left buttock.

No accidental tourist, I have in my checked baggage a supply of notebooks, ink pens, stationery and a Radio Shack Trash 80 portable computer that wasn't wired for international use and would be of about as much practical use as a paper weight. Nothing beats military issue, and thanks to the big Army-Navy surplus store near Times Square, I shelled out expense account money for a backpack, a snug sleeping bag and plastic canteens, because the aluminum ones would heat up in the desert and burn the lips. Also packed were a military utility belt, floppy desert hat, goggles, a pair of Hi-Tech hiking boots and a Maglite flashlight with interchangeable red and yellow lenses because an unfiltered white light can be seen for miles in the desert. In addition to bug repellant, sunscreen and diarrhea medicine, I also carried a towel, because a hitch-hiker through the galaxy always carried a towel. The checklist included some baseball caps and key chains with the AP logo on them to barter as goodwill trinkets. My soldier of fortune wardrobe consists of tan shirts and khaki cargo pants from the big Banana Republic Store on 59th Street. Richard Pyle, the colleague I was replacing, provided tips on what to bring. We first met when I was in charge of the Harrisburg office, and he came in to help during the Three Mile Island nuclear accident. He had covered the fall of Saigon during Vietnam, and he was on the ground in Bahrain during the 1986 Tanker War, so he knew the lay of the land. Funny story. He told me not to bring any porn or booze because they are banned in Saudi Arabia. Although I never traveled with a porn collection, I reluctantly left behind a bottle of Jack Daniel's.

The one item I lacked was a gas mask, which was a must given the real threat that Iraq would use chemical weapons, known in the arms bazaars of the world as the poor man's atomic bomb. The boss said not to worry. The London bureau was shipping protective gear being bought from British Petroleum. The last time I had a gas mask was during Three Mile Island, but it was useless because the company failed to provide the activated charcoal filters that made the air safe to breathe.

The comedians on the foreign desk provided a list of helpful phrases for journalists headed to the Arab world. It was compiled after AP staffer Terry Anderson was kidnapped in Beirut during Lebanon's civil war and held as a hostage by terrorists. Written in Arabic, the phrases were:

"Thank you, Excellency, for allowing me to ride in the trunk of your car."

"The bread crumbs were delicious. I must have the recipe."

"I agree with everything you have ever thought or said in your life."

No adventure comes without risk, especially for war correspondents, and only fools think of themselves as being bullet-proof. It's part of AP lore that Mark Kellogg, while working as a stringer, accompanied George Armstrong Custer to the Little Bighorn River, where he and those in the 7th Cavalry Regiment under his command were annihilated by Native Americans enforcing their own brand of homeland security. "I go with Custer and will be at the death," Kellogg wrote cryptically in his final dispatch. He was killed without ever having written a final report.

Any literature major knows that war has been written about since the dawn of human history, and I am following in the tradition begun by Heroditus, considered the father of history for preserving accounts of the ancient wars between Greece and Persia. Aeschylus, the father of tragedy in Greek theater, wrote of ancient battles and gave us this truism: "In war, truth is the first casualty." For the epic Greek poet Homer, the Trojan War was the back story for his *Iliad* and *Odyssey.* Shakespeare's vehicle for immortalizing the unbreakable bonds among those who put their lives on the line for each other was King Henry V: *We few, we happy few, we band of brothers; for he today that sheds his blood with me shall be my brother.* For students of iambic pentameter, The Bard also noted that life is tragic to those who feel and comic to those who think.

In the time before TV, the Blogosphere and the Twitterverse, being a war correspondent was considered an essential career step. In his writings about

war, Ernest Hemingway defined courage as grace under pressure. He also observed: "Never think that war, no matter how necessary or how justified, is not
a crime." Walter Cronkite was a print reporter during World War II and made
a glider landing with the 101st Airborne Division during Operation Market
Garden. The man who became the most trusted man in America as a CBS news
anchor called the experience "a lifelong cure for constipation."

The paradigm for war correspondents is Ernie Pyle, a one-time travel writer who ferreted out the hidden human emotion in every assignment. A dimin-
utive, humble man, Pyle called himself a bum with an expense account. As
a war correspondent subject to the rules of censorship in World War II, Pyle
provided the worm's eye view of combat by getting down in the dirt to chron-
icle the plight of the everyday infantryman. Commanders said that the morale
of their soldiers improved whenever Pyle was around because he conveyed
the hardships and depravations of those doing the fighting. While others wrote
of the sweeping movement of armies or the views of generals, Pyle wrote in
a folksy style about the bonds of brotherhood that came with the everyday
challenges of a soldier's life and the rigors of combat. He even died a soldier's
death. After writing extensively of the war in Europe, and being awarded the
Pulitzer Prize in 1944, Pyle took his notebook and typewriter to join the troops
in the Pacific. On an island off Okinawa, the last major battle before atomic
bombs incinerated two Japanese cities, Pyle was killed by a Japanese bullet.
He was buried with his steel pot helmet and laid to rest next to an Army private
in a long row of military graves. Pyle was one of the few civilians ever awarded the Purple Heart. A monument to him reads: "At this spot the 77th Infantry
Division lost a buddy, Ernie Pyle, 18 April 1945." The building that houses
Indiana University's journalism school is named after him, and the shovel he
used to dig his own foxholes is displayed there.

There was only one Ernie Pyle, but I can relate to being a bum with an
expense account. Boarding call. Time to go. A gateway to a different world
has opened.

A wistful feeling emerged as the coastline disappeared on a flight across the pond. The itinerary is to land in Amsterdam, and following a six-hour lay-over, take the final leg to Dhahran, Saudi Arabia. In the pre-digital age, the only free time was during travel. Editors had no way to get in touch, so all the office bullshit got left behind. The future bullshit was still off in the distance. It was a chance to sit back, relax and enjoy the flight. Then came another sign that this assignment was like no other.

While reading some background material on Iraq and Kuwait, the perks of first class presented themselves. A flight attendant appeared with a pair of slippers, some Dutch chocolate and a glass of white wine. After discovering I was on my way to a war zone, she fetched a full bottle of Chardonnay and sat down to talk. That never happened before. War has such an aura about it that flight attendants want to know your life's story.

Writing stories was my job, the demands of which cause an awful lot of stress on families. Leaving New York was no big deal. It's the best and worst of everything, all at the same time. What with the stench of human urine in the subway stations and the rotting garbage that piled up in plastic bags on street corners, The Big Apple is at times like Calcutta without the cows. It's no won-der that Gotham, with eight million hermits living elbow to elbow, has more psychiatrists per square foot than any other place on earth. Because she asked me about who I was leaving behind, I opened up fresh emotional scars result-ing from a bad break-up. At the height of a torrid but roller coaster love affair, a career woman and I agreed to have a life together in New York. But when I got there, she ran off with another man without telling me. She figured the less said the better. It was like one of those Mayan rituals where the high priestess cuts out your heart with a jagged piece of obsidian and shows it to you while it's still beating. Nothing like being a piece of bloody chum tossed into the big pond of sharks in the City From Hell. Or something.

It was the first time I laughed telling that story, and she volunteered that I sounded like someone who joins the French Foreign Legion to forget a lost love. Or maybe I was just a 40-year-old man going through a doozy of a mid-life crisis. Whatever. Conversation with a blue-eyed, flaxen-haired flight atten-dant was much better than the in-flight movie as the jumbo jet raced toward the sun.

Something nearly as extraordinary had happened my last night in New York. Packed and ready to go, I followed my Friday routine and squeezed in one last workout at Madison Avenue Muscle, a gym that drew its share of New York career women who are normally layered in seven layers of emotional armor. Then one who worked as an editor for a big New York publishing house struck up a conversation. When she learned where I was heading, she suggested having a spontaneous going away party at her East Side apartment. She called herself Lilith, the seductress. After donning a black lace body stocking, she opened a bottle of wine and danced in front of the wall-length mirror in her living room, teasingly saying that I wouldn't be getting anything like this where I was going. The evening sure beat drinking drafts of Pilsner Urquell at P.J. Clark's on 53rd and Third, before it became a tourist trap.

When the flight attendant got up to get back to her duties, she said in a disappointed tone that she had a connecting flight in Amsterdam. Before we landed, however, she gave me the phone number of her roommate and provided the names of a couple of coffee houses and dens of inequity near the Red Light District. A six-hour layover would hardly be enough time to cab it to Amsterdam, inhale the local ambiance and make it back to the airport in time. No sense in jeopardizing the trip. Besides, her roommate didn't answer the phone. I spent the time in the airport immersed in a book. A colleague had given me a copy of *Dispatches,* the book by photojournalist Michael Herr about Vietnam. One line stayed with me: "You don't cover a war. It covers you."

Then on the flight to Saudi Arabia, a fellow traveler struck up a conversation. His name was Yanni, a Saudi official who was returning home after a business trip to the States. His American wife, plus eight kids, were waiting for him at home in Dhahran. He must have dropped six grand on a pair of his and hers Rolex watches from the duty-free cart, and he knocked back double Scotches with a gusto. Booze was banned inside the kingdom, he explained, but outside the borders, you could drink to your liver's content.

In providing a crash course on Saudi culture, Yanni said the whole of Saudi Arabia is considered a sacred shrine by Muslims. It's where the Prophet Mohammad, peace be upon him, lived and died. Saudi laws are derived from the holy book of the Qu'ran, and everyone, including the rare Western visitor, is subject to Saudi laws. What outsiders do in private, as long as you keep it inside your tent, is their business. However, harsh punishment awaits those caught breaking the law. Anyone convicted of the capital offenses of peddling booze or drugs is executed in public. The authorities even encourage people to watch an executioner with a giant saber chop off the condemned person's head. They want it known that the most serious law-breakers will be beheaded. Any drunk who causes an accident can have his arm cut off, which led to the joke that first-time offenders are called "Lefty." Arab custom allows for a man to have as many as four wives at a time, Yanni explained. If one spouse gets a new car, however, all of the spouses must get a new car. Women wear veils in public because they are considered to be the property of their husbands. It was all good information.

About an hour away from landing, conversation ceased, and I became lost in my thoughts. Visible through the plane window was nothing but the dark, empty expanse of the desert floor at night. I wondered if the war had started while I was in the air.

Touchdown was at 11 o'clock at night local time, 25 hours after I left JFK. The first thing to greet me was a blast of hot air, accompanied by an odor that smelled like a mix of crude oil and sewer gas. Welcome to the kingdom.

After clearing customs, and having to promise that I would take the computer with me when I left, I was taken to the Dhahran International Hotel, which adjoined an airport that accommodated both civilian and military flights. The first thing to catch the eye was an enormous, ornate glass chandelier hanging from the ceiling in a spacious lobby. Having checked in but without unpacking, I met Richard Pyle in the hotel restaurant for a quick briefing. He ordered ice cream with chocolate sauce. I sipped tea. Clusters of Arab men, many from Kuwait, occupied nearby tables. What stood out beyond their robes and head-dresses were the AK-47 assault rifles they carried. U.S. military personnel were everywhere. Each carried a weapon, and each had a gas mask strapped to the left thigh.

So this is a war zone. Like Dorothy in the land of Oz, I wasn't in Kansas anymore. The only thing anybody knew for sure was that nobody knew what was going to happen next. Life on the edge had begun.

9

CHAPTER 2
A Pencil's World

My eyelids opened, but it was still darker than a coal mine at midnight. Whatever amount of sleep I had gotten wasn't enough. Music pierced the silence as I tried to remember where I was. The previous occupant of Room 132 had left the radio alarm on. The voice of Don Henley warbled out the song *The End of the Innocence.* Must be an omen.

Still jet-lagged, I stumbled over my luggage to open the window curtains. A blinding flash from the giant yellow ball of the sun ascending in the eastern sky burned my retinas. All I could do was squint. It was like the view from inside a terrarium. A flat, barren sea of sand, hard to look at but impossible to look away, seemingly went on forever. The spellbinding emptiness looked like the unfriendly, unforgiving surface of an alien planet.

Duty called, and I found the AP office in a suite occupying a prime spot on the hotel's second floor. Roomy enough for writers and photographers to share, it had a wall-sized map of the kingdom, a TV set that picked up Saudi news broadcasts, a sofa and a table against a back wall that served as a desk. The suite's door opened to a spacious ballroom where the Saudis and the U.S. military had established a Joint Information Bureau, or JIB, as the acronym-crazed bureaucracy called it. Saudi officials occupied one side of the ballroom, and all branches of the U.S. military had cubicles for public affairs officers in another.

In charge of credentialing foreign journalists were Mohammed Khayat of the Saudi Ministry of Information and a man called The Colonel, the liaison officer with the Saudi military. Anything resembling a tourist bureau was unheard of in the xenophobic kingdom, but the two men offered their assistance.

"As-Salaam alaikum," the men said in a welcoming greeting that means "peace be upon you."

"Wa-alaikum salaam," I replied, my limited Arabic able to convey a response that means "and upon you be peace."

After reviewing my papers, they processed my photo I.D. Written partly in Arabic, the credential requested that "concerned authorities offer all possible facilities to the bearer." Valid until the end of the assignment, it was to be worn at all times. On the back was the state symbol of Saudi Arabia — crossed swords beneath a palm tree. And, in a fortunate stroke of timing, I was invited to a reception that night in the outside area where the hotel swimming pool was located. The event had been planned for some time as way for the Saudis to welcome the contingent of American journalists covering the military build-up.

Next was an introduction to the U.S. military officers who coordinated news releases and fielded questions and requests from the media, starting with the ranking officer, Navy Captain Mike Sherman. World-class bitching is part of being in the media, and print reporters had already nicknamed him Hollywood Mike because they thought he was partial to the visual medium of television. Sherman had his job. I had mine. At least he never went as far as Union General William Tecumseh Sherman, who said famously during America's Civil War: "I hate newspapermen. They come into camp and pick up their camp rumors and print them as fact...If I had my choice, I would kill every reporter in the world, but I am sure we would be getting reports from Hell before breakfast."

My top priority was to get into the pool, but not the one behind the hotel. The pool system was conceived as a way of allowing a select group of reporters onto the battlefield under military escort. Whatever pool reporters produced in the way of stories or information would be subject to operational security and then shared with all other media. On paper, it seemed like a workable idea. In reality, it was something designed and agreed upon by people who would never have to use it. The pool system was created by news executives and the military brass after reporters were shut out of covering the U.S. invasion of Grenada in 1983. A committee recommended that future wars be covered by a pool of media representatives, who would have access to the battlefield but would operate under the rules of censorship. However, the pool of reporters assigned to cover Operation Just Cause, the 1989 invasion of Panama, never got out of the building where they were waiting to get in on the action. Anyway, the august minds at the Pentagon had determined that the desert was so vast and the forces so scattered that no reporters were authorized to venture out to visit troops without a military escort. I didn't invent the pool system, and I didn't particularly like it, but participation was like abiding by Saudi law. It was something you had to adhere to if you wanted to see the show. In its original configuration, the pool had nine slots. Two were for a wire service reporter and photographer, three for print journalists and a newspaper photographer, and three for a TV crew. Slots were to be allocated to those with the most continuous time in country, as long as they could pass a physical fitness test. Like every journalist sent to Saudi Arabia, I put in my name for a pool slot.

Then I learned my new job title was Pencil. During the military buildup, a system had been set up to take media out into the desert to observe military training exercises. The date and time of the exercises, plus the names of the reporters authorized to go, were posted on a message board. It just so happened that the Marines had scheduled an exercise for the next morning during which they would fire live ammunition. Because my predecessor had already signed up, I had the AP spot. My name was listed under the category of Pencils, the military term for those who write things down in notebooks. In military speak, an infantryman is called a trigger-puller or a bullet-stopper. A fighter pilot is a jet driver. And from now on, I no longer existed as a national writer for the world's largest news gathering organization, but as a Pencil. Geez, I missed the Army.

Following a round of introductions to the public affairs officers representing the branches of the American military, I explored the hotel. It was comfortable enough, maybe not a full-service Marriott but not the Flea Bag Motel either. It had a diner and a full-service restaurant, complete with room service. An arcade was lined with a dry cleaning shop for laundry, a place where one could smoke Turkish tobacco through a water pipe and a gift shop that carried newspapers and magazines, in which ads for booze and pictures of unveiled women were blotted out by Saudi censors with Magic Markers. Best of all, a gym was available for use in a building next to the hotel's swimming pool.

Arrangements had to be made to transfer the rental car to my name, and I was off on a drive into the adjacent community of Al-Khobar, which was home to a market district called a *souk*. It was 114 degrees outside. One traffic circle was adorned with a monument shaped like the Space Shuttle. It honors the Saudi prince, former Royal Saudi Air Force pilot Sultan bin Salman bin Abdul-Nazi Al Saudi, who flew as a mission specialist aboard the U.S. Space Shuttle in 1985. One of the most remarkable things about honoring a royal prince who orbited the globe was that, just 20 years earlier, the deputy rector at the Islamic University at Medina had supported a 14th Century theory that the world was flat. But then again, a desert kingdom that banned beer seemed flat.

Later in the day, Richard Pyle worked his contacts to file a story about the Navy's tracking of a cargo ship in the Red Sea. If it contained supplies headed for Iraq, the Navy would stop it and deny it entry. The situation required some monitoring, and because Richard was packing to leave the next day, I inherited the story. It was a chance to work with the Navy public affairs officers, and while I waited for events to unfold, a football game was on TV just outside the JIB. The military received TV broadcasts of National Football League games on Armed Forces Radio and Television Service, which happened to be carrying the game between the Houston Oilers and New Orleans Saints. Sunday football was a little slice of home.

The tracking of the ship turned out to be a non-story. Although the cargo wasn't bound for Iraq, the story on the wire had to be updated. My computer turned out to be useless, but I inherited a Toshiba model that transmitted stories on a phone line. For a journalist away on an assignment, the sweetest sound in the world is the screeching a portable makes when it connects to its mother computer. It means you're in business.

The procedure was to send stories to the AP Bureau in Cyprus, which would relay them to London and on to New York. Because New York was eight time zones behind, the deadlines were writer-friendly. It was not lost on me, however, that I was now single-handedly responsible for all the news coming from a foreign land where I didn't know much beyond the hotel. The knot in my stomach never did go away.

Well into the evening, and hungering for dinner, I ventured outside to the welcoming party. It could have passed for a scene from a Star Wars movie, except there was no wet bar. Bedouin tents had been set up, and a guy in a turban and an Arabian Nights outfit was dancing and spinning as he twirled a curved saber. The song he sang translated into, "My tent is your tent," which is the Bedouin way of welcoming visitors. A camel had been imported as a photo-op. Military personnel and reporters waited in line to get on the back of the humped beast and have their pictures taken. The only thing missing was a Flying Carpet and a mustachioed genie appearing out of a lamp. Rows of carpets had been unrolled in the sand. On each rug was a tray with a whole roasted goat, its head and legs still attached, atop a bed of rice. The eyeballs were supposed to be a delicacy, but I passed. The goat meat was a little stringy but edible. The meal was washed down with a concoction known as Saudi champagne, which despite the name had no alcohol content. It was a mix of apple juice, sparkling water, slices of apples and oranges, and sprigs of mint. While Saudi champagne had no kick, it was refreshing.

I left the party early. A Pencil's first day in the field awaited.

CHAPTER 3
On The Firing Line

It is zero dark stupid, the military term that denotes any time for being up and on the job in the wee hours. One has to be out of the sack early to train with the grunts. In civilian terms, it is just before 5 o'clock on Monday, October 22, and I'm the first Pencil aboard a mini-bus waiting outside the hotel's main entrance to take the media out with the Marines. The driver, an Air Force sergeant, says it would be a two-hour drive to where we were going. My gear was double-checked to make sure I had my credentials, notebook, pens, full canteen, floppy hat, sun screen, lip balm, sun glasses and insect repellant. Aware that the war could start at any moment, my seat felt like it was made of pins and needles, a feeling that would persist each day forward. Other media straggled aboard, looking bored and sleepy from the party the night before. The CNN cameraman wisecracked about stopping for doughnuts and coffee. My biggest concern is to avoid looking like the F.N.G., or Fucking New Guy, so I kept my mouth shut and my eyes open from my seat in the back as the bus departed.

From the window appeared commercial nurseries that sold palm trees, and a soccer field with nary a blade of grass. Herders tended their flocks of sheep and goats alongside the road. Then just outside of town, the road became a divided highway bracketed by desert on both sides, a ribbon of asphalt through an ocean of dun-colored wasteland. Off to the right, some distance away, was an enormous ball of roaring flame that could have passed for the gateway to Hell. The relentless fire consumed the waste gas at Ras Tanura, the port on the Persian Gulf where a continuous flow of crude oil was piped to be loaded onto oil tankers for export. The fireball churned with a raging mixture of orange and black colors.

In the absence of anything green or anything higher than scrub brush, the landscape had no distinguishable terrain features. Somewhere out there were a quarter of a million American troops who had already been deployed, and I'd have to find out where they were. The wide-open spaces of the desert can make anyone feel small. What difference can one person make in all of this? And why don't they ever fight wars in temperate climes? Questions, questions. It was a first-rate highway, though. Arrow straight, no hills, no potholes, no speed limits, no traffic.

In time, the bus exited the main road and drove by an air field occupied by Harrier jump jets. The runway was ringed with air defense guns camouflaged with netting, which was designed to make the weapons harder to see from the air. Before long, some graffiti-covered mud huts appeared as a hint that we were entering the town of Jubail. "It looks like Atlantic City, without the casinos," one of the TV crew deadpanned.

A seaport on the Persian Gulf, Jubail was the home of the two frigates that made up the entirety of the Saudi navy. It was also the headquarters of the 1st Marine Division. Sandbags and razor wire protected the entrance. Sections of concrete pipe were strewn about the ground to provide emergency duck and cover. A battery of box-like things that contained surface-to-air Patriot missiles was pointed north toward the Iraqi forces in Kuwait, which was only a couple of hours away. Their rifles locked and loaded, sentries stopped all traffic at a checkpoint. Marines used mirrors attached to poles to check under the bus for anything suspicious.

Security was tight because it was the day before the seventh anniversary of the 1983 terrorist bombing of the Marine barracks in Beirut, Lebanon. Back then, a Shiite Muslim suicide bomber drove a yellow Mercedes-Benz truck loaded with six tons of explosives into a building of sleeping Marines, who were sent to the region as peacekeepers. The blast destroyed the four-story cinder block building at the Beirut International Airport, killing 241 American troops. Those who were on guard duty that horrible night carried unloaded rifles because the politicians had ordered that they not appear to be war-like. The bloody aftermath sure looked like a war. It was the bloodiest single day in the Marine Corps since Iwo Jima in World War II, and the worst single-day death toll for the U.S. military since the first day of the 1968 Tet Offensive in the Vietnam War. The checkpoint was a sober reminder that danger lurks in the Middle East, where grudges have percolated for thousands of years. From the way the Marines searched under the media bus and all the other traffic, somebody had learned a lesson about being on guard.

After picking up a public affairs officer, we drove to what can be described as the middle of nowhere. Marines called it Cement Ridge because it was littered with concrete traffic barriers, and it was where the Marines had carved a firing range out of the desert.

Assembled were the men of Alpha Company, 1st Light Armored Vehicle Battalion, 1st Marine Expeditionary Force. From personal experience, a trip to the range to fire live rounds always spiced up the routine. It was also helpful to know that troops have their ranks and their names on their uniforms, which eased introductions. The highest-ranking officer there was Colonel James Fulks, the operations and training officer who would later lead the 1st Marine Division through the Iraqi obstacle belt during the invasion of Kuwait.

"Anytime there's live fire, the Marines are going to be excited. This is music to our ears, although other people get very nervous when they hear it. These guys are going to be so pumped, it'll take a week for them to come back down," Fulks said.

The company commander was Captain Mike Shupp, 31, of Bethlehem, Pennsylvania. He talked about the yellow ribbons that family and friends had put up for him back home, about how the spirit of his troops had recently improved because they were now receiving decent food and soda pop at base camp.

Shupp said to go talk to his Marines, who were tossing a couple of footballs around while the range was being cleared of Bedouins and any goats who might have wandered into the area. One dead goat carcass already littered the range. Although these Marines had been in country for almost two months, this was their first crack at shooting live rounds. Until now, they didn't have ammo to spare. They call themselves Devil Dogs, or Tuefel Hunden, a name given to Marines in World War I by the Germans, who said they fought like the Hounds of Hell, or so the story went. I introduced myself as a reporter, but they were the ones with questions.

"Who's No. 1 in college football?"

The University of Virginia. Honest.

"We heard that there are war protests back home," said Corporal Carlin

Walters, 21, of Vidor, Texas.

Well, yes, peace vigils had been held in some places, but for the most part, Americans support the deployment. The most requested song on the radio was Lee Greenwood's *God Bless The U.S.A,* and groups supporting the troops had sprung up everywhere. This new generation of warriors, however, was sensitive to the fact that troops in Vietnam were mistreated when they returned from a divisive war that had lost public support.

"If I come home from this and people decide to spit on me, ain't no telling what I'll do," Walters said.

Another Marine asked, "What are Saudi cities like?"

You've been here two months and you've never seen one? I'd have to get back to you on that. This is my second day.

The way they talked, the Marines made it sound like they were imprisoned, unable to go into any town for relaxation or to mingle with the opposite sex, unable to drink beer, unable to order a pizza. Their only link to home was mail, and that was spotty. Their main form of recreation was the hand-held GameBoy video game, if they could get one shipped from home and find the batteries to power it. Some Marines created diversions by capturing black scorpions in their canteen cups and pitting them against each other in gladiatorial contests to the death.

"If a scorpion can eat other scorpions, he's bad like us. He's our mascot," one of the Marines said.

The conversation stopped when the Marines were ordered to man their Light Armored Vehicles, each of which had a driver, a gunner, a commander and room in the back for six infantrymen. Such was the readiness of the American military in 1990 that these vehicles had been packed aboard supply ships that were pre-positioned at a port called Diego Garcia in the Indian Ocean, and when the order came to deploy to Saudi Arabia, the ships sailed into Jubail. Each LAV had a 25-millimeter cannon that moved in tandem with a machine gun. With eight wheels, an LAV could reach speeds of 60 miles per hour on a paved road, but it was designed to travel in all weather over all terrain. Night vision capabilities meant it could also operate in the dark. On the practice range, shots would be fired at 55-gallon drums as the vehicles motored down range. Some targets were as far away as the length of 10 football fields.

Among those eager to pull the trigger was Lance Corporal Anthony Uhler, 20, of Pontiac, Michigan, who had left a pregnant wife behind to go to war.

"Being on the range at least breaks the monotony," Uhler said. "We finally get a chance to go out and bust some caps, break the pressure a little bit and release some frustration. Every day in the desert seems like the day before and the day before that."

Uhler also talked about morale and the thoughts of the people back home while he and his fellow Marines coped in a hostile environment thousands of miles away from home and family.

"It's important for us to know that people support us," Uhler said. "Otherwise, we'd feel like we're all alone."

Other Marines flocked around CNN's Christiane Amanpour. They hadn't seen a woman in two months and just wanted to talk. Woman journalists had plenty of challenges on this assignment, such as not being able to drive cars under Saudi law, but troops who found it a rarity to talk to a woman volunteered for interviews.

The LAVs took turns on the firing line. One would rumble down range, firing its chain gun and machine gun at targets. And at some point, the vehicle would stop and the infantry in the back would dismount to fire away with their rifles. Two months worth of frustration went downrange with the bullets.

Around noon, though, the desert got to me. It was 106 degrees, and about 20 to 30 degrees hotter inside the infantry carriers. I had slathered on some sunscreen and gulped canteen water every time the Marines were ordered to do so, but I had began to feel light-headed and found a patch of shade in the shadow of one of the vehicles. Heat shimmers rising from the sand made the desert seem like it was boiling. Cripes, I felt like a REMF, which is an infantry term for Rear Echelon Motherfucker. These guys were grunts, which is a title of honor because a grunt can hack it, no matter the conditions or circumstances. Grunt is the sound an infantryman makes when he slings an 80-pound pack on his back. The Marines said not to worry. It took them a while to acclimate too, and they had learned to string out their ponchos to make shade.

A helpful sergeant produced a container of Tang, the orange powder developed for astronauts to use in outer space. It made warm water taste better. He was Gunnery Sergeant Leroy Ford, 39, a native of Alexandria, Louisiana. Gunny, as the Marines called him, was a father of four and he was father-figure to everyone in the company. He was here by a choice. A 19-year veteran of the Corps, he was a private in 1970-71 while serving in Vietnam and was pulled out of Beirut just before the truck bombing seven years earlier. He was due to retire in March and could have avoided deployment, but he didn't want to let his young Marines fend for themselves.

"This is my last hurrah," Ford said. "I didn't want to miss out. I didn't want to read about this in the papers and say, 'I should have been there.' The party's almost over. Like my father said, I'm going to have to get out of the Marine Corps some day and get a real job."

His responsibilities included making sure his troops had enough chow and spare parts and gear, and that they're ready for combat. He remembered what it's like to be a nervous 18-year-old private away from home for the first time. One of the fundamental lessons to learn is that war is long stretches of waiting interrupted by brief moments of sheer terror, and it was a good thing nobody knew how many more months of tedium were ahead.

"They ask me what it's like. All I can say is that it makes you grow up faster," Ford said. "They know what a bullet sounds like. I'm not worried about them. They'll know what to do when it's time."

Then he sang a few bars of *I'll Be Home For Christmas.*

One of his underlings said, "You'll have a White Christmas, Gunny. White sand."

When the training day ended, the Marines headed back to their camp, and the media bus began the two-hour drive back to Dhahran. I listened on my Walkman to a cassette tape given to me by an AP colleague, Jay Sharbutt, who had put the name Hamburger Hill in his copy about a battle in Vietnam and who had told me that a Marine squad includes nine infantrymen and a three-man camera crew. The play list began with the West Point Choir singing *Cool Clear Water.*

Dusk fell during the drive home. The sun was a blood red ball on the western horizon, the color produced by light beams passing through untold numbers of dust particles being kicked up by the desert. The sunset was spectacular, unless you've seen the same one night after night for months at a time. As the bus headed south, Arabs parked their big Mercedes, Audis and Chevrolet Caprices alongside the highway and placed their prayer rugs in the sand toward the direction of Mecca. As darkness fell, a crescent moon adorned the sky. The crescent moon is a good omen to natives.

It was dark when we got back to the hotel, just as it had been when I woke up. I typed out a story about the day's training and shipped it via a phone link. The glamour of being a war correspondent is working a 20-hour day and writing a story alone in a hotel room.

It was the first of many days in the desert to come.

CHAPTER 4
Off To See The Wizard

Wearing a crash helmet and life vest, I am harnessed into a seat facing backwards in the bowels of a propeller-driven plane called a COD, short for Carrier On-board Delivery. We're bound for the aircraft carrier *USS Saratoga* in the Red Sea to observe how the Navy is preventing Iraq from receiving war-fighting supplies by sea. Interdiction is another word for quarantine or blockade, which is another way of saying the Navy is already prosecuting the war. Photographer John Gaps III and I drove four hours through the desert at night to catch this flight from an air base in the Saudi capital of Riyadh. Also aboard the plane are sacks of mail, supplies and Navy essentials.

Without windows for sight-seeing, it was impossible to tell the route. A crewman from the cockpit yelled out over the drone of the engines that we were beginning our final approach. Gaps wanted to bet on which of the four arresting wires on the carrier would catch our tail hook. I took three. We lurched to a stop having caught the fourth and final one.

The door opened to a different world, one surrounded by the azure blue waters of the Red Sea aboard four-and-a-half acres of a floating airport that was sovereign U.S. property. Sailors hurried about their primary business of launching and recovering warplanes. What seemed like chaos was a carefully choreographed routine for crew members living aboard a floating city required to support an air wing of fighter jets, bombers, reconnaissance planes, air traffic control platforms, refueling tankers and helicopters. The color of the jersey indicated what a sailor's job was, such as safety, maintenance, bomb loading, emergency firefighting and the like. The average crew member's age was 19. I tried to get out of the way without bumping into anybody or anything, especially a stack of missiles adorned with a sign that said Do Not Touch. A greeting party herded us off the noisy deck while I gave a big "thumbs up" to the COD pilot, a female Navy officer.

Inside the bowels of the ship was the command-and-control headquarters. Even deep below decks, the muffled growl of the steam-powered catapult that sprung aircraft into the sky could still be heard. It sounded like being in the basement of a bowling alley.

Captain Joseph S. Mobley, the *Saratoga's* commanding officer, greeted us with handshakes and souvenir T-shirts. The Navy blue shirts were adorned with the Saratoga's motto — Invictus Gallus Gladiator, or Unconquered Fighting Gamecock. Because we had braved the landing, the captain also produced certificates making us honorary naval aviators.

A graduate of the U.S. Naval Academy, Captain Mobley was a former combat pilot who flew an A-6 Intruder from the *USS Enterprise* during Vietnam. On a combat mission over North Vietnam in 1968, his plane was shot out of the sky. Having ejected, he was taken prisoner and endured 1,724 days in the hellhole of a prison camp. With each day seeming like an eternity, he was released on March 14, 1973, after America's involvement in that war had ended and while I was in basic training. After everything Mobley had been through, his dedication to the Navy and his country remained unshaken. That's why he stayed in the service.

The subject came up about support of the folks back home during Operation Desert Shield, which was the name given to the ramp-up to the war with Iraq. Mobley recalled the experience of leaving San Francisco for Southeast Asia.

"War protesters were throwing garbage at us from the Golden Gate Bridge when we were on our way to Vietnam," he mused.

He pointed to the cards, telegrams and well-wishes now lining the walls of the ship.

"All military men like to feel the citizens are behind them. It makes the job a lot easier. That's a stark contrast to what most of us felt in Vietnam," Mobley said.

Casual talk aside, a briefing was given on the configuration of an aircraft carrier group, which included destroyers and guided missile cruisers. A description of the combat capabilities of the carrier's air wing was also given. Its Tomcats, Hornets, Prowlers and other flying gun platforms helped make the U.S. Navy the mightiest power on the seas.

Also explained was the Navy's standard operating procedure for interdicting shipping bound for Iraq. The Arabian Peninsula was surrounded on three sides by water, and the Navy controlled the seas with the same vigor as the Air Force controlled the skies. Much of the seagoing police work was done in the northern Red Sea, especially on traffic coming south from the Suez Canal and bound for the Jordanian port of Aqaba, where land routes led into Iraq. The Navy picked names from *The Wizard Of Oz* for this operation. The Red Sea was called Toto Station. The Suez Canal was the Yellow Brick Road. Sectors were code-named Emerald City, Wizard, Oz, Wicked Witch and Tin Man. There was no Cowardly Lion.

Then the journey continued. To get to a front-line ship enforcing the blockade, the photographer and I were whisked by a helicopter to the guided missile cruiser *USS Biddle*. Away we went, strapped inside the chopper as it lifted off the carrier and thundered over the open water. As we approached our destination, a crewman casually explained that the helicopter was too big to land on the *Biddle's* deck. We were to be harnessed up and lowered by cable. Like the saying goes, it's not just a job, it's an adventure.

With the helicopter hovering and the wash of its rotors whooshing down, I stepped out of the flying machine. One day you're wearing a suit and tie hanging on to a strap of the F Train during the morning commute in Manhattan office, then you're being lowered by cable from a helicopter to the floating deck of a warship in the Red Sea. Gaps captured the sequence on film, then took the same ride.

"Show these pictures to any woman, and I guarantee you her nipples will get hard," Gaps beamed.

Aboard the cruiser, a grinning crewman led us to the bridge for a welcome by Captain Louis F. Harlow. We were afforded the status of honorary crewmen and given an autographed picture of the *Biddle*, which was nicknamed Hard Charger and which had the Latin motto of Deus Clypeus Meus (God Is My Shield). An operational briefing was given over lunch. The Navy served tossed salad, French onion soup, roast beef, fried fish, potatoes, green beans, corn on the cob, iced tea and — get this — ice cream for dessert. It sure beat Army rations. Anyway, the Navy's mission was to check out every ship cruising into or out of the Suez Canal.

"It's a total roadblock. This is a very effective blockade," Captain Harlow said.

If the captain deemed it necessary, a boarding party would be dispatched to search a vessel. The enforcement arm included units such as Landing Team Alpha, whose members were specially trained by the Navy and Coast Guard. Carrying side arms or shotguns and wearing protective flak jackets, the 20-member team would scurry down a rope ladder onto a 26-foot whale boat for an open water trip to a suspect ship.

"We're the Red Sea Highway Patrol. We should put a red and blue light atop the ship with a siren. It's more police work than anything else. We're stopping contraband from reaching its goal," explained Gunner's Mate William Kitchens, 27, of Lakeland, Florida.

The waters, bluer than blue, were once the world's busiest shipping lanes. Since Iraq's invasion, however, there were now more warships than commercial traffic. No civilian ship passed without a challenge. One that had just been stopped was the Greek container ship *Zim Venezia*. It was bound for Eliat, Israel, not far from the Jordanian port of Aqaba.

In need of close-up pictures, Gaps accompanied the landing party, which had to go some distance through the chop to reach the vessel. The *Biddle's* officers made bets on when he would throw up his lunch. Whoever had 10 minutes won.

While the landing team was on its way, two F/A-18 Hornets were launched from the *Saratoga* as a projection of power. The roar of the sleek fighter jets as they raced overhead made the hair stand up on the back of my neck. Their presence made it easy to understand why every ship in the sea obeyed the Navy's orders to stop. In short order, the landing team climbed aboard the ship via rope ladders, checked the manifest and checked the cargo holds. Nothing out of the ordinary was found during the four-hour excursion, and Landing Team Alpha returned to report on the mission.

Arrangements had been made to spend the night aboard the *Biddle,* which provided first-rate accommodations. We had our own head, the Navy term for bathroom, complete with a shower.

Ships seem so big and menacing up close, but out at sea, they seem so tiny in the vast expanse. On a ship, you don't have to live in the dirt or eat bland rations. If your floating home was sunk, however, you'd be adrift and alone. That night, a bright moon reflected light onto waters that were as calm as a bathtub. Beneath a blanket of stars, I stood on deck in the solitude and tried to absorb it all.

When dawn broke, we were treated to another Navy tradition as a supply ship pulled alongside to deliver mail, food and fuel. Once such a transfer is complete, a Navy ship plays a breakaway song. The *Biddle's* song was *Bad To The Bone* by George Thorogood and The Delaware Destroyers. Ear-splitting rock 'n' roll thundered over the tranquil waters.

Morning exercises included gunnery practice. The *Biddle* fired the five-inch gun on its main deck, the one it uses to send a shot across the bow of a suspect vessel. The Phalanx system of guns fore and aft was checked. Bullets going out at 3,000 rounds a minute would knock any intruder out of the sky. The Phalanx was a response to a tragic event in 1987 when the U.S. flag had flown on Kuwaiti oil tankers during the Iran-Iraq war. The guided-missile frigate *USS Stark* was sailing off the coast of Saudi Arabia on its mission of protecting oil tankers in the Persian Gulf. But in what was likely a case of mistaken identity, an Iraqi jet locked its radar onto the warship. The pilot of the French-built Mirage fighter fired one Exocet missile from 22 miles away, then triggered a second missile at 15 miles out. Skimming 10 feet over the water, the first missile struck near the ship's bridge and ignited a fire. The second missile blew a gaping hole into the frigate's side. In all, 37 sailors, including two who were lost at sea, were killed, and 21 were wounded. Saddam Hussein apologized for what he called an accidental shooting. It was another reminder that this region is dangerous.

Crewman aboard the *Biddle* also fired M-60 machine guns at targets. It had been nearly 20 years since I fired a weapon the infantry calls The Hog, and I was invited to take a crack at it. I didn't see any harm in reacquainting myself with the weapon, just in case some emergency situation came up during the war. Target practice never gets old.

We were also taken to the Blue Room, which was the heart and soul of a guided missile cruise. Crewmen at various stations, the specific configuration of which is classified, had their eyes locked on radar scopes tracking air and sea traffic. The *Biddle* could launch guided missiles at multiple targets at the same time. It was a shield that protected it and its mother aircraft carrier, but it doubled as a sword that could strike hard at any opponent.

When it came time to leave, we did the trip in reverse, starting with being hoisted up by cable from the rear deck into a hovering helicopter. The scenery, like the experience, was breathtaking. Before landing on the *Saratoga*, we circled for a time to watch the ship launch and retrieve its jets. The crew make it look routine.

Once aboard the carrier, we boarded the same type of aircraft that delivered us and strapped ourselves in for takeoff. The engines revved to full power, creating a thunderous noise. Then — whoosh! The steam-driven catapult was triggered and, within a second and a half, we were airborne and headed home.

Back in Dhahran, when one of the Navy public affairs officers heard how the trip went, he laughed: "You did everything in the Navy but get a tattoo."

One unfinished chore remained from the trip. Aboard the *Biddle*, I met Chief Petty Officer Christopher Romei, who perked up when he learned I had already been to Jubail. His wife Nancy was an X-ray technician at Fleet Hospital No. 5 in Jubail, and he asked if I could deliver a message to her. They would be at separate duty stations for their 10th wedding anniversary, and he would be celebrating his 34th birthday without her. He was concerned about his wife's safety.

"This is our chosen profession. Being apart is just a fact of life. We just accept it and live with it, but I'm not comfortable with her being there. I feel a lot safer because I'm on a warship. I'm trained to fight. Where she is, a leaker (an untracked Iraqi missile) could get through," Romei said. "I don't have any doubts about who will ultimately win this fight, but..."

He had been at sea on a combat deployment for a couple of months now, and there was uncertainty over what was coming. Would there be a shooting war with Iraq? How long would the deployment last before it started?

"Our parents are asking why. Why are we here? Is it for oil? Or is it for principle? And if it's for principle, why haven't we done anything?" Romei said.

On my next trip to Jubail, I visited the fleet hospital, which was set up to handle war casualties and was a reminder that the deployment wasn't a recreational camping trip. The hospital had been packaged in 416 crates that came off a pre-positioned ship. Sixteen days after the crates had arrived at the port of Jubail, the contents blossomed into a 500-bed installation covering 28 acres, all inside tents. One of the hospital corridors was a mile long. In fact, it was now the largest naval hospital in the world, larger than first-rate Navy hospitals in Virginia, Maryland and California. The chief of surgery was nicknamed Hawkeye for the irreverent character on the TV show *M*A*S*H**. Three operating rooms could handle six patients at once, up to 60 patients a day. There were two intensive care units, an X-ray department and blood lab, plus individual wards to handle neurosurgery, skin grafts, psychological disorders and even obstetrics and gynecology if any female service member required such specific attention. The self-contained hospital also had its own commissary, security, laundry, recreation area and kitchens, plus a heliport to handle incoming wounded.

In the first two months of Desert Shield, the hospital had averaged 120 patients a day. Troops had been treated for scorpion and snake bites, broken legs, sprained ankles, heart attacks and appendectomies. The most serious injury so far happened to an Army captain who tripped over a rope while jogging and impaled his neck on a tent peg. The doctors saved him, and he returned to duty. Toothaches don't stop for war either. A two-chair dentist office was set up to handle every emergency except caps and crowns.

Lieutenant Commander Mike Mozzetti of Walnut Creek, California, specialized in emergency medicine and supervised a casualty receiving room. He and his staff have been told to expect lots of casualties and wounds of all sorts when the shooting starts.

"Being in the military is a dangerous profession. Our job is to snatch patients from the jaws of death and get them to surgery," Mozzetti said.

Anyway, Nancy Romei was located, and I delivered her husband's message. She had been stationed at a Navy hospital in Virginia before being sent to Saudi Arabia. She persuaded a friend to take power of attorney and pay the mortgage, take care of the couple's monthly bills and tend to their two cars. She and her husband had no children or pets, but most of their houseplants became casualties of war.

"It was like pulling my hair out trying to find someone to do these things, but this is part of the contract," Nancy said. "My husband always told me he was married to the Navy first. Besides, this separation won't last forever. The Navy trained me to do this job. Now it's time for me to produce for the Navy."

She appreciated knowing that he was thinking of her on their anniversary. I was glad to do my part. The media and the military may be at war with each other on a higher level, but in the ranks, we were all in the same boat.

On a personal level, my brief experiences with the Navy provided a greater appreciation for what my Old Man did in World War II.

CHAPTER 5
Gus

Everybody called him Gus, which was the shortened version of Augustine, his middle name. He may have been the most unlikely sailor in the world, given that his parents emigrated from a landlocked country in central Europe and, having worked their way out of the coal fields, owned a farm located in the foothills of the Appalachian Mountains about 50 miles south of Pittsburgh. Once in a great while, usually while sitting on my grandmother's porch on Sunday afternoons, he swapped stories over bottles of beer with a brother-in-law who was also a sailor during World War II. Gus also kept a cardboard box at home filled with a photo album and a ship's log of where he was and what he did. His scrapbook was his journal.

Gus was five years old when the Great Depression began, but the Roaring Twenties had never reached his corner of the world anyway. The only body of water he was familiar with was a meandering stream that bordered the family property. It was called the Sulfur Creek because acid mine drainage from surrounding coal mines polluted the water and tinted it orange. He wanted nothing more from life than the chance to work the land and hunt in the fields surrounding the farmhouse, but the Japanese attacked Pearl Harbor to push America into a global war while he was still in high school. An older brother had enlisted in the Navy shortly after war was declared. Four months after his father died in January of 1944, Gus, too, left school to enlist.

He had never been more than five miles away from home before he boarded a train in Uniontown, Pennsylvania, for basic training at the Great Lakes Naval Station near Chicago. Uniontown was also the home of Army General George C. Marshall, America's foremost soldier during the bloodiest conflict in human history. As the Army's chief of staff, Marshall advised commander-in-chief Franklin Roosevelt during the war. Gus did his part, too, because the entire nation mobilized to fight.

At the Naval Station that indoctrinated one million sailors, Gus graduated as a machinist mate and a gunner. Then he traveled by train to San Diego for deployment in the Pacific. Drawing a Navy paycheck, meager as it was, had provided him with spending money for the first time in his life. The first thing he bought was a camera. Although Navy regulations prohibited personnel from carrying such items, Gus stowed it away with his gear to document his journey. The first pictures he snapped were of Tijuana, Mexico, the first foreign soil he had ever stepped upon before shipping out on the world's largest ocean. His departure date was July 31, 1944.

A transport ship took him and his fellow sailors to Pearl Harbor, where they would be assigned to various ships of America's fleet. Gus reported for duty aboard the *USS Appalachian* (AGC-1), known affectionately to her crew as The Apple. She was the first of a new class of vessel, a floating command and control headquarters built to ferry Marines and soldiers to amphibious landings on islands held by the Japanese. Essentially, it was a floating city populated with 36 officers and 442 enlisted men, more than the entire population of Upper Middletown, the closest village to his farm. As a flag ship, The Apple was the floating headquarters of Rear Admiral Richard L. Conolly, commander of Amphibious Group Three of the U.S. Pacific Fleet. Before Gus became a crew member, The Apple had already participated in a couple of combat missions. It also did duty off the coast of Guadalcanal, site of big island battle in 1942. Most recently, The Apple's command center supervised the pre-invasion bombardment of Guam and disgorged some of the ground troops that took control of that island after a bloody fight.

Gus was at sea aboard The Apple when he turned 20 on August 24, 1944, the first birthday he had ever celebrated without a cake baked by his mother. As the ship steamed through the Pacific and back into the war, it crossed the Equator. Gus became part of a centuries-old tradition involving the realm of Neptunus Rex, or Neptune, god of the sea. Sea-faring newcomers like Gus were regarded as Lowly Pollywogs before they crossed the Equator. After the appropriate indoctrination ceremonies involving characters like Davey Jones, he became a Shellback. Anybody who could handle the initiation and come up grinning was said to be able to handle anything. Gus was now a card-carrying seaman.

On his first combat mission, he was one man aboard one ship in a giant armada, stretching from horizon to horizon, that helped Army General Douglas MacArthur fulfill a promise. After being driven from the Philippines by the Japanese in the earliest days of the war, MacArthur had vowed: "I shall return." The commander of all the ground forces in the Pacific, MacArthur was now aboard the *USS Nashville* on his way to reclaim the islands. The Apple actually led the convoy until it developed mechanical problems. The entire fleet passed it up before the engines were repaired, but The Apple caught up and did its part. Aboard the ship was Major General A.V. Arnold, the commanding officer of the U.S. Army's 7th Division. The general and his soldiers disembarked for the invasion of Leyte Island, climbing down rope ladders into landing craft that took them ashore.

On that mission, Gus got his first taste of the ever-present dangers of a war zone. Some ships in the convoy had to sweep away mines, and Japanese planes raided at dawn, dusk and during the night. With its job completed, The Apple departed on October 23 just as the Battle of Leyte Gulf, the largest naval battle in history, was getting started. Leyte marked the first appearance of Japanese suicide bombers known as kamikaze. Japanese pilots flew planes armed with a bomb and just enough fuel for a one-way trip. The kamikaze volunteered to crash their planes into enemy ships, which would mean the end of their own lives but would take as many Americans as they could with them. From then on, Gus and every other sailor in the Pacific knew that Japanese pilots were willing to die to sink American ships by serving as human bombs. At Leyte Gulf, 55 kamikaze pilots died sinking five American warships.

Meanwhile, The Apple was ordered to New Guinea to ferry the Army's 25th Division and other units to Lingayen Gulf as reinforcements for the invasion of Luzon, the largest island in the Philippines. The Apple was conducting pre-invasion rehearsals off Guadalcanal in the Solomon Islands when Gus spent his first Christmas ever away from the farm, an occasion that prompted him to write a tearful letter to his mother. The Apple headed toward Luzon the day after New Year's in 1945 as one of 57 ships participating in the invasion.

One day, the alarm was sounded for general quarters. The shrieking claxons meant Gus had to don his steel pot helmet and life jacket before manning his anti-aircraft gun. He was halfway across the open deck when he stopped dead in his tracks. A Japanese fighter plane buzzed The Apple and fired its machine guns. Gus stood like a statue during the attack, bullets whizzing on either side of him. The war becomes very personal when the realization sets in that someone is trying to kill you. His shipmates were in awe.

"Man, that was the bravest thing we ever saw," they told him.

"Brave?" Gus said. "I was so scared, I couldn't move!"

Having sustained no damage, The Apple delivered troops for the Luzon landings. The ship then headed back out to open waters on January 12 and was steaming through the South China Sea when it was attacked by Japanese planes. Again the alarm was sounded for general quarters. Gus grabbed his gear and ran to his battle station to defend the ship against a kamikaze attack. Aside from aircraft carriers, the kamikaze pilots targeted troop carriers like The Apple. Sinking such a ship would kill American troops before they could kill Japanese soldiers.

Gus had learned to shoot on the farm. He was especially adept at dropping ring-necked pheasants out of the air with his shotgun, aiming out in front of the bird to hit it. In his mind, shooting at Japanese planes required the same skill. He would fire up a stream of lead ahead of the plane, and the Japanese pilot would fly right into it. The way he saw it, he was shooting into open air, and the pilot killed himself by flying into his rounds. In a moment of kill or be killed, the only way for Gus to save his life and the lives of his shipmates was to knock Japanese planes out of the sky.

"I wanted to live for my country. They wanted to die for theirs," Gus would say.

The Apple and all the ships around her opened fire. Just off to the side, a kamikaze pilot crashed into the *USS Zeilin,* striking the starboard side of the superstructure and setting off several fires. In all, seven crew members were killed, three others were never found and 30 crew members were wounded. Determined to avoid a similar fate for his ship, Gus fired and fired and fired as fast as his crew could load. When the last plane had been shot down, Gus was surrounded by empty shells. The acrid smell of cordite filled his nostrils. Flaming wreckage littered the sea. When a man is fighting for his life, every fiber of his being joins the battle. And in the ferocity of this fight, Gus lost control of his bodily functions.

"I couldn't tell you if that battle lasted 20 minutes or two hours, but when it was over, I realized that I had shit my pants," Gus said. "I was so embarrassed that I ran down below decks to the shower. But I had to stand in line for 20 minutes behind every guy on the ship, including the captain, because they had shit themselves too."

He always laughed during the retelling. At its primary level, war is a shit storm.

Gus was from the generation that created words such as SNAFU (situation normal, all fucked up) and the related term FUBAR (fucked up beyond all recognition). One time, Gus and his shipmates pulled shore patrol after island battles. Everybody who has ever gone to war looks for souvenirs, especially things like a Japanese flag, a sword or a helmet. Sailors were warned, however, that Japanese soldiers sometimes played possum, pretending to be dead and then rising up to kill. Gus was walking along a beach and spotted a Japanese soldier face down in the sand with a rifle in his hand. Gus wanted that rifle, but he couldn't be sure if the guy was dead.

"I ran up and kicked him in the ass as hard as I could," Gus recalled. "I grabbed the gun and ran away as fast as my legs would carry me. I never did turn around to see if he was alive. But I got the rifle."

In the papers Gus saved from the war, there is an authorization signed by J.B. Renn, captain of The Apple, allowing him to mail home one Japanese rifle after its firing pin had been disabled.

More enemies than just the Japanese lurked in the Pacific, however. One time, The Apple got caught in a typhoon at sea. It bobbed up and down like a cork and barely managed to stay afloat in 30-foot waves. Crew members were so rattled that they said crazy things.

"One guy was so seasick he begged me to shoot him to put him out of his misery," Gus said. "I would have, but I was too seasick to pull the trigger."

Meanwhile, after Luzon and the Japanese air attacks, The Apple returned to Pearl Harbor and then headed back to the American mainland to be overhauled and repaired. The ship was at anchor between February 14 and April 10, 1945, at the Mare Island Navy Yard, 25 miles northeast of San Francisco.

The crew was allowed to take leave, and Gus headed East by transcontinental train to visit family and friends on the farm.

Much too soon, Gus had to get back to the ship. Before it returned to the war, The Apple threw a grand party in San Francisco on April 5 and 6 for Navy brass and civilian VIPs. Gus and the crew partied like condemned men being given one last opportunity to howl before being sent to the gallows. Four days later, The Apple was bound for Pearl Harbor again and the realities of war.

Following exercises at sea, The Apple steamed to Saipan, site of a bloody battle the year before. Sailors were aware that Japanese civilians were so afraid of the Americans that they leaped to their deaths off cliffs on Saipan rather than being taken captive. American sailors struggled to understand such fanaticism.

The Apple then set sail for Manila Bay in the Philippine Islands via the San Bernardino Straits. The ship reached port on July 13, just as the Battle of Okinawa, the largest amphibious assault in the Pacific, was in its final stages. Gus and his shipmates were making physical and mental preparations for the final assault on the Japanese mainland. While they had survived the war thus far, everybody pretty much figured they'd get it from a kamikaze or a Japanese submarine when it came time to invade the home islands.

Training was being carried out in Subic Bay when word came that a single bomb had destroyed the city of Hiroshima on August 6, and a second bomb had incinerated the city of Nagasaki three days later. After being subjected to the most horrible weapon ever used in war, Japan surrendered.

The Apple was ordered to do its part in the occupation of Japan, ferrying ground troops that would enforce the peace. Gus and The Apple anchored off Northern Honshu and Hokkaido along with 23 other transports carrying troops from the Army's 77th and 81st Divisions. The Apple later sailed into the Japanese naval base at Ominato and assisted with the occupation of Hakodate and Otaru. With all occupation troops now ashore, The Apple visited Tokyo Harbor, among other places. Sailors were told their own rations were being cut so that the Americans could feed the starving Japanese.

"One minute, you're trying to kill the bastards who are trying to kill you. Then we had to eat less so we could feed them," Gus said.

On September 24, The Apple dropped anchor in the bay off what used to be Hiroshima. Patrols were put ashore in the atomic ashes. Although sailors were warned not to bring anything back, nobody understood the risks of radiation. On one shore patrol, Gus took a series of photographs of the flattened city. One frame showed a human skull that was devoid of flesh but had an upper jaw filled with gold teeth. Gus put the skull in his bag and headed back to the ship. Gold teeth were prime souvenirs and could be used to barter for other goods.

"We had to pass by this contraption I had never heard of, a Geiger counter, and it made a whole lot of noise. Before any of the officers could find out what set off the alarm, I tossed my bag and the skull overboard. Whoever the poor bastard was, his skull is forever buried in Hiroshima Bay," Gus said.

The morality of dropping a bomb that was more powerful than all the bombs dropped before it never phased him at the time. It meant that he was going home alive. Throughout the advance through the Pacific, Americans were motivated by one battle cry: "Remember Pearl Harbor." It was a terrible thing to incinerate an entire city populated by women and children and old men, but war is a terrible thing. If it took a weapon of mass destruction to force an unconditional surrender from the people who started it, so be it. He was convinced that the weapon was so terrible that nobody would be stupid enough to start another war.

When Gus was discharged on June 4, 1946, two years and nine days after he stepped forward and took the oath of enlistment, he wore the Pacific Theater Ribbon with two stars, the American Theater Ribbon, the Victory Medal and the Philippine Liberation Ribbon with two stars. Some veterans used their savings to buy new cars or motorcycles. Gus applied for and received a veteran's priority for purchasing a new piece of farm equipment, a Farm-All H Series tractor. He also received a letter of thanks on White House stationery from President Harry Truman, the commander-in-chief who made the decision to drop the atomic bomb. Gus returned to the farm to resume a life in peace as best he could. He left as a boy and came back as a man, scarred by the cruelty and insanity of total war. Sometimes when he got angry, it was as if he was still fighting kamikazes.

A pretty girl conquered his heart and forced an unconditional surrender of a romantic kind. He married Marcella Garcher in 1947 and contributed nine children to the Baby Boom. Later, those who endured the Great Depression and fought in the deadliest conflagration in human history were called the Greatest Generation. Gus would have laughed. He did what had to do, the same as so many others.

Then came a long and costly Cold War against Communism, and shooting wars in Korea and Vietnam. His oldest son and namesake would be caught up in a conflict in Southeast Asia. Gus died of a massive heart attack in 1977. I wonder what he would have thought if he knew another of his sons went off to write about another war in 1990.

CHAPTER 6
The War Within

A swirling cloud of dun-colored sand and powdery dust swallowed the giant Chinook helicopter as it descended and hovered before touching down on the desert floor. From the vantage point through a portal inside the flying workhorse, the beating lades of the signature twin rotors had created a brown fog that blotted out the sun. The back ramp opened to a world of soldiers in battle, but instead of the snapping bullets and bursting shells of a firefight, this war was being waged against one of the most inhospitable environments on the planet. The battle with the desert had begun the moment the first troops set foot in the kingdom, and it would be waged continuously before, during and after the balloon went up, which is military jargon for when the actual shooting started. We had landed at a desert camp of the Army's 1st Cavalry Division, the final piece of firepower deployed in Operation Desert Shield, the name given to the defense of Saudi Arabia from the Iraqi threat.

The Cav, which calls itself the First Team, had brought its main battle tanks, armored personnel carriers and helicopter wing from Fort Hood, Texas. Its awesome firepower supported the three components of the Army's XVIII Airborne Corps already on the ground — the 101st Air Mobile Division, the 24th Mechanized Infantry Division and three infantry brigades of the 82nd Airborne Division, which had drawn the original line in the sand back in August. In the final days of October, the Cav had invited the media to its desert encampment as a way of announcing its arrival.

Throughout eastern Saudi Arabia, Army camps had been given various names by their creative occupants. One was called Camel Lot. Another was christened Bedrock because it was as primitive as Fred Flintstone's Stone Age town, minus the foot-powered cars and rocky bowling lanes. For troopers in the Cav, this new home was called Six Flags Over Saudi Arabia. It's no amusement park, but a dry sense of humor helps.

"We're waiting for our grass to grow, but since we don't have a lawn mower, we hope it doesn't," deadpanned Private Scott Tenhagen, 19, of Burlington,

Kentucky, and a member of the 92nd Field Artillery Regiment serving with the Cav.

Six Flags Over Saudi Arabia had elements common to Army camps throughout history. On a signpost planted in the sand, hand-made wooden directional markers noted it was 6,500 miles to Brooklyn, 7,013 miles to Chicago and 8,066 miles to San Antonio, the city closest to Fort Hood. Because its real home is located in the arid American Southwest, the Cav was used to heat and dust. Still, it took time to get acclimated to the furnace-like conditions.

Rows of canvas tents, their olive-drab color now covered with layers of desert dust, dotted the landscape. Soldiers did what they could to make the camp livable. Protective bunkers were constructed of, what else, sand bags. Mail boxes were built from scraps of wood. A cardboard box that once contained Army rations was a storage compartment for a soldier's personal gear. Water bags raised on poles served as a crude shower, although soldiers are sent back to rear occasionally for real showers. A staple of this camp, or any other army camp in the field, are the rows of four-hole outhouses for calls of nature. A football gridiron had been marked off in the desert. There was also a volleyball court for R&R (rest and relaxation). Overturned stretchers served as card tables. Scraps of wood were laid down as flooring, which kept sleeping cots above the sand. A TV with a VCR was set up in one tent designated as a movie theater. In the absence of a fitness center, soldiers made barbells out of sand bags attached to metal bars. These crude gyms drew a lot of traffic. The volunteers in the new modern Army worked to stay in peak physical shape without being ordered to do so.

"These guys really know how to adapt. They'll do anything they can to make life a little easier," said Lieutenant William Moore, 23, of Orange County, California.

The Cav had long ago traded in its horses for tanks. Part of its muscle came from the multiple launch rocket system, or MLRS, which is supposed to be faster, deadlier and more accurate than traditional artillery. The tubes can fire 12 rockets in 36 seconds, each capable of taking out a different target. Their radars can track any incoming rounds, plot the trajectory back to the source and fire back before a shell hits the ground. Warrant Officer Francisco

Merced, 36, of Gary, Indiana, said it packs quite a punch: "If you have a rocket land within 24 yards of your position, commit your soul to God."

When the time came to board the Chinook for the flight back to Dhahran, I introduced myself to the crew, whose motto was "Fly The Hostile Skies." Having informed them that my oldest brother was in the Air Cavalry Troop of the 11th Armored Cavalry Regiment in Vietnam, I was invited to ride up front in a jump seat just behind the pilot. A set of headphones was provided for listening to the chatter.

Cruising above an expanse devoid of vegetation provided a better idea of how much military stuff occupied the kingdom. The withered landscape was a stark contrast to the rice paddies and triple canopy cover of Vietnam, where treetops 150 feet off the ground masked everything beneath them. Troops had referred to the magnificent desolation of the endless desert by various names, such as the world's largest ash tray, the world's largest kitty litter, the world's largest beach, the world's biggest sand trap or the world's largest unpaved parking lot. My personal favorite was the Sand Box because it resembled a child's play area filled with toys.

For mile after mile, from horizon to horizon, the machines of war — some American, some British, some of undetermined origin — maneuvered and took up positions. Ancient routes carved out by camels had been obliterated by a crazy-quilt pattern of ruts left by tanks, trucks and Humvees, the latest incarnation of the Jeep. While convoys snaked along the highways, engineers bulldozed new roads or gouged out spaces for encampments in the burning sand. Gusts of wind gave rise to whirling clouds of dust. There was something captivating and dreadful about this, all at the same time. These weren't toys, and this wasn't child's play. Commanders intended to use all this stuff in bloody battle. It didn't take a military genius to realize that whoever controls the skies in a desert war has the upper hand. There's nothing to hide behind. Like they say in the Air Cav, you can run, but you'll die tired.

The American army last fought a desert campaign in World War II in the wastelands of Libya and Tunisia in North Africa. The military foe back then was the Afrika Korps of Germany's Erwin Rommel, the Desert Fox, who had observed: "First, you must defeat the desert." Major John Little, the transportation officer of the U.S. Army's 82nd Airborne Division, voiced this modern addendum when paratroopers ventured onto the parched landscape: "And the desert is an ass-kicker."

Human life is unsustainable on most of the Arabian Peninsula, which sits on the same parallel as the Sahara Desert. There are more mirages than watering holes, and the blowtorch heat can drive a man insane. Little wonder the desert has such a purgative effect on the human psyche.

From above, it looked as if some higher power had rolled up the topsoil and exposed a wasteland devoid of anything green, watery or familiar. One definition of Arab is desert, concocted by someone with a definite grasp of the obvious. The tortured landscape was a carpet baked by an unrelenting sun radiating heat and producing a glaring light in a cloudless sky. The constant compressing of the eyelids to withstand the white-hot glare resulted in a condition known as the Saudi squint.

A war of words existed from the time American troops first landed in the kingdom. A statement attributed to Iraqi dictator Saddam Hussein and broadcast on Iraqi radio said, "If the spark of war is started, many will be burned. We continue to pray and pray hard to God that there will be no confrontation whereby you will receive thousands of Americans wrapped in sad coffins after you had pushed them into a dark tunnel."

As more and more troops arrived, a female voice known as Baghdad Betty mocked their ability to adapt. "For all you Americans, go home. The desert heat will kill you, and the sand will swallow you up. Your families back home are insecure, and handsome men have taken your wives away," she said.

Saudi sand did have its own peculiar texture. Boots that walked on it, or military vehicles that drove over it, would easily break through a thin surface crust. The sand turned into a pulverized powder, as fine as talcum, that finds its way into everything from nostrils to eyelids to every body cavity, not to mention weaponry and gear boxes and air filters on engines. The abrasive powder is particularly tough on helicopter blades. So alien and fascinating was this withered landscape that soldiers put scoops of sand in the mail they sent back in order to give the home folks an idea of what they were living in. To appreciate what the battle against the environment was like, you had to taste the grit in your teeth.

Taking two steps in the sand is exhausting for even the fittest of troops. Combat boots, which were leftovers from Vietnam, were ill-suited to the desert. A steel shank in the boot's sole guarded against nasty booby traps a foot soldier might step on, but in the blazing heat, the metal heated up and cooked the bottom of the foot. On the instep were small holes with wire screens. They were designed to let out water that could get in from rice paddies and jungle pools. In the desert, all they did was let in powdery sand, which made it feel like marching on sand paper.

Whatever life was out there was of the nuisance variety. Everyone wondered how an empty wasteland could be the realm of flies as big as Chinook helicopters, not to mention the scorpions, snakes and sand fleas. Each morning, soldiers shook out their footwear to empty them of scorpions or other undesirable creatures who may have wandered in during the night.

The key to sustaining an army in such a harsh environment was logistics. The Army manual for desert warfare considers food and water to be tactical weapons. Judging from the gripes, troops wondered if the food weapon was aimed at them. No topic got more growl time than prepackaged rations called the MRE, which stands for Meal Ready To Eat but which is derisively called Meal Rejected by Ethiopians. Troops were also under orders to drink six quarts of water a day to avoid dehydration, and every bottle of water had to be imported.

An improvement on previous field rations or canned items such as Spam, each MRE came in a chocolate-brown wrapper as a 2,500-calorie, prepackaged portion that can be eaten anywhere. The main courses included ham omelet, spaghetti, escalloped potatoes and ham, chicken a la king, diced turkey, tuna casserole or frankfurters with bean component. Other goodies in the packets included crackers, peanut butter, jelly, a freeze-dried dessert, powdered chocolate, instant coffee, a pack of matches and toilet paper. One rarity and a sure-fire favorite in the packs was M&Ms candies. If someone was lucky to get M&Ms, a big whoop usually followed. Some MREs came with a tiny bottle of Tabasco sauce, which added a little spice to a bland diet. Troops loved the bottled hot sauce so much that they would say, "In case of emergency, break glass."

Spartan desert camps lacked amenities such as clubs for off-duty soldiers seeking a beer to slake their thirst. Even though booze was already banned for religious reasons in Saudi Arabia, the military high command doubled-down by issuing General Order No. 1. It prohibited the consumption of alcoholic beverages in the kingdom.

Arriving American troops were told that they were ambassadors of the United States. Saudi religious places and practices had to be respected. To avoid cultural friction, chaplains were renamed morale officers. Troops were also told not to photograph mosques, military installations or the local population without permission. A crash course in Arab culture was taught. For example, troops were told not to read anything into it if two Arab men held hands in public. That's their custom. It was emphasized never to extend the left hand to an Arab. In the absence of toilet paper, that's the hand they wipe with after they defecate. Another no-no would be showing the sole of the foot to an Arab. It's considered a major insult. And by all means, red-blooded American troops must never show any interest in Arab women. With no cultural or other exchanges between the sexes, this might have been the first war in American history when GIs did not leave behind a new batch of babies.

Any amount of time spent with soldiers brings up references to Murphy's Laws of Combat, a compendium of war wisdom that explains both the obvious and the unexplainable. And Murphy was a grunt. The first rule is that anything that can go wrong, will go wrong. A popular one making the rounds during the build-up was: Remember, your weapon is made by the lowest possible bidder.

The desert creates a feeling of isolation, that nothing exists outside one's field of vision, and that field of vision was boundless. Although the information was classified, troop formations were arrayed with a definite purpose. As part of Desert Shield, the 1st Marine Division was closest to the Persian Gulf. The Army's 101st and 24th divisions occupied the northern front in the interior, their attack helicopters and mix of tanks and armored personnel carriers best suited to meet an Iraqi invasion. The 1st Cavalry Division's tanks were positioned to counterattack any Iraqi movement. And the three infantry brigades of the 82nd Airborne were arrayed in reserve in case they were needed to be dropped anywhere on the battlefield. Also out there somewhere was the Army's 197th Mechanized Brigade, the 3rd Armored Cavalry Regiment and the tank-killing Apache helicopters of the 12th Combat Aviation Brigade, not to mention support units and supply dumps.

Military intelligence, a sure-fired oxymoron if there ever was one, noted that the Iraqi army on paper was larger than the Werhmacht forces deployed in Western Europe prior to the D-Day landings. With one million soldiers in uniform, Iraq had the fourth largest army in the world. It had 4,000 tanks of various models. Its artillery, according to the range it could fire, was some of the best in the world. Many of its 56 divisions had fought in a catastrophic eight-year against Iran, during which it has used chemical weapons and during which America was an unofficial ally of Saddam Hussein. Although front-line infantry was basically cannon fodder, Iraq's regular army was composed of divisions equipped with tanks and armor. Then came the elite Republican Guard, which had 28 brigades in eight divisions. The Guard had the best of everything — higher pay, better food and equipment such as top-of-the-line Soviet tanks. The Iraqi air force had 750 aircraft, including fighter jets. And overall, the Iraqis had shorter supply lines and would be fighting on their home turf.

The logistical wizard overseeing the effort of bringing all troops and equipment into the kingdom was Major General William (Gus) Pagonis, who would earn his third star during the war. He was from Charleroi, a blue-collar Pennsylvania steel town along the Monongahela River south of Pittsburgh. A Penn State man, he earned a bachelor's degree in transportation and traffic management and a master's degree in business administration.

When the first planeload of troops had landed in August, Pagonis was already on the ground. In those early days, he slept right off the tarmac. He also oversaw the construction of the first four-hole outhouse in the kingdom. It was the same type he had learned to build in Vietnam, where he had earned the Combat Infantryman's Badge.

An interview was arranged through channels. I had never talked to a general before, but I had attended the Army's Quartermaster School at Fort Lee,

Virginia, so I asked why he was in logistics.

"I failed tactics," he deadpanned.

Perhaps. But in the words of Napoleon, an army travels on its stomach. What's the key to logistics?

"You have to remember who your customers are," Pagonis said.

Not only did the operation mean bringing troops in, it meant finding them food, water and shelter as soon as they got there. As a Greek-American, Pagonis was inspired by an ancestral figure, Alexander The Great, who conquered the world by living off the land and creating the concept of the mobile firebase. With supply lines stretching thousands of miles back to the States, Pagonis applied the concept of brute-force logistics. In the first 80 days of deployment, 101 ships and 677 airplanes had delivered 230,000 troops. Now planes and ships were bringing in spare parts, stockpiles of ammo and recreation gear for the long haul.

Military supplies got priority, but the pipeline also included mail. Seventy tons of the stuff was coming in every day, and the volume of letters to any soldier, newspapers, books and packages of cookies grew by the hour. Drives were organized in the States to boost the morale of the troops. Once the stuff reached Saudi Arabia, reservists sorted the incoming mail packages and put it on trucks for delivery to the troops in the field. The goal was to have a letter delivered within 10 days of arrival. Given the distances Pagonis was up against, it was a miracle to get it delivered that fast. For troops so far from home, mail was their oxygen.

"It looks like America has gone super patriotic in support of the troops," Pagonis said. "Priority is given to moving stuff needed for battle, but I know how important mail is. It wouldn't be fair to say the system doesn't have some problems, but we're improving every day."

In the early months of the deployment, logisticians stockpiled ammunition that would be needed for war, but there wasn't always enough to fire rounds during training exercises. On one occasion when Marines practiced assaulting a mock bunker, infantrymen who lacked live rounds raised their rifles and shouted "butta-butt-butta," just like a kid would mimic the sounds of bullets being fired from a toy. Staff Sergeant Charles Woods, 31, of North Glenn, Colorado, said drilling with sound effects instead of bullets was one way grunts adapted to any situation.

"We're proud of being grunts. You have to earn the name. Until we set foot on the ground and say we control it, the battle's never over with," Woods said.

The genius in the Washington bureaucracy who labeled this the 100-hour war never spent a day in the desert. Unseen battles raged everywhere.

One trip into the desert involved an overnight stay with the Marines, who had scheduled a joint exercise with the Saudi troops they may be fighting alongside. Part of the purpose was to ease cultural frictions, and because pork is forbidden in Islam, the Marines had removed MREs containing ham and pork. Marines had also been told to clean up their colorful language so as not to offend their hosts, the King Abdul-Aziz Brigade of the Saudi Arabian National Guard.

Religion was a sticking point. When a chaplain spoke to a formation about the need to be sensitive to the Saudi belief that Islam is the one true religion, a corporal named Michael Collins spoke up. "I don't see how the Marine Corps can ask any man to hide his religious faith. We're here defending them. Why are we kissing their butt?" he said.

Lunch was spent with Major John Bates, executive officer of the 1st Battalion, 3rd Marine Regiment, which had deployed from Kaneohe Bay, Hawaii. Trying to be helpful, he said not to worry about the flies buzzing around as a chicken a la king MRE was being consumed.

"We don't start waving them off the forks until four or five flies land at once," Bates said.

Were the Marines getting everything they wanted?

"Maybe not everything we want, but everything we need," Bates said.

What did he want that he didn't have?

"Beer and ice water," he laughed.

The major's domain was the infantry, variously known as ground-pounders, foot-sloggers or grunts. And every Marine is a rifleman first.

"After all the tracked and wheeled vehicles are crippled, it's up to the infantryman. No matter how high-tech we become, the infantryman is still the one who wins it or loses it," Bates said.

A native of Little Rock, Ark., Bates symbolized the legacy of America's conflict in Vietnam, both the price paid and the determination to drive on. He was wounded three times — once by a grenade that took a chunk of his left knee, another time through his left foot when he stepped on a pungi stick and the third by a machine gun round through his chest that robbed him of a lung. The last wound forced him to retire from the Marine Corps when he was 21. Determined to get back in, he spent seven-plus years rehabilitating. He passed a physical test by running three miles with one working lung. Then one year after putting the uniform on again in 1975, he ran the Marine Corps Marathon. He ran 29 marathons in all before he moved up to ultra-marathons. He was physically stronger than he was before he shed blood for his country.

The emotional scars were a different story. When the American public turned against that war, it also turned against the troops. For the first time in American history, those who bled in war were being blamed for it.

"They didn't separate the war from the warrior. The military doesn't make policy. We only enforce it. People were pointing the finger in the wrong direction," Bates said.

On that same exercise was a first sergeant who had the Marine Corps emblem tattooed on his left arm. He was Chuck Woodruff, 38, of Oroville, California, who said he was on the second to last helicopter to leave Saigon before the capital fell to the North Vietnamese army on April 30, 1975. Vietnam was always in the back of his mind.

"The question keeps coming up because there's nothing to compare this to except Vietnam. I think it will take generations and decades before people forget," Woodruff said.

The new breed of Marines was aware of Vietnam too. They were willing to fight for their country, but they could not imagine doing so without public support. Said Corporal John Vaughn, 23, of Bravo Company, who was nicknamed "Lifer" by his fellow Marines: "I'd feel betrayed if people turned against us."

Spend any amount of time on a ship, on the firing range or in the field and the subject of Vietnam invariably came up. It was as if that experience was being carried in foot lockers, duffel bags and rucksacks.

Vietnam divided the country more than at any time since the Civil War. In hindsight, it had all the ingredients of a disaster from the start, a war fought for an invented reason and with a bad battle plan, all hatched by the civilian masters who hold the power of deciding when to go to war. It was sold to the American public as a war against communist aggression and to liberate South Vietnam. The reason given for intervention were two attacks on the destroyer *USS Maddox* in the Gulf of Tonkin in 1964, but the architects of the war later conceded the second attack never happened. No matter. The United States had essentially committed itself a year earlier when President John Kennedy supported the overthrow of South Vietnam leader Ngo Dinh Diem, who was killed in a coup. By orchestrating a regime change, U.S. leaders became responsible for trying to build a nation while fighting a war.

Ground troops figured they'd be greeted as liberators while they handed out chocolate bars to appreciative citizens freed from the yoke of oppression, just as their fathers did in World War II. But when combat troops were committed by President Lyndon Johnson, Americans who answered their country's call found themselves propping up the South Vietnamese army with one hand and confronting a foe that included regular army units from North Vietnam and insurgents in South Vietnam, who saw themselves as freedom fighters against foreign intervention. What's more, instead of massing firepower and taking territory, American units were fed piecemeal into a battle with the objective of racking up body counts. Troops found themselves fighting guerillas in the form of the Viet Cong, who blended in with the civilian population, and North Vietnamese regulars, equipped by the Soviet Union and China, who could hide in tunnels or find sanctuary in neighboring countries. An enemy skilled at setting booby traps and employing hit-and-run tactics was nowhere and everywhere, all at the same time. Hilltops were taken with a steep price in blood, only to be abandoned for enemy forces to take back. Vietnam became a quagmire that cost Lyndon Johnson his presidency, and his successor turned the fighting over to the South Vietnamese while bringing U.S. troops home.

Vietnam was fought at home too. I was completing my third year of college when, on May 4, 1970, during an anti-war protest, four unarmed Kent State University students were killed and others wounded by members of the Ohio National Guard in a 13-second hail of bullets. The guardsmen were of the same generation as the students. They fired M1 rifles, the assault weapons that G.I. Joe carried to kill Germans and Japanese in World War II. The day after those shootings, I was on the first tee at the local golf course, sporting shoulder-length hair and wearing a Captain America shirt. Some guy behind me said they should have killed them all, and he was staring at me when he said it. That was a moment of clarity. You could get your ass shot up in Vietnam, or on a college campus for questioning the legality and morality of an unnecessary war, or for just looking like somebody who didn't conform. The only way to stop the killing and the unrest was to stop the war. Wars are like relationships. They don't work out if one party is misled at the start.

It wasn't just that returning veterans were called baby killers or greeted with the cold shoulder of apathy. Veterans of Foreign Wars Post 47 in Uniontown, Pennsylvania, was once the largest post in the country. The commander refused membership to Vietnam vets, however. By his way of thinking, they were involved in an undeclared conflict, not a real war. Inevitably, the post's World War II members died off. When new VFW leadership reached out to those who it had once rejected, Vietnam vets had formed their own social network, saying in essence: "You didn't want us then, we don't need you now." Post 47 is now shuttered. Vietnam vets vowed no generation of warriors would ever be forsaken again. A line from a song of the times noted: *The country I grew up in fell apart and died.*

Reminders of Vietnam went all the way to the top. President George H.W. Bush, who had cobbled together a 34-nation coalition to confront Saddam Hussein, knew what it was like to face enemy fire. He was a Navy pilot who had been shot down in the Pacific in World War II. Although he would have the final say as commander-in-chief, he left the planning in this war to the professionals in the military.

"This will not be another Vietnam," the commander-in-chief had promised.

One could only hope. My oldest brother was in that war.

CHAPTER 7
A Brother's Battle

If the Age of Aquarius dawned in the Sixties, San Francisco was party central, a magnet for gentle people with flowers in their hair who wanted to change the world. Baby Boomers, dope-smoking Hippies and long-haired Peaceniks flocked by the tens of thousands to the city's Haight-Ashbury District by the summer of 1968. It was hardly the only city in America where sex, drugs and rock 'n' roll held sway, but in no other place did the counterculture reach such critical mass in its rebellion against authority. It was as if the city, built atop a seismic fault line, had become the epicenter of a social earthquake ripping America apart. Timothy Leary, that guru of the counterculture, had come to San Francisco to advocate the use of psychedelic drugs such as LSD and advised his adherents to "turn on, tune in, drop out." The undeclared war in Southeast Asia was seen as unjustified and therefore immoral, and significant numbers of Baby Boomers rejected it by saying "Make Love, Not War" while the establishment was saying, "America — Love It Or Leave It."

San Francisco was also the place where a different segment of Baby Boomers gravitated to do what they thought was their duty. One of them was my oldest brother Edward, who was ordered to the City By The Bay, not with flowers in his hair and not to take part in a summertime love-in. He reported to the airport, Army duffel bag packed, to board a Flying Tiger Airlines charter that would whisk him to Vietnam.

A private first class trained as a helicopter crew chief, he was the oldest of nine children of hard-working descendants of Slovak immigrants who farmed the rolling hills of Appalachia. Like most kids, he played at war with his younger siblings, wondering about how he would perform in combat during make-believe scenarios. An avid outdoorsman and natural athlete, his first love was baseball. Standing 6-foot-4 and 220 pounds, he was nicknamed Tree and pitched with a high leg kick in the style of Juan Marichal. To anyone in a batter's box, it looked as if his left leg reached home plate just ahead of his fastball. He also played football, basketball and threw the javelin on the track team at Uniontown High School. He was drafted into the Army on June 9, 1967.

Taking the step forward meant reporting to Fort Jackson, South Carolina, for basic combat training and to Fort Eustis, Virginia, for advanced training at the Army's helicopter school. He married his high school sweetheart before he left for Vietnam. On the day of departure, his father told him: "Don't be a hero." And the Old Man, who we all thought was the strongest man on the face of the Earth, broke down and wept as the car drove away. Call it an accident of history, but Eddie's flight to Vietnam departed San Francisco on July 31, 1968, 24 years to the day after his father left San Diego to fight the war in the Pacific.

The flight path went over the North Pole to the Bien Hoa Air Base about 20 miles north of Saigon, Vietnam. Cobra helicopter gunships flew next to the arriving aircraft as protection during descent. Then it was a short hop aboard a twin turbo-prop Mohawk, a rugged airplane designed to land on crude airstrips, to a place called Xuan Loc. There, in a clearing between the triple canopy jungle and the rice paddies, was the base camp for the Air Cavalry Troop of the 11th Armored Cavalry Regiment. The Mohawk cruised at about 2,500 feet, then seemed to fall out of the sky for a landing in the middle of nowhere.

The arrivals were greeted with encouraging news. "Welcome to the safest place in Vietnam. We haven't been hit in months," they were told. Eddie and the other newcomers, known as Cherries because they were virgins to combat, lugged their gear to their quarters, an olive drab Army tent surrounded by protective sand bags.

That first night, at about 2 o'clock in the morning, the whistle of incoming mortar rounds shattered the quiet. One round exploded outside Eddie's tent, with pieces of jagged shrapnel tearing through the canvas and lodging into the wooden tent poles. A fireball set the tent ablaze and prompted a mad dash to the nearest bunker. The sudden realization that someone was trying to kill him was a nightmarish experience. Eddie was a bundle of nerves for the next two weeks. This was nothing like he had ever experienced before, and nothing like the war he expected. There was no front line like in the war movies he had grown up watching. The surrounding territory was infested with Viet Cong insurgents and North Vietnamese Army regulars. He vomited a lot and stopped eating. Finally, gripping the Saint Christopher medal he wore to protect him on his journey, he came to terms with it.

"This is crazy. You're killing yourself. If you're going to get killed, make them kill you. If they get me, they get me. At least go down fighting," he told himself.

From that moment on, nothing else mattered but his buddies and the thought of returning to his wife and family. Earlier in 1968, the North Vietnamese and the Viet Cong, also known as Victor Charlie, had launched the Tet Offensive, which struck a psychological blow back home. President Lyndon Baines Johnson, the commander-in-chief who had escalated this war, had already announced he would not seek re-election and would leave the war's future to his successor while he tried to negotiate a peace.

Eddie served as the crew chief on an OH-6 helicopter, generically known as a Loach (light observation chopper) or Flying Egg. The pilot and crew chief sat side by side on seats surrounded by a Plexiglas bubble. The crew chief's job was to keep the aircraft in flying shape and to man a grenade launcher or a machine gun if firepower was needed. Each of the little choppers flew in tandem with a Cobra gunship, which meant there were a total of 22 helicopters comprising 11 teams in his unit at Xuan Loc.

As the new guy, Eddie was assigned to fly with the platoon commander. This Army captain was a capable pilot and a capable leader. Instead of recklessly endangering the lives of his men, he believed his helicopters should serve as eyes and ears but leave the heavy fighting to the regiment's tanks and the grunts in their armored personnel carriers. Using a light helicopter for scouting missions was a rational and militarily sound approach. Too bad the arrangement was short-lived.

His captain went on a recon mission in a fixed wing aircraft. The plane either crashed or was shot down, and the captain was missing in action. When the wreckage was spotted two weeks later, ground troops brought back the captain's body. The force of the crash was so severe that the captain's .45 caliber pistol was jammed into his punctured abdomen. Because that pistol was government property, the Army ordered that it be recovered and cleaned. The grisly task fell to Eddie.

Blood, guts and putrefied flesh made a gory mess of that firearm. Eddie grabbed a stiff brush, some JP4 jet fuel and a cleaning kit to begin a day-long task. He stopped only when he had to puke because of the unbearable stench, which was stronger than the odor of the jet fuel. He got the job done. But that night in the shower, no matter how much soap he applied or how long he stayed under the stream of water, he just could not get that smell off his hands or out of his brain.

A new commanding officer arrived. Carrying pistols on his hips and flashing a gunslinger's look in his eye, he also had a new vision for the Air Cavalry Troop's mission.

"We're here to kill gooks, and kill gooks we will," said Major Hard Ass, which was the name the enlisted personnel gave him.

This approach was hardly new in Vietnam. Instead of gaining and holding territory, the idea was to rack up a big body count by killing so many of the foe that they would be bled of their strength and give up the fight. Killing gooks, a derisive term given to the Vietnamese, was also in keeping with the philosophy of the regimental commander, Colonel George S. Patton, the son and namesake of the World War II tank commander. The M-48 tanks in the 11th Armored Cavalry Regiment, which called itself the Blackhorse Cavalry and had a shoulder patch depicting a rearing black stallion on a red and white shield, were even called Patton tanks. Like his father, the younger Patton brandished pistols with ivory handles. The regiment's standing order was: "Find the bastards, then pile on." Some officers hated war but fought it to get it over with. Patton embraced it. He once said: "I do like to see the arms and legs fly." But as a consequence, some of the flying arms and legs belonged to the troops under his command.

Eddie's helicopter unit, which called itself The Gnat Patrol, began spearheading combat missions. The light choppers would fly at tree-top level, about 150 feet over the floor of a triple canopy jungle, to scout for enemy forces, bunker complexes, trails and equipment. Essentially, they were bait, sent up to draw fire from the enemy on ground. When they were shot at, the scouts would drop smoke grenades to mark the location. Then the AH-1 Cobra gunships will roar in with their rockets and guns blazing. They reaped a deadly harvest, but almost daily, scouts would be hit by enemy fire. It was not a question of who would be shot up or shot at, but when. They were bullet magnets.

Scout choppers routinely returned to the flight line with bullet holes in rotor blades, Plexiglas shields and aluminum hulls. On these search and destroy missions, carnage was everywhere. Casualty rates in the Gnat Patrol reached 50 percent. Every other man or ship was hit. Furthermore, the Loaches learned to paint the top of their helicopter blades orange — so the Cobras wouldn't mistakenly fire at them.

Eddie learned to fly the machine from his second pilot. On a mission, the pilot would release the controls and shout to Eddie to take over. He wanted his crew chief to be able to handle the machine in case he was hit.

In addition to assault missions, the scout helicopters sometimes assessed bomb damage following missions by Air Force B-52s, affectionately known as BUFFs (Big Ugly Fat Fuckers). Each warplane carried tons of bombs in its belly, and any area hit with a B-52 strike was reduced to a smoldering ruin. One time, air traffic controllers cleared Eddie and his pilot to fly in and take a look around after a bombing run. The smell of cordite filled the air while the jungle blazed with fire below. All of a sudden, objects that looked like falling logs dropped by the chopper. There was an explosion with a nerve-rattling shock wave, then another, and another. A second wave of three B-52s were dropping lethal payloads through the same air the chopper was flying in. Over the deafening din of hundreds of exploding 500-pound bombs, Eddie's pilot radioed the Air Force controllers, cursing at the top of his lungs while bomb fragments struck the chopper.

"It was a miracle we made it out of there. I felt we had cheated death," Eddie said.

In time, Eddie gave the name Day Tripper to his chopper. An officer gave him shit because he thought it was a reference to an LSD acid trip. Eddie explained it was the name of a Beatles song, and his ship was going out on combat trips daily. The name stuck.

Day Tripper was out on another run that was supposed to provide assessment of damage done by an artillery strike on an enemy position. The artillery unit had radioed in the "all clear," and Day Tripper charged in fast to avoid enemy fire. The ship was within 50 yards of the site when — Wham! — a fireball exploded and spewed dirt and shrapnel into the air. An artillery shell had exploded right in front of the helicopter. Shrapnel damaged the ship, but Day Tripper returned to base. Death had been cheated again.

In the midst of all this insanity, Major Hard Ass went out on an assault mission, and in violation of all regulations, he invited a date. Flying in his command-and-control chopper, the major brought along a female friend who was a nurse in Saigon. Nothing engorges a woman's nipples or gets her juices flowing like taking her on a bomb run, the major reasoned. It would have gone down as just a stupid idea, but during the mission, ground fire hit the major's ship and one of his crewmen was killed. As the pilot maneuvered to avoid more rounds, the woman's purse fell out into the jungle below. Back at base, the major ordered someone to retrieve it. The mission fell to Day Tripper.

"This is fucking great," Eddie muttered to his pilot. "We'll get killed trying to find a purse."

Lo and behold, they spotted the purse from the air and landed to retrieve it. Eddie was firmly convinced that the purse had been booby-trapped by the Viet Cong. He poked the purse with a stick, then grabbed it and raced back to Day Tripper for the flight home. The grateful major rewarded Eddie with a bottle of Crown Royal. The crewman who got killed on that ill-conceived mission would later get his name etched on The Vietnam Memorial Wall.

On occasion, observers would ask to go on search and destroy missions. They could be Cobra pilots or pogues who weren't required to fly combat missions. Day Tripper could be configured so that another seat could be folded down behind the crew chief and pilot, which accommodated passengers. But the observers weren't used to flying tight circles at low altitude for hours at a time while looking for targets. Without fail, these observers would puke all over the aircraft. Upon landing, the job of scrubbing out the ship fell to Eddie.

One time, an Army combat photographer talked his way into taking Eddie's seat on Day Tripper so that he could snap some pictures. At tree-top level, the photographer leaned out to get a better view. Then a couple of AK-47 rounds fired from the ground found their mark, ripping off the top of the photographer's head and spewing blood, brains and skull fragments through the ship. By the time Day Tripper returned to base with the photographer's lifeless body, blowflies were already feasting on the blood and gore. Eddie had to wash out the mess.

"People who weren't assigned combat missions thought war was an adventure. I thought it was too at first, until somebody starts shooting at you. Then it's not fun anymore," Eddie said. "The worst part was going up day after day after day after day. It wears on you. It was an everyday sight to see burned up bodies, guys with no limbs, dead gooks. Death was everywhere."

His primitive base camp was called Hud after the title of a movie in which Paul Newman portrayed a rebellious Texan. Eddie never saw the movie, but he liked the name. Home was a bunk inside a shelter surrounded by sandbags. When it rained, which it did often, the red clay soil turned into mud that clumped up on combat boots. It was impossible to scrape off completely.

Breakfast was almost always powdered eggs and powdered milk. Other meals came from C Rations, which were leftovers from World War II. In time, K Rations appeared and were a little better. The Air Cav also had the same rations as those carried by Long Range Recon Patrols (LRRPs). These precooked packaged meals could be heated up and served out of a pouch.

There wasn't much in the way of recreation, but one guy had captured a python in the jungle and brought it back to base. Once or twice a week, soldiers would feed the snake a Vietnamese duck.

As the days passed, Eddie marked his 21st birthday on September 9, 1968. Richard Nixon was elected president and promised to end the war. Thanksgiving, Christmas and New Year's Day came and went. Nothing provides a greater appreciation for America than being away from home at war during the holidays.

Then on January 23, 1969, on a search and destroy mission, Day Tripper spotted three enemy soldiers on the ground. Turning in an instant, the pilot flew back over the targets, and Eddie fired the M-79 grenade launcher. Two were killed, the third one ran for cover. Day Tripper was ordered to land and secure any papers that might provide intelligence. Gathering intel was one thing, but a jungle landing was always a terrifying prospect. Wary that one enemy might still be lurking in the bush, Eddie reached the two dead soldiers. His grenade had exploded just behind their heads, and hot metal fragments exited through their faces. It was hard to tell they were human beings. Looking for anything that might be of use, Eddie was surprised to discover that one of them was a woman. A lieutenant in the North Vietnamese army, she carried a picture of her husband among the maps and papers she carried.

Eddie received an Air Medal with "V" device, one of three Air Medals he earned, for bringing back the information. The citation said he distinguished himself with heroism by spotting two enemy trying to evade advancing ground forces. War saps the humanity right out of a person, but Eddie couldn't help but wonder about that woman and her comrades.

"I felt sorry for them at times. We were there for a year. They were in it for the duration. When they got sent south, it was either win or die. There was no going home for them until the whole thing was over," he said.

He also started to question the strategy of body counts. The cavalry would clear out an area, but before long, the enemy would move back in. Then they'd have to go back and kill again. Nothing was being gained.

"How are you going to beat these people? They were like termites coming out of a log. The more we killed, the more would come out," he said.

In time, a semblance of normalcy presented itself when the Army supplied a basketball and a rim for the troops at Xuan Loc. Soldiers nailed the basket to a pole and installed a plywood backboard. The court surface was tarmac. Basketball was a welcome respite from the stress of combat, and among the grunts who played was an African-American from Mississippi and another really good athlete from Kansas. Eddie got to know them during their one-on-one or half-court games. A bond of brotherhood developed. No matter the race or creed, no matter if a guy drove helicopters or was a grunt on the ground, they were all in it together.

Then one day, on a joint mission, Eddie went up in Day Tripper to provide air cover for a foot patrol that included his basketball buddies. Mississippi walked the point, with Kansas right behind him. In the jungle, a booby-trap had been rigged from an American Claymore mine, an ingenious killing device that is packed with pea-sized metal pellets and rigged to an explosive charge. Mississippi tripped the wire, shouting a warning in the split second before the mine exploded. Scores of pellets rent the air. Both of Mississippi's legs were blown off below the knees. The deadly blast also pelted Kansas from head to toe.

At the same time, the ground patrol captured an enemy soldier. Day Tripper was ordered to land, pick up the wounded prisoner and fly him back for interrogation. Raging inside Eddie and his pilot was the white hot anger that comrades feel when two of their buddies are blown apart. On the flight back, Eddie and his pilot were so pissed that, as payback, they planned to dump the prisoner out of the chopper and send him to his death. Unbeknownst to them, however, they were talking over an open radio channel. The commanding officer heard the chatter. Although he understood the desire for payback and he didn't mind adding to the body count, he ordered them to return the prisoner to base alive or face court-martial.

Not long after that, a third pilot was assigned to Day Tripper. He was an ex-Cobra pilot who wanted to experience missions in a scout helicopter. The new pilot was good at his job and knew enough not to take unnecessary risks on combat flights. He fit right in with the Gnat Patrol, making friends with the crews. Then one of their mutual friends, another Cobra pilot, asked to go on a mission in Eddie's seat. As an observer, he wanted to learn how Day Tripper performed missions. During the flight, however, a firefight broke out. Enemy rounds zipped up from the ground, and the guy sitting in Eddie's seat was hit. He was wearing a protective piece of armor called a chicken plate, which would stop a .30 caliber round fired from 100 yards away. But the slug came up under the chicken plate, tore through the left side of the observer's stomach and exited the right side of his neck. He died instantly. When Day Tripper returned to base, Eddie scrubbed another comrade's blood and guts from the aircraft.

"By not being on that mission, my life was spared again. My buddies had started calling me Lucky because I missed out on some real hairy missions, but I didn't feel very lucky. Was my time coming up soon?" Eddie mused.

Unnerved by the killing, Eddie's pilot was unfit to fly future missions. While flying at tree-top level, he would constantly turn Day Tripper in zig-zag patterns to avoid ground fire. This was extremely hard on the aircraft and on Eddie. Over the rice paddies, the pilot would fly at ten feet off the ground at

110 miles per hour to keep from getting hit. Nobody could shoot at them, but the helicopter spooked up swarms of birds. The birds would splat against the Plexiglas windshield, and to this day, Eddie has flashbacks every time he sees a flock of birds. Aware of the pilot's behavior, the commanding officer had him transferred out.

In seven months of combat, Eddie was promoted twice and held the rank of Specialist 5, the equivalent rank of a sergeant. Now he had to break in a fourth pilot, a 19-year-old who was fresh out of flight school. Green, nervous and unschooled in tree-top search and destroy, the pilot was jittery about going up, and it showed on the remarkable day of March 4, 1969.

Day Tripper got a distress call that a member of the regiment was badly wounded in a fierce ground fight. The wounded soldier and his fellow grunts took cover inside a hole in the jungle created by an exploding bomb. The crater was about the size of a swimming pool. A medical evacuation helicopter would be too big to attempt a rescue, but Day Tripper just might be able to squeeze its way in to fetch the wounded man. As the small ship descended through an opening in a thicket of bamboo trees, Eddie leaned out of the cockpit to guide the pilot left, right, forward and backward. At the same time, rounds from enemy ground fire zipped through Day Tripper's thin aluminum skin and whizzed around Eddie's head.

The first attempt failed, and Day Tripper could have flown off. But soldiers look out for one another. Who the hell else will? Day Tripper attempted a second descent, with rounds whistling by Eddie's head again. The helicopter pulled up again.

Then came a third attempt at lowering a helicopter down an opening hardly bigger than the size of an elevator shaft. Day Tripper dropped down and hovered at a height just off the jungle floor. The wounded soldier tried to crawl aboard, but the pilot employed evasive maneuvers to avoid being hit by gunfire. Again, the rescue attempt failed.

Day Tripper hovered above the jungle before a fourth attempt could be made when small arms fire crackled through and around the helicopter. In the hundreds of hours he had flown, Eddie's constant companion was the buzz of a helicopter engine droning in his ears. Now there was dead silence. An enemy round took out the engine, and Day Tripper plunged like a damn brick. To brace for a hard landing, Eddie raised himself out of his seat and tried to absorb the impact through his legs. The ship crashed with a thud. Shards of plastic from the shattered shield tore into his arms and legs.

Eddie's first act was to unbuckle the pilot's harness, and the officer raced out of the cockpit. Eddie then turned off the battery and fuel supply to keep the ship from bursting into flames. Bleeding and banged up but alive, Eddie popped yellow smoke to mark the position. Ground troops reached them in about 30 minutes.

The grunts escorted them back to the very bomb crater where the wounded man was located. Then a firefight erupted, with the opposing sides no more than ten yards apart. Troops inside the crater were ordered to lay down suppressing fire, but that consisted of rattled troops poking rifles atop the crater and firing blindly. Eddie grabbed a weapon and fired back at the muzzle flashes coming toward him. Enemy forces were so well entrenched they couldn't be dislodged. Finally, tanks were called in and rolled over the enemy positions, crushing whoever remained.

"It was one of my worst days ever. There were two miracles. I survived the crash and survived the firefight," Eddie said.

When he reached the infirmary, Eddie was bandaged up, given a set of crutches and ordered off-duty for ten days. His wounds qualified him for a Purple Heart, an award created by George Washington in the Revolutionary War to honor those who spill blood for their country.

For his actions in attempting to save a wounded man, Eddie was awarded the Distinguished Flying Cross, a medal rarely given to anyone who is not a pilot. But as the citation said, he had distinguished himself while participating in aerial flight and performing above and beyond the call of duty.

"Disregarding the possibility of return fire, Specialist Dvorchak leaned out of the aircraft to place suppressive fire on hostile positions and mark them with smoke grenades for helicopter gunships and advancing ground troops," the citation read. "On three occasions when the helicopter attempted to evacuate friendly soldiers wounded in fierce ground fighting, he exposed himself to intense enemy fire as he guided his pilot into an extremely small and hazardous landing zone...(His) outstanding courage and quick thinking were in keeping with the highest traditions of the military service and reflect great credit upon himself, his unit and the United States Army."

While he was recuperating, Eddie was introduced to his fifth pilot in seven months. The new guy would serve as his platoon's commanding officer, and he and Eddie hit it off immediately. A religious man, the lieutenant was well-respected by all members of the team, but their time together was limited to just one flight.

On the ninth day of Eddie's recovery, the Blackhorse Cavalry discovered an enemy bunker complex while conducting a mission in the Michelin Rubber Plantation near Lai Khe (pronounced Lie Kay). The gunships had a field day. The enemy was caught so off guard that they didn't even return fire. Returning air crews reported high body counts. One ship had 31 confirmed kills. Another had 25, and a third claimed 21. Body counts were sometimes exaggerated to make units look good, but these enemy kills were legitimate.

The Air Cav's commander was so fired up at the prospect of an even a higher body count that he couldn't wait to go back the next day. *Find the bastards, then pile on.* He ordered all combat teams into the fight. Still unable to walk without crutches, Eddie was supposed to see the doctor the next day about his previous wounds. No matter. He was ordered to fly too.

"You don't have to walk. You'll be flying," the commander told him.

A sick feeling grew in the pit of Eddie's stomach. He knew the enemy, now stung in battle, would be ready the next day. There was still a chance that Day Tripper would be grounded. The ship required a new blade on the main rotor, and normally, that would take several days to replace. Although ground crews had a spare blade and worked all night to install it, a helicopter blade is a tricky thing. Putting on a new one was like putting a summer tire on a car equipped with three snow tires. The ship would probably rattle and shake and be unworthy of flight. But Lucky's fortune had run out. During a test flight, Day Tripper performed flawlessly.

"Shit, that son of a bitch was so smooth it was as if that blade was custom-made for that chopper," Eddie said. "Man, I knew I was fucked. There ain't no way I wasn't going to get hit. I just knew it."

Nevertheless, Eddie limped on crutches to his helicopter and buckled up. Day Tripper, its companion Cobra and ten other teams took off before dawn. In addition to the air umbrella, tanks and armored personnel carriers carrying infantrymen roared over the ground. Before the sun was up, the force encountered enemy soldiers in open-faced bunkers. The helicopters circled their prey. So many ships were flying in close quarters that it looked like a traffic jam in the air.

When a crash seemed inevitable, Day Tripper pulled away to look for other targets. Sure enough, Eddie spotted a North Vietnamese Army pack on a bicycle leaning against a brush pile. Without knowing that two enemy soldiers were hiding under the brush, his pilot ordered him to take out the bike with a grenade.

Eddie raised the M-79 grenade launcher, which looked like a sawed off shotgun, into a shooting position. Because a tree blocked his sight, he told the pilot to pull up.

As soon he had a clear line of sight, Eddie fired. Simultaneously, rounds from an AK-47 pierced through Day Tripper, two going on either side of the pilot's head without hitting anything. However, a round tore through the fleshy part of Eddie's right forearm and punched through his right biceps, ripping out flesh, muscle and nerve endings. As blood spurted everywhere, the grenade hit the brush pile, and the two enemy soldiers flew up into the air. Eddie got them just as they got him. It happened in an eye-blink.

"My right arm went numb. I was bleeding like a stuck pig. I looked over at the lieutenant, who had come within a whisker of taking a head shot. If he had been hit, that would have been curtains for me too, because I couldn't fly the ship with a useless right arm," Eddie said.

The pilot rushed back to the infirmary. Eddie had never known such pain, but his overwhelming feeling was one of relief.

"Thank God. My time in Hell is over," Eddie thought to himself. He had earned a second Purple Heart within ten days, and regimental commander George S. Patton signed the citation.

While awaiting evacuation to a military hospital in Japan, some of his buddies stopped by to visit. In a continuation of the same battle Eddie was in, one of his brother crew chiefs and his pilot got into a fierce firefight. Shot out of the air, the helicopter crashed and burned. Both men died. Rushing in to help them, another chopper was shot down and its crew chief and pilot were killed. Within two days of getting wounded, four of Eddie's comrades were dead.

A military aircraft evacuated Eddie to a hospital in Yokohama, Japan. The butcher's bill of the war in Vietnam was right in front of his eyes. Hundreds of young men his own age, each with fresh wounds, lined the wards.

When he was well enough to travel, Eddie was placed aboard a C-130 cargo plane converted into a flying hospital for a return flight to the States. The aircraft had canvas seats lining each side of the fuselage, and Eddie strapped himself in. Also in the belly of the ship were guys on stretchers, moaning, groaning and crying for their mothers. Eddie was thankful he was able to sit up. The flight lasted 22 horrible hours. He ended up at the Valley Forge Veterans Administration Hospital outside of Philadelphia.

By this time, a telegram from the Defense Department had arrived back on the farm. The brief message said Eddie had been wounded but was ambulatory. That meant he was at least able to walk, which seemed of little comfort to his distressed parents and siblings.

Because I had the best car, a 1966 Chevelle hardtop with an eight-track tape player, I drove out with his wife to see him at Valley Forge. I had been writing to him in Vietnam, and I knew that a war had been going on. Nothing prepared me for that hospital scene, however. To reach him, we walked through eight wards, each filled with guys my age who were maimed, disfigured, castrated, shot all to hell. The smell of bloody wounds and rotting flesh almost knocked me over.

When we reached Eddie for a tearful reunion, his arm was in a sling and he looked like a scarecrow, some 60 pounds lighter than his football playing weight. He didn't have a room, just a slot in a ward with sheets put up around some of the most severely wounded. He had a gift for me — a cigarette lighter shaped like a hand grenade. Pulling the pin triggered the flint and lit the flame. I was playing with my new toy, pulling the pin again and again, thinking this was really neat. Then I looked to my right and there was a kid my age with a thousand yard stare and tears in his eyes because both his arms had been blown away by a grenade. Ashamed, I put the lighter away and tried to look invisible.

Eddie faced eleven months of recovery and recuperation in that wretched place. His body healed, but the emotional and psychological damage got worse. Living in a hospital with young men who had been blown to pieces, whose noses and ears and been burned off, whose faces had been blown away, took a toll. The crying soldiers and the horrible smell that permeated that warehouse of the wounded would get to anybody.

"What a waste of humanity," Eddie thought.

He qualified for disability pay for his damaged right arm, which would never be the same. On Memorial Day, four weeks after the Kent State shootings, Eddie donned his uniform and his medals to ride in a parade in the small Fayette County town of Connellsville. His wife said somebody came out of the crowd and spit on him. He took the uniform off and seldom spoke of the war again until he received counseling for Post Traumatic Stress Disorder decades later.

A footnote: The American Army never lost a major ground battle in Vietnam before turning the fighting over to the South Vietnamese army. In March of 1975 at Xuan Loc, the place consecrated with the blood of Eddie and his comrades, the South made its last stand against the North and lost. After Xuan Loc fell, the road to Saigon was open. The fallen capital was renamed Ho Chi Minh City.

For his attempt to rescue a wounded comrade in the action that earned him the Distinguished Flying Cross, Eddie was inducted in 2015 into the Joseph A. Dugan Hall of Valor at Soldiers & Sailors Hall, a Pittsburgh military museum that has honored qualifying veterans from western Pennsylvania in all branches of the service since the Civil War. Having retired to South Carolina, he can wear his medals again.

CHAPTER 8
Beneath The Veil

What are Saudi cities like? Like the Marine who asked that question, any Westerner deployed to the peninsula operated in a cultural desert. The responsibilities of the assignment left almost zero time for sight-seeing in a kingdom that veiled itself from the outside world. Even though the glance may have been cursory, we existed in a strange juxtaposition of the ancient and the modern. The dominant features of the withered landscape are the ubiquitous mosques of Islam adorning centuries-old Arab communities sprinkled with a mix of fast food restaurants, shopping malls and new-fangled conveniences.

As good a start as any for peeking beneath the veil of Saudi life are the Bedouins, the nomads who wander the endless sands in search of water and scattered pockets of life where their flocks of goats, sheep and camels can find enough to eat and drink. Through the Ministry of Information, I asked to interview a Bedouin and was told "insh'allah," or God willing, which usually means "fat chance" unless there's some kind of divine intervention. Then lo and behold, a Saudi interpreter and driver appeared one day to take me and a photographer into the wilderness.

We drove north on the inner highway and took the exit to a place with the tongue-twister name of Nuariyah. The photographers referred to Arabic signs as being written in "worms and squiggles," but license plates are easy enough to read because it was the Arabs who popularized the numeric system familiar to the world. We left the pavement to drive across the open sand, and in time, we came across a desert dweller who had recently moved his herd of 240 goats from the north because military camps had intruded on centuries-old rhythms and squeezed him out of his traditional grazing areas.

His name was Fulayyih Al-Azmi, who with his wife and children, lived inside a tent made of burlap and camel hide. With the flaps up to welcome the breeze, the dark brown tent provided tolerable shade and a haven from the unrelenting sun. In a display of Bedouin hospitality, he served tea and dates while telling a story. Recently, the quiet of a starry night was shattered when he peered outside his tent to see a metal monster rumbling past his goat pen. It had to be an American tank or armored vehicle out on night maneuvers.

"My wife was afraid because it had no lights, and she didn't know what it was. I couldn't speak their language, so I lit a lantern to let them know I was here. After that, I don't move my herd at night anymore," the man of the desert said through the interpreter.

I was writing it down with my notebook perched on my right knee. When more tea was offered, I instinctively reached out with my left hand to take the cup. One of his children, his face covered with flies, laughed. A fundamental cultural faux pas had been committed. Never extend the left hand to an Arab because it's the hand used to wipe themselves. Profuse apologies were extended and accepted.

At any rate, Al-Azmi was willing to put up with the inconvenience of moving his goats. He understood that foreign troops had been invited into the country by the king, himself a descendant of Bedouins, to reverse the Iraqi invasion of a fellow Arab country.

"I thank God the government is having people come to defend the kingdom. Saddam Hussein attacked people who did him no harm. Allah will punish him," Al-Azmi said.

The Bedouin lived much like his forefathers, barely subsisting from water hole to water hole as herds of goats, sheep and camels nibbled on what little vegetation they could find. The nomads have meager possessions such as rugs, cushions and cookware, but even they have been affected by the march of progress. It was common for Bedouins like our host to have luxuries like Toyota pickup trucks, which are now as much a part of tribal life as the camel once was.

Guided by whim and the weather, Bedouins pay no attention to political lines drawn on the map. They don't have gadgets that plot their position by using satellites or reconnaissance flights. They rely on the stars or the blowing sands to guide them. The desert is their home, back yard and pasture. But now the U.S. military needed space to operate and to test-fire its artillery and other long-range weapons. Home on the range has become home on the firing range.

Attempts were made to make sure there were no desert wanderers out and about when the guns opened up. Accidents were inevitable, though. On one artillery range, the big guns splattered one camel and wounded two others that had roamed into the kill zone. It's a big loss to a Bedouin because a camel can fetch $2,500 at market. Reparations were paid.

A short time after interviewing the Bedouin, I was on a night exercise with the Marines. In getting acclimated to the desert, they maneuvered their amphibious assault vehicles, which were similar to the machines that ferried Marines from ship to shore during the island-hopping campaign of World War II. The vehicles had tracks, not wheels, and were known as AAVs or amtracks. Now the machines carried infantry on maneuvers in a sea of sand.

At first, I rode in the back with the grunts, being jostled as the amtrack rolled and pitched over the dunes. One Marine actually slept during the ride, proof that troops can sleep anywhere. Then an invitation came to ride up front. Someone lent me a set of night vision goggles, which amplify starlight to allow the user to see in the dark. I could see well enough to know there was an AAV on our left and on our right as we cruised over the sand. Suddenly, I spotted a Bedouin tent that was in our way. A man scared out of his wits jumped out of the way. His goats scattered everywhere. We just missed running him over.

"Did you guys see that?" I yelled.

"See what?"

Nothing was hit, but I can still see that poor Bedouin running for his life.

The birth of the modern kingdom of Saudi Arabia reads like a fable. It began with the family that was on the losing end of a fight late in the 19th Century. The clan sought safe haven in Kuwait, one reason the Saudis were so keen on overturning the Iraq invasion. A future king, Abdulaziz ibn Abdul Rahman al Saud, or ibn Saud as he was known, hid in his father's saddle bags for a long trek across the desert to a safe haven.

A Bedouin warrior, horseman and hunter, the future king became skilled in the use of the dagger, the sword and the rifle. After years of exile, at the age of

21, he returned to Arabia with 40 able men on camelback and captured Riyadh in 1902. His forces then fought warring tribes in region after region. One of the ways he unified the peninsula under the House of Saud was to marry women from the conquered tribes, but following Islamic custom, he never had more than four wives at a time. In the span of three decades, he declared himself king. Saudi Arabia became a country in 1932, with Riyadh as its capital and a family as its ruler. The king surrounded the city with walls to protect inhabitants from potential invaders.

Like the desert, the kingdom hides its secrets well. No tourist bureau exists because the kingdom is leery of outsiders to the point of being xenophobic. The country's founder set the tone when he said: "My kingdom will survive insofar as it remains a country difficult to access, where the foreigner will have no other aim, with his task fulfilled, but to get out." We were all just passing through.

Understanding Saudi Arabia is impossible without knowing at least something about Islam, which means to submit oneself to the will of God. The king's most cherished title is Defender of the Two Holy Mosques, the hallowed sites at Mecca and Medina that mark the birth and death of the prophet Mohammad, peace be upon him. As an Arab who once made his living on cross-desert caravans, Mohammad received the word of Allah, the Arabic name for God, the Merciful and the Almighty. The revelations were ultimately written down in the Qu'ran to be shared with all the tribes on the Arabian peninsula. The holy book serves not only as a blueprint for the Arab way of life, it is Saudi Arabia's Constitution. The Saudi flag, in green, has an image of a sword and an edict written in Arabic: "There is no God but Allah, and Mohammad is the messenger of Allah." No other religion is openly practiced.

If they are able during their lifetimes, Muslims are required to make a pilgrimage to Mecca, a practice the pilgrims call the Hajj. Mecca and Medina are off-limits to non-believers, however. Road signs dictate that all non-Muslims exit the roadways leading into the cities.

It's their country. They have the right to believe what they want and live the way they want to live, and we wouldn't care, except for the complications of oil.

Within a week of my arrival, representatives of ARAMCO (the Arab-American Oil Company) organized a tour of Saudi Arabia's first oil-producing well for the visiting media. It was called Damman No. 7, or Lucky No. 7. Pioneering geologists worked on it in 1933, but it wasn't until 1938 that the wildcatters and roughnecks tapped into a reservoir of crude oil 4,700 feet below the surface.

In a story told by an American oil executive who now lives in Dhahran, a 43-mile pipeline was constructed between this "mother of wells" and the new port of Ras Tanura, where the precious crude is pumped onto tankers for export. The first king of the House of Saud led a caravan of 2,000 people in 500 cars across the desert from Riyadh to check out the new discovery. The country's founder turned the valve to open the pipeline on May 1, 1939.

No. 7 was just the start. One-fourth of all the oil in the world lies beneath territory claimed by Saudi Arabia. In addition to 167 billion barrels of recoverable oil reserves, drillers have found 135 trillion feet of recoverable natural gas. The incredible riches from the underground treasures transformed Saudi Arabia from a Bedouin culture to a modern economic dynamo in the space of a generation.

Although no military alliance existed between America and Saudi Arabia, a special relationship anointed with oil dated back to the last months of World War II. President Franklin Delano Roosevelt, returning from the Yalta Conference in Crimea, arranged a meeting with the king of Saudi Arabia. The two leaders met aboard the *USS Quincy* in Egypt's Great Bitter Lake on February 14, 1945. The Saudi king brought sheep to be slaughtered for a formal meal. The patrician president proclaimed that the kingdom's security was a matter of fundamental interest to America. Under this informal arrangement, America military might would protect Saudi oil fields. The two countries were the oddest of odd couples in so many ways, but one needed to sell oil, and one needed to buy it, and they would have to reconcile the friction between them.

Dhahran, my new home, was actually one of three cities that made up an urban area of about 300,000 residents. The other communities were the seaport city of Dammam and the market area of Al-Khobar. Most of what was seen on a daily basis didn't exist a half-century ago.

Dhahran was nothing but an uninhabited hill of sand and scrub brush until the late 1940s, and its growth was spurred when the Americans were allowed to build a military base with an airstrip that is now the international airport. Dammam had a spring that supported a single tribe, its water allowing an extended family to exist in the barren desert. With the advent of the oil boom, things changed dramatically. In 1946, Dammam was selected as the site of a deep water seaport on the Persian Gulf, which the Saudis called the Arabian Gulf. Dammam also was chosen as the starting point of a railroad line built across the desert to the capital city of Riyadh.

Al-Khobar, which historically was a small fishing village, became a blend of the old and the new after the oil boom. A modern business center sprang from the traditional bazaar where rugs and trinkets were sold in shops near the fish market. Western influences could be found in such places as the photo shop the photographers discovered to develop their film. It was sandwiched between a doughnut shop and a Baskin-Robbins ice cream store. Other establishments offered that most American of expressions — the T-shirt. With the kingdom on a war-footing, shirts were adorned with diverse images such as a camel wearing a gas mask while riding on a flying carpet, a tank named Camel Smoker, and for someone with a real sense of humor, the Hard Rock Cafe of Al-Khobar. No such place existed.

Al-Khobar had Western influences such as Burger King, Kentucky Fried Chicken, Dairy Queen and the Pizza Sheikh. Supermarkets offered fresh produce. Just like back home, the place to hang out was the mall, in this case a two-story building that had a Radio Shack and stores that carried pricey Rolex watches, high-end cameras and TVs. My favorite was the music store. The kingdom has no copyright laws, so cassette tapes were available for the equivalent of one American dollar apiece. Shelves were stocked with the greatest hits of The Beatles, The Rolling Stones, Jimi Hendrix, Bob Seger and Frank Sinatra.

All commerce ceased, however, during prayer time, which is announced by the melodious chant of a muezzin. Shopkeepers hang out a sign that says "Closed For Prayer." Business resumes once prayer time is over.

Suffice it to say that nobody comes here for the night life. Normally on an assignment, the thing to do to get a feel for a new place is to find a watering hole and befriend the bartender, but there are no bars. Non-alcoholic beer is sold in stores, but O'Doul's offers little in the way of consolation. No movie theaters or dance clubs are permitted.

Some decent restaurants offered an alternative to the hotel fare. My favorite was the Thai place with the spicy seafood soup. There were, however, cultural clashes in something as simple as going out to eat. One night, as a group of media went to a Khobar restaurant, I was walking behind two women journalists who, unlike Saudi women, were not wearing head scarves and were not covered from head to toe in black robes. An agitated Arab came up from behind and tapped me on the ankles with a long stick. He was a member of the religious police, formally known as the Committee for Encouraging Virtue and Discouraging Vice. These enforcers were called mutawwa, a word than means volunteer, and they looked for infractions of the law like going out in public with improper attire. Instead of reprimanding the women, he targeted me because a man is supposed to be in charge. With all the civility I could muster, I told him it wasn't my place to tell American women what to do, and he could beat my ankles until they bled, or break both my legs, but I still couldn't tell an American woman how to dress. The guy had the sense of humor of a diseased camel, but he let us pass.

On another occasion, about ten of us were seated at a table in an Indian restaurant. The maitre d' ordered that a portable screen be put up around the table so that we would be walled off from other patrons, who objected to seeing American women out in public.

Going out beat sitting in the room to watch TV at night. There was only one channel of state-controlled news. An anchorman wearing a headdress would read the news in English. No sense in listening to the weather forecast either. It's the same every day — brutally hot and sunny, with no chance of rain.

But get this. Dhahran has a golf course called Rolling Hills Golf Club.

There's nary a blade of grass to be found. Golfers hit their shots off a patch of artificial turf that they carry around with them. The greens are actually brown. The putting surface is sand that is rolled and then coated with oil or kerosene. The sand traps are remarkable. The kingdom may sit atop one of the largest expanses of sand in the world, but the texture of the sand is such that it turns to powder when disturbed. Sand for the bunkers is actually imported. It would be like Eskimos importing snow. I never found time to play, but I did get a golf shirt with the club's logo.

Public executions were suspended during the deployment. I never got the chance to see an executioner chop off a criminal's head with a curved sword.

My one opportunity for tourism grudgingly presented itself one Thursday morning. The photographers wanted to take a trip to a traditional camel market at Hofuf, a 90-mile drive from the hotel but a step back into time. Despite worries that the war might start, they talked me into going.

"How can you pass up a chance to see Larry's Camel Lot? Same location for two thousand years," one of them said.

Hofuf is one of the oldest inhabited settlements in Arabia, mainly because the ancient place had the largest spring-fed oasis in the world. In the middle of the arid plain stood 30,000 acres of gardens and a forest of date palm trees.

If the camel is the ship of the desert, the camel market in Hofuf was one giant boat yard. Camels were available for buying and selling. I helped one Bedouin unload a camel from the back of his pickup, and I also got my picture taken sitting in the saddle atop one of the dromedaries. Part of the market is devoted to breeders. Owners bring their female camels to be impregnated for a fee by some magnificent stud.

The Arab version of a go-anywhere, do-anything mode of ground transportation was the camel. They may be ornery critters that spit and bite, but no other animal had a more significant hand in shaping Arab culture. Their ability to carry heavy loads across the forbidding desert opened up ancient trade routes. The trading of frankincense and myrrh for silks, spices and gold would have been impossible without camels, which have feet made of broad leathery pads that don't sink into the sand. Camels are especially adapted to the desert. They have extra eyelashes to keep out blowing particles during sandstorms, and they can close their nostrils to keep out the grit. The hump stores fat, so they can go for days without drinking or eating and can lose one-third of their body weight without consequence. When they do come upon a watering hole, camels can drink up to 15 gallons at a time — the capacity of some gas tanks. When walking, a camel moves both legs on one side, then the two on the other side. It makes for a gentle rocking motion, which contributes to their reputation as the ship of the desert. A camel is an Arabian commissary. It provides milk, cheese, meat and hide. Even its dung can be burned as fuel. Like the locals say, a camel has many parts. To keep them from wandering off at night, camels are hobbled at night with a black cord that is also worn over the traditional Arab headdress. We called it the radiator belt.

Our stay in the camel market concluded, we ventured into Hofuf to stroll through the marketplace. Shops offered jewelry, colorful cloth, watches, house wares, tea pots, cups, cardamom, cloves, ginger, curry powder, savory spices, fruits, rugs and tobacco. It was a good place to buy souvenir tea sets and engage in the Arab custom of negotiating. If you say *wajid* — too much — an Arab trader will usually come down in price. Nobody pays retail.

Because we were unescorted, the religious police appeared and demanded to see our credentials. Just when I thought we were going to be arrested for being where we weren't supposed to be, the police cornered one of the AP photographers who was based in Germany. After a brief encounter, the police became quite friendly and let us go about our business.

What had he said to turn an angry encounter into a friendly conversation? His media credential identified him as being from Germany, the land of Hitler, and Hitler killed Jews. The encounter was the embodiment of the Bedouin proverb: the enemy of my enemy is my friend. The Middle East is a harsh, complex place.

One Saturday afternoon after completing an assignment with the Marines, photographer Dave Martin and I drove through Jubail. The community embodied the transformation of Saudi Arabia from a centuries-old culture of Bedouin herders and traders into a modern country built on oil riches. Jubail in Arabic means mountain, but in reality, it sat on a small hill. Once a small fishing village and once the home of a slave market, Jubail had morphed into an industrial center that supported the businesses of exploration and drilling for oil. Foreign workers had been recruited to build the modern city. One of its current attractions was a big smoke shop, where the locals gathered to enjoy a brick of Turkish tobacco through a water pipe while sipping tea and discussing the issues of the day. It was like a sports bar, without TVs or beer. Dave wanted to snap a picture of the colorful water pipes lined up in an open courtyard. After getting permission from the owners, he put his camera to work. Then the fun began.

A good ol' boy from Alabama, Dave suggested we smoke a bowl. It cost the equivalent of a dollar to buy a brick of tobacco, and, well, even condemned men get a last smoke. Escorted inside, we procured a couple of water pipes and leaned back on the pillows. The smoke is inhaled through a tube that served the same purpose as a pipe stem. The water pipe, also called a hookah or hubbly-bubbly, cooled and filtered the smoke as it passed through. Dave took a deep pull and felt an immediate nicotine rush.

"Hey, I'm getting a buzz. This must be hashish," he said.

"No, it's not," I told him. "Drugs are illegal in the kingdom. You're just getting high on the tobacco. Take it easy on that stuff. It's really strong."

Under Saudi Arabia's civil and criminal code that was based on religious law, drug trafficking and drug smuggling are punishable by death. Those caught dealing drugs will have their heads cut off in public. Miscreants can receive 80 lashes just for processing or distributing the stuff. But Dave took another long pull, and another, and another, thinking he was getting a high. The water pipe bubbled as if it were boiling. He finished the whole brick in short order. Then his face turned green before becoming as white as his T-shirt. The stuff had made him sick.

"I think I'm going to throw up," he said.

So much for a relaxing smoke.

"Don't you dare. They'll probably arrest us and put us in jail. We'll be thrown out of the country, and I won't be able to cover the war. Whatever you do, do not throw up," I insisted.

The words were barely out of my mouth when he barfed the first time. Puke splattered everywhere.

"Take off your shirt and tie it around your mouth," I told him. "Whatever you do, do NOT throw up again."

As he gagged his mouth, the commotion had attracted the attention of the other patrons. Some were laughing and pointing. You didn't have to understand Arabic to know they were quite amused by an outsider struggling with one of their customs. Then Dave let go with another heave, and the stuff exploded out of the sides of the temporary gag.

"Let me know the second you think you're strong enough to stand, and let's get out of here," I said.

After he had gathered himself and some color returned to his face, I put his arm over my shoulder and walked him to the door, paying for the tobacco and tea as deferentially as I could and offering to pay the cleaning bill.

I got him into the car, but he didn't have a spare shirt. He had to wear the soggy one he had just ruined. With the windows down, we drove the two hours back to Dhahran at 120 kilometers per hour. I threw in a Jimi Hendrix tape and cranked up the volume, listening to *All Along The Watchtower* as Dave slept it off.

The story got funnier and funnier as time passed.

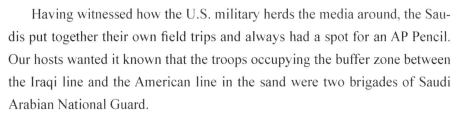

Having witnessed how the U.S. military herds the media around, the Saudis put together their own field trips and always had a spot for an AP Pencil. Our hosts wanted it known that the troops occupying the buffer zone between the Iraqi line and the American line in the sand were two brigades of Saudi Arabian National Guard.

To visit them, we boarded a military transport plane in Dhahran for a flight to a place called Hafr al-Batin. The town, located about 60 miles from the Kuwait border, was once a desert stop for pilgrims passing through on their way to Mecca. Water wells had been dug in the 7th Century to refresh them on their journey. The town sits along a dry bed of the ancient Pison River, thought to be one of the four rivers of the Garden of Eden. Once the largest river in Asia, the waterway had dried up thousands of years ago. The only hint that a river once existed were the rocks dotting the withered channel.

Yellow school buses ferried us over miles of flat, pebble-strewn, hard-packed sand before we reached the Saudi camp. The troops were the latest incarnation of the White Army, a group of tribal forces that once served the country's founder. They were there to defend the kingdom but had never practiced large-scale battlefield maneuvers.

The trip was arranged as an inspection tour by three-star general Khalid bin Sultan, the commander of the Saudi Air Force and a nephew of the king. As the kingdom's top military commander, he was the Norman Schwarzkopf of Saudi Arabia and as physically imposing. Technically, he was co-commander of Desert Shield, and the top commander of the Egyptian, Syrian and other Arab troops who had planted their flag in the sand to stop Saddam Hussein. Khalid reinforced the point that Saudi troops were positioned in front of the American, British, French and all the other forces in the kingdom.

"If our friends are here to shed their blood with us, the least we can do is put our forces right in front. If any blood is shed, I can assure you Saudis will spill it before our friends," the general said.

One Saudi soldier invited me into his tent. His sandy floor was covered by a huge carpet. The tent's center pole had a TV antenna bolted to it so the occupant could spend free time watching the tube. Tea was brewing on his personal stove. These creature comforts were non-existent in American military camps.

At noon, the Saudi troops stopped whatever they were doing and rolled out their prayer rugs in the sand. General Khalid led them in the religious ritual. When prayers concluded, a military truck drove up and served trays of whole roasted chickens on beds of cooked rice. Bottled water and soda were provided. At least this army lives and eats well.

But could the Saudis fight? Would they be of any use in a war with Iraq? Only combat could provide the answer. One British officer was already dismissive, sniffing: "They're not worth the sand they're sitting on."

———————————✦———————————

Just days after Iraq's takeover of Kuwait, Khalid had been part of the high-powered meeting that resulted in the unprecedented decision to allow American troops inside Saudi Arabia. He and other members of the Saudi royal family greeted U.S. officials such as Secretary of Defense Dick Cheney and H. Norman Schwarzkopf, the four-star Army general whose command watched over the Middle East. In an ornate royal palace, the Americans displayed satellite photos showing Iraqi tanks poised to strike south across the Saudi border. Military options were outlined if Saudi Arabia agreed to become a staging area. King Fahd, a son of Saudi Arabia's founder, listened politely but had already made up his mind. Iraq's invasion of Kuwait, a stab in the back by one Arab state into another, was like an occupation of the Saudi capital of Riyadh.

"The Kuwaitis delayed asking for help, and now they are our guests. We do not want to make the same mistake and become someone else's guest," the king reasoned. He agreed to allow U.S. forces onto the holiest ground in Islam to protect Saudi Arabia's sovereignty and its oil reserves.

Khalid expressed similar views. "The nationality of the troops that came to our aid was our least concern. If your house is on fire, you are not too concerned about who helps you extinguish the flames," he wrote in his war memoir *Desert Warrior.*

Unknown at the time, however, the seeds for a future war were planted even before this one began. Call it Murphy's Law of Unintended Consequences.

A Saudi militant approached King Fahd with an option that would have negated the need for American intervention in the kingdom. This warrior offered to unleash his militia network to defeat Saddam Hussein, just as he had gone to Afghanistan to take on the Soviet army in a previous war. His name was Osama bin Laden, scion of a Saudi billionaire and an Islamic fundamentalist who believed in jihad, or holy war. Osama, a name that means young lion, was born in Riyadh in 1957 to Mohammed bin Awad bin Laden and one of his

22 wives. Osama's father owned the largest construction company in Saudi Arabia and, as a favorite of the royal family, he had earned riches beyond his wildest dreams. He sired 53 other children, but Osama was the only one born to Alia, a Syrian wife. Osama was educated and steeped in Wahhabism, a puritanical, anti-Western strain of Islam that dominates Saudi thinking. When the Soviets invaded Afghanistan, Osama was part of a coalition of Muslim fighters who had been supported by the United States in a fight against the Red Army. At the moment, however, Osama thought it a sacrilege to allow Americans on the sacred soil of Islam. When the Saudi king opted for the unmatched military might of America's professional army, Osama vehemently opposed the royal family's decision. In time, he was deported and his Saudi citizenship was revoked. Ultimately, he created a radical movement called al-Qaeda, an Arab name that means The Base. Even though America stepped in to defend Saudi Arabia, Osama later waged war on America because its troops had landed on Saudi soil. When America was attacked with commercial jets that had been turned into guided missiles on Sept. 11, 2001, 15 of the 19 hijackers were Saudis. The Middle East is a complex place.

What was Saudi like? On the surface, the locals were polite enough, but there always seemed to be an underlying friction. Some Saudis objected to the presence of outsiders, even if those outsiders were there to defend the kingdom. I heard it more than once during the deployment — the guns were pointed in the wrong direction.

CHAPTER 9
Hoo-ah!

Monday, November 5. The phone rang at the AP suite at the Dhahran International Hotel. On the line was headquarters in New York, and a sinking feeling took hold. One look at the clock indicated it was just about the time the news executives were emerging from the morning news meeting brimming with story ideas. And sure enough, they had marching orders.

The voice belonged to Marty Sutphin, one of my favorite editors on the general desk. Listening was difficult because of a triple echo on the phone, which we just assumed was due to the Saudis tapping the lines. First off, he said the gas masks were due to be shipped any day from London, a welcome update because anyone who didn't carry a personal defense against the threat of chemical or nerve gas attacks felt naked. He also asked how things were going. At the moment, I was the lone AP staffer in a country where I didn't know the language or the culture, the war could start at any minute, there was no happy hour anywhere and it wasn't exactly a target-rich environment when it came to the opposite sex, but other than that, I was having the time of my life. He chuckled.

The real reason for the call was a story idea based on the premise that troops might be losing their fighting edge after being hunkered down for three months in the desert. The request, which in reality was an order, coincided with a live-fire training exercise scheduled for the next day by the 82nd Airborne. I told Marty to consider it done. A day in the field should provide all the fodder necessary to satisfy the editors. Only in retrospect did the significance of that day come into focus. In a Pencil's world, the real story often unfolds while the brain trust wants something else written.

Even those who have never been in the Army have some understanding of the long, proud tradition of the Airborne. When the 82nd Infantry Division was formed in World War I, its members came from every state in the Union. They called themselves All-Americans, leading to the distinctive Double-A every soldier wore as a shoulder patch. The division's most famous soldier in that war was Sergeant Alvin York, who was awarded the Medal of Honor in France and who was portrayed in the movies by Gary Cooper. Sergeant York was a country boy who objected to killing but who did his duty in the trenches in order to get the war over with as quickly as possible. Then in World War II, the division became the Army's first Airborne unit, with elements making combat jumps at Sicily, Salerno, Normandy and Holland during Operation Market Garden. Division commander James "Jumpin' Jim" Gavin noted: "Show me a man who will jump out of an airplane, and I'll show you a man who will fight." When General George Patton saw the division marching in Berlin, he said he had never seen a finer honor guard. The Airborne adopted the compliment for its slogan: "America's Guard of Honor."

My first experience with the Airborne came in 1973 at Fort Lee, Virginia, where a contingent of paratroopers was on temporary duty to practice packing giant parachutes for dropping heavy equipment and big guns from cargo planes. The rest of the Army would rise before dawn, begin the day with physical training (P.T.), scarf down breakfast in the chow hall in 15 minutes and then march to duty stations. The Airborne did a little extra. Instead of marching, they ran, singing a spirited cadence.

Everywhere we go, people want to know, who we are, where we come from. So we tell them. We are Airborne. Lean and mean Airborne. Rough and tough Airborne. Hard to fight Airborne. Fit to fight Airborne. Fit to win Airborne. One mile, no sweat. Better yet, two miles. One, two, three, four. Run a little, run a little, run some more. There's two things that I can't stand, a bow-legged woman and a straight-legged man.

A soldier who lacked wings on his chest, a designation earned by completing five practice drops at Jump School in Fort Benning, Georgia, was a lowly leg. My buck sergeant was so inspired by the Airborne spirit that he made us run everywhere we went too. Even if he was a living blob of chicken shit, he knew his order would be obeyed because he had one more stripe than the rest of us. The Airborne had a reputation for being mouthy braggarts who thought they were better than everybody else, which was annoying because they were. Paratroopers are the best light infantry in the world. Just ask one of them. They got an extra amount of money for jumping out of airplanes. So when payday rolled around every other Friday, or when the eagle shit as they say in the Army, paratroopers had jump pay to spend.

On one practice drop, the chutes failed to deploy properly and a piece of government-issued equipment crashed to the ground. Somebody was filling out paper work for months for that error. Before they left to return to their home in Fort Bragg, North Carolina, the Airborne had a party in the mess hall they shared with us. They served beer, and to top it all off, they hired a stripper. Legs were allowed in, as long as we kept our mouths shut and stayed in the back. No worries. I co-existed with them, and they never messed with me. Besides, in the professional Army, strippers were as non-existent as draftees. And there wasn't any beer in the chow hall, except for the non-alcoholic stuff available in grocery stores.

Anyway, a day of training with the Airborne meant boarding a media bus for an hour's ride to a town called Abqaig, then a right at an intersection to a firing range that paratroopers built to practice assaults against Iraqi-style bunkers built in the sand. On the trip was Major Baxter Ennis, the public affairs officer for the 82nd Airborne. A native of Coats, North Carolina, Ennis would become a much closer acquaintance in the future. Some public affairs officers still harbored grudges because they thought the media unfairly portrayed those serving during Vietnam, and to be fair, some journalists considered public affairs officers as nothing more than the propaganda arm of the Big Army. But Major Ennis was a likable sort and a credible source.

Before Desert Shield even had a name, the Airborne had one of its three brigades ready to react to any trouble spot within 18 hours of notification. When given an order, a paratrooper salutes smartly and responds, "All the way, sir!" One of the division's officers even had a business card that read: "No Mission Too Tough. You Call. We Fall. Service Anywhere In The World In 18 hours. Our Work Is Permanent." In a nutshell, their mission is to take the fight to the enemy. Their patron saint is Michael the Archangel, who dropped into Hell to confront Lucifer and his fallen legions. Even the Almighty needs a contingency force.

The toughest job for a paratrooper is to squat and hold, but Major Ennis said there was no danger of the Airborne losing its fighting edge. "We train the way we fight, and we're doing the most realistic training we've ever done over here," he said.

The major also explained the meaning of "hoo-ah," a word I had been unfamiliar with until Desert Shield. Among soldiers, hoo-ah was a synonym for acknowledge. Although it had various meanings, it was usually a response indicating that troopers understood their situation, were motivated to perform, that they understood an order and would carry out their duty no matter what. With a chance to vent some frustrations by firing live ammunition, this would be a double hoo-ah day.

Paratroopers stand out even in the way they dress, such as the spit-shined jump boots they are authorized to wear with their dress uniforms. While other units opted to wear the more comfortable floppy hat in the desert heat, division commander James H. Johnson Jr. ordered the Airborne to wear Kevlar combat helmets at all times to underscore a "go to war" mentality. A two-star general, Johnson was the first man out the airplane door during Operation Just Cause in Panama. For making a combat jump, Johnson had a splash of gold thread on his parachutist wings. Paratroopers call it a mustard splat, but despite the pedestrian name, the gold thread is a coveted award. While it was a pain to wear the heavy helmets in the sauna-like heat, having it strapped on was a reminder that paratroopers could be in combat at any moment. A combat helmet was a defensive precaution that would protect them if the bullets start flying. No floppy hat had ever stopped a bullet. The headgear had changed from the steel pot worn by GIs from World War II through Korea and Vietnam. Those helmets could be used as a wash bowl or a vessel to make coffee or cook eggs. The Kevlar version was a synthetic material that offered more protection than steel.

On the firing range were troops of the 1st Battalion of the Third Brigade, nicknamed the Panther Brigade but historically known as the 505th Parachute Infantry Regiment. Their forefathers made four combat jumps during World War II, and the regiment liberated the first town in France at St. Mere-Eglise as part of the D-Day invasion. And in 1967, elements were also sent to quell race riots in Detroit while a war was being fought in Southeast Asia.

The brigade's current commander, Colonel Glynn Hale, had served three tours of duty in Vietnam and participated in the 1989 operation in Panama. The way the nation had responded to troops in this crisis was something new to him.

"It's almost overwhelming the support we've gotten from back home. That's something we didn't get in Vietnam. It never really struck me until we started getting all the letters and cards over here. It's quite a change. These guys know they're being appreciated over here," Hale said.

Hale, 46, dismissed that notion that troops might be losing their edge.

"We've always had a combat focus. We're a fast-reaction force. These guys know we can get thrown into combat any day now. They're ready. They've been ready. Now go talk to them. They're the best soldiers the Army has ever had," Hale said.

One private in Bravo Company, machine gunner Jimmy Phipps, was in a platoon that had been adopted by the Rural Retreat Elementary School in Wytheville, Virginia. He was receiving sacks of mail because his father was the school's principal and a Vietnam vet.

"If you don't have people that care and you don't have people behind you, you ain't got nothing," Phipps said.

The purpose of the day's training was to have squads of infantry mount a 300-yard assault in full combat gear on mock bunkers and trenches. In an infantry assault against a fixed position, the last 300 yards are the toughest. Even though this was training, machine guns fired live rounds over the heads of the infantry to get them used to the whiz of lead in the air. What soldiers do in training is hardly indicative of how they'll perform in combat, but training teaches soldiers how to stay on mission in the chaos of combat. Each one of these squads, in their turn, kept their proper spacing and poured a steady rate of fire into the target. During basic training in the Army I was in, some guys would jam their rifle muzzles into the sand and fire, intentionally blowing up their own weapons as a symbol of destroying the thing they hated the most — the Army. I had never seen a real combat unit train, and the difference was striking. I walked behind them at what I thought was a comfortable pace, but they left me in the dust, littering the desert floor with spent bullet casings. It was a lesson in how a real combat unit trains.

During the exercises, the deep voice of Master Sergeant J.R. Kendall of Bravo Company provided commentary over the gunfire. With a leathered face and rock-hard build, he looked and spoke like a super-dooper paratrooper. Kendall, who called Fayetteville, North Carolina, his home, carried a 12-gauge Winchester shotgun loaded with buckshot shells.

"Ain't no sweeter sound in the world than a shotgun going off in a bunker. It's an infantryman's friend," Kendall grinned.

No one had lost an edge, the master sergeant insisted.

"The only way you lose your edge is if you sit on your ass and don't train. We keep from getting bored by training hard. If the decision is made to go offensive, these paratroopers are ready. We've become acclimated to the desert. Besides, you tell a paratrooper to do something, and it'll get done. We lead the way," Kendall said.

As one rifle squad got ready for its assault, a six-pack of non-alcoholic beer was offered to the first machine gun crew that could wipe out the bunker. The winner was Sergeant Ben Perkins, 23, of Greeley, Colorado, who poured such a steady, accurate stream of 7.65 millimeter rounds from his M-60 machine gun that he set the bunker ablaze.

He preferred Pepsi over near beer, however. "Drinking that stuff is like kissing your sister," Perkins said.

Perkins also shared an infantryman's secret. Everything carried into battle is government issue, except for a personal item tucked inside the combat helmet to maintain a connection with the real world. It could be a snapshot of a significant other or a lock of hair from a baby born while they were away. Perkins kept a pair of his wife's panties in his Kevlar.

"They remind me of what I'm fighting for," he grinned. "We're ready to do what we've got to do."

On another portion of the firing range, Private Alonzo Range, 21, of New York City fired an anti-tank, bazooka-like weapon called a Dragon at a target 500 yards away. When using the shoulder-fired weapon, the gunner must keep the target in his sights to guide it on its path, which means he could be exposed to return fire. The naked eye can follow the projectile as it dips and weaves down range. The rocket exploded on target in a ball of orange flame, accompanied by a thunder-like roar. Fellow paratroopers congratulated the gunner by whooping: "Beautiful! Airborne!"

"It was better than sex. Almost," Range said.

Still, an antsy tone could be heard in conversations. Feeling imprisoned, they wanted to get the show on the road so they could go home.

"Morale ain't that good. What are we waiting for?" one of them said.

"Let's go. Let's jump into Kuwait and get this over with. We've been out in this desert all this time with no beer and no pussy, eating shitty food and drinking warm water. It's inhumane," another added.

"Schwarzkopf calls us 'Glory Boys.' But when the time comes, we'll get the job done. We just need the word to turn us loose," another said.

Nobody has earned the right to bitch more than a soldier. If you ask a man or a woman to put their lives on the line, and then put them in a hostile environment where they're cut off from civilization, bitching was understandable. But as far as losing their edge? Actually, the ordeal was like rubbing a knife blade against a whetstone. The Airborne was sharpening its edge, and the sharpness would become more pronounced in the days and months to come.

P.S. I mentioned to New York that the new volunteer Army was head and shoulders above the post-Vietnam force I was in. The editors said to keep gathering string for a story, but the tone indicated that they weren't about to take a risk of saying how good the Army was following the stigma of Vietnam. Maybe you had to be in the Army of 1973 to appreciate how good these guys were, both the quality of the weaponry and the quality of the troops, and not just the Army.

On one overnight trip with the Marines, the sound of a platoon doing calisthenics in the sand was my wakeup call. Prior to doing a three-mile run, Marines did a four-count movement to complete 25 jumping jacks, then added, "And one for Connie Chung." Lo and behold, I heard someone call my name. It was the platoon leader, David (Spike) Myerson. He played football at Yale University with my cousins, Kenny and Donny Lund. After a homecoming game against Harvard that I attended, we all hung out one night drinking my uncle's homemade wine. Now he was a lieutenant in the Marines. He asked if I wanted to run too, but I took a rain check. I tried to hook back up with him several times but never could pull it off. But imagine that. The Marines had Yale graduates as officers. And the Marine version of Hoo-ah is "Oooo-rah!"

CHAPTER 10
Old Testament Stuff

A billboard on the main drag in Fayetteville, North Carolina, identifies Fort Bragg as the Home of the Airborne and Special Forces. No such pronouncement existed for desert headquarters at the King Fahd International Airport, located about an hour's drive north and west of Dhahran. The lone hint that the command existed was a guard post outside the airport's main gate. Even the flying of the American flag was unauthorized, lest the citizens of the host country get the impression foreigners had taken over. The Airborne called the place Champion Main. Some soldiers called it Epcot because its fancy radars and high-tech electronics made it look futuristic. Inside the perimeter, troops could be seen wearing full backpacks on 20-mile marches. They were trying to stay in shape for Ranger school when they returned home from deployment.

An interview had been arranged with Colonel Jesse Johnson, the officer in charge of Special Operations Command. Just three years earlier, Special Ops had been officially recognized as the fifth branch of the military. In meetings at the highest level, the colonel sat in the only seat not occupied by a general or an admiral representing the Army, Air Force, Navy and Marines.

"I'm a Chihuahua surrounded by pachyderms," was the way Johnson introduced himself.

Still, Johnson reported directly to Norman Schwarzkopf, an indication of his status as the officer in charge of a single command that included the Army's Green Berets, the Navy's SEALs and the Air Force's Search and Rescue. The command had evolved from the disaster of Desert One, the failed attempt by the Army's Delta Force to bring back 53 Americans being held hostage by Iran in 1980. Eight Americans died in that attempt, which ended in a fireball in the Iranian desert when a helicopter collided with a transport plane.

Johnson, 51, had been in the Army for 33 years. Originally an enlisted man, he received a field commission in Vietnam and served his second tour as commander of an infantry company. Jump qualified, he was a battalion commander in the 82nd Airborne before joining the Special Forces.

Johnson wouldn't and couldn't talk about specific missions, like the secret assignment of determining whether or not the southern Iraqi desert could support the movement of heavy tanks. He noted, however, that not a single Johnny Rambo served in his ranks. The role of Special Ops included desert survival and navigation, assisting coalition troops in adapting to the American command structure, breaking down language barriers, practicing things like calling in air strikes and the mundane chores of watching and listening to gather intelligence on the 430,000 Iraqi troops reportedly facing the international coalition. Almost all of the work was done without media attention.

"If we do our jobs right, nobody knows about it. If you're not successful, that's when you get the publicity," Johnson said. "We're not snake-eaters. We're not spies. We're quiet professionals."

Like all Desert Shield commanders, he was keenly aware of the challenges facing an American army waging a daily battle against the desert.

"There's nothing to hide behind out here, and you have to be much more mobile. It's a harsh environment, but it's not insurmountable," Johnson said.

Even the mightiest military can get tripped up and bogged down in a war if the foe is underestimated. Johnson shared a nugget of information contained in a profile the Special Forces had compiled on Saddam Hussein. When he was an up and coming strong man and assassin, Saddam was a member of a hit squad assigned to kill Iraqi dictator General Abd al-Karim Qasim in 1959. That attempt failed. However, despite being wounded in the leg, Saddam resisted arrest and fought on until he ran out of bullets.

"This is a guy who fights to the end. Even after he was shot, he emptied his weapon. That tells us a lot," Johnson said. "He sees himself as a direct descendant of Nebuchadnezzar. He's positioned himself as a god. Gods don't back down. He's capable of almost anything."

Saddam was also the ultimate survivor. He did jail time, but following various coups and internal conflicts, he emerged from prison to become Iraq's president in 1979 and positioned himself as the power to be dealt with in the Middle East.

On the ride back to the hotel, the link between the ancient and the modern kept churning in my mind. The parched landscape appeared to be flatter than water on a plate, baked by the sun and devoid of anything familiar, but the history of thousands of years ran deep beneath the sandy carpet. Prophets and holy men through the ages ventured into the emptiness to sandblast away the trappings of the world as a way of getting in touch with their spiritual centers. Little wonder the desert is a metaphor for a purgative. I could see why three of the great religions of the world evolved in this region. Anyone who wanders out in the desert long enough will see visions and hear voices. Saudi Arabia is the birthplace of Islam, yet the roots of Judaism and Christianity were apparent. All three faiths have a patriarch in Abraham, who professed his belief in a single God. All three trace their origins to the beginnings of civilization.

One needn't be able to cite the Qur'an or Old Testament chapter and verse, or be an expert in World Cultures, to be familiar with the tale of Nebuchadnezzar II. He was the king of Babylon, one of the empires of Mesopotamia, a Greek word that means, "land between the rivers." From his palace between the Tigris and Euphrates rivers, Nebuchadnezzar ordered the conquest of Jerusalem and the destruction of Solomon's Temple, bringing the children of Israel back to Baghdad in bondage. The king who controlled all of the Near East, Nebuchadnezzar also left a legacy as a builder. It was Nebuchadnezzar who built the Hanging Gardens, one of seven wonders of the ancient world. And according to Daniel in the Old Testament, he went insane and lived as an animal in the wilderness for seven years.

The ancient king was Saddam's inspiration for inscribing his own name on the bricks, tiles and marble of buildings and monuments in modern-day Iraq. One of his elite Republican Guard units was the Nebuchadnezzar Motorized Infantry Division.

Despite all the talk of high-tech gadgetry and whiz-bang wonder weapons in the coming war, a different way of looking at Saddam and the conflict was to take the long view. The borders of modern-day Iraq were drawn by the British and French from the butchery of the First World War and the breakup of the Ottoman Empire. Iraq was administered by Britain, which cobbled together a kingdom made up of Sunni and Shiite Muslims, who had been fighting a religious civil war for fourteen centuries, and an ethnic group of Kurds. Winston Churchill described Britain's early relationship with Iraq as costing millions in treasure "for the privilege of living on an ungrateful volcano out of which we are in no circumstances to get anything worth having."

Some ancient stories pre-date the Bible. The oldest known writing comes from Sumeria, where an early culture preserved the past with cuneiform symbols on clay tablets. Sumeria was where agriculture took root and where a ruler named Hammurabi codified a system of justice, including the notion of "an eye for an eye" before it was written in the Old Testament. To defend its harvests in what was part of the Fertile Crescent, Sumeria created the first armies. Go figure. The cradle of civilization is also the cradle of conflict, a metaphor for what happens when matter and anti-matter are locked in a deadly duel in the same space. Modern war was now brewing in a region where the first ones were fought five thousand years ago.

Iraq is thought to be the likely location of the Garden of Eden, home to Adam and Eve. It was the place where the first man and first woman ate the forbidden fruit from the Tree of Knowledge and fell from grace, being banished from Paradise to earn their daily bread by the sweat of their brows. Iraq, then, would also be the site of the first recorded murder, where Cain slew his brother Abel, and the killing was just beginning.

The ancient city of Ur, the capital of Sumeria, is believed to be the home of Abraham and his monotheist beliefs. Abraham is also the source of the never-ending conflict between Arabs and the Chosen People. Unable to have an heir with his aging wife, Abraham fathered a child with an Egyptian servant named Hagar, or Hajjar. The heir's name was Ishmael. Then Abraham's wife Sarah miraculously conceived a son named Isaac, who became the favored son of Abraham. God demanded that Abraham sacrifice his own flesh and blood to prove his faith, only to be stopped at the last second by an angel of the Lord. In the Old Testament version, Isaac was placed on the sacrificial altar. According Islamic versions, the son to be sacrificed was Ishmael. At any rate, Ishmael and his mother were sent away to a wilderness that is now called the Arabian Peninsula, and Ishmael became the father of all the great desert peoples. Isaac claimed the full inheritance of Abraham, and his descendants created what is now Israel. That ancient feud between their descendants over who was the rightful heir rages on. No conflict is bloodier or more heated than battles between brothers, and more people have been killed in the name of religion than any other cause.

But in the modern age where attention spans struggle to last 15 minutes, who remembers or cares about any of that? The way to avoid getting bogged down in this quicksand of a region was to stay out, or get in and get out as quickly as possible.

CHAPTER 11
Mission Change

Thursday, November 8. The first commandment of journalism is write what you know. The worst feeling on an assignment like this is not knowing very much. A Pencil feels more like a Mushroom — kept in the dark and fed a lot of manure. Weeks have been spent trying to wrap my arms around this story while waiting for the war to start. The information gap breeds uncertainty, and not knowing does nothing but feed the knot in my stomach. Ask anybody to explain the battle plan or the timetable, and the answer is, "That's above my pay grade." Or, "That's classified. If I tell you, I'd have to kill you." Little wonder that one of the most often-used expressions in the military is, "First to go, last to know." It's the nature of war. No one can see what's coming, like a change in mission.

While I was still grappling with finding out how troops were arrayed, policy-makers believed that the force encamped in the desert was sufficient to defend Saudi Arabia from an Iraqi attack, but the cost in blood would be unacceptable if the force was sent to evict the Iraqi army from Kuwait. To create an offensive option, Commander-in-Chief George H.W. Bush ordered additional troops to the Gulf and essentially doubled the size of the war machine. It was a prudent decision. The best time to order a surge is before battle, not during one when things have degenerated into chaos.

My job would have been a lot easier if I had known about the most important meeting on the path to war held right under my nose at the Desert Inn, a dining facility in Dhahran, but it was top secret. Assembled within a week of the president's announcement were 22 generals and admirals who collectively had a galaxy's worth of stars on their collars. Among them was Gus Pagonis, the logistics mastermind who would have to make sure all the pieces got into place. In the first 90 days, logisticians had moved the equivalent of a city the size of Richmond into the desert, including their trucks, vehicles, tanks and tools plus the life support required to feed, water and house them. The new task would be to move the equivalent of a city the size of Des Moines into the kingdom, all under the guns of the world's fourth largest army. If it took three months to bring in the fast reaction forces, it would take at least that long to bring in the heavier stuff.

Additional firepower for the offensive came with the deployment of the 2nd Marine Division, three more Navy carrier groups, 300 more Air Force warplanes and the deadliest land force on the planet — an Army formation of 146,000 soldiers and 1,400 tanks called VII Corps.

The way the Army is organized, a group of soldiers make up a squad, which is part of a platoon. Platoons are the building blocks of companies, which are then grouped together to form battalions. Battalions are arranged in regiments, or brigades, which form a division. When two or more divisions fight together, they form a corps, which carries a Roman numeral. Two or more corps form an army. The two Army corps in the Kuwaiti Theater of Operations now comprised the U.S. Third Army, which was George Patton's outfit in his drive across France into Germany in World War II.

VII Corps was designated as the maneuver force needed to smash Iraq's best troops, the Republican Guard. The muscle that provided the armored thrust into Germany in World War II, the corps was stationed in Europe to deter any Soviet invasion, the immediate threat of which had vanished because the Soviet empire was disintegrating. The forces included the 2nd Armored Cavalry Regiment (Always Ready), the 1st Armored Division (Old Ironsides), the 3rd Armored Division (Spearhead) and the 1st Infantry Division (Big Red One). On paper, it currently packed more combat punch than any corps ever fielded by the Army.

The master of ceremonies at the Desert Inn was H. Norman Schwarzkopf, the four-star general in command of all the forces. A 15-foot wide map of Kuwait and Iraq was displayed. It showed the deployment of Iraqi forces — 26 divisions, 450,000 troops and thousands of tanks — dug in behind obstacle belts and the Saddam Line, a defensive alignment that extended westward for 175 miles from Kuwait City into the desert. When the shooting started, the Iraqis were expected to use everything in their arsenal, including chemical weapons.

Under the battle plan now being refined, air power would isolate the Iraqi army from its command and control in Baghdad. After gaining control of the skies, the Air Force would provide an umbrella of cover, depriving the Iraqis of knowing what was coming or from what direction. Bombers and fighters would also destroy factories capable of producing nuclear, biological and chemical weapons of mass destruction. Then ground forces would wipe out the Iraqi army. Details of the meeting were provided in Schwarzkopf's postwar autobiography *It Doesn't Take A Hero,* and the strategy was totally different from the Vietnam thinking of incrementally feeding forces into battle.

"Forget the defensive bullshit," the commanding general told the assembled officers. "We're going to talk offense from now until the day we go home. All you tankers, listen to this. We need to destroy — not attack, not damage, not surround — I want you to destroy the Republican Guard. When you're done with them, I don't want them to be an effective fighting force anymore. I don't want them to exist as a military organization. We're not going to do this with one arm tied behind our backs. We're not going to say we want to be as nice as we possibly can, and if they draw back across the border, that's fine with us. That's bullshit. We're going to destroy the Republican Guard."

The ground war would involve two supporting attacks while the tank corps swooped around from the left to smash the Iraqi flank. Under the plan, two Marine Divisions and the Saudi-led Arab forces would breach defensive lines and drive straight north for Kuwait City. Two Egyptian divisions and other Arab forces would seize a road junction west of Kuwait City, blocking any retreat by the Iraqi army. Far to the west, the Army's XVII Airborne Corps would attack deep into Iraq and cut Highway 8, preventing reinforcements from coming in and preventing the Iraqis from trying to escape. Positioned between the Marines and the XVIII Airborne Corps, VII Corps would strike north through a breach in the defensive line by the 1st Infantry Division, then wheel to the east to hit the Republican Guard. Like a heavyweight boxer smashing the ribs of his foe with a single wallop, it would be a devastating left hook.

"Once they're gone, be prepared to continue the attack to Baghdad because there isn't going to be anything else out there," Schwarzkopf continued.

The attack would be in mid-February. Time was required to bring in the new forces, and troops would also need time to acclimate to the desert. To keep the Iraqis in the dark, movement into attack positions would come only after the air campaign had started.

"In order for this to succeed, because the enemy is still going to outnumber us, it's going to take, for lack of a better word, killer instinct on the part of all our leaders out there," Schwarzkopf said. "There's going to be none of this bullshit, 'Well, I think we're going to go in and probe a little bit and see if we can get through.' We need commanders in the lead who absolutely, clearly understand that they will get through. And once they're through, they're not going to stop and discuss it. They are going to go up there and destroy the Republican Guard. I cannot afford to have commanders who do not understand that it is attack, attack, attack and destroy every step of the way. If you have somebody who doesn't understand it, I would strongly recommend that you consider removing him from command and putting in somebody that can do the job. For our country, we dare not fail. We cannot fail, and we will not fail. Anybody in here who doesn't understand that, get out of the way. Any questions? Okay, good luck to you. You know what needs to be done," he said.

Schwarzkopf bade farewell by quoting from Shakespeare's *Henry V:* "And gentlemen in England now a-bed shall think themselves accurs'd they were not here."

Details still needed to be worked out with the international forces. Originally, the British were attached to the Marines, but they preferred to be part of the main attack. Under the modified plan, Britain's Challenger tanks and 28,000 troops would be assigned to VII Corps as part of the armored punch. To make up for the loss of British tanks, the Marines would be given the armored might of the First Brigade, or Tiger Brigade, of the U.S. Army's 2nd Armored Division (Hell On Wheels). The Army had the top-of-the-line M1A1 tanks. The Marines were equipped with M60A3 tanks, which were leftovers from Vietnam. Schwarzkopf still had to figure out the mission of a French division.

The Saudis were briefed two days after the war council at the Desert Inn.

It may have seemed like the war was a long way off, but Americans were already dying in Desert Shield. The first casualty was Air Force Staff Sergeant

John Campisi of West Covina, California, who perished on August 12 when he was hit by a truck on the darkened runway at Dhahran International Airport. He was an aircraft maintenance technician with the 55th Strategic Reconnaissance Wing from Offutt Air Force Base, Nebraska.

On August 28, a C-5A transport plane — the free world's largest aircraft — was bringing food, medical supplies and maintenance equipment to the Gulf. It crashed near Ramstein Air Base, Germany, killing 13 and injuring four. Shortly after taking off, the plane clipped the tops of some trees before crashing and breaking apart. Nine of the dead were reservists from Texas who had volunteered instead of waiting for a call-up. The flight crew was from the 433rd Military Airlift Wing at Kelly Air Force Base in Texas.

Another deadly accident occurred at the end of October on a Navy ship at the beginning of a 10-day exercise during which Marines would practice assaulting a beach in Oman. After being in port for five days to repair a leaking steam valve, the *USS Iwo Jima* was one mile from its pier in Manama, Bahrain, when a bonnet blew off the balky valve. Superheated steam from two boilers flooded the boiler room, killing 10 crewmen. Six died immediately, and four died later after being flown to the hospital ship *USS Comfort* operating in the Gulf.

The *Iwo Jima*, an assault ship and helicopter-launching pad, was the oldest ship of its class. Steam heated to 850 degrees at 600 pounds per square inch was piped through a turbine to spin its propellers. The ship had gained a bit of fame during the Apollo 13 space mission for plucking the command module Odyssey from the water near American Samoa. In the Gulf, it had a 685-man crew and 1,100 Marines on board.

After the accident, a 40-minute memorial service was held on board. An honor guard fired a 21-gun salute, and a lone bugler sounded "Taps" as Marines in battle dress and sailors in dungarees honored the dead. A table on deck served as an altar. Vice Admiral Henry Mauz Jr., commander of the naval contingent in Central Command, said, "The price of freedom is high. May God bless them and keep them."

Captain Michael O'Hearn delivered the eulogy. "Our resolution to go on and restore this ship and ourselves, so that we can restore our combat readiness, is within itself a tribute to our fallen shipmates," he said.

One of the dead, Daniel Lupatsky, 22, of Centralia, Pennsylvania, had written home about the poor structural integrity of the ship.

"He really hated that ship. He really thought it was a dangerous ship. It was always breaking down," said his father, Michael, a carpet installer.

It would not be last time the Navy, or any other of the services, mourned losses.

CHAPTER 12
Diversions

I was in for the long haul anyway, too busy and too worried to be bored. However, the sending of additional troops to the kingdom triggered an Army phenomenon centered around the outhouse lawyer, the name given to the guy who knows everything and feels free to dispense what he thinks at the latrine. A rumor starts when one guy said he had a buddy at battalion who knew somebody from brigade who got it straight from division that the forces already in country would be rotated home now that the main battle tanks and armored divisions were coming in. The virus of a rumor spread so swiftly through the ranks that some commanders addressed formations to tell the troops they weren't going anywhere.

Major Dan Grigson, public affairs officer for the 101st Airborne, described the reaction when soldiers got the news. "They said, 'Ain't going to be a rotation, huh?' Then they pulled out their whetstones and began sharpening their knives," he said. All of the troops who had been hunkered down for months were now in it for a longer haul, continuing their battle against the arid wasteland and cultural desert for however long it would take for the offensive to begin.

Saturday, November 10. A birthday party complete with cake and music was held in various locations in the desert for Marines marking the 215th anniversary of their founding by the Continental Congress in 1775. At the Tun Tavern in Philadelphia, authorization was approved for two battalions of Marines capable of fighting from the sea or on land. From that moment on, Marines thought of themselves as America's original protectors. The top-ranking Marine in Saudi Arabia, three-star general Walter Boomer, cut a birthday cake with his ceremonial sword, the oldest weapon still in service in the U.S. armed forces.

"Marines, you're a special breed. There are no others in the world like you.

And like previous generations of Marines, you celebrate our birthday preparing for battle," the lieutenant general told his charges.

The traditional drink of rum was missing because alcohol is taboo in Saudi Arabia, but Marines delivered as much pomp and ceremony as they could. At headquarters, the Marine band slung rifles as they played their trumpets and tubas. Escorts carried a three-tiered birthday cake on a stretcher. And a color guard adorned in chocolate chip camouflage rather than dress blues paraded with the American and Marine Corps flags. According to one unconfirmed report, a Marine had called a hotel in Iraqi-held Kuwait City to make dinner reservations for 30,000 — the number of Marines in the desert.

"We'd have to be up to our ears in firefights to keep from celebrating," said First Sergeant George Spear of Coleman, Alabama. He recalled a time 21 years ago when he was pulled off a hill near Da Nang during the Vietnam War and put on duty as a cake carrier. "No matter where we are, we're going to take time out to celebrate who we are and what we are," Spear said.

As far as being prepared for the coming war, Spear noted: "We feel a lot of tension, like a tight spring."

Helping to mark the occasion was Gary Luck, the three-star general who commanded the Army's XVIII Corps. Once the leader of a Special Forces "A" Team in the Vietnam War, Luck had been awarded a Purple Heart for wounds received in battle. He had previously served as assistant division commander of the 101st Airborne Division, was the former commanding general of the 2nd Infantry Division and former commanding general of the U.S. Army Special Operations Command. As he wished the Marines well during a ceremony in the desert, Luck also spoke of the forces gathering to evict Saddam Hussein's army from Kuwait.

"He's gotta be dumber than a stump if he doesn't know what's coming," Luck said.

Marines in the remotest desert foxholes took time to celebrate the birthday. The Marine Corps band was flown by helicopter to 18 desert stops to play the Marine Corps Hymn.

Thursday, November 15. In an unmistakable sign that the dynamic had changed, a media pool – me included — was assembled to witness a Marine amphibious exercise called Imminent Thunder. The six-day exercise had everybody in a lather. It felt like a dress rehearsal for what was coming. The Marines had practiced amphibious assaults on three previous occasions without much fanfare, but this was the first one since the offensive option was put on the table. On Baghdad Radio, Saddam Hussein called it a provocative act, as if invading Kuwait wasn't a provocative act. It gave him something else to worry about. Every armchair general in the kingdom figured the Marines would hit the beaches in Kuwait City when the war started.

As part of the exercise, about 500 to 800 Marines aboard ships in the Persian Gulf were scheduled to take part in a mock assault beginning 30 miles from shore. About 1,100 aircraft were involved, including 14 CH-46 Sea Knight helicopters and an undisclosed number of AV-8B Harrier jump jets, F/A-18 Hornets, F-14 Tomcats and A-6 Intruders. The British added their own arsenal of Nimrod surveillance planes and Tornado and Jaguar attack jets.

The media pool choppered to the deck of the USS Nassau, a steam-powered amphibious assault ship operating in the waters off Saudi Arabia. Troops and equipment were supposed to be launched from sea to shore on high-speed hovercraft called LCACs (landing craft, air cushioned). One M-60 tank making the trip from ship to shore had the name So Damn Insane written on its gun barrel. After the first hovercraft was launched, however, nature complicated the drill. With waves reaching 14 feet in height, the hovercraft actually disappeared from sight as it bobbed in the chop. If this had been a real combat situation, the full assault would have been launched, but it was canceled as a safety precaution. Instead, Marines and media flew to shore aboard helicopters.

My chopper landed at Foxtrot Surgical Support Hospital, the northernmost of five field hospitals set up by the Marines. To prepare the medical staff for what could be coming, and to underscore the reality of war, a mass casualty drill was held involving 80 Marines with simulated wounds.

"People get hurt. Occasionally, they die. We have to learn to handle both. The Marines have a saying that we fight the way we train. Well, we treat patients the same way," said Captain Robert Chaney, the man in charge of all the medical assets assigned to the Marines in Saudi Arabia.

When a siren wailed, stretcher bearers raced into action. The mock wounded were carried through clouds of powdery sand kicked up by helicopter blades. One of the Marines brought to the emergency room was Lance Corporal Jimmy O. Hall of Atlanta.

"Marines practice everything. We even practice dying," he said. The tone of his voice and the look on his face said he didn't care much for the prospect of getting shot up.

Lieutenant Commander Chris Kahn of Bremerton, Washington, one of four orthopedic surgeons at Foxtrot, said even the knifings and shootings seen in American emergency rooms won't compare to combat wounds because the weaponry is much more lethal. He had a new name for triage.

"We're used to seeing gunshot wounds, but not at such huge, huge volumes. This will be meatball surgery. It's fast and dirty. We used to call it slash and dash," Kahn said. "Are we scared? Absolutely. Can we handle it? Yes."

In this field hospital, the triage floor was desert sand. Operating rooms and intensive care units were set up under olive drab tents camouflaged with netting. One tent was designated as the morgue, where two corpsmen volunteered to work. Overheard was this exchange.

"If we're still here a year from now, without beer or pussy, I'm going to go after him myself."

"Who? Saddam?"

"No. Bush."

He was joking, but he could have been disciplined for saying it.

Because the schedule of Imminent Thunder had changed on the fly, the possibility existed that we might be stranded overnight without sleeping bags or gear. The blood-red ball of the sun was sinking fast on the western horizon. Stars were already visible in the eastern sky. Arrangements were made for us to sleep on stretchers in the morgue. Perish the thought.

Then off in the distance came the dull thud of chopper blades beating the air. It was our ride, and I was never happier to see a helicopter in my life. In the gloaming, we boarded it for the flight south to Dhahran.

It was after midnight when I finished my pool report. Dinner was an MRE of diced turkey. A Pencil crosses some sort of threshold when an MRE for dinner was as good as room service.

Got another call from New York about a page one story in *The New York Times* about soldiers bitching to Secretary of Defense Dick Cheney about having to spend more time in the desert while additional forces were being deployed. Having invited a Times reporter along, but no other media, Cheney had visited the 24th Division to explain the new situation. What he got was an earful from those living in the sand and drinking desert-temperature water. Editors get their ideas reading stories in the papers, and they wanted me to match this one. It took several days to go through channels to request a visit to division headquarters. After what was published, commanders had already ordered their troops not to sound off to reporters. The comments I got were from soldiers saying that, despite being far from home in a hostile and desolate environment, they were resolutely doing their duty without complaint.

The trip wasn't a total loss, however. A field exercise was staged involving a company of 14 of the Army's main battle tanks assaulting a mock trench line. There to explain things was a battalion commander, Lieutenant Colonel Bill Chamberlain, a 1972 graduate of West Point whose forefathers had been in the Army for a century. In the exercise, the 72-ton tanks were given a seven-minute window to cross a trench, which would presumably be filled with burning oil during the real invasion. While the tanks released clouds of white smoke to mask their positions, a specialty vehicle on tracks moved up to unfold a metal bridge across the obstacle. Once across, the tanks were supposed to fan out and continue a charge, guns blazing. This was the modern-day cavalry, charging into battle with steel behemoths powered by twin 1,500-horsepower jet turbine engines.

"That's America right there!" said Chamberlain, 39, of La Plata, Maryland. "I'll admit it. I love it. When you get the maneuver going, it's just an old-style cavalry charge. When you get the tanks and halftracks going together and you slam into an objective, it's awesome."

The cavalry was in his blood. His great-grandfather, Jack Corbett, was a sergeant major in the 18th Infantry Regiment in the Philippines in 1898. George C. Marshall and Douglas MacArthur, both five-star generals in World War II, once served together in the same regiment.

"I like to say that they were both raised by my great-grandfather," Chamberlain said.

Chamberlain's grandfather liked telling a story during World War II when he was sent to Australia as a Pentagon staff officer to meet with MacArthur. It took two weeks to get there for a 15-minute briefing, and he was headed out the door when he said something over his shoulder.

"Hey sir, best regards from Old Jack."

"Colonel, do you know Old Jack?"

"Yes sir, he's my father-in-law."

MacArthur invited him back, and the two men spent the rest of the afternoon together. All those stories Chamberlain's great-grandfather had been telling for years were true because McArthur told the same stories.

During World War II, Chamberlain's father was itching to join the fight, but he was too young at age 16 to enlist. So he went to Skid Row in Washington, D.C., and paid a bum to pose as his guardian and tell recruiters he was old enough to serve. He made it through basic training but the war ended before he could leave the States. He did, however, serve four tours in Vietnam.

Chamberlain himself never made it to Vietnam because America's involvement ended, but he knew that soldiers must have public support if they ever went to war again.

"I think the American people can see why we're here. You know, every day they go fill up their cars with gas so they can go to work. Our whole economy is still driven by fossil fuels. There are some who are wondering why we're here, but how could you look at our lifestyle and our economy and even begin to question why. This is our vital interest. This is how we live," Chamberlain said.

And in the coming war, America would be fielding the best standing army it has ever had, Chamberlain said. These volunteers were a true cross-section of America. No army had ever been better trained, better equipped or better led.

"They are smart. They are better disciplined that we've ever had. And they care. They really care. I love soldiers. The day they tell me that I will no longer be able to be with soldiers is the day I will put in my retirement. They've always been loveable through the years, but this group of soldiers, you can't believe how good these guys are," Chamberlain said. "We're ready to fight. We're just waiting for somebody to tell us which way to go."

He also provided a clue of what was to come. Using the toe of his boot, he sketched a vertical line in the sand representing the enemy's positions. Then he drew a line around to the left to show how attacking tanks would hit them in the flank.

Chamberlain was one of those guys you remember. New York passed on a story about him, though. It didn't have any bitching in it.

The unexpected could be found in the kingdom the way a Bedouin, through word of mouth, might chance upon a watering hole. I found a source of liquid refreshment in the form of moonshine, courtesy of the photographers and the Filipinos who waited tables at Saudi restaurants. Foreign workers came to Saudi Arabia on multi-year contracts that were a form of indentured servitude. The imported workforce complained bitterly that their hosts abused them, but hey, slavery existed in the kingdom until 1962, nearly a full century after Abraham Lincoln's Emancipation Proclamation during the Civil War.

Always an inquisitive and resourceful lot, the photographers befriended the wait staff at a popular Khobar restaurant. Through casual conversation, and generous tips, they learned of the existence of a black market — there's always a black market, even in a veiled society — that sold illicit alcohol. Call it white lightning or homemade hooch, but a clear alcoholic beverage was available for sale in a place where booze was forbidden. The restaurant was a perfect front because the stuff was packaged in plastic bottles labeled as water. Somebody bought a whole case of moonshine and brought it back to the hotel. I got a bottle and kept it hidden in my room. If the Saudis knew, they would have deported us, or cut off our hands. To be honest, the stuff tasted like radiator fluid. Beggars can't be choosers.

Then it got even better. One photographer who had covered the war in Vietnam befriended an Air Force supply sergeant who was like a real-life version of Radar O'Reilly from *M*A*S*H**. With hundreds of tons of supplies coming in from the States every day, the Air Force could bring in all sorts of stuff, including a hidden stash of Johnny Walker Scotch. With the right goods to trade, the enterprising photographer procured a couple of bottles, and he shared one with me. Scotch is an acquired taste. I acquired it. And a bottle of real whiskey, secreted away in my hotel room, beat the hell out of the homemade stuff. In a private toast, I blessed the photographers and wished the Marine Corps a happy birthday.

As new arrivals entered the kingdom, those who had been in the desert for months were sometimes given a rare break from the routine. One such place was the Marine Corps Rest and Relaxation Center, informally called Desert World, and it welcomed all branches of the military. The place had originally been built by the Saudi Royal Commission for foreign oilfield workers. It was reopened and dusted off for use by U.S. troops after it sat idle for six years. A busload of media was invited to visit, and it turned out to be a most eventful field trip.

Surrounded by palm trees and shrubbery, Desert World had an Olympic-sized pool, volleyball courts, a place to lift real weights, an area to ride a camel, a movie theater, a video game parlor, phones to call home, a store to buy souvenirs, a library to read books and a walking path through what seemed like a mirage — a patch of real green grass on an irrigated lawn. About 1,200 troops a day were trucked in for a chance to unwind.

Master Gunnery Sergeant John Kulick of Pawtucket, Rhode Island, ran Desert World. "It's one of the biggest morale boosts I've seen. We get long faces in the morning and smiles at the end of the day," he said.

Corporal Michael Flaga, 25, of McHenry, Illinois, who served with the 3rd Battalion of the 9th Marine Regiment, also enjoyed a chance to walk on a real lawn. "The green almost hurts my eyes. We're used to seeing no colors in the desert. I couldn't believe they had something like this," Flaga said.

Surprisingly, a voice called out. It was Marine Lance Corporal Anthony Uhler, who I had met on my first day during the live-fire exercises. This was the first time he had been off duty too, and we chatted about how things were going. He said his Light Armored Vehicle battalion was secretly running recon missions into Kuwait. The information was filed away for future reference.

A couple of soldiers stood out because they wore their Kevlar helmets, which identified them as members of the 82nd Airborne. One was Staff Sergeant Craig Colberge, 29, of Aurora, Ohio. "This is the first day I had off in 119 days. This is the first time I've seen anything that resembles grass," the sergeant said.

Also enjoying the off-duty time was an Airborne chaplain. He asked that I not use his name because chaplains were under orders not to talk to the media, lest they offend the sensibilities of our Saudi hosts by talking about the spiritual health of the troops outside the realm of Islam. Chaplains were now called morale officers, and religious services had to be held in private. No coverage of services was allowed. Schedules were in code. The C-Word meant Catholic mass, and the J-Word meant a Jewish service. The Saudis didn't mind anything that happens inside the tent, but they would have reacted forcefully if Jewish services involving the ram's horn were conducted out in the open. The Airborne chaplain had mixed feelings about having to take the cross off his uniform collar.

"To me, that cross is a symbol of what I am and who I am. It offended me that I would have to hide who I am, but in retrospect, if it was the only means of carrying out our mission as chaplains, no sacrifice is too great. In a quiet, unassuming way, the soldiers are being ministered to. We don't want to draw attention to what we're doing, but we're able to provide," the chaplain said. He even gave me a small cross that I could wear on the chain of my media credentials.

A Desert World attraction that caught my attention was called Better Than A Letter. A bank of eight video cameras had been set up, and troops could record a message on videotape to send back home.

Lance Corporal Will French, 24, of Johnstown, Pennsylvania, demonstrated how he put on his gas mask.

One soldier taped a message for his girlfriend. "Don't forget me," he pleaded.

Another soldier made a tape for his wife by saying into the camera, "I love you." Then he got up and kissed the lens.

Chief Warrant Officer Randall Anderson, 33, of Swainsboro, Georgia, took advantage of the occasion to send home Christmas wishes because he didn't know if he'd have another chance to do so. Wearing his Marine Corps gym shorts and shower shoes, he also donned his Santa Claus suspenders and a red and white stocking cap that looked totally out of place in the desert. "I'm doing fine, and I'll be home. Someday," Anderson said into the camera.

I wasn't the only reporter taking in this scene. By this time, correspondents from all over the world were gathering in the kingdom to write about the coming war. One of them was an ex-patriate American working in the Middle East for a big paper in the States. Her name was Cleo, and we sat together on the two-hour bus ride back to the hotel.

She was interested in getting photos for her story, and I hooked her up with the photographer to make sure she got what she wanted. She was staying in the hotel, and I invited her over for a sip of Scotch after work. It was the only Happy Hour in Dhahran.

We spent a pleasant evening chatting about this assignment and the difficulties of working with the U.S. military while being under the thumb of the Saudis. Because she couldn't drive, she spent a fortune in cab fares to get around. And going out to restaurants was an adventure. She was good at her job, and it didn't go unnoticed that she had attractive dark hair, pretty dark eyes and a comely smile. After a cordial conversation, she thanked me for the drink and left.

On Sunday nights, the hotel offered a buffet dinner set up on tables by the outdoor swimming pool. The food was decent and reasonably priced, but invariably, a giant water gun battle would break out between some of the military types who worked in the JIB. It was a little too grab-ass for me, but the buffet made for a convenient dinner.

Cleo appeared at one such gathering. She was leaving the next day to return to her home base and was looking for something to do on her last night.

She wanted something more than dinner, however. She asked if I would take her for a drive in the desert.

"Do you have a blanket you can bring?" she asked in a lilting voice.

My sleeping bag sufficed. So as not to call any attention to ourselves, or to raise the suspicions of the religious police, she went out to the front parking lot and I went to the room to collect the essentials. We met at my rental car and headed west into the desert toward the oasis at Hofuf. I knew of a side road that led to a secluded spot. Hell, ten minutes into the drive would have been a secluded spot, but this was perfect. Not too far, but far enough, and perfectly private.

Under the stars, and in hushed tones, we talked about careers. The desert at night does have a mystique about it. It's so quiet and peaceful under the stars, which shine even brighter because there is no light pollution to dim their brightness. After telling me how she always wanted to be a foreign journalist, she asked about my story. Becoming a reporter was a bit of serendipity for me. I earned an academic scholarship to go to college, and the local newspaper was looking for someone who was good in English, so I landed my first newspaper job ten days out of high school when I was 17. Getting paid to write stories for a living was a revelation, and I stuck with it. Besides, my Old Man had a beagle named Nellie that he absolutely loved because she never failed to bring back a rabbit on a hunt. My way of earning appreciation was to be a news hound as good as Nellie.

Because I hadn't been with a woman since I left New York, it was a joy to flirt. One thing led to another, and before long, I was touching her hair, holding her close and pressing my lips against hers. We got lost in the moment.

After a particularly long, passionate, wet kiss to set the mood, our hands roamed and unfastened each other's buttons. Our mutual, unfettered lust sparked an emotional fire. Opening up like a desert flower in bloom, she knew just how to grind her hips and arch her back. She liked being on top. She liked every position. And I knew just where to touch and where to flick my tongue to find the wettest spot in a parched environment. Like a wildcat in heat, she brought herself — and then me — to explosive delight. Our chests still heaving, we lay there in blissful repose, my arm under her head, her hand rubbing my chest as she draped a thigh over my leg. The stars twinkled radiantly.

I was already having the time of my life, but this tryst enhanced my great adventure. Then, as if driven by the fickle desert wind, we drove back to the hotel. She was gone the next morning. War may be hell, it can provide little slices of heaven.

CHAPTER 13
Giving Thanks

The invasion is on. It is as unmistakable as it is unstoppable, but it was not of military variety. A new multinational force was entering the kingdom to cover the troops at Thanksgiving, that most American of holidays. Media from ABC to the Voice of America, from the American Spectator to The Wall Street Journal, from the alphabet soup of CBS, NBC, CNN, BBC and ITN descended on the hotel. Reporters from Britain, France, Germany, Japan, Italy, Greece, Portugal, Brazil and Egypt had applied for credentials. Among them were the network anchors — Peter Jennings, Dan Rather and Tom Brokaw.

The hotel's miniature golf course and a garage roof were converted into satellite alley because so many of the dishes would be bouncing signals off orbiting satellites to audiences in America. NBC trucked in sand as a backdrop to make it look like the set was in the middle of a desert. Reality TV, huh?

O.J. Simpson arrived. He was doing the pre-game show from the kingdom for the National Football League game between the Denver Broncos and Detroit Lions, which was being played at the Silverdome in Pontiac, Michigan. The Juice did his show in the company of the Marines. A couple of years later, he would make headlines and would search for what he said were the real killers of Nicole Brown Simpson and Ronald Goldman.

On Thanksgiving Day, the 82nd Airborne had a 10-kilometer run. Air Force units in Oman had a mock Macy's Thanksgiving Day parade, which included eight floats, several marching units and a band playing makeshift instruments. AT&T offered free phone calls if troops could find a phone.

Troops in the field were to be treated to a traditional dinner with all the trimmings, courtesy of Uncle Sugar. On the menu were 90,000 pounds of turkey, 70,000 pounds of roast beef, 45,000 pounds of baked ham, 32,000 pies and 17,000 pounds of fruitcake. The Saudi royal family donated 230,000 Mars and Snickers candy bars as a way of saying thanks to the American troops defending the kingdom.

President Bush, with about 300 members of the White House press corps in tow, visited the kingdom. The commander-in-chief handed out horseshoes to soldiers, stood in a chow line and ate turkey at a sandbag and plywood table. The Army's 197th Brigade built him his own private presidential outhouse, but it went unused because his schedule kept him away. The president also attended religious services aboard the *USS Nassau*, which was operating outside territorial waters and therefore would not infringe on Islam-only rites in the kingdom. From there, he made his last stop at a Marine outpost 65 miles south of Kuwait.

"We won't pull any punches. We are not here on some exercise. And we are not walking away until the invader is out of Kuwait. That may well be where you come in," the president said. The Marines cheered and barked like Devil Dogs.

Among media insiders, presidential visits are called goat fucks. Events are staged to produce images and sound bites, and the media horde tumbles all over itself to get in position. Because the AP's Washington crew traveled with the president, I opted to spend my Thanksgiving with the grunts in the field. Captain Bill Taylor, a public affairs officer from New Jersey, took me out to a field kitchen cooking up turkey for their brothers and sisters at their desert camps. It was, by the way, the largest Marine field kitchen in operation since World War II. With the turkey placed into containers, a supply truck provided a bumpy ride to Headquarters and Service Company of the 1st Battalion, 5th Marine Regiment, deep in the sandy expanse.

On a day of light duty, and on their 100th day in the desert, these Marines tended to personal chores. Some wrote letters home. Others played volleyball or softball, using sandbags for bases. Groups gathered around to watch the gladiatorial contests involving captured scorpions. First Sergeant Alonzo Sledge, a 20-year veteran from Memphis, Tennessee, stood by his horseshoe pit just in case President Bush came by. He never did.

As one formation gathered in the desert, Chaplain Paschal Dawson of Homer, Louisiana, led ranks of Marines in a chorus of *God Bless America.* Marines doffed their floppy hats and sang along. Kate Smith never sang it with more feeling. Tears welled up even in the most cynical eyes.

"One of the things we have to be thankful for is we're Americans. Although we're here, it's not the end of the world. We're here to do what we gotta do," the chaplain said after the singing concluded. He declined to be interviewed, however, citing the ban on chaplains talking to the media.

At chow time, Marines stacked their rifles and sat in the shade of their Humvees to savor their turkey. Each one got two cans of soda pop. Each gave thanks in his own way.

"People would be fools not to want to be home for Thanksgiving and Christmas, but we have a job to do. I'd rather be with the Marines. It's where I belong. They don't care if you eat your salad with the wrong fork," said Corporal Ed Walsh, 21, of Las Vegas, Nevada.

One thing about being so far away from home on a Thanksgiving is that it deepens one's appreciation of America, with all its bounty and all its freedoms and everything we tend to take for granted.

Back at the hotel, the restaurant went out of its way to offer a turkey dinner with all the trimmings. It wasn't like what mom makes, but it was pretty darn good.

New York sent a message of thanks for doing a tough job far from home. The message also said the gas masks and chemical suits would be shipped any day now.

What's Thanksgiving without football? The day after the holiday, a flag football game was played at an old soccer stadium in Jubail. Some called it the Scud Bowl. Others preferred the name Turkey Bowl. The game featured two teams of women — the Desert Foxes, made up of Navy nurses from Fleet Hospital No. 5, versus the Wrecking Crew, made up of women Marines. Some names on the back of jerseys were Killer, Spaz and Rocky. Male cheerleaders in combat boots shouted through orange traffic cones and waved pink paper pompoms. Every play on the grassless expanse kicked up a cloud of dust in the 90-degree heat. Off-duty Marines stacked their rifles and did the wave as they watched. The spectators roared, barked, howled and booed the refs. No beer was present, but it didn't prevent them from shouting "Less filling" and "Tastes great." Overall, the event was a great morale boost.

"When the women play, people come out of the woodwork to watch. Besides, there ain't no place else to go. You can't go to town. There's no alcohol. We're pretty isolated," said Sergeant Chris Dempsey, 25, of Cleveland, Ohio.

The Marines won, 20-13, but the Navy nurses made it competitive.

Lieutenant Commander Raelene Hoogendorn of McDonald, Pennsylvania, was proud of her Navy team. Known as Killer, she was assigned to casualty receiving at the fleet hospital and wore a white T-shirt adorned with Red Crosses. "We didn't know the first thing about football. I thought we were going to get trounced," she said.

A sporting event involving women was unheard of in Saudi Arabia, which forbids the public mingling of sexes. The Saudis bitched when they saw the pictures and story, and in turn, the public affairs officers bitched at me. It was a small price to pay for a good story.

News from abroad often featured reports about peace delegations meeting to avoid a war. Robert Fisk, the award-winning British journalist, once walked through the JIB trumpeting a mock headline: "War Hopes Fade; Peace Looms."

Then came the green light.

On November 29, the United Nations passed Resolution 678 demanding Iraq's unconditional withdrawal from Kuwait by January 15 or "all necessary means" would be taken to evict its army. The deadline had been set. Force was authorized.

For reaction, I went out to the flight line at the airport where troops were always coming and going. I spotted a member of the 82nd Airborne because, as he waited for a flight, he was wearing his Kevlar helmet.

"It gives the soldiers a focus for the future. People now have something to key on. It looks like we've got a mission again. Guys want to kick some ass," said Captain Michael Langman.

Setting a deadline brought some clarity to an uncertain situation.

"The worst part of all has been not knowing. We're not here to babysit. We'd just like to get on about our business and go home," said Lieutenant

Jackie Jones, 25, of Springfield, Virginia, who was assigned to a Patriot missile battery in the XVIII Airborne Corps.

Marine Lieutenant Colonel Michael Brooks, 45, commanding officer of the 1st Force Reconnaissance Company, said the deadline allows people to get psychologically prepared for battle. "There's some ambivalence. There's a dark side to this. We know what the human costs are going to be," he said.

Seaman Steven Simpson of Hartford, Connecticut, part of a Construction Battalion, said it was about time. "Who knows if there's a Kuwait left? Saddam Hussein stripped it down. He pillaged the whole country. He deserves what's going to happen to him," Simpson said.

What was left of Kuwait? Although there were some horror stories that turned out to be false, the invading Iraqis behaved like animals on a wild binge. Medical equipment was taken from hospitals and sent to Baghdad by truck, plane or barge. More than a million ounces of gold was hauled away from the Central Bank of Kuwait. Jewels and gold were stolen from the city's markets. Looters ransacked 170,000 houses and apartments. They took porcelain sinks, toilets, light fixtures, rugs, drapes and light bulbs. Also part of the loot were seven marine ferries and 20 shrimp trawlers from the Gulf ports. Fifteen airliners were stolen from the international airport, along with runway lights. Carcasses of beef hanging in storage freezers were shipped to Iraq. Also plundered was the granite facing of Kuwait City buildings, along with 20,000 plastic seats from the Kuwait University Stadium. Funeral hearses and grave-digging backhoes were taken from cemeteries. Half a million cars, buses and trucks were stolen or stripped. Mercedes-Benz sedans and BWMs gracing the showrooms of car dealerships were driven off. Eight movie theaters and 17 sports clubs were vandalized. Stolen by the Iraqis were TV sets, chairs, sofas, new shirts in plastic wrappers, carpets, cutlery, artificial flowers, scuba gear, hair spray and red nail polish from various stores. Ransacked were Kuwait's Parliament, government ministries, hotels, department stores, telephone exchanges and the emir's palace, which Iraqi soldiers desecrated by defecating on the rugs. Ox-like, spiral-horned elands and buffalo in the Kuwait City zoo were slaughtered and eaten or left to rot. More than 300 captive birds and most mammals died of neglect. A resident Indian elephant was shot and killed. Artwork was destroyed, and 19 libraries were stripped of their collections.

In addition, 1,330 oil wells and 26 gathering stations were packed with explosives to be blown up as a deterrent to an invasion.

The Iraqis intended to erase Kuwait. Many of country's written laws, its library collections, its maps and even its constitution disappeared in a campaign of looting and burning. Saddam Hussein even sought to wipe out the history of a nation. The Central Library, Kuwait's version of the Library of Congress, was gutted. Nearly half of the 3.1 million books and documents housed in 600 schools nationwide either vanished or were destroyed in bonfires. Maps delineating Kuwait's national borders and the location of its oil fields disappeared along with every copier and every computer in the country. Two million government documents and bank records were destroyed. But for a lucky break, the central registry of Kuwait's citizenry might have disappeared too. A copy was made on magnetic tapes and smuggled into Saudi Arabia. Kuwait's identity was preserved.

Kuwait, the country with the highest standard of living in the region, was being plundered and dismantled.

CHAPTER 14
Splendid Carelessness

It's remarkable what can bloom in the desert when conditions are right, and the spark of life extends beyond the dormant vegetation thirsting for moisture. Two unexpected things happened on a Saudi-arranged field trip to Hafr al-Batin, where Egyptian special forces and Kuwaiti troops were on display for a day of training arranged for the benefit of the international media.

Surprise, surprise, surprise. For the first time in the deployment, rain fell to provide a break from the sun and heat. Water puddled in tire tracks and boot prints. Even the Saudis were amazed.

"Because we have sunshine all year round, we have picnics in this weather," said Mohammed Khayat of the Ministry of Information. "We love this weather. There is no dust. The men will feel fresh. They won't feel exhausted from the heat." He also explained that plants and flowers would appear in the desert within days after being supplied with life-giving rain.

Most of us were in shirt-sleeves, but Kuwaiti tank commanders wore parkas with fur-lined hoods. Rust-colored mud stuck to boots and tires. Sentries wrapped themselves in blankets. The most interviewed person on the trip was Captain Ali, a Kuwaiti tank commander who refused to give his full name because his wife and four kids were still in their home country and under Iraq's thumb. During the chaos of Iraq's invasion in August, two of six companies of the Kuwaiti army escaped with 22 of their 80 tanks. Ali's force had been reorganized into the 35th Armored Brigade, which he renamed the Martyr Brigade. It had subsequently been reinforced with 80 tanks purchased from Yugoslavia. But when Ali tried to start his tank for a demonstration, the engine wouldn't catch. Even after a crewman hit the engine with a wrench, it still wouldn't start. Nevertheless, Ali said he and those under his command were more than ready to have a go at the Iraqi army.

"We want to go back now, but our orders keep us here. I don't know why they are waiting. We must have revenge," Captain Ali said. "We ask that we be in the front. I prefer to be killed than kept out of Kuwait. I feel some shame because I wanted to stay on the battlefield. I could have done more. We want to fight."

Khalid Bin Sultan, the three-star Saudi general who was again part of the field exercise, was asked how Saudi and coalition troops could defend the wide-open spaces of the endless desert.

"Well, I can assure you of this, if anyone touches my land, you will see a vicious soldier who will do his job well," Khalid vowed.

The big treat for me, however, was the presence of a statuesque Italian journalist who had her dark hair wrapped in an Arab scarf. One of the photographers poked me in the ribs after noticing her and said something about a target-rich environment at my three o'clock position. Her name was Sophia, and after introducing myself, we exchanged small talk about the assignment and where we were from. When the time came to fly back to Dhahran on a military aircraft, I did some skillful but subtle maneuvering to land the seat next to her. Although this was her first time in the field, she had spent time aboard an Italian warship that was enforcing the shipping embargo. She mentioned that the sailors, while patrolling in international waters, had provided her with Italian red wine. With her dark eyes and classic Roman facial features, it was easy to see why she would be popular with sailors in any navy. During this rather pleasant flight, she said that she was staying at the hotel. I still had some liquid refreshment in my private stash, and I invited her over for a drink if she was so inclined.

Within a week, the Saudis arranged a day-long train trip for the media from Dhahran to Riyadh and back. The tracks were built through mostly empty desert between the two cities. I felt obligated to take the trip, but it was quickly apparent that little news would be generated. A whole day would be wasted while work was left unattended. Therefore, after about an hour's ride to the oasis town of Hofuf, I disembarked and tried to find a taxi for a ride back to Dhahran. Sophia was on the train and had the same idea. We were on the platform ready to make our escape when our Saudi host stopped us. Back on board we went.

The Saudis wanted to show off parts of their country that had nothing to do with the coming war. Around noon, the train stopped at a dairy farm that existed in the forbidding desert. The farm was something of a miracle. The Saudis pumped water from artesian wells 800 feet below the surface to grow crops that fed the cows, which were American Holsteins that had been bred to adjust to the desert heat. There was a demonstration of artificial insemination that kept the milk flowing, but seeing some farmhand with his arm deep inside a cow didn't produce much in the way of news. For lunch, we had roasted goat on trays of rice. I passed on the eyeballs again.

Thanks to Sophia, the train trip was a pleasant one. We had some witty conversation and shared a few laughs while talking about the news business. It was after midnight when the train got back to Dhahran. She took me up on the offer for a drink, which concluded an otherwise uneventful day. Nothing happened, though. Things take time to bloom in the desert.

My visa had expired long ago, and it probably wouldn't have made any difference to the Saudis, but I wanted to get my paperwork in order so that nobody had a reason to remove me from the kingdom before the war started. Heaven forbid that I would miss the war after investing so much time. Getting a new visa meant leaving the country to have a passport stamped at a Saudi Arabian embassy. The closest one was in Bahrain, an island country in the Gulf connected to the kingdom by the 20-mile long King Fahd Causeway. The one-way cab fare was 50 bucks, and the trip included a mandatory stop at a border post stationed halfway along the causeway. Because the visa process took 24 hours, an overnight stay was required.

The trip over went smoothly enough. I checked into a hotel that was filled with off-duty British jet pilots who lounged by the swimming pool. The next stop was the Saudi embassy, which would have a new visa ready the next day.

Bahrain was much more liberal than Saudi. The sale and consumption of alcohol were legal, which worked to the benefit of the U.S. Navy's Fifth Fleet that was headquartered there. My room had a mini-bar with real booze, and the hotel bar served real beer. Inside the lounge were some Navy officers I had met, and we had a rip-roaring time consuming pints and singing Christmas carols. Coincidentally, PBS had recently aired a mini-series on America's Civil

War, and some of the Navy guys wondered why we hadn't attacked the Iraqis yet. "Schwarzkopf is the new McClellan. He has an army, but he won't use it," said one. That kind of bar talk chapped Schwarzkopf's ass.

Bahrain also had liquor stores, and I got to thinking. What if I bought some vodka and poured it into the two military canteens I had brought along in my backpack? Yeah, there was a checkpoint, but the border guards seemed to gloss over military gear. Who would look inside a canteen? Against my better judgment, I bought two bottles of vodka and poured the contents into the canteens for the return trip.

The next day, with a new two-week visa in my passport, I hailed a cab back to Saudi Arabia. At the border post, I figured the guards would be suspicious if I tried to conceal anything, so I hid the canteens in plain sight. After presenting my paperwork, the first thing I placed on a conveyor belt leading to an X-ray machine was the backpack with the canteens. Carlos the Jackal would have been proud. The guards checked my luggage but pushed the canteens through without so much as a glance. Breathing a huge sigh of relief, I got back into the cab and was off.

It was a stupid, reckless stunt. If the border guards had been more thorough, I could have been denied entry and sent home in disgrace, or possibly faced arrest and a Saudi lashing. Either way, the chance to cover the war would have been over, and I would have sabotaged the whole assignment. I didn't even care about having booze. Maybe I was tired of someone else telling me what I could and could not do. Maybe I thought I could out-smart the system. Whatever. That's the thing about war. It messes with the brain. It makes one take risks that would never be considered under normal circumstances. Some call it the "we're-all-going-to-die syndrome." English playwright Noel Coward, writing about World War I, described it this way: "That strange feeling we had in the war. Have you found anything in your lives to equal it in strength? A sort of splendid carelessness it was, holding us all together."

My secret stash now included vodka. Splendid carelessness, indeed.

Just after I returned from Bahrain, Sophia stopped me as I was walking through the ballroom occupied by the American military. She and some women journalists had been invited to a party that night, and she asked if I would escort them. A vibe was in the air, and my radar locked on. How could I say no? But rather than driving, I insisted we take a cab. Drinks would be served, and I wasn't about to take any chances by drinking and driving. Our destination was a walled, gated compound housing British nationals who worked for British Petroleum. Inside the compound, away from Saudi eyes, was a club that served real alcohol.

No pub in the British Isles could have been more splendid. We played darts, sipped Scotch, laughed with our hosts and had the best time. For the women, it was their first night of leisure in a country that offered none.

Apparently, the booze lowered some inhibitions, and human nature started to take over. As we sat at the bar, Sophia draped an arm around me and conversed over the din by whispering into my ear.

The barkeep noticed. "Man, you're going to get lucky tonight," he winked.

At closing time, I herded my little group back into a cab for the ride back, with Sophia sitting on my lap. At the hotel, she asked if the invitation for a nightcap still stood. Not that she needed another drink, but, well, one thing led to another, and she showed up in my room. This time, she chased down her cocktail with a wet kiss, and we stripped off each other's clothes to jump between the sheets. Her carnal cravings were unfettered. You have to love a comely woman who wants it as badly as you do, especially among two people thrown together by happenstance in an environment that discourages intimacy. We couldn't get enough of each other until we reached the point of exhaustion, falling asleep in each other's arms.

When morning came, she asked me what had happened. If she truly didn't remember, the evidence was in the pile of clothes on the floor and the naked flesh in the bed. As I filled in the blanks, she giggled playfully and said she wanted to repeat everything so she would remember this time. She was as eager as she was the night before, and it was a healthy sex drive, not booze, that got her motor going.

This was more than a wild romp. Companionship in a faraway land was part of it, but so was the pleasure of the company of someone swept up by the same tides and carried to the same place. Conversation was an unexpected treat. So were the unspoken moments of two kindred spirits brought together under harrowing circumstances. For a brief time that morning, there was no deadline to meet or stories to chase. The blissful escape extended into the shower and over coffee delivered by room service.

Afterwards, she snuck out the door to avoid being seen by the religious police and made her way back to her room. The best part was, she wanted to get together again when our schedules would permit.

This adventure just kept getting better and better.

It's a shame to say, but information had gotten so ridiculously tight, it was easier to get out in the field with the Saudis than it was with the American military. Trips were scheduled on Thursdays or Fridays, the Muslim weekend. Each trip had a spot for an AP Pencil. It would have been an insult to our hosts not to go, even if the news value was marginal.

Several flights were arranged between Dhahran and Yanbu, an industrial city with a deep-water port on the Red Sea. It was 800 miles each way over the forlorn landscape, and I wish I had qualified for frequent flier miles. The purpose was to get pictures and TV footage of Egyptian and Syrian tanks, all part of the international coalition, rolling off transport ships to defend the kingdom and to stand up to the aggression of one Arab state against another.

One arriving unit was an armored brigade of 5,000 soldiers and 94 tanks from the Egyptian 4th Armored Division, which was trained to fight urban battles. Established in 1956, the division fought against the Israelis that year and in subsequent wars in 1967 and 1973. It was the unit that crossed the Suez Canal in the 1973 war, surprising the Israelis who thought the maneuver was impossible. It had also trained with U.S. Army's 24th Division in 1988. Its combat power came from American-made M60 battle tanks, M113 armored personnel carriers and M109 self-propelled howitzers.

"If peace doesn't arrive, and if we're ordered by our supreme commanders, we can teach Saddam a lesson he'll never forget," General Khalid said.

Overall, the Arab-Islamic international force numbered 100,000 troops. In addition to Saudis, Egyptians, Syrians and vengeful Kuwaitis, troops from Pakistan, Morocco, Bangladesh, Niger and Senegal, among other nations, planted their flags in the sand.

Also in the coalition was a chemical decontamination unit from Czechoslovakia, my ancestral homeland. I happened across them by chance on one training mission.

With 170 members, it was the smallest of the foreign forces deployed. It had five different teams to clean up vehicles, equipment and airstrips if Saddam used chemical weapons. This former Eastern Bloc country had aligned itself with the West, and it was the first time in history they had ever been deployed in the desert. They wore caps with earflaps and had brown combat boots.

"If we don't stop Saddam now, there will be war in the Middle East and maybe in the world," said Major Ivan Pavlov, the unit commander.

———————————

Another obstacle has been removed on the path to war. After holding hostages for four months as human shields, Saddam Hussein told them on December 6 they were free to go.

The reaction of troops was mixed.

"I don't want to go to war, but if we have to, I think it's better than the alternative of letting Saddam develop his nuclear weapons capabilities, which I see as the ultimate evil," said Lieutenant Brian Ratchford, 26, of Spartanburg, South Carolina, a member of the 39th Tactical Air Squadron.

Air Force Staff Sergeant Chester Smolarczyk, 28, of Jacksonville, Arkansas, said he was more than willing to wait it out in the desert to allow diplomacy to work. "Ask yourself, which is cheaper, blood or oil?" he said.

———————————

American traditions take on even more meaning for those who are away on duty in a war zone. Take the December 8 college football game between Army and Navy. Even though a sports event seems insignificant under the circumstances, the games had a way of bringing people together and putting on hold the grim reality of what's coming.

Lieutenant Commander Tim Traeen of Gig Harbor, Washington, a former tight end at the Naval Academy, left his duty station as supply officer aboard the *USS Blue Ridge*, the flagship for the U.S. Navy Central Command, to watch the game live on Armed Forces Network in Dhahran. He once listened to the Army-Navy game during strategic operations in a missile submarine, and he wasn't about to miss this opportunity.

"If there was one game I had to pick — the Super Bowl, the Orange Bowl, or whatever — this is the game I'd want to see. It incorporates all the reasons why I'm in the Navy — the challenge, the competition, the spirit," Traeen said. "You can beat the heck out of each other on the football field, but when the shit hits the fan, we pull together."

Army Colonel Bill Mulvey, a 1968 graduate of West Point and the new director of the Joint Information Bureau, remembered listening to the game on the radio in Vietnam. At the time, he was pulling guard duty behind a .50 caliber machine gun mounted to an armored personnel carrier.

"The 12th man isn't just the cadets in the stands. We're all part of the Army team. These Navy guys get to watch the game in an air-conditioned wardroom off the coast. In Saudi Arabia, the Army has to listen on the radio because they're in the desert," said Mulvey, 44, of Clarksville, Tennessee.

Army and Navy representatives whooped and cheered and taunted each other during the game. Army won, 30-20, in a contest played at Veterans Stadium in Philadelphia. For the moment, the all-time series was tied, 42-42-7.

Instead of working in the hotel office, I've started taking the portable computer out by the swimming pool. I can write just as well while soaking up rays from the comfort of a lounge chair. On one such venture, two sleek fighter jets took off from the Dhahran runway and kicked in the after burners. They climbed into the sky and broke the sound barrier before they were out of sight. The background scenes can't be beat.

Despite the limited access to U.S. troops, I did manage to run across some

American forces while in the field on the Saudi trips. My fellow journalists gave me a lot of grief for writing this, but military operations in desert warfare would be like fighting at sea because of the vast open spaces. Erwin Rommel, Germany's Desert Fox, applied naval strategies in his North African campaign, deploying his tanks like battleships and his armored personnel carriers like destroyers. The empty desert, with its room to maneuver, was more amenable to long-distance fighting rather than close-in firefights. What most of us failed to grasp was how quickly the engagements would be over.

Colonel Doug Starr, 47, commander of the five tank squadrons of the 3rd Armored Cavalry Regiment, predicted that the fighting would be like those naval battles where the two sides opened fire without ever seeing each other.

"The distances and the space look a lot more like the sea than any Westerners see in the places we normally live. It's an entirely different maneuver scheme than you'd see in Europe. The tank battles have the potential to be at longer distances and ranges," Starr said.

Ground troops employed maritime equipment to simplify their battle strategies. One device was Loran, or Long Range Navigation, which is normally used to fix a position of a ship or an aircraft with electronic pulses sent out by two radio signals. A new innovation was the Global Positioning System, which could pinpoint a location on the earth to within ten yards by receiving signals from satellites in orbit.

"Our armored formations are a lot like ships at sea," said Captain Sean McFarland of the 3rd Armored Cavalry Regiment: "There's no place you can hide. You have to rely on speed and firepower."

P.S. I can happily report my place on the media pool designated to cover the war is now secured. The final hurdle was passing a physical fitness test during which journalists had to do a certain number of push-ups and sit-ups in one minute. We also had to run a mile in a prescribed period of time. It wasn't as tough as the workouts I was doing in the hotel gym, but the military required that those of us going onto the battlefield meet basic standards in case we had to run to a helicopter in the heat of battle. I was even interviewed for a segment on Ted Koppel's *Nightline* about the physical fitness test and the media pool. In the words of the troops, I am good to go.

CHAPTER 15
Reserve Power

New York was still keen on getting a story about disgruntled troops who left their homes and their families to find themselves plopped down in a desert war zone, and the obvious candidates were the reservists who were plucked from civilian life and called to active duty. What they said and did, however, was an indication of how far the reserves had come since Vietnam. Stereotypes die hard.

Having spent some time in various Army reserve units, I knew from personal experience why the term weekend warriors had come into vogue. Although some reserve units did stand shoulder-to-shoulder with those who did the fighting in Vietnam, the reserves were never formally mobilized. Therefore, a person could be drafted and fulfill a military obligation, no questions asked, by joining any reserve unit that had an opening. There was a huge difference between draftees who did a two-year hitch on active duty and those who opted for a six-year term of attending meetings every month and reporting for two weeks of summer camp every year. Military insiders acknowledged the difference by establishing their own pecking order. In basic training, for example, draftees and Regular Army soldiers were always moved to the front of the chow line. Reservists and those in their state's National Guard were treated like second-class citizens and ate last. Still, reservists could qualify for the same honorable discharge as those who served in combat. No matter what anyone says, the overwhelming majority of reservists from that era found a safe haven in which to ride out the war. Those who failed to show for meetings faced the potential penalty of being called to active duty, but enforcement of that regulation was hardly ever imposed. Besides, it was common practice to show up for roll call in the morning, skip out to the doughnut shop, return for lunch and another roll call, and then spend the afternoon at a nearby watering hole. The two weeks of summer camp often meant a running poker game, keg party and softball tournament. Some skirted the regulation of having military haircuts by wearing short-haired wigs over their long locks. Not that the duty was much of a burden either. In one public affairs unit, which produced stories about how the reservists were serving their country, the motto was: "Retreat, hell! Backspace."

Policy-makers who were appalled by the system vowed to avoid repeating the same mistakes. A turnaround began with the all-volunteer military following the report of an Army study group that called Vietnam "a particularly dismal period" for the Guard and Reserve and concluded its "ability to go to war was near zero." When the military transitioned to the all-volunteer system in 1973, a Total Force Policy was adopted. Essentially, it meant that the country could not go to war again without the reserves, because part-time soldiers were given key assignments essential to a wartime mission. Desert Shield was the first real test of the new policy, and not since Bunker Hill had America depended so heavily on its citizen-soldiers. While serving behind the scenes, reservists provided the military with truck drivers, mechanics, postal workers, doctors, nurses, lawyers, pilots, aircrews and water purification specialists.

For a story on readiness before leaving the States, I spoke with Herbert R. Temple, former head of the National Guard Bureau. He said the changes that had occurred in the last 20 years were like night and day. "It was not but a few years ago that they said we couldn't fight our way out of a wet paper bag. Baby, we've come a long way," he said.

As one example, the Army's 24th Mechanized Division was comprised of two active-duty brigades and would be rounded out by a National Guard unit. The reserve brigade was the 48th Mechanized Brigade of the Georgia Army National Guard, headquartered in Dalton, Georgia. The brigade had trained for its combat mission at the National Training Center in the Mojave Desert, and it had received its Abrams main battle tanks and Bradley armored fighting vehicles even before its parent unit. Its ranks were all volunteers too.

Harry Heath, spokesman for the Georgia Department of Defense and a retired Army colonel, said: "Annual training used to be an open-ended poker game and beerfest. Today, the Army and Air National Guard are prepared to accept any challenge and will acquit themselves competently and professionally."

Alton Key, 41, a sergeant in the 48th Brigade, had this to say: "Most people's image of a reservist was of an individual trying to beat the draft, or a bunch of drunks and card-players. There's been a complete turnaround. We signed on the dotted line. We're ready to stand in the ranks."

The brigade never did receive combat certification or make it to Saudi Arabia, however. It says right there in Murphy's Laws of Combat that no combat unit has ever passed inspection, and that no inspection-ready unit has ever passed combat. In its absence, the 197th Mechanized Infantry Brigade rounded out the 24th Division.

Still, the 35,000 or so reservists who were called to active duty and deployed in Desert Shield sacrificed much to do their duty. One of them was George Phelan of Fall River, Massachusetts, a member of the 46th Judge Advocate General Detachment, the first reserve unit to be activated. Phelan had left his family and his law practice to serve as a major in Desert Shield. His new home, located off the Dhahran airport runway, was a cot in a tent pieced together with ponchos, shelter halves and plywood boards. He had missed his infant daughter's first birthday and celebrated his 40th birthday on September 4 at gas mask school with his army buddies at Fort Devens, Massachusetts. When his orders came, he didn't have time to tell all his clients he was leaving. He wrote letters and took out a newspaper ad saying he'd be away for an indefinite time. His gripes were not out of the ordinary.

"When your country calls you to defend it and defend its interests, I think it's a small sacrifice to pay. It's my duty to be here. You've got to put the inconvenience aside and put your mind to work," Phelan said. "As simplistic and naive as it might sound, I'm proud to be over here. It's something you've got to be willing to do even though it might be unexpected and certainly inconvenient from a business and personal point of view. The thing that eats at me is not being able to enjoy things I'll never be able to recapture, like my daughter's first birthday, the first teeth, walking for the first time, saying her first words. Those things you can't get back because they only happen one time."

Staff Sergeant Paul Boyd, 37, of Murfreesboro, Tennessee, was a National Guardsman assigned to the 130th Rear Area Operations Center. He said something that any veteran, or future defense secretary, could relate to when talking about military bureaucracy.

"I despise the U. S. Army bureaucracy. It's the most screwed up, disorganized organization I've ever been associated with," Boyd said.

Nevertheless, he was committed to the job at hand.

"The biggest battle is within ourselves, keeping our minds right. One of the things I've learned here is what's important. It's not a house, a boat, a car. None of the material things mean anything. It's my loved ones that count," Boyd said.

Gerald McCormick, a reservist who was now an Army sergeant, was losing money after being converted from a financial planner to a soldier. His wife was expecting their first child in December, and being away took its toll.

"It's just lost time you won't ever make up. When I get home, I'll never complain about living conditions again," McCormick said.

The strain put on reservists was voiced by Johnny Speel, 46, of Autryville, North Carolina, who ran an appliance store founded by his late father. He was activated on August 31 and was deployed to the kingdom two weeks later as a staff sergeant with the Army's 382nd Public Affairs Unit. He barely had time to straighten out business details, change some things in his will and give his wife power of attorney. He would miss Thanksgiving and Christmas at home, and he'd be away for his wife's birthday on December 7.

"It's harder on the citizen soldier. We had to leave a job, and we had to leave our families. Being self-employed, it's just a tough situation to deal with," Speel said. "But don't misunderstand. When you sign the dotted line, you know if the time comes like this you have to go and do your duty. I'm not bitter about being here. I just miss home and I miss my business like every person does. This may sound corny, but I wanted to do my patriotic American duty. I wanted to serve. We have a job to do. Everyone over here regrets not being at home. I guess that can't be helped."

Fighting the war would have been impossible without reservists. And one reserve detachment would pay a bloodier price than any other unit, active or otherwise, in the war.

CHAPTER 16
'Tis The Season

Something was afoot the morning Mohammad Khayat of the Saudi Ministry of Information visited the AP suite to say that a package had arrived from the States, and that I should accompany him to the Post Office to claim it. I figured the gas masks and chemical gear had finally arrived, or maybe New York had shipped fresh supplies, so off we went. It took stops at three different post offices around Dhahran before we located the right one. Bureaucracies must be the same everywhere.

A postal official took us to a back room stacked to the ceiling with incoming boxes. A package with my name on it was found. Inside a cardboard box that had already been opened by Saudi inspectors was an artificial Christmas tree, a wreath and a box of chocolates. A well-intentioned AP colleague from San Francisco figured a touch of home would make the assignment more tolerable. While the gesture was appreciated, it had unintended consequences. As far as the Saudis were concerned, the tree was a religious symbol, and all religious symbols not associated with Islam were prohibited in the kingdom. Hoping to avoid any trouble, I told the postal supervisor to keep it or trash it, and I'd be on my way.

"No, no," he said. "Don't be ashamed of your religion. You can have it. Just don't display it in public. And sign this promise that you'll take it with you when you leave the country."

Arguing would have been pointless. I signed the form and handed out the chocolates to the Saudis for their troubles. The tree was brought back and set up on a table inside the AP office where it was out of public view. Decorations were unique to the circumstance. The base was adorned with the metal casings of spent shells fired during target practice. Some sun-bleached camel bones retrieved from the desert floor also seemed appropriate as decorations. All in all, the tree was a touch of home. Media colleagues and even some of the military guys stopped in to see it. This would be a Christmas like no other, even if it definitely did NOT feel like the most wonderful time of the year.

Although the Qur'an recognizes Jesus as a prophet, the Islamic religion does not celebrate the accepted birthday of the most important figure in Christianity. Merchants in the local shops, however, stocked their shelves with what they called cards of the season. A popular one depicted three Arab noblemen on camelback heading toward a star while bearing gifts of gold, frankincense and myrrh. Well, the Three Wise Men did come from the East, according to what I was taught. Strings of twinkling lights could also be purchased, but snow was out of the question. Still, a season of peace, minus the crass commercialism, was approaching in a time of war.

Would there be an outbreak of Christmas blues in the ranks, given that U.S. troops were far from home and unable to mark the holiday the way they do back home? The psychologists on staff at Fleet Hospital No. 5 conceded that Christmas was a delicate subject, but they were counting on the inner strength of the troops to get them through. What helped were personal things sent from home — a card, a trinket, a snapshot, Yule decorations, Nativity scenes, fake snow, candy cane houses, artificial trees or anything to suggest that someone back home was thinking of them.

"There will be a kind of blue haze over everything. It's kind of a funk. But the average person will find a lot of solace being among friends, sharing Christmas dinner, singing a couple of carols," said one of the psychologists, Captain Frank Mullins, 54, of Mobile, Alabama.

"The troops should try to have as normal a Christmas as they can, with as many customs and rituals as they can get from home," he added. "Don't get me wrong. People are upset. If you don't feel upset, maybe there's something wrong with you. People may get depressed. They may cry a little. But they'll be fine the next day. We don't expect to be overflowing with psychiatric casualties on Christmas Day."

One thing for sure, there would be no rum in the eggnog. The absence of booze was even seen as a blessing by those in the mental health field, but I kept the existence of my private stash to myself.

"I'll be the first to say I'm glad there's no alcohol," Mullins said. "What it does is cut down on the mental health business. Without alcohol, the troops are going to engage in more adult behavior and operate in their environment more realistically."

He even encouraged soldiers to vent.

"How many times have you heard that morale is good when people are bitching? More is good when people are bitching. When people get too depressed to bitch, you've got problems. They withdraw socially, go into themselves," Mullins said. "For a lot of the young people here, this may be the major growth experience in their lives. Don't forget, World War II was that way for the people of that generation. And years from now, when somebody says something about this war, they can tell people they're full of shit because they were over here."

Footnote: Some members of the 101st Airborne tried to make some home-brew out of antifreeze, and the batch made them sick. Eight of them were hospitalized, half of them with damaged livers.

Even since Thanksgiving, the Christmas crush of mail had been non-stop. Coming from the States were letters, cards, care packages, bottles of water, cookies, banners and Brooklyn bagels. From 90 tons a day in October, the mail hit a single day record of 211 tons just prior to Thanksgiving. Then it built to a peak of 400 tons a day, partly due to the Christmas rush and partly due to the doubling of size of the force. The volume was enough to fill three wide-bodied commercial jets — just for the Army alone. For comparison purposes, the U.S. Post Office in Newark, New Jersey, handles 400 tons of mail per month with 800 workers. The Army moved that much in a week, with 300 reservists working 12-hour shifts each day. The mail, that gossamer bridge that keeps troops connected to home, was especially important at Christmas.

"It's really the only contact we have with our families. From the generals on down to the lowest private, mail is the lifeblood of the morale system. Getting a letter is like a drink of water for troops who have been in the desert for days. If the troops didn't have their mail, they'd go bonkers," said Lieutenant Colonel Fred Nichols of Atlanta, the deputy commander of the organization that handled the Army's mail.

The hundreds of thousands of Americans deployed to the region were also sending stuff home — prayer rugs, gold jewelry, blankets, trinkets, video tapes and snapshots. The most popular gift was something that validated their deployment and provided a hint of the alien world they now inhabited. It was a pinch of Saudi sand. Never more than a reach away, sand was scooped up and put inside an envelope to be mailed home. The unintended consequence was that sand spilled out as letters were processed by the postal machinery in the States. Sending sand clogged up the works.

"We would like to discourage that as much as possible. It tends to leak out of the envelopes and fouls up the automated sorting equipment back home," Nichols said.

Last-minute shopping could be done at Cindy's Saudi Store, set up just behind the military post office at the Dhahran airport. In a trailer housing the Army and Air Force Exchange, a computerized shopping network allowed troops to pick gifts from a catalog and ship them to their loved ones.

One of the most popular items for those deployed was a wax bust of Saddam Hussein. The package came with a hammer, which allowed troops to vent their frustrations by whacking the image of the Iraqi leader. President Bush had referred to Saddam as "Hitler revisited," and troops that had been here the longest had worked up the most hatred for him.

If Thanksgiving dinner was a big deal, the menu for Christmas topped it. Chief Warrant Officer Wesley Wolf, who served as a cook in Vietnam and was now the food adviser for the U.S. military in Saudi Arabia, insisted on something extraordinary for the occasion.

"Santa Claus is not going to be around to bring presents, so we're going to have to do something to make it a special day. This is really an important meal for us. We're trying to get a hot meal to everyone," Wolf said.

The menu included 35,000 pounds of shrimp plus cocktail sauce; 108,000 pounds of canned ham (kept low key because pork is forbidden in the kingdom); 172,000 pounds of roast beef; 150,000 pounds of rolled turkey; 4,000 whole turkeys with cranberry sauce and stuffing; 280,000 pounds of glazed sweet potatoes; mashed potatoes; assorted veggies; a fresh salad of tomatoes, lettuce and cucumbers; assorted breads; 35,000 pounds of fruitcake; apple, peach, pecan, pumpkin and minced meat pies, 150,000 in all; candy, mixed nuts, oranges, grapes, tangerines and pears; coffee, tea, milk, soda pop and egg nog. Also part of the spread were 500,000 Mars and Snickers candy bars donated by the Saudi royal family.

New York ordered up another story, this one on the mission. What did those in the ranks think they were fighting for? Was it to defend Saudi Arabia or liberate Kuwait from Iraqi occupation?

The simplest answer was voiced by Marine Lance Corporal Bournet (Hollywood) Huddleston, 20, of Los Angeles, who volunteered his opinion from the sidelines of the Scud Bowl football game at Thanksgiving.

"We're here to kick some ass. Let's free these people so we can go home and be free again," Huddleston said.

The top commander of all Marines in the Gulf, three-star general Walter Boomer, had an answer tempered by his service in Vietnam, where he was awarded the Silver Star for valor while serving as a company commander and later returning as an advisor to a battalion of South Vietnamese marines.

"There are things worth fighting for. A world in which brutality and lawlessness are allowed to go unchecked isn't the kind of world we're going to want to live in," Boomer said.

Army Lieutenant Jackie Jones, 25, of Springfield, Virginia, a member of a Patriot missile battery, believed the purpose of the coming conflict was to stand up to a tyrant.

"We're here to show the rest of the world the United States is not going to stand for bullies trying to wipe other countries off the face of the earth. If we let him get away with this, who knows what's going to be next?" she said.

Airman Julie Taylor, 20, of Lake Tahoe, California, thought that the confrontation boiled down to oil. Although protecting the flow of oil was a vital interest of the United States, she wondered about the cost in blood. "Thousands of people are going to die if we go to war or if we get gassed. I don't think a quart of Valvoline is a good reason for it," she said.

However, Master Sergeant J.R. Kendall of the 82nd Airborne Division said it was more than just stopping a dictator before he could threaten other countries by getting his hands on more money and more weapons. As a soldier about to go to war, he believed he was making a difference.

"We're here for more than just the price of a gallon of gas," Kendall said. "What we're doing is going to chart the future of the world for the next 100 years. It's better to deal with this guy now than five years from now. One way or another, he's got to be dealt with."

The view of the mission depended on who you asked, however. Staff Sergeant Jerome McReynolds, 39, of Montgomery, Alabama, was a reservist with the Army's 1241st Post Unit. He had left his home and his family to deploy to a land 8,000 miles away to work 12 hours a day, seven days a week, unloading mail in Dhahran and without ever getting a day off.

"I actually don't know why we're here," said McReynolds. "The mission? I'd really like to know. What is it?"

December 21, the first day of winter, was a sunny, 80-degree day. It was also the day that Secretary of Defense Dick Cheney and Colin Powell, chairman of the Joint Chiefs of Staff, visited the kingdom for an inspection tour of the troops. Two media pools were organized to follow them, and I was assigned to Powell.

Our bus took us to the port of Dammam, where the equipment of VII Corps was pouring in. Parked on the docks were row after row of armored personnel carriers awaiting deployment to the field. In the desert, tanks and armored vehicles are dispersed. Here, they were concentrated. The sheer numbers were remarkable.

Next came a helicopter ride to Operating Base Eagle, headquarters of the 101st Air Assault (Airborne) Division. The base was located near a desert town with the tongue-twister name of An Nuayriah, where five roads intersected in eastern Saudi Arabia about a hour's drive south of Kuwait. The road junction conjured images of the Belgian town of Bastogne, where the Screaming Eagles fought in the Battle of the Bulge despite being surrounded by attacking

Germans.

As a show of readiness for the visiting general, a company of Screaming Eagles assaulted a mock bunker complex. On display were the infantrymen's skill at fire and maneuver in taking a defended position. Not far away from the exercise, a staff sergeant in an artillery unit was filling sandbags to strengthen his position. While on his inspection tour, Powell picked up a shovel, stepped into the sergeant's fighting hole and lent a hand filling the bags. A four-star general who was chairman of the Joint Chiefs of Staff actually got down in the dirt to help a startled sergeant perform a menial but necessary task. This was different than the Army I knew.

Finally, Powell lunched inside a tent with rank-and-file infantrymen. Eating a cold MRE, the chairman of the joint chiefs fielded questions.

Would Israel get involved?

What are the geopolitical ramifications of the mission?

When do we get going?

Powell answered them as he ate, and then politely asked the media to leave the tent so he could have a moment in private with his soldiers. Like Eisenhower before D-Day, Powell wanted the troops to know that he understood what the country was asking them to do, but he also wanted them to know the mission was essential.

Powell, a division commander in Vietnam, was on the record as saying that never again would the United States ask its soldiers to fight a limited war like they had in Vietnam. He believed that wars are to be avoided, but if combat became unavoidable, overwhelming force should be applied to get it over with as quickly as possible. The concept became known as the Powell Doctrine, and it was impressive for an infantryman to hear it from the top.

A husband and wife in the 82nd Airborne who were both deployed and trying to make plans to have a Christmas dinner together made for a good story. Private First Class Bruce Krot, 21, of Dearborn, Michigan, was pulling guard duty at a sentry post at division headquarters. He had a mustard splat on his airborne wings for making the combat jump into Panama a year earlier. This would be his second straight Christmas away from home.

"We were separated last year. She didn't want it to happen again, but I consider my company to be part of my family," said Krot, who served in a company of Airborne Military Police.

One of the networks picked up on the story and arranged for Bruce and Melissa Krot to be interviewed on TV. As a fringe benefit, the network put them up in a hotel for Christmas. Hoo-ah!

Death never takes a holiday, but the timing of it worsens the pain. On December 22, the *USS Saratoga*, the carrier from which I made a tail-hook landing and catapult take-off, was anchored a mile from the Israeli port of Haifa in the Red Sea. With the crew eagerly anticipating Christmas liberty, about 1,920 sailors from the *Saratoga* and three escort vessels went ashore. Haifa, or God's Vineyard, offered amenities such as a USO canteen with a library and sitting room. Some wives and girlfriends had flown to Haifa to be with their loved ones, who had been out to sea for months. The backdrop to the city was the sacred Mount Carmel, the site of the prophet Elijah's confrontation with pagan priests. Because it was only 75 miles from Jerusalem, some of the crew embarked on tours to the Holy Land at the holiest time of the year.

When leave was over and it was time to return to the *Saratoga,* the deadliest moment of Desert Shield happened. Even though I had only been on the carrier for one day, it felt personal. About 150 returning sailors were aboard the ferry *Tuvia*, which was licensed to carry 131 passengers. The 57-foot long ferry was plying through the Red Sea, about 200 yards from the ship, when it was swamped by two large swells. With many of the passengers gathered in the stern, water rushed in, and the ferry rolled over.

Flares lit the night sky as survivors scrambled for their lives, clinging to life jackets and other debris. While 81 sailors who found themselves adrift in 65 feet of water survived, 22 perished and 47 more required medical care.

The next day, on a Sunday morning, the *Saratoga's* shipboard complement gathered in an aircraft hangar converted into a chapel. They sang *America The Beautiful* and the Navy Hymn. Two sailors dropped a wreath into the gray sea, and a Marine honor guard fired a 21-gun salute. The flag-draped coffins were then flown to a mortuary in Dover, Delaware.

Solemnly acknowledging the toll, Captain Joe Mobley addressed those under his command. "Every man on this mighty ship has had his heart in his throat, tears in his eyes and a knot in his stomach since that event," Mobley said.

In the desert, Christmas spirit was harder to find than a reindeer at the camel market, but training went on as usual. On December 23, the 1st Calvary Division invited the media to watch its battle tanks on the firing range. The metal beasts would charge ahead at 30 miles per hour, firing the tank's main gun while on the move. A giant ball of orange flame would leave the barrel as the shell was fired, followed by an angry blast. The concussion kicked up clouds of sand.

"It's just another day in the desert," said Private First Class Mark Idleman, 19, of Wilson, Oklahoma, a tank crewman in the 32nd Armored Regiment.

Still, everyone in the division would have a gift to unwrap on Christmas, thanks to the efforts of Major Steve Stacey, the division's personnel officer.

"It might be a pair of green socks. It might be a Frisbee. But we've got one gift for every one of the 20,000 soldiers in the division."

And he asked that a message be sent back home to loved ones.

"Although we're homesick and we miss you, we're with you in spirit. We can't send any presents, so we send our love," Stacey said.

CHAPTER 17
Birthday Gifts

It's Christmas Eve, the 41st anniversary of my entry into the world, and I find myself at the pinnacle of my profession, right where I'm destined to be, eight time zones from home, running the Dhahran Bureau of a global news agency, part of an international media corps covering the biggest story in the world, living on the expense account, prepared to go to war, straining to see what's coming but tuned in to today. I am keenly aware that enemies often attacked around the holidays because troops might let their guard down, certain only that Christmas is tomorrow for a half a million Americans encamped in an Islamic kingdom, connected in spirit to loved one back home, having the time of my life and appreciative for the surprising gifts that made this birthday like no other.

Anyone born on December 24, the day before the birth of the most famous person in human history, gets used to being overshadowed. Everyone's too busy preparing for Christmas and Santa Claus to throw a party or bake a cake. Getting shorted applies to presents too, like getting a right glove as a birthday gift and the left glove for Christmas, or a right skate and then a left skate. Not this time.

My AP colleagues surprised me with a new sleeping bag bought at the Khobar shopping mall. It was a replacement for the military-strength bag I left in the trunk of the rental car, which became a total wreck when one of the photographers took it out on an assignment and rolled it into a heap of crumpled metal and broken glass just days before. We never did find the car. Saudi authorities had already towed it to a junk yard, with the sleeping bag still inside. The photographer who was in the accident survived, but he cracked a couple of vertebrae and was being sent home without having covered the war. Receiving a replacement bag was much appreciated, but it was a poor quality foreign model.

Out of nowhere, Cleo reappeared. She had returned to the kingdom to write the same kinds of stories I was looking to do about men and women preparing for war in a season of peace on Earth, goodwill towards men. She stopped in at the AP suite to check out the tree and the decorations, which I can safely say was the best display in the Eastern Province. Discreetly, she invited me back to her room, saying she had something for me. The birthday gift was a Persian rug woven in a timeless tradition, but it had modern touches such as images of an assault rifle and hand grenades as part of the pattern. To make the most of the moment, she rolled out the rug and cooed something about how comfortable it was to kneel on. This birthday surprise sure beat a cake with candles, and it was even better than that night under the stars in the desert. Somewhere in between the heavy breathing and the moaning of an eager woman, it occurred to me that hundreds of thousands of other Americans deployed to the desert would love trading places. Nothing beats having something so precious when the supply is so short. As consenting adults, we fell into each other's arms for carnal pleasures on the rug. I would have stayed there all day for more horizontal refreshment, as soldiers refer to it, but duty called. The news cycle is a hungry beast, and it must be fed even on holidays.

Numerous requests to be out in the field with the troops had gone unfulfilled. Military brass wanted to respect their Saudi hosts by downplaying Christmas, but I argued with the officers at the Joint Information Bureau that families back in the States would want to know how their loved ones are faring. Dealing with an Islamic theocracy ruled by a king on a desolate peninsula ranks right up there with trying to work with a military bureaucracy that wants to guard its own secrets and doesn't want to make waves with the host country. Then the 82nd Airborne delivered its own kind of gift. Paratroopers had scheduled a 10-kilometer run called the Jingle Bell Jog at division headquarters at Champion Main at the King Fahd International Airport, and media representatives were invited to board a military van to take us to the event.

The Jingle Bell Jog was a perfect story. Running was part of the daily training regimen for the division's soldiers, yet this one was enhanced with nuances about the true meaning of Christmas. At the starting line, the jump-qualified division band played a somber rendition of *Deck The Halls*. Chief Warrant Officer Willie James Lockett, 35, of Jacksonville, Florida, led the musicians while playing his saxophone.

"We don't want the soldiers to be lonely and think about what it's like back in the world," Lockett said. "My Christmas tree will be up whenever I get back to the world. If it's ten years from now, that sucker will still be up."

Santa Claus was played by Lieutenant Colonel Bob Murphy. The 43-year-old resident of Fayetteville, North Carolina, handed out cheer from a brown plastic garbage bag that substituted as a gift sack. Distributed were razor blades, candy, Frisbees, yo-yo's and other gifts. It's the thought that counts, and the troops appreciated even the most meager gift.

"Christmas is where the heart is, and in the 82nd Airborne Division, everybody's heart is in the right place. Sure, we'd all love to be home with our loved ones, but my gosh, we've got an important mission to do over here. Right now, we're at peace. That's the reason we're here, to preserve that peace," Murphy said before bellowing out a "Ho! Ho! Ho! Hoo-ah!"

The starting gun was an artillery piece. With the boom of the cannon, runners took off on a circular course that would take them around the airbase and back to where they started. Some ran singing cadence, just like they would if it were a duty day at Fort Bragg: *All the way. Everyday.*

Captain Michael Thomas, 30, of Trenton, New Jersey, ran the route wearing a Santa's cap and a pair of Bart Simpson shorts. While serving Uncle Sam, he had been away from home for Christmas six times in the last eight years, and he had learned to look at the bright side. For this Christmas, the desert had sandblasted away all worldly distractions.

"Actually, out here, we're away from the commercial side of Christmas. You have to look inside yourself to find the real Christmas spirit," Thomas said.

The sacrifice some soldiers made in being away from home was apparent. Lieutenant Lisa Titus, 27, jogged with her husband, Greg, who was commander of an artillery battery. With both of them on deployment, they were separated from their 14-month old son, who was staying with a nanny in Grand Rapids, Michigan.

"That's the worst part, being separated," she said. "But a lot of people made a lot of sacrifices to be here. We'll make it up when we get home."

Specialist Lee Etris, 25, of Greenville, South Carolina, talked about the camaraderie in the 82nd Airborne and the special bond that paratroopers share.

"When you're away from home, these guys tend to become family. We all put up with the same hardships. We're all in it together," Etris said.

Sergeant Duane Barker, 23, of Mansfield, Ohio, was away from home at Christmas on a deployment for the fifth time in six years. But nothing compared to being sent to the desert waiting for the combat mission to begin.

"It's been a roller coaster. The worst part of all is not knowing. Nobody minds doing the job. Nobody has a fear of fighting. The frustration comes in not knowing when it's going to happen," Barker said.

Sergeant Elton Moto, 25, of Newport News, Virginia, said being away for Christmas was part of being a soldier. The contract calls for sacrifices.

"It's a trying time. Everybody would love to be back home with their families and loved ones, but we have to carry out our mission. You live with it, accept it. We're all volunteers. We all signed on the dotted line," Moto said.

Some of the more dedicated, motivated troopers ran the course wearing a fully loaded, 80-pound pack on their backs and carrying their rifles at port arms. None of them knew what they might be called upon to do or when they might do it, but they were physically and mentally prepared to parachute into combat in the not too distant future.

The bus ride back provided time to reflect. The more time spent with troops in the field, especially the Airborne, the more I appreciated their earthy wisdom and their willingness to live up to the responsibilities of being in a war zone far away from home. Stereotypes were being sandblasted away. Even with allowing for the existence of the odd psychopath, the Airborne was a tight-knit, professional organization that knew what the business of war was all about, and they did their duty without lording it over anybody. It didn't hurt that they were open to the media, but it was more than that. They all seemed to believe in something bigger than themselves, and their very existence reflected what it meant to be an American soldier. To understand what makes paratroopers tick, there's a poster that reads: "I chose to do this. Nobody forced me. Not for King or Glory, but for the man next to me, and the Country that holds my family…And this we'll defend." The Army had come a long way.

More birthday surprises when the work was done. My AP colleagues and a gaggle of fellow media enjoyed a sit-down meal in the hotel restaurant. Our hosts had prepared a superb turkey dinner for journalists who had adopted each other as their own second family. Fiercely competitive when it came to getting stories, we were all in this together too. One topic of conversation was an item in *The Arab News*, an English language paper that had been running a countdown to the January 15 deadline for war. It published this poem in its Christmas Eve edition: '*Twas the night before K Day, And all through Kuwait, No Iraqi was leaving. They had sealed their fate.* The feast was even better because Sophia was there.

"Are you serving drinks later? I have something for you," she whispered at one point.

We rendezvoused at my room. She brought along birthday gifts in a Desert Shield bag — an ink pen, a kitschy plastic bubble containing camel dung, a display case containing a droplet of Saudi oil, a Closed For Prayer sign and prayer beads. It was the thought that counted, and it counted a lot. After sipping a drink but lacking mistletoe, we toasted birthdays and Christmas. One thing led to another, and we fell into each other's arms for a long night of passion. She fulfilled all of my wishes, and I returned the favor. Cripes, a half a million horny troops in the desert were going nuts without sex, and I enjoyed the company of two different women on my birthday. I almost felt guilty. Almost. It was the most meaningful Christmas Eve ever.

CHAPTER 18
The Holidays

Dashing through the sky, in a chopper not a sleigh, cruising o'er the dunes, what a lovely Christmas Day. Although nothing was on the schedule, the military arranged a last-minute field trip to spend the day with the troops. Having argued to get out into the field on Christmas, I had no special desire to spend the day in the hotel. Access to units always seemed like a gift. Weather conditions have made for a white Christmas, but not because of snow. A sandstorm is kicking up clouds of dust. We had been told to expect such conditions in winter. In what the Arabs call a *shamal,* winds of up to 50 miles per hour can whip up trillions of sand granules into dust clouds. As abrasive as sandpaper, a *shamal* can strip the paint off a car. Instead of being in a snow globe, this was like being inside an hourglass.

After a two-hour flight, a twin-rotor Chinook landed at Operating Base Eagle. If this wasn't the Army's northernmost camp, you could probably see it from here, except visibility was maybe 50 yards when the back door opened in the world of the Army's 20th Combat Engineer Brigade (Airborne), a self-contained unit deployed from Fort Bragg, North Carolina.

Above the whoosh of the wind, the brigade commander, Colonel Robert Flowers of Kane, Pennsylvania, delivered holiday cheer with a welcome and the gift of a T-shirt adorned with the unit logo and the slogan Proud To Be American. Thankfully, I brought along some key chains with the AP logo on them, and I had something to give in return. It's the thought that counts.

Combat engineers are in the business of construction and destruction, all at the same time. First in and last out on a battlefield, they build things like roads, bridges, fortifications and camps. They also blow up things like obstacle belts and bunkers, and their real test was coming soon. The Iraqis were notorious diggers, having hunkered down behind the 175-mile long Saddam Line extending from the Gulf into the desert. Taking advantage of sand berms the Saudis had built to deter smugglers, the Iraqi army burrowed in behind obstacle belts, mine fields, trenches and ditches filled with oil. Engineers would have to breach those nasty hurdles to accomplish the liberation of Kuwait.

In a nearby tent, without any intent to offend anyone else's religious beliefs, a Christmas worship service was conducted. Elements of the 37th Engineer Battalion (Airborne), whose forefathers landed in the first wave on Omaha Beach on D-Day, marked the occasion in their own quiet way. The unit's motto is *Fortuna Infortuna Forti Una*, which translates to mean, "To a man of stout heart, luck means nothing." Their hearts had to be stout this day as soldiers, standing shoulder to shoulder with their rifles slung and gas masks at the ready, paused in prayer in a war zone. Hanging over a folding table decorated with camouflage cloth and converted into a makeshift altar was a Christmas star painted red, white and blue. Captain Todd Hann, commander of Alpha Company, handed out candy and Christmas cards to his troops.

"If Christmas means anything, it's this. We're one big family here, and that's what's going to pull us through. Think of it as a day of thanks for being together as a family," the captain said.

The night before, troops said they held midnight services atop a nearby windy bluff, huddling together to protect flickering candles with their boonie hats. A chaplain said some appropriate words, and four troopers sang *O Holy Night* a cappella, just as a shooting star made a fiery trail across the sky. It was a night they would always remember.

In other areas of the camp, and despite the relentless storm, some troops played volleyball on a sandy court. A tent converted into a movie theater offered showings of *It's A Wonderful Life* and, as a way of expressing pent-up emotions about Saddam Hussein, *How The Grinch Stole Christmas.* In his living quarters, First Sergeant Charles Rio, 39, of Fayetteville, North Carolina, showed off a gift mailed from the States by his son. It was a fishing lure, entirely out of place in a country with no lakes or rivers, and everybody laughed. "It's for catching sand bass," Rio grinned.

A family support group from Fort Bragg had sent tiny plastic trees, twinkling lights and plastic Santas to their loved ones. A VCR and a TV monitor were set up in one tent for soldiers to watch videos of their wives and children opening gifts back home. There wasn't a sound except for the wind whipping outside. Some soldiers, heads down and faces long, walked out silently after catching a glimpse of their families. Private First Class Raymond Waldorf, 25, of Greenville, Michigan, had a different reaction. After seeing his wife, two-year-old son and five-month-old daughter on tape, he said: "It brightened up an otherwise gloomy day."

Christmas dinner, courtesy of the commander, was served in a giant mess tent filled with rows of tables and folding chairs. The aroma of hot turkey with all the trimmings filled the air. A tray of assorted nuts and holiday candy provided a special treat as a recording of *O Come All Ye Faithful* wafted over loudspeakers at a dirge-like pace.

In the motor pool, 20-year-old Specialist 4 John Davidson from Detroit, Michigan, vented to a stranger. Away from home for the first time in his life, he was afflicted with the Christmas blues. "Everybody here is down and depressed," Davidson said. It was hard not to be. Even the toughest soldier, having endured all the hardships of the deployment, felt a pang of homesickness on Christmas.

As dusk approached, and with the sandstorm making flying conditions hazardous, the unwelcome word came that we might be stranded. Lacking any gear other than a notebook, I was scrambling to find a place to sleep. Then, just as the window nearly closed on all military flights, the distinctive noise of helicopter blades thumping through the air could be heard. Santa's sleigh couldn't have brought more relief. A Chinook helicopter arrived and whisked us back to Dhahran.

I typed up the details of the day, but New York opted for a story about Bob Hope. Just as he had done since World War II, the old troubadour entertained troops. The venues were outside the kingdom so as not to offend the Saudis.

Yesterday had been such a high. Today was emotionally draining, swinging the mood like a pendulum to low. I turned in and slept for 12 hours, the longest single stretch of sack time since I got here. The whole day was a metaphor for flying through a sandstorm. You just had to get through it. Nevertheless, it was a Christmas for the ages.

Catching up. If it wasn't already clear, the only way to do this story justice will be to write it after the fact. A big meeting was held between the media destined to be on the combat pool and the military public affairs officers who would serve as escorts. Like most of these sessions, it got bogged down in the details. For print reporters, stories from the battlefield were to be crafted on manual typewriters. Before the pages could be sent back, a military censor would insure that the contents complied with the strictures of operational security. If approved, a story would be placed in a military pouch and put into the system for delivery to the Joint Information Bureau in Dhahran. Once received, the story would be available to any news organization that wanted to use all or part of it. The military promised to do the best it could in getting the stories back. That meant that combat units would have to devote resources to deliver stories from the field, whether it be by truck, helicopter or cargo plane. Therein lay one big flaw. Even if you drew a unit with a public affairs officer who allowed access to combat and you could write what you saw, the delivery system was in the military's hands.

Ground rules were open to interpretation. If strictly applied, a reporter couldn't say where a unit was, what it was doing and where it was going. If we followed the rules to the letter, we wouldn't be able to report anything. It came down to a matter of common sense — don't reveal anything that might jeopardize your own safety or the safety of those you're with. Despite reservations, I signed my name on the dotted line of a form saying that I agreed to adhere to the ground rules, including censorship. A pool slot depended on it.

December 29. The Army's 75th Artillery Brigade out of Fort Sill, Oklahoma, home of the big guns, invited the media to a field exercise intended to demonstrate its firepower and prowess. On a desert firing range, the unit unlimbered its cannons and took aim at targets eight miles away. In previous wars, one round would be sent down range and a spotter would radio back with adjustments. It usually took two rounds to bracket a target, then the third would land close enough to do some harm. Now, however, a laser beam painted targets and provided pinpoint accuracy. One crew on an eight-inch gun, commanded by a lieutenant who was a West Point graduate, hit a wrecked car designated as a target with the first shot. Fired from a distance of eight miles, the projectile blew the target to smithereens. When the lieutenant ordered the gun to fire and the lanyard was pulled, the concussion from the blast slapped my trousers against my legs. Awesome blast.

The brigade commander, Colonel Jerry "Gunner" Laws, had flown helicopters in Nam and was one of the true-believers who stayed in to rebuild the Army. During an interview, the subject came up about how troops prepare mentally for battle. He explained that one of the reasons the military trains so hard and so often, doing the same things over and over and over again, is to make the job second nature. Soldiers don't think, they react.

"Combat is so violent that you can't describe it. You can only talk around the periphery. They've got to go through the black hole and experience it themselves," Laws said. "The fear of the unknown is the biggest factor. Before the fight, you're going to be afraid. During the fight, you get angry. Then after, you're so afraid your knees are knocking so bad you can't hear anybody talking to you. That's all right if the soldiers understand that."

The brigade's top enlisted man, Command Sergeant Major Rufus Taylor, 47, of Birmingham, Alabama, was an artilleryman in Vietnam. He was confident the new generation of soldiers would handle the mental part of the job.

"My first combat experience was about survival. No other thought, just survival," Taylor said. "But somebody out there was depending on us to put some steel on the target. So we just got up and fired those rounds as quickly as we possibly could."

As evening approached, my education about the extremes of the desert grew exponentially when the sun disappeared and the temperature sank like a stone. The earliest days of the deployment posed challenges such as searing heat and the plague of sand fleas, flies, scorpions and vipers. Now it was teeth-chattering cold, and it wouldn't have been so bad if I had my original all-weather sleeping bag. The one I got for Christmas failed to provide sufficient warmth. Even though I slept in all my clothes, including a Gortex ski jacket, I could never get comfortable. The night became an endurance test. It was so chilly, I kept waking up every 20 minutes or so. I know, it wasn't exactly the Chosin Reservoir in Korea when temperatures plummeted to an inhumane 30 degrees below zero, but if you're used to 100-degree temperatures and then the mercury drops to 34, believe me, it's cold.

Soldiers on guard duty that night were wrapped up like mummies as they tried to ward off the cold. Specialist Hector Macias, 25, of El Paso, Texas, looked like something out of a sci-fi flick patrolling the perimeter. He wore his long johns, his battle dress uniform and a night parka with insulated liner, held snugly in place by his body armor. He wrapped a T-shirt around his ears and wore arctic mittens with a notch for the trigger finger. Even so, a frigid wind cut like a knife through the layers of clothing.

"You can feel it down to the bone," Macias said.

Warming tents with kerosene heaters were set up. Those coming off guard duty were fed hot soup and hot coffee. I made a mental note to start gathering up cold weather gear.

One of our Saudi hosts had proposed taking a media group by cab to Bahrain for a wet New Year's Eve party, but the plan never materialized. Instead, an improvised gathering was held in the AP suite. Any journalist who had remained in the kingdom for the holidays was invited, and a core group of about a dozen journalists had formed a collegial work environment over the past months. Nothing stronger than Saudi champagne was served, but we had some room service food to snack on. The Christmas tree provided cheer. Larry Jolidan of *USA Today* brought a surprise guest. The comedians at his paper had mailed him a blow-up doll. He named her Desiree Shields, and the plastic doll occupied a place on the sofa.

A footnote: My doll was more than plastic. After the party, Sophia came over to my room. The pleasures of soft, inviting female flesh presented themselves at our own private get-together. I would have rather been here than in Times Square watching the ball fall. I couldn't imagine a better way to ring in the new year. A man can fall in love with lots of thing. I had been in love with writing when, at the age of 17, I was making the minimum wage of a buck-forty an hour on my first newspaper job, and an editor thought enough of what I had written that he put my byline on it. This assignment ranks as the greatest love of all. As the calendar page turned to a new year, war clouds thickened.

CHAPTER 19
Countdown

Wednesday, January 2, 1991. The penetrating wail of an air raid siren set in motion a prescribed sequence of emergency procedures. Dhahran's airport, and hotel, were within range of Iraqi Scud missiles and air attacks, and Saudi Civil Defense officials in the Eastern Province had developed defensive plans. On the floor of the hotel corridors, arrows made of white tape pointed the way to a stairwell that led to a bomb shelter in the basement. With the rising and falling tones of the siren blaring, I fell in with everyone else and headed for the shelter. In some small way, this must have been how Londoners felt while living under the German threat in the time before D-Day. The alarm was just a drill, but it was an unmistakable sign that war was approaching. Taking shelter brought a heightened sense of awareness. It did not go unnoticed that just about every other journalist in the bunker had a gas mask. The ones for the AP staff had yet to arrive.

The road to war led to Riyadh. The military planned to do a test run on conducting briefings for the media from a hotel ballroom, and the Air Force scheduled a side trip to publicize the existence of a new base from which it would launch missions. The two-day trip meant taking a commercial flight to the capital on Saudia Airlines, which was an adventure in and of itself. Before takeoff, a mandatory prayer was said over the intercom to Mohammed, The Traveler and The Prophet, peace be upon him. Women in the media who were part of the trip had to acquire letters of transit from the Ministry of Information. The letter basically said that even though they were traveling alone, they were on official business and were not whores.

Riyadh had the look of a city living under the sword of Damocles. Security checkpoints were everywhere on the roads leading from the airport. The hotel we were taken to had been taken over by military brass. All the officers were wearing the new desert boots designed by Norman Schwarzkopf, but troops in the field were still wearing jungle boots.

Briefings were planned in a spacious main ballroom. Chairs were lined up in neat rows to seat reporters who would be asking questions. Officers would speak from a podium located on a stage, and it goes without saying that stages are for actors. After all, this was the Kuwaiti Theater of Operations. No real news came out of the trial run. I did my part and asked a softball question about the differences in range between American and Iraqi artillery. A long-winded, non-answer followed that wasn't worth writing down. I swear, I would rather drag my balls over ten miles of broken glass than cover briefings from a hotel ballroom. Reporters who covered Vietnam said the set-up reminded them of the Five O'Clock Follies, where briefers at a Saigon hotel would say how well the war was going while the U.S. sunk deeper into a quagmire.

The next morning, an Air Force bus took us on a 60-mile ride to a town called Al-Kharj, the name of which had been Americanized to Al's Garage. Although we were forbidden to disclose the exact location for security reasons, a sprawling air base now operated in the middle of nowhere. The infrastructure was already in place. The Saudis had built a 15,000 foot runway and parking aprons in the middle of the desert in 1989, figuring it would make a top-notch military base if it were ever needed. The base was scheduled for completion in 1994, but Iraq's invasion accelerated the timetable. Although no permanent buildings had been completed, the Air Force erected a city of tents — air conditioned, no less — to accommodate pilots and crews.

Al's Garage had 4,000 inhabitants. Its 600 tents included four kitchens, an air transportable hospital and living quarters. The base had its own water supply, power generators, sewage disposal system, garbage collection, a police department, shops, laundry, barber shop, post office, a chapel with a stained-glass window, a movie theater, a library and a club that featured two live bands but no alcohol. The air base covered 200 square miles, about the size of the Dallas-Fort Worth International Airport in Texas.

Four fighter squadrons of the 4th Tactical Fighter Wing were housed in hangars administered by the 4th Civil Engineer Squadron from Seymour Johnson Air Force Base in Goldsboro, North Carolina. Wing commander Colonel Hal Hornburg said his F-15 Strike Eagles and F-16 Falcons were capable of striking Baghdad without having to refuel in the air. His warplanes could deliver one million pounds of bombs a day.

"The main advantage to being here is proximity to targets. We can go to our target areas and back on our own internal fuel," Hornburg said, speaking on the record.

He also predicted, that if it came to a shooting match, American pilots would gain air superiority quickly.

"I'm not saying it's going to be easy, but I think the skies are going to be clear in just a matter of days. I think it's going to be a few days before the surface-to-air-missile batteries are taken care of also. We're going to be able to take down Iraqi defenses if not in short order, at least in due course," Hornburg said.

The mission would be to hit airfields, missile sites, air defenses, communications points, railroads, bridges, Iraqi tanks and troop formations in the desert.

How many planes might be lost in the effort?

"I don't plan to lose any. I'd be very disappointed if I do," Hornburg said.

He stressed, however, that air power alone would not defeat Iraq.

"The business of winning a war has to do with capturing territory. That's what the Army and Marines are for. If we can keep bombs off them, if we can kill tanks, then we've done our job. Air doctrine is to provide an umbrella under which there's tactical and strategic advantage for ground forces," Hornburg said.

One of his pilots was Colonel David Eberly, deputy commander of operations for the 4th Tactical Fighter Wing. In his flight suit, he seemed to strut standing still. A native of Brazil, Indiana, Eberly got into the Air Force through the ROTC program in 1969. With a hint of regret in his voice, he said he had just missed Vietnam. Now his time had come.

"We have gone from absolutely nothing out here but powdery sand to the largest tactical wing in the modern Air Force," Eberly said. His crew chief was a staff sergeant, who matter-of-factly noted that he owned the Strike Eagle but let Eberly fly it.

Al's Garage was also home to the 169th Tactical Fighter Group of the

South Carolina Air National Guard, known as the Swamp Foxes. The reservists arrived just before New Year's in their F-16 Falcons, and 12 of the 40 pilots flew commercial jets in civilian life. One of them, Captain Dave Seawell, was recently cruising above the U.S. East Coast in a McDonnell Douglas MD-80 jetliner, the twin-engine, medium range, single-aisle update of the DC-9. One week later, he was zooming over the tortured landscape in a Fighting Falcon.

"A pilot's job is to make a passenger jet like a family bus so they don't feel the landing or the takeoff. Here, our job is to find, fight and destroy the enemy. There's a tremendous mental adjustment," Seawell said.

Among the reservists in the Swamp Foxes were real estate agents, dairy farmers and bankers. Whatever they did in civilian life, they could drive jets. In 1989, the Swamp Foxes won the Air Force's Gun Smoke competition, beating 15 teams from around the world in a six-day contest flown over the southern Nevada desert. The competition tested a pilot's skills in strafing, bombing and navigation. No other Guard unit had ever won the award. The top gun award went to Major George Robert "Jet" Jernigen.

"I think the U.S. Air Force is the finest in the world, and we beat them. We can stand toe to toe with anyone," the 37-year-old Jernigen said.

He was asked what makes a good fighter pilot.

"Most of them aren't all that thrilled by winning. They expect to win. But they hate to lose at anything," Jernigen said. "The kind of guy you want in a fighter jet is not someone who has self-doubts or is satisfied to be second best. They're hard to live with sometimes because they know the best way to do everything. It's like having a bunch of thoroughbreds. You got to ride herd on them a little bit, but when you got them pointed in the right direction, they're a pretty awesome force."

On the parking aprons, gunmetal gray fighters looked like birds of prey. Their cockpits were a maze of screens, scopes and controls. In a preview of air combat, Lieutenant Colonel Bob Gray of Asheville, South Carolina, said that traditional dogfights are now called "swirling fur balls" because they are contested at dizzying speeds.

"Your engagement lasts maybe 30 seconds at the most. Either you win or lose in that length of time. Things happen in a hurry," Gray said.

Lieutenant Colonel John Marshall, commander of the Swamp Foxes, said time slows down when somebody is shooting back.

"The world sort of stands still. The closer the bullets come, the longer they seem to be there," Marshall said.

The day at Al's Garage made for a good story. New York called to verify that Hornburg was speaking on the record. Editors were worried he might get fired for being so candid. Back in September, four-star General Michael Dugan, the Air Force chief of staff, was fired by Dick Cheney for saying that Saddam was "the focus of our efforts." Dugan had violated military rules by publicly discussing military targets.

―――――――――

January 4. Military gear was issued to those in the media pool. The first order of business was to get a Department of Defense identity card, which meant being photographed and fingerprinted. The card identified the bearer as a civilian accompanying the military as a non-combatant who should be accorded privileges stipulated under the Geneva Conventions if captured. It was written in English. Would an Iraqi captor understand English?

Next came a dog tag. Stamped on the metal plate was the name, religious preference, blood type, date of birth and social security number of the bearer. It would be useful for medical treatment, getting Last Rites or assisting those working in the morgue.

Getting military equipment means standing in line, just like it did in basic training. Various stations handed out a Kevlar combat helmet, goggles, body armor, a night desert parka with insulated liner, a regulation sleeping bag, a backpack that came in a forest camouflage pattern, web gear and a utility belt, a canteen, a personal first aid kit complete with bandage, a sealed bag containing overgarments lined with activated charcoal as protection in case of a chemical attack, and a gas mask (finally!) complete with a dose of atropine and a blister pack of 21 white pills. Atropine is an antidote to a chemical attack. Its name is derived from Atropos, one of the three Fates in Greek mythology who chose how a person was going to die. The stuff is made from nightshade (belladonna), jimsonweed and mandrake. Designed to block the effects of chemical weapons, it comes in a container that looks like a Magic Marker. If you get hit, you're supposed to take off the cap and jab a spring-loaded syringe into the large muscles of the thigh. Although nobody could say exactly what was in the white pills in the blister pack, they were pyridostigmine bromide, or PB, which was supposed to keep the neurons of the brain firing in the event of a nerve gas attack. PB had a cumulative effect. The more pills you took, the more neurons would fire. PB had been used since 1955 to treat patients with a medical condition known as myasthenia gravis, but it had never been tried in combat. Side effects included nausea, abdominal cramps, urinary urgency, headaches and erectile dysfunction. No wonder they didn't tell us.

We were on our own for other clothing. Someone asked Sergeant Steve Smith of the Marine Corps public affairs office what would be appropriate, and the good sergeant replied, "Ask yourself. What color is sand?"

In my personal inventory were notebooks, pencils, pens, binoculars, a watch cap for warmth, long underwear, a green towel, a flashlight and short-wave radio with extra batteries for picking up BBC news broadcasts. I had also purchased a portable manual typewriter, which I called my Combat Olivetti. A manual typewriter was more practical than a portable computer. Batteries would be dead within hours, and there would be no outlets for recharging. Besides, you'd need a phone line to transmit unless you had a satellite phone, and they were in short supply. Also included was a supply of typing paper. The photographers also equipped me with a small Nikon camera with some rolls of film. That way, if I was near a big event, I could snap pictures. All film, however, was subject to government control.

Without giving any specifics, the Saudis arranged a media trip up north to Hafr al-Batin. At an airfield somewhere in the desert, cohorts representing the nations who had joined the coalition stood in formation. About 1,000 American troops from the Army Support Command were present, including the band and color guard of the 1st Cavalry Division. Also on hand were combat engineers, a hospital company, quartermasters, a signal battalion and the 766th Transportation Company of the Indiana National Guard.

Then came the arrival of King Fahd and General Norman Schwarzkopf, the two most powerful men in the kingdom. The Saudi monarch wore a gilt-edged headdress. The commander-in-chief of the combat forces wore his battle dress chocolate chip fatigues and the new desert boots. Together, they rode in the back of an open Jeep to review the troops. The ceremonial gathering was the final inspection of troops as the countdown to war clicked down.

Schwarzkopf mingled with U.S. soldiers, shaking hands and telling jokes and mugging for pictures. It was like seeing Eisenhower inspecting paratroopers just before they jumped into Normandy on D-Day. Known as The Bear, Schwarzkopf had dual personality. He told an earlier interviewer that he was a teddy bear with his troops but a grizzly bear when it came to the enemy.

Pausing to take a few questions, Schwarzkopf told the assembled media the purpose of this ceremony was to show world solidarity against Saddam Hussein.

"It's a demonstration that we're all in this together," Schwarzkopf said. He also insisted the force under his command would be ready to go on the January 15 deadline.

King Fahd inspected the international forces. Then he moved to an enormous tent set up for the dignitaries, who sat in giant overstuffed chairs atop rugs placed over the sand. The king talked for two hours, telling a Bedouin story about how one brother was punished for stealing from a fellow Bedouin.

He also answered questions from the media, a rarity for a monarch. War, he said, could only be avoided by an Iraqi withdrawal.

"I hope that Saddam Hussein would take this important step and withdraw from Kuwait and spare everybody the bloodshed and the catastrophe of war," the king said through an interpreter.

The ceremonies done, we were driven to a place called King Khalid Military City, or KKMC. Informally known as Emerald City because of its modern buildings and flowing fountains, it could have passed for an otherworldly setting in *Star Wars*. KKMC, located about 37 miles south of Hafr al-Batin, was built by the U.S. Army Corps of Engineers and completed in 1987. It had 21 water wells, five mosques, 3,400 houses, an airport and a military academy. The place was now crawling with U.S. troops.

In a January 6 speech from Baghdad marking the 70th anniversary of the founding of the modern Iraqi Army, Saddam Hussein said the coming war would be "the mother of battles." Iraq's state-run broadcasts would now be airing over Mother of Battles Radio. In no time, the phrase would become the mother of all clichés.

Eight days before the deadline, the media pool was activated for a trial run. I was assigned to the Marines, and being with the grunts was fine by me. My first assignment to the field had been with the Marines, and I had been along on several of their training exercises and got used to working with them. One of the best public affairs officers I got to know was Captain Bill Taylor, a New Jersey native. He jokingly explained that U.S.M.C. stands for "U Signed the Mother-fucking Contract."

With everything needed for war packed in the back of a Humvee, we drove north toward Jubail and then left the highway to travel across the open desert. The staff sergeant in charge got lost. Even the Bedouins get lost. After stopping to check his map, we reached the headquarters of one of the two main assault forces the Marines had assembled for the attack into Kuwait. The force was called Task Force Ripper, comprised of three infantry battalions of the 7th Marine Regiment, 1st Marine Expeditionary Force. A self-contained fighting force, the Marines had their own tanks, combat engineers, anti-tank missile batteries, a motor pool of amphibious assault vehicles and light armored vehicles, artillery units and an air umbrella provided by Cobra helicopter gunships and Harrier jump jets, all of it there to support the infantry.

A welcome was provided by Lieutenant Colonel John Hines of Dayton, Ohio, executive officer of 7th Marines and a veteran of Vietnam and Beirut. He said the Marines had never been this close to Kuwait before.

"You're the chosen ones," Hines said.

How so?

"Marines are an elite group of fighters, and not many outside observers have accompanied them in war," he answered.

So you don't mind having media along?

"I don't view the media as adversaries. We make the news, you write it. The American public is entitled to see exactly what is taking place," Hines said. "We want you to become part of our family. When push comes to shove, these Marines will put their lives on the line for you all."

What's your state of readiness?

"We have not holed up and died in the desert. We have thrived," Hines said. "Morale is phenomenal. You wouldn't expect a Marine to say anything less. This is no longer a conflict of world powers and Saddam Hussein. This has become a personal thing. You coop up any Marines, deprive them of their freedom, liberty, families and special occasions, how could it not become something personal? When we come to get him, he's got to understand that."

How will this new generation of Marines react when the bullets start flying?

"Every Marine who's ever gone into combat has asked that question, from the commandant of the Marine Corps on down," Hines said. "You just assure them they'll do fine if they rely on their training, their equipment and their fellow Marines. You just overcome it. You get through it."

There was a marked difference between how troops in the field and those at headquarters accepted the media.

"Having people on the ground to get a first-hand look of what it was like, and to report it accurately, is important," said Captain Brett Shoemaker of Hollis City, Maine, commander of an infantry company. "If the American public doesn't think they're getting their money's worth, they're not going to support it. We've got something to say, and we're not afraid to say it."

Having been granted access to those who would be doing the fighting, and without being told any specifics about the battle plan and the timetable for war, I pursued the idea of troops making mental preparations for combat. Anyone who stereotyped Marines as a bunch of mindless Jarheads would have been disappointed in the responses. I did get a chuckle out of an inside joke, though.

Q. Why does a Marine have an I.Q. a few points higher than a horse?
A. So he knows not to shit during parades.

"When the first round comes down range, who's to say how we'll react. It all depends on how hard these people fight," said Corporal Michael Roundtree, 28, of Chicago, Illinois, who was a machine gunner assigned to Task Force Ripper.

A 1985 graduate of University of Illinois with a degree in mathematics, he worked for Benefit Trust Life Insurance Company before enlisting. His older brother had served in Nam, and he wanted to prove he had the right stuff too. Going into combat wasn't exactly at the top of the list of things he'd like to be doing at the moment, but Roundtree had rationalized it.

"We're up to the job. If we don't deal with this now, I wonder if one of my nephews or my son will have to do it. I'm not going to shit you. We'd all rather be home, but morale is good. Nobody was forced to come here. If our air holds up, his troops will be out there for the plucking. Ain't no turning back now," Roundtree said.

Processing fear was part of the contract, according to Captain Brent Smith, 33, commander of a company of Marine infantrymen based in Camp Pendleton, California.

"You're supposed to be scared to death. That's the way it works," he said. "But I know this. If you call upon a Marine to do something, it'll get done."

Going into battle is what a Marine is trained to do from the first moment in the Corps, according to Chief Warrant Officer Charles Rowe, a 1981 graduate of Bates College and a public affairs officer with the Marines.

"When the time comes, they'll get up on their own. They won't need some fiery speech from us. They'll know what to do," Rowe said. "Fighting the Iraqis is what stands between us and going home. God help them."

A forward patrol moved out before dark, the pennant of a Jolly Roger flying from the last vehicle in the column. From the back of our Humvee at camp, I pecked out a story on the portable Olivetti. The pages were handed to the Marine public affairs officers, who checked them for operational security before they were placed in a pouch and sent back to the JIB in Dhahran.

The Marines in Ripper had taken over a camp formerly occupied by Saudi forces, whose discipline in the field left a lot to be desired. The Saudis left behind a bunch of garbage pits. We stayed overnight, and my new government-issued sleeping bag passed muster. In the middle of the night, however, I got up for a call of nature and made my way to the latrine. Some distance behind our tent, plastic tubes had been driven into the sand for use as a urinal. It was so dark, I couldn't see my hand in front of my face and got lost on my way back. A sentry led me back to my cot.

We drove back the next day. On the trial run, at least, my story made it back before we did. I'd go to war with the Marines any day.

Fuck. I'm so angry I can hardly write. Just when everything was set, I got bumped from my slot with the Marines because some asshole from the Reuters News Agency pointed out something in the fine print of the media guidelines. Regulations said that members of a pool were supposed to be rotated when they returned from the field so that other reporters could go out on the next one. I argued that this was only a trial run. Reporters were supposed to bond with units in the field, and I had already made my contacts. Rotating me off the wire service slot made no sense. No luck. This objection only involved the wire service slot. Reuters didn't even get the slot. It went to a UPI reporter. But I was taken off the Marine pool.

Then I pulled rank to make the best of this bullshit. As the senior wire service representative in Saudi Arabia, I placed an AP staffer on the Air Force pool and another with the Navy aboard the aircraft carrier *USS John F. Kennedy*, figuring that the war would start with air attacks. I also secured slots for other AP staffers with other military units. My own fate was undetermined. Whatever unit I would be assigned to was up to Valkyries, the figures in Norse mythology who decide who lives and who dies in battle. You don't get to pick and choose in war.

The last story I filed before heading out to the field was about a piece of equipment in the arsenal that was as important as any conventional weapon in

Desert Shield. The successor to the Jeep, it was an ungainly, box-like contraption with a jaw-breaking name: the high utility, multipurpose, wheeled vehicle, officially known as the M-998 cargo/troop carrier, but popularly known as the Humvee.

Faster, stronger, safer and more versatile than the Jeep, the Humvee is a cross between a fat car and a squat truck. Having entered the service in 1985, the four-wheel drive vehicle came with independent suspension and power steering. It had a low profile on top and 16 inches of clearance underneath. A Humvee could climb a 60-degree grade and was almost impossible to overturn or get stuck. During trials, it ran in ice, mud and snow. Now it's leaving tire tracks in the sand. It came in five basic models — cargo or troop carrier, anti-tank missile or machine gun carrier, ambulance, shelter carrier and light artillery prime mover. The models could be configured 15 different ways.

If a tire went flat, the Humvee could keep rolling because it had magnesium doughnuts inside the rubber. During Operation Just Cause in Panama, one 82nd Airborne commander noted how valuable it was in saving lives during an ambush: "All four tires were shot out, (but) able to drive another two-plus miles to safety. Awesome vehicle. Saved the six soldiers riding in it."

Built by the AM General Division of LTV Missiles and Electronics Group, Humvees had been shipped to 18 countries, including Luxembourg, Djibouti, Abu Dhabi, Thailand and Saudi Arabia. China had five for hauling oil exploration equipment. One was even in Baghdad. The Middle East salesman for AM General was in Iraq with a demo model on August 2. He escaped to Jordan but had to leave the vehicle behind.

Although it only went nine miles on a gallon of gas, the Humvee drew raves from Army Captain Mike Wilber, 37, of Fort Carson, Colorado. "Looks be damned. How its looks is part of its attractiveness. It's the right vehicle in the right place at the right time," he said.

About 20,000 Humvees were sent to Saudi Arabia. Only a dozen of them broke down. It was perfect for the open spaces of the desert. It was never designed for urban warfare, but only a military novice would get bogged down in urban warfare. The vehicle was made commercially after the war and was a favorite of actor Arnold Schwarzenegger.

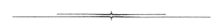

January 12. Congress authorized the use of force to evict Iraq from Kuwait. The House vote was 250-183. In the Senate, it was 52-47. Military action had been approved for the first time since the Gulf of Tonkin Resolution in 1964 authorized the war in Vietnam.

January 14. The day before the deadline, word came that the pools were being activated again. I left instructions for the AP staffers who would be coming into the war zone about who would be on what pools and where to find the keys to the rental car. Along with making my last calls home, I packed and re-packed all my gear, ate a last supper at the best restaurant in Khobar and finished off the remaining vodka with Sophia in my room. Not knowing when she would see me again, she gave me a royal sendoff. We spent the last evening as if it would be the last thing we did on Earth. As a way of staying connected, she told me to find Polaris in the night sky when I went into the field, and that she would look at the same star.

The sand has run out of the hourglass.

CHAPTER 20
We're At War

Tuesday, January 15. The day of days had arrived. It seemed like a lifetime ago that I had landed in the kingdom, each passing day building to this moment. With the world spinning out of control, the only thing to do was put one foot in front of the other and get on with it. My orders were to take the back stairs from the hotel and board a bus that would take me to wherever. Colonel Bill Mulvey, the commanding officer of the Joint Information Bureau, bid farewell and did a quick equipment check.

"I seen a thousand packs of soldiers heading off into the field, and yours is as tight as any of them," he grinned. "Godspeed."

About three dozen other journalists climbed aboard the bus with their equipment. Few words were spoken, but the eyes said a lot. We hadn't driven very far at all before we reached Desert Dragon, the processing station off the Dhahran airbase where the first ground troops received their marching orders five months earlier. My name was called. I was on Army Combat Pool No. 1, assigned to the 82nd Airborne.

Holy shit. They're the guys who got here first. Will they be jumping? Will I be jumping with them? This is fucking great, I told myself. Under the supervision of Major Baxter Ennis, the division public affairs officer, we drove to the Champion Main headquarters at King Fahd International Airport. Epcot was on a heightened war footing. Extra concrete barricades and sandbag walls had been erected at the entrance. A coil of razor wire blocked all traffic while sentries, with their war faces on, checked the vehicles. After stowing my gear, we headed off to the field in a maroon Mitsubishi Pajero, which had been donated by the Japanese as part of their contributions to the war effort.

The driver was Captain Clint Esarey, the son of an FBI agent and an Airborne Ranger who had been in the Army for nearly 17 years. A native of Indianapolis, Indiana, he would assist Major Ennis in shepherding Combat Pool No. 1. Without prompting, he broke the silence.

"In our minds, the war has started," Esarey said.

With permission, I pulled out my notebook and started writing.

"The awareness of soldiers is definitely heightened. Today is the day. Training's over with. This is the real thing. It comes down to survival. I dictated a living will on a cassette tape I sent back home to my wife. If I don't make it back, I want to be buried in my military uniform. I'm a soldier. It's my life. The uniform is part of me," the captain continued.

What mental preparations had he made?

"There's always a concern about how you're going to react in combat. Those fears get locked away. It comes down to survival. It's abnormal to kill another human being, but it's not normal to jump from an airplane either. You react. It becomes instinctive," Esarey said. "You're fighting for the man next to you. You don't want to do anything that gets your buddy killed."

Airborne infantry had gone through their own checklists. Weapons had been cleaned, oiled and triple-checked to make sure they were in good working order. Expiration dates had been checked on things like filters in the gas mask. And in an unseen but timeless ritual, soldiers had boxed up everything they didn't need for combat and sent it home. Their packs were down to government issue. Anything else would be extra weight they'd have to carry.

"You make your load as light as you can. Anything you don't absolutely have to have to live or fight with, you get rid of because you want to make your rucksack as light as you can get it. Most likely, you'll have to carry it on your back. I sent three packages back right after Christmas," Esarey said.

What's the mood?

"Somber would be a good word for it," he said. "Soldiers are mulling this stuff around in their minds."

After an hour's drive, we arrived at a camp near the camel market town Hofuf that housed an aviation battalion of Apache attack helicopters and their crews. The scent of kerosene was thick in the air. It had been sprayed over the sand to keep down the dust, which could adversely affect the sensitive instruments of a flying machine that looked like a giant angry hornet.

On the headquarters tent were two hand-made signs. One said: "Lost Dog. Three legs. Blind in left eye. Missing right ear. Tail broken. Recently castrated. Answers to the name of Lucky." The other said: "Wanted. Woman to cook and clean fish, dig worms and make home. Must have good boat and motor. Please enclose recent photo of boat and motor." I love Army humor.

From behind the dust-covered canvas stepped the battalion's executive officer, Major Lee Stuart, 43, of Jonesboro, Georgia. Part of the Army since 1967, he served in 173rd Airborne Brigade (The Sky Soldiers) in Vietnam, worked special ops for five years and was with the Apache battalion in Panama. His body language indicated that he considered journalists to be as useless as tits on a bull. The media had painted an unfair picture of how soldiers served in Vietnam, he believed, and those who fought and died there suffered because of it. One of his favorite quotes was: "Do not fear the enemy, for your enemy can only take your life. It is far better to fear the media, for they will steal your honor." Nevertheless, he answered questions when asked about Apache crews.

"They are the finest aviators you will find. They are part of the infantry. They live in the dirt like grunts," Stuart said.

What were his thoughts today?

"Either Saddam Hussein leaves or we go in. The sooner, the better. The sooner I get to go home. He's made me waste five months of my life in the desert. It's come down to the two big kids on the block," the major said.

Then, just to be clear, he added something.

"I want peace more than anybody. GIs are the last ones who want to go to war. They're the ones who have to shed their blood. We don't want to kill anybody, but I want it settled and settled now. I don't want my young one to have to come back years from now and do it," he said.

Parked along a nearby apron were Apache helicopters capable of fighting in day or night. The machines had a tandem cockpit for the pilot and gunner. In the nose was a 30-millimeter chain gun connected to the gunner's helmet-mounted display. When he turned his head, the gun turned with him. He could shoot whatever he was looking at. Side pods were armed with 16 Hellfire missiles, the most aptly named weapon I had ever come across. Each missile, laser-guided for pinpoint accuracy, could kill an enemy tank. Rocket pods for taking out bunkers and buildings were also part of the helicopter's arsenal.

Working on one of the Apaches was Specialist James Cox, 21, of Houston, Texas, whose deployment to the kingdom meant five months away from his wife and son. As a supply technician, he knew every part on the sophisticated machine. With a piece of chalk, he wrote messages on the Hellfire missiles.

This is for the unwanted vacation. Hey Saddam, Kiss My Ass. Up Yours, Saddam. I Am Gonna Get You, Sucker. Any Last Requests? The Last Thing To Go Through An Iraqi's Mind Is A Hellfire.

Throughout history, warriors have sent messages to their foe. Soldiers from ancient Greece and Rome etched their unit numbers on the stones they slung at their enemies, just to let them know who was coming. It wasn't just a practice of enlisted men, either. During their inspection tour, Dick Cheney and Colin Powell wrote messages in chalk on bombs being readied for the opening wave.

"We know he'll never be able to read these messages. No matter," said Cox. "It's like a personal vendetta. It's a state of mind. I gave him my two bits worth. He's going to know I was here, no matter what."

Cox had shipped home his souvenir Arab headdress but hung on to pictures of his wife and kids to carry with him.

"He's taken five months away from us. He took a lot of guys away from their wives and girlfriends," Cox added. "I'm at war right now. I'm here to do my job, no matter what. If I have to give my life for my country, that's what I signed that piece of paper to do."

Nearby, Chief Warrant Officer Timothy D. Bricker, 26, of Downingtown, Pennsylvania, explained that Saddam personified the frustrations the paratroopers felt for having to endure the desolation of the desert, the boredom, the flies, the heat, the grit, the beerless nights and the time ripped away from wives, children and loved ones.

"I don't think there's a guy on the line who wouldn't want to put a missile on Saddam Hussein's house," said the pilot of an Apache named Bricker's Revenge. "Nobody wants to die. Nobody wants to see their buddies die, but we're all ready to get it done. We've been here so long. We know some of us aren't going to make it. We've come to terms with that."

Also on the flight line was Ron Moring, 32, wearing his pilot's flight suit and his infantryman's combat boots. A chief warrant officer, Moring had spent four of his 12 years in the Army flying Apaches. He had already shipped home his hand-held computer game and his beach shorts, but he kept a slice of the real world in his pocket — photographs of his wife and two children. His flying machine was called the Virginia Regulator.

"We're a bunch of racehorses that smell the barn right now," Moring said. "There's a lot more excitement in the air today. We're a lot more serious about what we're doing. It's time to quit the pre-game show."

Chief Warrant Officer Cleveland Simmons, 35, of Lawtey, Florida, flew Apache missions in Panama the year before and spent his second straight Christmas away from home and away from his wife and three kids.

"I'm not anxious to kill anybody, but we've got a job to do," Simmons said.

The trip concluded, we drove back to division headquarters. I typed out a story that was approved by the censors, then slept in my bag on cot inside a hangar that housed a couple of hundred paratroopers.

Morning came, the U.N. deadline for Iraq to leave Kuwait had passed, and still nothing. A company of paratroopers arose for their morning run, singing cadence along the way. Then they played a game of touch football outside the hangar. A nearby mess tent served a breakfast of hot coffee, breakfast rolls and corn flakes.

Specialist Jeffrey Helm, 21, of Chicago, Illinois, looked skyward. "I hoped there would be B-52s on the way to their air space. I've been here too long. The quickest way home is through Baghdad," he said.

Specialist 4 Ed Dingus, 21, of Nicklesville, Virginia, said he would be cheering the planes on. "I don't want to sound bloodthirsty or anything, but let's get it done. All hopes for peace are about gone. Now that they've decided on war, let's not sit here for another five months," he said.

A training day was scheduled for Bravo Company of the 3rd Battalion of the First Brigade, historically known as the 504th Parachute Infantry Regiment. In World War II, during combat around the Anzio beachhead in Italy, the regiment had acquired the nickname "Devils in Baggy Pants." It came from a German officer who had written in his journal: "American parachutists...devils in baggy pants...They pop up from nowhere and we never know when or how they will strike next. Seems like the black-hearted devils are everywhere."

Troops boarded trucks at 8 o'clock in the morning for a drive to a place called Michelin City, a practice range that included a two-story structure built from old tires. The structure was based on the design of a typical Iraqi home, complete with a courtyard. During the drill, nine-man squads would enter and clear one room at a time, tossing grenades around a corner to eliminate potential enemies who may be lying in wait. The exercise was called Military Operations in Urban Terrain, or MOUT, and if paratroopers train the way they fight, they were preparing for action in a city. One squad invited me to run through the drill with them. When the grenade was tossed, we all hugged the wall until it exploded. The soldiers then rushed in and shot at targets made of sand bags and balloons.

During an MRE lunch, Sergeant Michael Gensler, 26, of Fayetteville, North Carolina, said a betting pool had been started on when the war would start. Gensler picked January 17.

"I've been counting down the hours," Gensler said. "There's telltale signs that something is going to happen. Some guys have gotten real quiet, but you can see it in their eyes."

Staff Sergeant Jeffrey Wheeler, 28, of Lansing, Michigan, noted: "The light at the end of the tunnel is Baghdad."

It was the second time today the Iraqi capital was mentioned. Are these guys going to Baghdad? The answer was, "Where else would be going, numb nuts?"

Lieutenant Colonel Paul Trotti, 39, of Atlanta, George, said about 60 percent of his men were veterans of the Panama invasion and were trained to a fine edge. "Paratroopers are ready to see this whole thing come to a head," said Trotti, a 1973 graduate of West Point.

Back at Champion Main, we again settled in for the evening. On a TV set attached to a VCR, paratroopers watched the movie *Predator*, which starred two future governors, Jesse Ventura of Minnesota and Arnold Schwarzenegger of California. Troops snickered at Ventura's line: "I ain't got time to bleed." And they laughed at the combat scenes because the actors never had to re-load while they fired machine guns from the hip, Rambo-style.

In other parts of the hangar, troops got hair cuts, wrote letters, read paperbacks or pumped weights. Sergeant Dan Eller of Headquarters and Headquarters Company provided a crash course on living in the field, sharing some infantryman's secrets that would make my life better in the weeks to come.

For example, the waterproof wrap for my sleeping bag could be turned into a field expedient for washing laundry. Fill the bag with water, add detergent and dirty clothes, then tie it tight and shake vigorously.

Among other helpful tips, he showed how to store a spare set of clothes by rolling them up in a sleeping bag. It's called a tanker's roll. For calls of nature in the field, Eller said, dig a hole and place the cardboard sleeve of an MRE box sleeve over it. Then you can squat over it like a crapper and bury the excrement in the sand. Eller also squared away my web gear, putting black tape on the metal fasteners so they wouldn't shine or make noise. He donated a length of rope that could be used as a clothes line or for tying things down.

Just as I was ready to hit the sack at 10 o'clock, Major Ennis said to take a little white pill from the blister pack, the ones that were a defense against a nerve gas attack.

Oh, shit. What for? What's going down? I asked.

"It's a general upgrade. A precaution. The deadline has passed. He might launch a pre-emptive strike," Ennis said. "If we play it right, we'll all survive."

Comforting news, that. All of the military personnel in the Gulf were under orders to take the pills. The major also said, that from now on, to wear the Kevlar helmet and carry the gas mask everywhere, even the latrine.

The menacing roar of jet engines interrupted my sleep. This growl was made by packs of warplanes heading north. This was it. Air strikes had begun.

The major said to turn on the short-wave radio. With several paratroopers gathering around to hear the official word, we learned that Desert Shield was over. As of January 17, troops had become the thunder and lightning of Desert Storm. Hundreds of sorties had been launched. Baghdad was being pummeled.

From the back of the hangar, a major growled: "Turn that goddamn radio off. People are trying to sleep."

"Hey, we're at war, fucker," Major Ennis shouted back.

"We've been at war for five months," the voice said. "Now turn it off!"

With the volume lowered, a group of us continued to listen to the historic words of President Bush. In his speech, the commander-in-chief quoted Hollywood Huddelston, J.R. Kendall, Jackie Jones and Walt Boomer, people who I had quoted in my December story about the mission. Bush said the troops voiced the sentiments more eloquently than any president or prime minister ever could.

"Hey, he's reading from one of my stories," I said to no one in particular. People looked at me like I had a foot growing out of my forehead, but you can look it up. One of his speech writers had borrowed what I wrote for the president's speech.

"It's almost a relief the dam has finally burst after more than 160 days in country," Major Ennis said. "Americans want war the least of anybody in the world, but there's a glimmer of light at the end of the tunnel. Before, it was just a question mark, an open-ended calendar. We're not naive enough to think it's all going to be over quickly. If it comes to a ground war, it could be very costly. We hope and pray the air war will succeed."

The protocol called for taking a nerve gas pill every eight hours, and I popped a second one at 6 o'clock. For the first time in my life, I headed to an Army chow hall for breakfast during an actual war. As troopers lined up, I wondered why everybody wasn't boarding airplanes to join the attack against the Iraqi army. The answer was that this was only the opening strike, that it might be a while before the ground war started. That made sense. Let the fly boys do their job and soften up the enemy. At least the start of the war brought a sense of clarity.

"It's about time," said Sergeant Michael Senter, 24, of San Antonio, Texas. "After five months, there's a sense of relief. We're part of something that's going to be in the history books."

"It had to start to come to an end. Now we can see the end," said Private

First Class William Weaver, 20, of Cherry Hill, New Jersey.

Staff Sergeant Henry Rouse, 40, of Waynesboro, Georgia, said the war of nerves since August was like standing up to a bully, and the air war meant the physical fight had begun. "That was just the first punch. Now we dance," said Rouse. "The wait, wait, wait is over."

A medical doctor in the First Brigade, Major Larry Burns of Cabot, Arkansas, noted: "It was the biggest poker game in the world. Bush just called."

As I scribbled in my notebook, Specialist Janet Moore of Many, Louisiana, walked over. One of about a dozen women in the 118th Military Police Company, she didn't wait for a question. She had something to say.

"It's about time. We're been here for five months just sitting and waiting. You get frustrated," she said.

Then she added: "Those protesters back home can kiss my ass. We're here for a good reason. Americans shouldn't be fighting each other. We're here to fight Iraqis. I don't want to die, but we're here to get the job done."

One of the soldiers on duty in the chow hall wore a paper cap that said: "Baghdad or Bust." On a bulletin board, the training schedule for the day said: "Going Out Of Business." Training was over. All leaves had been canceled.

Colonel Keith Kellogg, the division chief of staff, said it was time to confront an aggressor, and he said it in an Airborne way.

"If you're going to piss on a tree, you had better be a pretty big dog," Kellogg said. "I'm proud of the quiet professionalism of our paratroopers. I'm proud to be an American. And Americans are really going to be proud of their army. This is how the big boys play."

Later, we came across several Kuwaiti volunteers who had been attached to the 313th Military Intelligence Unit as translators. In one of the few outward displays of emotion witnessed that day, they hugged and kissed each other as the bombing waves continued. One was Mohammed, a 24-year-old who didn't want to give his last name because his parents, a brother and two sisters were under Iraqi control in Kuwait City. He had been studying in Fresno, California, then volunteered for service with the U.S. Army. After a crash course in basic training and chemical warfare, he was given a uniform and a rifle.

"No matter how much is destroyed, we can rebuild. Kuwait is being destroyed on a daily basis anyhow. Looting, destruction, burning," Mohammed said. "That man chose war. Simple greed, simple evil. Finally, we get a chance to get back at these people. They thought they could get away with it. They all deserve what they get. I don't need a weapon. I can kill with my own hands."

From a room that served as the office of the public affairs officers, I wrote up a story, using the dateline of Army Combat Pool No. 1. The commanding general, Major General James H. Johnson Jr., stopped by to say welcome to the Airborne.

The pool report wasn't sent back in a pouch. We gathered up all our gear and drove back to deliver it first-hand to Dhahran. What a strange atmosphere. Military traffic was bumper to bumper on the highways. Horns were honking. It was impossible to tell if drivers were exchanging "V" for victory signs or peace signs with their fingers. Being at war was like entering a different dimension. The countryside looked the same, but some invisible force had crawled out of Pandora's box. Where would it take us? Fortune, surprise and the fog of war mean that no one is master of events.

The hotel was crawling with hundreds of new journalists. They had just landed after taking a flight from Washington, D.C., and they all demanded to get out to the field and into the war. The pools were filled, however, and they would be relegated to writing from reports or covering the briefings. I stopped by the office to make sure the story had gotten through, which it had, and read all the stories on the wire about the start of the war. The placing of AP reporters with the Air Force and Navy turned out to be an inside victory. Take that, Reuters. Details from Al's Garage and the carrier *USS John F. Kennedy* added much to the copy. No need to thank me. I did an interview with AP radio about taking the pills and troop reaction. The time I was investing with the Airborne would pay off later, or so I thought.

The gas masks the AP had promised still hadn't been delivered. The package with the protective gear arrived the next day. It was a personal comfort to have military issue strapped to my left thigh. I went to sleep the way I woke up, listening to the sounds of fighter jets taking off and landing from Dhahran.

CHAPTER 21
Instant Thunder

Day Two. I'm on the road to an unknown destination to do my part in the war, traveling West instead of North in a Humvee with my Airborne escorts, wearing a flak vest with my helmet and gas mask at the ready. Self-preservation is the order of the day. The lingering question is what really happened at H-Hour of D-Day, and a burning curiosity led me to find out later. Jet drivers from the Air Force, Navy, Marines and coalition partners performed their roles. The big surprise was the most powerful air armada in the history of warfare was led by Army pilots in Apache helicopters, and the first blow landed far from Baghdad.

The opening gambit was a choreographed, comprehensive, coordinated effort called Instant Thunder. The name contrasted sharply to the on-and-off, limited air campaign of Rolling Thunder in Vietnam. The challenge was to defeat Iraq's formidable air defenses that were linked together by computers, which were designed as a trip wire that would allow Baghdad to activate a network of surface-to-air missiles, thousands of anti-aircraft guns and multiple airfields with fighter jets waiting to be scrambled. The defensive ring, purchased at a cost of billions of dollars from France and the Soviet Union, was called KARI — the French word for Iraq spelled backwards. Early warning radars were linked to Interceptor Operations Centers, which in turn were plugged in to five Sector Operations Centers surrounding Iraq. Smashing down the door into Iraq began with taking out two early warning radars. The mission fell to the 101st Airborne, the unit that had parachuted into France as part of D-Day nearly a half century earlier.

Code-named Task Force Normandy, eight Apache helicopters under the command of Colonel Dick Cody had practiced the plan for months. In six secret live-fire exercises against mock targets, the gunships honed their skills at infiltrating Iraq air space to take out two sites simultaneously. Timing was of the essence. Both sites had to be destroyed at the same time if Baghdad was to be kept unaware of what was coming.

In the days leading up to the state of the war, Task Force Normandy moved into position in the open desert of western Saudi Arabia near a town called Ar Ar. By nightfall of January 14, the Apaches were outfitted with external fuel tanks to increase their range by an extra 400 miles. The extra tanks meant the number of rockets each carried was reduced, an acceptable tradeoff because it eliminated the need for a risky refueling. Only when the green light was given for the wee hours of January 17 did Cody tell his pilots and gunners what the mission was. The first maps and photos of the targets were shown. The actual route had never been flown before.

Liftoff for the two Apache teams was one o'clock in the morning, local time. Off they went into a moonless sky under strict radio silence and without running lights. Cody commanded the four attack helicopters in White Team, and four Apaches in Red Team followed. Guiding them were Pave Low helicopters of the Air Force's 20th Special Operations Squadron from Hurlburt Field in Florida. Pave Lows were chosen for their superior ability to reach and pinpoint targets using the Global Positioning System. The Apaches flew at 120 miles per hour, 50 feet above the ground, their engines baffled to keep noise behind them. Forward looking infrared sensors and night vision goggles allowed crews to see in the dark. When the task force crossed the Saudi border into Iraq, they took fire from the ground, with the tracers streaking into the inky darkness. Nothing was hit, but pilots and gunners were on heightened alert. People on the ground with guns were trying to kill them. Nine miles south of the two targeted radar sites, the Pave Lows dropped chemical lights on the desert floor to mark the route. As they peeled away, the Apaches came on line and locked on to their targets.

First to be hit would be the generator building of Iraq's first line of defense. Blow it up and the radars would lose power. At 10 seconds before launch, from a distance of four miles, 1st Lieutenant Tom Drew in the lead Apache broke radio silence. "Party in 10," he said. When the countdown ticked down to zero, laser-guided Hellfire missiles left their racks.

"This one's for you, Saddam," said Apache pilot Chief Warrant Officer 3 Dave Jones when his first Hellfire was launched.

The Hellfires hissed away and then exploded in a ball of flame when they found their targets. Some Apaches closed to within 800 yards, taking out back-up generators and satellite dishes. Also filling the air were rockets and 30-millimeter rounds from the Apaches' nose guns. Anti-aircraft guns on the ground were obliterated. In four minutes of mayhem, the first site was flaming rubble. A similar result was produced 20 miles away at the second radar site.

Their mission accomplished, the Apaches flew back to Saudi Arabia. Cody transmitted the code words — Alpha, Alpha, Alpha. It meant that all targets had been destroyed. There were no casualties. The attack was on. The gate was open.

The next target was the Interceptor Operations Center, which was tied in to the two early warning sites and linked to Iraq's defensive ring. The mission belonged to a new generation of stealth jets called the F-117, which the Saudi's called Shabah, or Ghost, and which in time would be called the Night Hawk. A stealth jet gave off such a small electronic signature that defenders had no clue about what was coming.

From an airbase in Khamis Mushayt, hidden high in the Saudi mountains between Yemen and the Red Sea, an order came to "Execute Wolfpack." Ten Night Hawks had the green light to take off at midnight

Major Gregory A. Feest and his wingman headed to western Iraq while the other eight black jets in the strike package flew toward Baghdad. Feest, whose F-117 had dropped the first bomb during Operation Just Cause in Panama, had flown the first Night Hawk to Saudi Arabia in August from a secret base at Tonopah, Nevada. As the success of the Apache strike was being confirmed, Feest was bearing down on his target. This particular Interceptor Operations Center was connected to four air bases and the central command in Baghdad. Its continued existence posed a threat to every plane headed north.

Operating without lights and under strict radio silence, Feest passed his check points and changed his heading frequently just in case any Iraqi radars tracked him. During the countdown to war, the Air Force had been flying a tanker up to the border of Iraq, and each time, the tanker had turned back. The Iraqis paid it little heed. But this time, Feest and his wingman accompanied the tanker and kept going.

Feest's pulse and breathing rate increased as he neared the point where he would release his bombs. After checking all his instruments, he armed his weapons. Infrared sensors picked up terrain features and the well-hidden IOC bunker. Feest compared what he saw on his displays to a reconnaissance photo strapped to his leg. Using a fingertip target designator button located on one of his jet's throttles, Feest placed the cross hairs on his aim point, which was the center of the top of the bunker. At the same time, he began painting the target with an invisible laser beam. By reflecting the laser energy from the target back to the plane, the so-called smart bomb would be ride the beam to the ground. Instruments instructed Feest to fly left or right to correct for crosswinds. When a symbol showed he was within range, he depressed the red button at the top of his control stick. The weapons door opened, released a bomb and snapped shut. A 2,000-pound bomb, designed to penetrate deep into a target before exploding, followed the laser beam to the ground. A split second after penetrating the roof, the bomb detonated and the bunker doors blew out. Half of the air defense center had been obliterated.

As he headed to his next target, Feest saw ground fire filling the sky behind him. It started after his first bomb hit, which told him nobody knew he was there until he had left. But his wing man had to fly through an imposing wall of tracers, flashes, flak and missiles. Undaunted, Feest found his second target, repeated the procedures and released a laser-guided bomb. He confirmed the hit, then turned for home. Impact occurred at 2:51 a.m., right on schedule.

Meanwhile, eight Night Hawks bore down on Baghdad, intent on taking out command centers, air defense points and communications centers. Flying at 480 knots, the black jets had flown past the Iraqi capital and turned around to come in from the north, where they would be least expected. At three o'clock, Night Hawk pilots placed their cross hairs on the Al Karakh International Tele-communications Center, known informally as the AT&T building. More than half of the Iraqi military's land communications ran through the commercial telephone lines, and the building was neutralized with one bomb. To take out a similar target in World War II, it would have taken 10,000 bombs, not to mention lost pilots and crews, civilian deaths and the destruction of buildings that had no military value. At Air Force headquarters in Saudi Arabia, Lieutenant General Chuck Horner dispatched an aide to watch CNN. The TV signal from

Baghdad stopped precisely at H-Hour. The plan was working. Night Hawks also took telecommunications towers, command bunkers, Iraqi air force head-quarters, two air defense command posts and Saddam's suburban retreat. In the first wave over Baghdad, 13 of the 17 bombs that were dropped hit their targets.

Now bearing down on Iraq was an eclectic mix of Strike Eagles, Falcons, Aardvarks, Wild Weasels, Warthogs, Stratofortresses, Hornets, Tomcats, Prowlers, Harriers and Tornadoes. Next to arrive in Baghdad, between 3:06 and 3:11 a.m., were Tomahawks. The initial barrage of 100 cruise missiles, each costing $1 million, came from Navy ships. The *USS San Jacinto* in the Red Sea fired first at 90 minutes before H-Hour. Once fired, it could not be recalled. The precision-guided missile exited the launch tube and hung suspended for a moment. It then rode a tail of rocket flame on its 700-mile journey to Baghdad. Shortly thereafter, the *USS Bunker Hill* in the Gulf launched its first Tomahawk. Adding to the high-tech hailstorm were missiles fired from nine cruisers, five destroyers, the battleships *Wisconsin* and *Missouri,* and two nuclear-powered attack submarines. Eight Tomahawks hit the presidential palace. Six more hit the headquarters of the Ba'ath Party, the Sunni organization that ruled Iraq under Saddam Hussein. Thirty pounded an air defense complex at Taji. The Tomahawks obliterated power generating plants. In 20 minutes, Baghdad went dark. Grid by grid, the power died. The heart of the city died too. Kept in the dark, Iraqi defenders opened up their defensive guns. While they pulled their triggers with a gusto, they were firing but not aiming.

Then suddenly, the defenders of Baghdad detected what looked like a fleet of bombers bearing down on the city. Tracking radars, which had been inert up to now lest they give away their positions, were turned on. Missiles were launched. Iraqi commanders were convinced they were knocking down scores of planes. It was, however, all part of a planned deception. Instead of bombers, the blips were made by drones designed to show up as big as a warplane on a radar scope, and the Iraqis had unwittingly taken the bait. Just minutes behind the drones, and 40 minutes after the first bomb fell on Baghdad, came a picket line of 70 F-4G Wild Weasels. The Wild Weasels were designed to pick up an enemy radar signal and then fire a HARM missile that rode the signal back to the source. The tactics were developed during the Vietnam War and later used by the Israelis. In Baghdad, to turn on the radar system was to die, and the HARMs reaped a deadly harvest. British pilots joined in with their own version of radar-seeking missiles.

In less than an hour, KARI had been eliminated as a coherent, unified defense. Surface-to-air missiles and anti-aircraft artillery would fill the skies for weeks, but coordinated air defenses were effectively suppressed in the time it takes an average motorist to drive 60 miles.

Meanwhile, two more waves of Stealth fighters arrived. Because of strict radio silence, pilots new nothing of the success of the first strike, but what they saw was a city flailing to defend itself. While only 15 of their 32 smart bombs hit their targets, the fresh wave hit air defense headquarters, presidential retreats, biological weapons bunkers, TV towers, ammo dumps and radio transmitters.

In addition, a total of 53 F-111 Aardvarks bombed chemical bunkers and airfields and control towers in Iraq and Kuwait.

Joining the fray were the B-52s, the giant strategic bombers known as BUFFs (Big Ugly Flying Fuckers). Older than the crews flying them, the bombers loosed missiles and bombs on four airfields. They also rained destruction on Iraqi army formations. One flight took off from Barksdale Air Force Base in Louisiana, refueled in the air en route, struck targets in Iraq and returned home. The 35-hour, 14,000-mile round trip set what was then a record for longest-distance combat mission. B-52s also flew from bases in Saudi Arabia, Great Britain, Spain and the island of Diego Garcia.

Also in the air were 160 refueling tankers, stacked three deep with 500 feet of separation on carefully arranged flight paths over Saudi Arabia. Three flying command posts, called E-3 Airborne Warning and Control System (AWACS), provided air traffic control in the skies.

An RC-135 Rivet Joint spy plane eavesdropped on Iraqi communications. A U-2 spy plane tracked the air battle from 11 miles above the desert floor.

Combat Air Patrols, circling like birds of prey, waited for Iraqi jets to take to the skies. Air Force Captain Steve Tate launched at 1:30 a.m. from the 1st Tactical Fighter Wing, headquartered at the King Abdul Aziz Air Base, to lead

F-15C Eagles into the fray. During his four-hour mission, while over an airfield in southern Iraq, a flying radar platform reported a Iraqi plane in the air. It was a hostile F-1 Mirage climbing to 8,000 feet and heading west. A system known as Identification Friend or Foe confirmed the French-made jet was a bogey. Tate got tone lock from 12 miles out, fired his AIM-7 Sparrow at four miles away, then saw a huge fireball. The Iraqi plane disintegrated.

The Navy's role went far beyond launching Tomahawks. Two Navy E-2C Hawkeyes provided additional radar coverage and flight control, one for the four Navy carriers in the Arabian Gulf — *America, Theodore Roosevelt, Ranger* and *Midway* — and one over western Saudi Arabia for two carriers in the Red Sea — the *Saratoga* and the *John F. Kennedy*.

On one mission, four F/A-18 Hornets from the *Saratoga* were on their way to bomb an Iraqi airfield when two MiG-21 interceptors were detected seven miles away. The Hornet pilots switched from bombing mode to an air-to-air mission, downing both MiGs with Sidewinder missiles. Then the Hornets switched back to bombing mode and scored direct hits on their original target. The Navy's only air-to-air kills of the war happened on that mission.

British Tornadoes dropped bombs that cratered runways and neutralized Iraqi airfields. Marine Harrier jets hit a railroad depot in Basra. Air Force, Navy and Saudi planes also bombed an airfield in Basra.

It wasn't perfect. Some missions went awry. Some bombs missed. Some missions were aborted due to heavy return fire or maintenance problems. Still, the success of the onslaught, accomplished by 668 coalition aircraft, was incredible. Only a superpower could have landed such a blow.

Planners anticipated losses of 100 aircraft or more, and Special Forces teams were on standby to rescue downed pilots. They all came back, all except one. Lieutenant Commander Scott Speicher of the *USS Saratoga*, flying under the call sign Spike, was shot down by an Iraqi missile. It took 18 years to find out what happened.

Given the go-ahead by a crewman called The Shooter, Speicher launched into the sky with a boost from the *Saratoga's* catapult. Climbing to an altitude of about five miles and zooming along at speeds just below the sound barrier, his F/A-18 Hornet flew over the Red Sea and across the Saudi sands toward a target about 100 miles west of Baghdad. When his fellow pilots formed up to head back to the ship, Spike failed to answer. An Iraqi missile had locked onto to him and knocked him out of the sky. Although no search-and-rescue mission was sent to find him, then-Secretary of Defense Dick Cheney addressed a news conference the following day in Washington and announced Speicher's death.

A model aviator whose father had flown combat missions in World War II, Speicher was married and the father of two children. Flying was in his blood. In his youth, he collected model planes and hung posters of jets in his room. He flew for the first time at the age of five with his dad. In addition, he set swimming records before his graduation from Nathan Bedford Forrest High School in 1975. At Florida State University, where he received a degree in management and accounting, he was captain of the swimming team. He joined the Navy to fulfill a dream of flying jets off an aircraft carrier.

At the time the *Saratoga* lost crew members in the ferry accident at Christmas, Speicher made a pilgrimage to Bethlehem. Back in the world, he was a Sunday school teacher at a Methodist church. Speicher wrote a letter home to his pastor, the Reverend Paul Dickson that described his visit to the scene of the Nativity as his "holiest moment."

Because Speicher's body was not recovered, the incident haunted the Navy. Two years after the shoot-down, a military official from Qatar roaming the desert discovered the wreckage of Speicher's plane but could provide no information on the pilot. The canopy was a good distance away, which meant Speicher had ejected. Unbeknownst to anyone, a Bedouin subsequently wandering the desert chanced upon Speicher's body and buried him. In 1996, the Secretary of the Navy reaffirmed the presumptive finding of death, and Speicher was honored with a tomb at Arlington National Cemetery. Five years later, however, Speicher's status was changed again to missing in action. It was the first time in history the Navy had made such a reversal. Speicher was even promoted to commander, then to captain. As rumors persisted that Speicher was being held prisoner by Saddam Hussein, his status was again changed to missing/captured.

Finally, on August 2, 2009, more than six years into the Second Iraq War, Speicher's remains were found. Marines operating in the area exhumed his unmarked grave, and a jawbone recovered from the crash site was sent to the Charles C. Carson Center for Mortuary Affairs at Dover Air Force Base. Tests confirmed that it was Speicher. His remains were returned to Florida and interred at Jacksonville Memory Garden. The first lost and the last found of Desert Storm had, at last, come home to rest in peace.

In the meantime, Speicher's name was given to a fortress that was originally built as the Al Sahra Airfield, located near Saddam Hussein's home town of Tikrit and the home of Iraq's Air Force Academy. After its capture by U.S. troops in the Second Iraq War, the place was refurbished by contractors of Kellogg, Brown & Root Inc., a wholly owned subsidiary of Halliburton Co., and it was renamed Contingency Operating Base Speicher. The base housed a U.S. Army brigade and served as a supply and distribution center. In addition to a large kitchen that fed hot meals daily to the troops, the base also featured American fast food restaurants such as Subway, Burger King and Pizza Hut. COB Speicher was turned back over to the post-Saddam Iraqi government two months before the Second Iraq War was officially declared over on December 15, 2011.

In June of 2014, however, COB Speicher was attacked by an army of religious radicals who claimed the area as part of an Islamic State that included broad swaths of territory in Syria and Iraq. An off-shoot of al-Qaeda that didn't exist when Speicher was shot down, the Islamic State aimed to establish an independent caliphate through a grisly campaign of terror and blood.

In response to the Islamic State's advances, the Pentagon dispatched the aircraft carrier *USS George H.W. Bush* to the region. The carrier is named after the commander-in-chief who prosecuted the war in which Speicher died. Bush's son, George W. Bush, was the president who waged the Iraq war during which Speicher was found.

On August 8, 2014, Navy pilots in their F/A-18Cs roared from the deck of the carrier named after the elder Bush in the first of their strikes against the Islamic State, whose jihadists decapitate and murder in the name of God. Then in retaliation for the air strikes, two American free-lance journalists who had been covering the civil war in Syria — James Foley and Steven Sotloff — were beheaded on video by a radical who warned, "Our knife will continue to strike the necks of your people."

Instant Thunder may have been the most remarkable first strike in the history of warfare, but it still came with a price. War always comes with a price.

CHAPTER 22
All the Way

Friday, January 18. I'm on my sleeping cot in a warehouse filled with paratroopers, scheduled to board a transport plane in the morning to an assembly area up north. Mission undetermined, destination unknown. Oh, and as the only way to get the story I came over here to do, I am now a member of the 82nd Airborne. I may be the least likely and least qualified member in the history of the Airborne, but I have the shoulder patches to prove it. It's a long story.

Every other time I had been to Abqaig, we turned right at an intersection to go to a firing range. This time, a left turn took us into a walled compound guarded by sentries and razor wire. Inside the front office of a large warehouse was the headquarters of the 82nd Airborne's Second Brigade. With maps lining the walls, officers had gathered for a situation report. Conversation stopped as a welcome was given by Ronald Rokosz, the 45-year-old colonel who commanded the brigade. Just as I had every other time I met anyone in the military, I introduced myself as an AP national writer from New York City. Then came a moment of truth.

The colonel agreed to take the media to war with his troops, to go wherever they went and live like they did, under one condition. He insisted I join the unit. With that, he looked me square in the eye and held out two sets of All-American shoulder patches, complete with Airborne tabs, one set in the red, white and blue that adorns dress uniforms and the other in olive drab for combat wear.

While a journalist operates under the code of arm's length objectivity, joining the unit meant crossing an invisible line from observer to something else entirely. But my mission was to get as close to war as possible, and the colonel was offering a front row seat. This wasn't some way to control the media or compromise journalistic integrity. No conditions on reporting would be imposed, other than those agreed to regarding operational security. He just didn't want reporters coming around to do quick stories and then leave without being accountable to those who were being written about. The way I saw it, I had two choices. If I said no, I'd be driven back to the hotel and would cover the war from the briefing room with the rest of the pogues. If I said yes, I'd be going all in. War forces you to make decisions. After a split second, and with a dry mouth and a knotted stomach, I agreed.

No oath was sworn. No step forward was taken. No formal induction papers were signed. The colonel offered a handshake, and I accepted. Those shoulder patches were heavy with responsibility. Known informally as the Falcon Brigade, the unit is historically known as the 325th Parachute Infantry Regiment. Its motto is "Let's Go!" Pool reporters were supposed to bond with combat units, and a future generation of war correspondents would be embedded. Joining the Airborne was a step beyond. *All the way, sir.*

The briefing resumed with a status report on the readiness, concluding with a comment from Captain Brad Nelson, the brigade adjutant. "Another day in the KSA," said the captain, using the abbreviation for the kingdom of Saudi Arabia in a phrase that he had been repeating for months.

Weather reports were discussed about a particular area up north. The time had come to move to a location from which to launch the ground invasion.

"We're repositioning to a tactical assembly area north along the Iraq border to conduct offensive operations if we're told. The main movement starts tomorrow," Colonel Rokosz said. "The pre-game show is over."

The mere fact that they were moving north was a big deal, and he did say Iraq, not Kuwait. Then the colonel took some questions.

"This is the best morale has been since day one," Rokosz said. "Morale was skyrocketing the last few days. The men are very confident. They're very resolute. They're very confident. They just want to do it and go home."

What about casualties?

"They know some people are going to get killed, and they're accepting it," he said somberly. "The first five months were about coping with uncertainty, adjusting to Saudi Arabia, getting used to the desert. They kind of got resolute about it. Now we're going to do what we have to do."

Under his command were three infantry battalions, one company of combat engineers, an air defense company, a military intelligence unit, a platoon of military police, a civil affairs unit to deal with the local population, a signal platoon for communications, a battalion of towed 105 millimeter howitzers, a company of 12 Sheridan light tanks and a battalion of Apache attack helicopters, roughly 2,500 troops in all.

What were his thoughts about the ground war, now that air strikes had started?

"Nobody wanted to go to war. If we have to, that's what we'll do. There is no historical precedent for what we're doing," the colonel said. "I don't want to see soldiers killed in any army. I've got a vested interest in coming home in one piece."

What's the timetable for the invasion?

"We might be going for the long haul. This thing's not going to end in two days. If the Air Force keeps doing what it's doing, they're going to make our job a hell of a lot easier," he said.

What's the mission?

"The best use of a light force is in support of a heavy force," Rokosz said.

It was a non-specific answer, but he meant that the infantry's role in a desert war would be to work in tandem with armor. Instead of being fed piecemeal into a fight, the combat power of the entire brigade had been consolidated.

"The unit has never been better trained. We've got artillery, tanks, mortars, helicopters. It's one of the few times it's all been assembled," the colonel said.

At the briefing was the colonel's right hand man, Command Sergeant Major Steve Slocum, the top enlisted man in the brigade who serves as a liaison between commanders and the trigger-pullers. Leery of the media, Slocum politely declined an interview. He said he would talk after everything was over. In his quarters that were connected to the briefing room, however, Slocum kept a wall-sized poster that spoke to Airborne history. It pictured a grizzled infantryman from the 325th Regiment during the Battle of the Bulge. With a sleeping bag draped over his shoulders to ward off the winter cold, the soldier had his rifle slung on one arm and a bazooka on the other. A signature paratrooper knife was strapped to his leg. A picture of him was taken December 23, 1944, when the 82nd Airborne moved forward even as other American units were in full retreat from a German offensive. As a tank destroyer rolled by, the infantryman said: "Are you looking for a safe place? Well, buddy, just pull your vehicle behind me...I'm the 82nd Airborne, and this is as far as the bastards are going."

Rokosz and Slocum, both veterans of Vietnam, had traveled a long road to get to this point.

Rokosz, 44, grew up in a Polish Catholic neighborhood on Chicago's South Side. He was commissioned through the Reserve Officer Training Program at Loyola University in 1968, the same year demonstrators opposed to the Vietnam War roiled Chicago streets outside the Democratic National Convention. At a time when it wasn't exactly popular to have an Army haircut or wear a uniform, Rokosz served in the triple canopy cover of Vietnam with the Army's 1st Cavalry Division. He was among the veterans who stayed in the Army to oversee the transition to an all-volunteer force, rising to command a company of elite Army Rangers before becoming deputy commander of the 75th Ranger Regiment. From years of carrying an 80-pound pack on his back, his shoulders stooped. Underlings called him Rucksack Ron, but not to his face.

One month after his 18th birthday, Slocum was fighting in Vietnam with an Airborne infantry regiment. And five months into his tour of duty, during an ambush in which his best friend was killed, Slocum took two AK-47 rounds in the groin. After recuperating at a military hospital in Japan, Slocum returned to his comrades in Charlie Company just in time for the Tet Offensive of 1968. The company's mission was to block a route, which troopers called the Yellow Brick Road that ran east to west from the notorious A Shau Valley to the city of Hue. Slocum and 109 fellow paratroopers were hit by a North Vietnamese regiment attempting to reinforce communist forces. After a daylong firefight, Slocum was one of only 32 paratroopers who were still alive and unwounded. He, too, stayed in the Army to oversee its rebirth.

Just before Iraq invaded Kuwait, the unit commanded by Rokosz and Slocum had assumed the role of being the 82nd Airborne Division's Ready Brigade, on call to respond to any crisis. The order to deploy to Saudi Arabia came late on August 6, four days after Iraq invaded Kuwait. At about 11 o'clock at night, the sergeant on duty at Airborne headquarters in Fort Bragg received a message from the National Command Authority, another name for the commander-in-chief. Formally known as a Red X-Ray message, it alerted the Second Brigade to a mission. The Airborne calls itself America's 9-1-1, so when the order came, it was like an operator handing over the phone and saying, "Here, it's for you." A thunderstorm broke over North Carolina that night, but like they say in the infantry, "If it ain't raining, we ain't training."

A practiced sequence flipped the switch on the war machine. All members of the Ready Brigade had to leave a phone number where they could be reached. If they heard the code word Corvette, they knew it was time to report, don their combat gear and draw weapons and ammo. Phones rang in barracks, off-post housing and the bars and strip clubs off Bragg Boulevard in Fayetteville, North Carolina.

Minutes later, cars began arriving at Airborne headquarters on Ardennes Street. Officers at the division, brigade and battalion levels reported for a briefing at midnight in a room known as the Puzzle Palace. Clocks in the briefing room were set to various time zones around the world, including the time in Saudi Arabia. Tension was in the air as map were rolled out. The first order of business was to make sure the Saudi airport in Dhahran was secure for follow-on flights, and that the neighboring seaport of Damman was safe to receive arriving ships loaded with equipment and supplies.

Whatever troopers needed would be carried on their backs. Long lines formed as rifles, mortars and ammunition were drawn. Troops were issued two sets of desert camouflage uniforms. One was worn, the other was the only change of clothing they would have. Also issued were extra canteens, gas masks with activated charcoal filters, first aid kits and MREs. Their sleeping bags would be their beds.

Soldiers were then herded onto 40-foot long trucks and moved to a marshalling area. For security reasons, they were locked in behind a fence, unable to call home to say where they were going. Even if they could have called, they would be unable to say how long they'd be gone.

From this assembly point, paratroopers marched via the Green Ramp to the adjoining Pope Field Air Force Base to await their ride. The word came early on that they would not be parachuting in, which was a major letdown.

Still, they were prepared to fight their way in, if necessary, in the event the Iraqi army had moved south. They were also told they would be making history because no American combat force had ever deployed to Saudi Arabia. Given the fluid situation, plans would be refined while they were in the air. It was just the beginning of a long period of not knowing what would happen next.

By the time the first flight was cleared for take-off, it was August 7, which was designated as Callout Day, or C-Day. Although most troopers would travel by military aircraft, the first flight to Saudi Arabia was a civilian Trans-America DC-10 airliner chartered for just such an emergency. There were 210 soldiers aboard, including Rokosz and Slocum.

The first flight, designated Chalk One, was wheels up at about one o'clock in the afternoon, fourteen hours after the alert was sent out. Troopers stored their Kevlar combat helmets, body armor, gas masks, web gear, rucksacks and weapons in the compartments above their heads or in the space under their seats. When the clock officially starts for the start of a war can be open to debate, but for a paratrooper on a mission, the battle starts as soon as the plane leaves the ground. It took 24 hours of flight time to get to Dhahran.

The aircraft had flight attendants and even an in-flight movie. Some troopers slept. Some wore that Airborne grin that comes from the adrenaline rush. Some stared out the windows, alone in their thoughts. About an hour out from their destination, all the idle chatter and Army jokes stopped. Things got really serious when paratroopers slathered their faces with camouflage paint. The flight attendants painted their faces, too, to break the tension. The order came to lock and load their rifles.

Master Sergeant David Leary, the non-commissioned officer in charge of air movement for the division and a father of four, recalled the moment. "It was so quiet, you could have heard a pin drop. Nobody knew what to expect, and not knowing was the worst," Leary said.

The landing in Dhahran was uneventful. A welcoming party of Saudi officials in their light cotton robes and head dresses looked on quizzically as paratroopers ran off the plane and, weapons at the ready, took up defensive positions around the runway. Although no Iraqis were in sight, the arriving troops were greeted by their first enemy — a blast of lung-searing desert air.

"It was like stepping into an oven," said Specialist Chris Totten of Sumner, Washington, who was aboard the first flight. Camouflage paint melted off as sweat streamed down his face.

Paratroopers had been in the air when President Bush declared he was drawing a line in the sand. The first arrivals from the Second Brigade, undeterred by their limited numbers, drew that line the moment their combat boots stepped on the ground.

It took four days to move the entire brigade, but even as troops poured in, the next step was to secure the deep water port of Jubail to make sure it was safe for arriving troops and equipment. Colonel Rokosz was the first paratrooper to make that two-hour drive north, and the brigade quickly took up defensive positions.

Quarters for some troops were found in a trailer complex that once housed the foreign laborers who built the modern Jubail. Because the trailers had been vacant for years, it would take some sprucing up to make them habitable again. The complex did have air conditioning, hot and cold running water, indoor toilets, showers and coin-operated washers and dryers. It served the purposes of the vanguard of the Army while it became acclimated to a hostile environment.

From Jubail, paratroopers ventured northwest into the desert where a couple of Saudi highways intersected. If the Iraqi army invaded, they would likely move through the crossroads located at An Nuayriyah, about 80 miles south of the Kuwait border. The Airborne occupied the area on August 23 and promptly named it Camp Essex.

This is as far as the bastards are going.

Having dug hasty fighting positions, paratroopers were prepared to take the fight to the Iraqis. Like his comrades, Sergeant First Class Gary Hammond of Fayetteville, North Carolina, was aware of the arithmetic.

"The 82nd Airborne can do a lot of things, but it can't defend against 4,000 tanks. It made you do a lot of thinking. We knew we didn't have anything to stop all those tanks if Saddam came south," Hammond said.

Because they might only be able to slow down an attack or serve as a tripwire, paratroopers adopted a new name.

"We were calling ourselves speed bumps. All we could have done is slowed him down," said Specialist Mark Matson, 30, of Port Huron, Michigan.

To acclimate themselves to the harsh environment, paratroopers donned gas masks and practiced such things as drinking water through a straw in the mask. As hot as it was, the wearing of a rubber gas mask under the desert sun made things worse. Still, a gas mask was mandatory at all times as troops faced the prospect of confronting a weapon no U.S. serviceman had confronted since the trenches of World War I. Poison gas had been outlawed by a 1925 Geneva Protocol, but Saddam Hussein's army had used mustard gas in its war with Iran and against Kurdish dissidents inside Iraq. Iraq was also thought to possess nerve gas and biological weapons such as anthrax and botulinum. Fitted with full protective gear, an American soldier looked like a lunar astronaut.

Then, as the Army rushed in more troops with more firepower, the Second Brigade was pulled back about 130 miles to the south to the town of Abqaiq, about 40 miles southwest of the Dhahran airport where they had entered the kingdom. Their mission was to defend against terrorist threats to the Ghawar Oil Field, an underground geological giant that is 174 miles long and 16 miles across. The largest oil field in the world, it accounted for half of Saudi Arabia's considerable oil production. A portion of Abqaiq was a camp, surrounded by a security fence, for employees of the Arab American Oil Company (ARAM-CO). The camp also had an airstrip that could be used to move paratroopers anywhere they might be needed.

The Airborne's new home was a vacant warehouse, which had a concrete floor and a tin roof. Some improvements were needed, however, before it became a barracks. The only creatures that had been living in it were flocks of pigeons that found the rafters to their liking. Over time, pigeon droppings piled up on the floor like a deep carpet. As practice for cleaning areas that could be poisoned by chemical weapons, soldiers trained in decontamination rolled up the layers of pigeon shit and sanitized the floor. Sleeping cots were installed, and about 700 paratroopers moved in.

I grabbed my pack and a cot and settled in for the night on the same floor once layered in pigeon droppings. Some troops wrote letters home. Others lightened their load. Everything that wasn't essential to the mission was packed up and placed in storage boxes that would be left behind. Some passed the time tossing a football. Some gravitated to a far corner of the open room where a bench press had been set up for pumping iron. A few wondered why somebody in civilian clothes was pecking out a story on a manual typewriter.

That evening, while strolling around the warehouse, a medic stopped me. He asked if I had gotten any precautionary inoculations.

"Some gamma globulin when I left New York in October," I said.

"We're going to be living out in the field for who knows how long, and there are some nasty things out there. Let me fix you up," he said.

In what might be called a hasty doctor/patient consultation, he convinced me that it would be to my benefit to get a booster shot of gamma globulin. It's what the AP nurse had given me when I left New York. All the other members of the brigade already had received a shot as a precaution. Another split-second decision led to another yes.

Dropping my trousers and leaning against a table, I took a syringe into my buttocks. Forget the colonel giving me shoulder patches and shaking my hand. Getting a shot in full view of my new comrades was the real moment I joined the Airborne. Well, I had agreed to do this. I am good to go.

CHAPTER 23
The Grounded Bird

Saturday, January 19. A C-130 Hercules transport plane, its engines running, waited for the go-ahead to roll down the airstrip. The question of access seems to have been answered satisfactorily. Harnessed up inside, I'm going where the Airborne goes. Five flights have already departed to the assembly area on the Iraqi border, and this is Chalk Six. It's not a jump. We'll be landing at some undisclosed airfield. Over the din of the engines, a noise made tolerable by wearing earplugs, one of the Air Force crewman just announced a temporary delay because of bad weather at the landing site. How far north are we going? I'll find out soon enough when the bird takes to the skies…

———————◆———————

The day began with the ritual of climbing out of the bag, shaking out my boots to make sure no scorpions or other nasty things crawled in, making a call of nature in one of the outhouses, brushing my teeth and shaving at a bank of outdoor sinks, packing up, turning in the cot and moving out to the airstrip.

Members of the Second Brigade assembled on the apron, providing the opportunity for interviews. One was Staff Sergeant Steve Brown, 23, of Kent, Ohio, who had a paper plate of Army scrambled eggs and potatoes perched on the hood of a Humvee as he listened to news on a short-wave radio. "We're on the way home now. We're just taking a detour through Iraq," he said in an upbeat tone.

Having been caged up for months, troops just wanted to get this over with. Staff Sergeant Joseph Hafner, 25, of Tulsa, Oklahoma, was in the lean-and-rest position against his pack, rifle in hand. "Once we got the word it was on, morale soared. There's no a doubt in my mind Saddam Hussein is history. It's time," Hafner said.

This battle had become personal. Forget the stuff about fighting for the nation's vital interests, or to correct an international injustice. The target was the Iraqi leader responsible for pulling them away from home to fight in the desert.

Specialist 4 John Hague, 29, of Oakland, California, spoke of a chance for some payback after all the waiting and training. "He made the last five months of my life miserable. Now it's his turn. Finally. Finally. The sooner we go, the sooner we can wrap it up. No more training. It's all for real," Hague said.

Master Sergeant John Torre, 33, of Guam, lit up a handmade Padron Cuban cigar he had been saving for the occasion. A comrade suggested he should have saved it for when the brigade entered Baghdad, but it seemed as good a time as any for a last smoke.

Private First Class Aaron Smith, 20, of Denver, Colorado, carried a 7.62 millimeter round in his shirt pocket for his M-60 machine gun. The bullet had Saddam Hussein's name on it. "I've been saving this one. It's going to be my first round down range," Smith said.

First Sergeant Jim Southerly, 39, of Fayetteville, North Carolina, said his Delta Company, informally known as the Junkyard Dogs, was ready for anything that might come their way. "It's all for real now. We're pumped. We just want to get it on so we can go home. The way home is through Iraq," Southerly said.

An Army operation almost always involves forming up and then having to mark time. Captain Dave Smith of Leesville, Louisiana, the brigade intelligence officer, expressed impatience. "When I get back to the world, I'm never going to wait in another line. That's all we've done since we've been here," Smith said.

After what these guys had been through in the preceding five months, the latest wait seemed miniscule. Specialist 4 Michael Merchant, 30, of Tulsa, Oklahoma, who called himself the mortar man from hell, had a 65-pound pack on his back and a 25-pound mortar in his hands. "We were the first ones in country. It's only right we get their ass first," Merchant said.

One paratrooper of particular note was John R. Vines, a lieutenant colonel who commanded the 650 soldiers in the 4th Battalion. He earned a mustard splat on his Airborne wings for making a combat jump into Panama with his battalion during Operation Just Cause.

"We'll be making coffee in Saddam's backyard before he knows it," Vines said.

Vines was a symbol of the post-Vietnam Army. A graduate of the University of Alabama, he had previously served as a company commander and staff officer in the 75th Ranger Regiment. And he had a story to tell about this deployment.

Back on August 2, the day Iraq invaded Kuwait, the training schedule at Fort Bragg included a four-mile training run for officers in the XVIII Airborne Corps. Participating in what was called a Green Tab Run were generals, colonels, lieutenant colonels, majors, captains and lieutenants. While it was still unclear what Iraq's invasion would mean for the Airborne, soldier talk that day centered on the death of a member of the Fort Bragg family who was killed when his parachute failed to deploy during a night training exercise on the last day of July. He was Colonel Dick Malvesti, a veteran of the Army since 1967 and a Green Beret who was director of operations for the Joint Special Operations Command. The Airborne goes to great lengths to insure safety, with jump masters triple-checking equipment at every turn. Still, it's a dangerous profession. Even practicing for a mission can get you killed. Vines was among those who would attend Malvesti's funeral in Cape Cod, Massachusetts. When he returned to weekend duty at Fort Bragg, Vines was walking by a TV set on Sunday, August 4. President Bush said of Kuwait's occupation: "This will not stand." To a combat veteran, Bush's words meant war.

"The hair stood up on the back of my neck," Vines said. "I knew the president of the United States had just committed the United States politically and militarily."

The official word came two days later. Vines' duties on August 6 called for him to evaluate a battalion from the 29th Infantry Division, a National Guard unit that was training at Fort Bragg. Early in the afternoon, he was summoned by Lieutenant Colonel Dan McNeill, the 82nd Airborne's officer in charge of synchronizing readiness, operations, training, mobilization and plans. The Second Brigade was being called up, and Vines was told that his 4th Battalion would be first to go to Saudi Arabia. No specifics about timeline or mission were available, but the best guess was that the alert would come within a day or so. Returning to his headquarters, Vines quietly prepared plans for what troops and equipment to send first.

After landing in Saudi Arabia, Vines led his 4th Battalion on the journey to Jubail to make sure the port was secure for arriving forces and equipment. He was at the dock to greet the first Marines deploying to the kingdom, and he had a picture to prove it.

Then it was out to the desert to draw the line in the sand before the Airborne was pulled back to Abqaig. It was true, Vines said, that paratroopers did their most realistic combat training in their time spent at a firing range carved out of the sand.

"There sure wasn't anything else to do," the battalion commander said.

The throttle of Chalk Six never moved forward. After an interminable wait, word came that the bad weather had settled in up north and it would be unsafe to land. Today's mission was scratched, which meant unbuckling and grabbing another cot for a Saturday night stay in the warehouse. Part of being a soldier means switching gears from ready to take off to standing down. The bird doesn't always fly. *Another day in the KSA.*

CHAPTER 24
A Crazy Job

Sunday, January 20. Censorship sucks. I've just had material blotted out of a story. It had nothing to do with operational security. It wasn't a violation of the rules I had signed. It was a quote from a chaplain officiating a worship service for paratroopers seeking spiritual solace before they went into combat. The major who did the censoring would have let it go, but he was overruled by a lieutenant colonel who served as the brigade's highest-ranking chaplain. The chaplain I quoted had made some poignant remarks about how taking a life is a crime and a sin in civilized society, but soldiers in time of war faced circumstances in which they might have to kill to get the war over with. Lieutenant Colonel Lawrence Krause, however, pointed out that chaplains were prohibited from granting interviews to reporters under the general orders issued during the deployment. Our Saudi hosts might take offense if any religion other than Islam were practiced. I tried to argue that things were different now that the war had started, but Krause was adamant. I wasn't about to win a fight with a by-the-book lieutenant colonel. When an editor deletes material from a story, reporters call it "killing the babies." When an Army censor does it, it feels worse. It was the last time I bothered talking to a chaplain, but it didn't matter. Enough of the story survived to get the point across.

It was my idea to attend Sunday services in the first place. A tent that doubled as a chow hall served as a chapel. Paratroopers brought their rifles and gas masks to the non-denominational service, sitting on folding chairs that served as pews. A wooden table doubled as an altar.

Staff Sergeant Timothy Alspach, 33, of Groveport, Ohio, the senior medic for the Second Brigade, assisted at the service. He said a steeple and other niceties weren't required.

"Christianity is not about being in a fancy church. Christianity is like having a personal relationship with God. My faith is a source of strength for me," Alspach said. "I've gone over my equipment a hundred times. I got a lot of quiet time to reflect, to think about what's going to happen, how it's going to go down. I wonder how I'm going to react to seeing one of my best buddies dying. It's scary to think about. This isn't about the flag and apple pie anymore. What you think about is the buddy next to you."

Unprompted, he also added: "We don't want anybody spitting on us when we go home. That means we'd have to kill them."

At the service, paratroopers sang hymns and bowed their heads in prayer while armed guards in Humvees patrolled the camp perimeter and mechanics readied vehicles for the move north. In a sign that things had taken a serious turn, attendance at such services had peaked. Just like their fathers and grandfathers before them, the infantrymen made inner preparations. Protestants, Catholics and Jews attended. Some gathered in tight clusters to read and discuss Scripture. Others read Bibles in silence. They were even mindful of what the guys on the other side would be up against.

"I've said prayers for the Iraqi soldiers. When you come right down it, their plight isn't much different from ours," Major Ennis said.

With my flight north still grounded, I took the time to stroll around the camp and get acquainted with the soldiers who were taking me to war. In one stretch of sand next to a bank of four-hole outhouses, a lone figure was writing letters on a makeshift desk made from the sleeve of an MRE box. He was Sergeant Rick Gonzales, 24, of San Antonio, Texas, who sat alone among the flies. Because the latrines were nearby in the sand, the area was called Shit Beach. It was devoid of foot traffic because the smell discouraged casual visitors. Only people who had to go ventured into it. A senior medic attached to Bravo Company of the 2nd Battalion, Gonzales was engaged in the soldierly ritual of shedding emotional baggage.

"I wrote a letter to my ex-wife telling her I really did love her even if it didn't work out. I wrote a letter to my 4-year-old son explaining what war is. I wanted to give him some insight if I don't make it back for some crazy reason," he said.

The gravity of the situation was apparent to anyone tasked with treating the wounded.

"I don't want to see these guys get chewed up. I know these guys. I live with them. Undoubtedly, we will take some casualties. I'm hoping they're not that bad. But this ain't like the movies. They're going to get shot, maimed, have holes in them," Gonzales said.

In a nearby barracks area, some paratroopers passed the time by sharpening their knives, and everyone seemed to have a two-handed, Rambo-style pig-sticker just in case they had to cut their lines away if their chutes got tangled. They were members of Bravo Company in the 2nd Battalion. They called themselves "The Nasty Boys" because they get the job done, no matter what, and with as much fury and viciousness as they can muster. One Bravo Company scout, Specialist 4 Kevin Strickland, 21, of Shreveport, Louisiana, had shaved his head for a practical reason.

"The medics will have an easier time treating me if I get a head wound. They won't have to go through my hair," Strickland said. "But hey, I'm ready for it to kick off so I can go home."

Another member of The Nasty Boys, Specialist 4 Daryl Smallwood, 21, of Gainesville, Georgia, spent his Sunday afternoon making death cards to place on the Iraqis he might kill. One of his cards said "Personal Debt Paid." Another was, "Died Like The Pig That You Were." A third one said, "Fuck you. We're arrogant."

"I made 50 so far, but I know I'll need more," Smallwood said.

The name Abqaig had been Americanized to Butt Cake because the austerity of the camp had all the appeal of someone's posterior. Niches of the camp were called The Projects, The 'Hood, The Ghetto and The Dog Pound.

In his home area, Lieutenant Richard White, 23, of Sand Mountain, Alabama, prepared himself in his own way. A platoon leader of Alpha Company in the 2nd Battalion, he explained that one of his responsibilities was to write letters home to next of kin if one of the company's soldiers got killed in combat. He had the same task in Panama but didn't have to write the dreaded letter.

"If you have a casualty, what can you really say? You can tell them you appreciate the sacrifice their son made, but there's not a whole lot you can do to console them for their loss," the lieutenant said.

White didn't mind the delay. He was content to let air power do the preparatory work.

"The Army, the Air Force, the Marines, the Navy — we all fight each other in bars. But when it comes down to business, we're all one big family. The more the Air Force does, the more of my guys I can take home with me. No matter how bad soldiers think they have it in camp, it's going to be worse up north. Once they leave, they'll be hating life. They'll be cold, tired, hungry and worried about lead poisoning," White said.

Lead poisoning is a euphemism for taking a bullet.

Not far away, Staff Sergeant Gary McLaurin, 32, of Fayetteville, North Carolina, had a fire going in a 55-gallon drum. He was burning letters that he had received during the deployment. Should he be captured or worse, he didn't want the Iraqis to be able to find the return addresses on the envelopes. He, too, was lightening his load.

"That's just the hard copy," McLaurin said as flames consumed the paper. "I got all the emotions and feelings out of it. It's all stored in my personal databank. It's no hardship to burn it."

Elsewhere, the most unusual trooper of Alpha Battery, 2nd Battalion of the 319th Field Artillery Regiment was Honas P. Dicklicker. He had an Airborne patch, a camouflage desert scarf, a name tag, the rank of command private first class and a spot on the manifest for the flight north. Everybody called him Dick. He wasn't a two-legged creature, though. He was a raw-boned hound dog that paratroopers adopted three months before.

"He's been living with us for so long, he's one of us. Everybody calls him, knows him, feeds him. He lends an air of normalcy," said Sergeant First Class Philip Lemon, 33, of Denver, Colorado.

Lemon found the skinny mutt in the desert. Dick was a saluki, a cousin of the greyhound. The dog's paperwork was signed by Lieutenant Colonel Gerald Cummins, commander of the artillery regiment. Dick didn't take up much room. His gear included a rubber ball and a food dish for leftover Spam and MREs. Dog food has a different meaning over here.

"His favorite dinner is chicken a la king. It works out for both of us. He gets plenty to eat. We get rid of the stuff we don't want," Lemon said.

Even the Airborne cooks were battle ready. The most unusual weapon in the brigade belonged to Sergeant First Class Cameron Woodson, 35, a mess sergeant from Detroit, Michigan. It was a polished axe handle engraved with his nickname "Hog Head." Woodson took it with him on walks around the compound.

"I'm going to carry this through the war. This is my ticket home. If it comes down to hand-to-hand, I'm going to bust one of them Iraqis with my axe club," Woodson said. "They're ruthless. They're barbarians. They caused me undue hardship. I've been locked up for too long. The only way out is to fight."

During an evening update, we were told we would be leaving on Tuesday, not on a plane, but in an overland convoy. Major Ennis said to be patient because the Iraqis were absorbing punishment from the air.

"It's like a boxer with a 44-inch reach against one with a 36-inch reach. We're just going to stand off and hit him. Pop, pop, pop," he said.

A crash course in weaponry was given in case of an emergency. Basic training may have been 18 years ago, but I was still familiar with the workings of the M-16 rifle. There had been one significant modification. When the weapon was set to full automatic, which was also called rock 'n' roll or the John Wayne, the rifle could fire a 20-round magazine in 3.2 seconds with one pull of the trigger. Now it fired in bursts of three before the trigger had to be pulled again. Also part of the refresher course in weaponry was how to load and cock the Army's new sidearm , the 9 millimeter Baretta that officers carried. It didn't hurt to know how to use it, just in case.

Near my cot, Sergeant First Class Aubrey Butts, 31, of Elizabeth City, North Carolina, squeezed all of his equipment in his pack. It must've weighed 120 pounds, and he grunted as he swung it on his back. He said that's why the pain-killer Motrin, which relieves back aches, is called Airborne M&Ms.

"If I had a choice between going home and going north, I'd go north. Somebody's going to pay for this suffering," Butts said.

Sergeant Jim Noyes, 26, of Fayetteville, North Carolina, was among the paratroopers who was curious about meeting a war correspondent. A member of the 21st Chemical Decontamination Company, he asked the questions and I gave the answers. The same conversation was subsequently held on five or six occasions with different paratroopers.

"Did you volunteer to be here or were you ordered?"

My boss said he wanted me to go to Saudi Arabia, and I wanted to be in on the biggest story in the world. Instead of covering the war from the hotel, I wanted to be in the field with the troops. I chose to do this.

"Are you getting paid extra money?"

No, we don't have combat pay, but the AP did double the payout on my company life insurance policy if I get killed.

"Where's your weapon?"

As a non-combatant, I'm prohibited from carrying a weapon under the protocols of the Geneva Convention, but I do have this I.D. card identifying me as a civilian. It's written in English, though. I hope any potential Iraqi captor can understand it.

"If we jump, are you going to jump with us?"

Absolutely. I'm going to do whatever you guys do. Other reporters in other wars have made combat jumps. The American people have a right to know what's really going on.

"So let me get this straight. You don't have to be here. You're not getting paid extra. We're going to war, but you don't have a weapon. And if we jump, you will too? Damn, mister, you're crazier than us."

I couldn't argue the point.

CHAPTER 25
Troop Movement

Tuesday, January 22. On the road again, this time in an Army convoy of Humvees, two-and-a-half ton trucks loaded with troops, fuel tankers, ammo carriers and enough 18-wheeled flatbed trucks to tax the Pennsylvania Turnpike. The move north has begun, not on a C-130, but in an unbroken line of vehicles moving along at the convoy speed limit of 45 kilometers per hour, or just under 30 miles per hour. There's no scenery to break the monotony, just a sea of dun-colored sand. Music blares from a cassette player broadcasting Sinatra and his rendition of *That's Life,* and if there's nothing shaking come this here July, I will definitely roll myself up in a big ball and die. My ride is the Japanese Pajero, slathered in mud as camouflage to keep down the glint from sunlight reflecting off glass, chrome and shiny paint.

The day began with a sense of anticipation. Not knowing when the next chance might come to take a shower, I shook out my boots and wrapped my towel around my waist to trudge 50 steps to reach a bank of tents. In the sand were the boot prints of legions of paratroopers who had made the same trek in the preceding months. Showers had been installed inside canvas tents that had floors made of bare wooden pallets. Water flowed from overhead tanks through a nozzle. Cold was the only water temperature. Soaping up and rinsing off as quickly as possible was a prudent strategy. Overheard in the showers was talk about a big Acey-Deucey card game the night before.

"I'm jumping clean," somebody said. "I lost everything, but who needs money where we're going?"

In the warehouse, a giant big pile of discarded clothing and equipment littered the concrete floor. Items were free for the picking, and I grabbed a brown wool Army sweater and an extra set of long johns. It might be cold where we were going. One man's trash is another man's treasure. We also packed our sleeping cots and some discarded aluminum wash bowls from the bank of outdoor sinks.

The last chore before leaving was to mix water and dirt in some wash bowls to make mud. The goop was spread over the roof, the hood, the back and the sides of my ride, the Japanese-made Pajero. Bumpers got a heavy dose. Even the windshield and the outer mirrors got a coating. It may have been the only time in the Army a soldier could get yelled at for having a clean vehicle. The idea was to prevent us, like all the other vehicles, from reflecting any glare that the Iraqis might detect. As Murphy's Law says, "Never draw attention to yourself. It invites enemy fire." Then we saddled up, fell in with the convoy and gave the warehouse in Butt Cake back to the pigeons.

Trucks for the troop movement were provided by a couple of Army Reserve units — the 253rd Transportation Company of Cape May, New Jersey, and the 1122nd Transportation Company from Arkansas. One of the trucks was decorated with an image of the Grim Reaper.

I had a new compass that fit on the band of my wrist watch. The Airborne had recently received a shipment of them from the States and handed them out. The arrow showed that we were heading west, deeper into the desert and deeper into the unknown on a ribbon of asphalt, before we turned north. The miles disappeared beneath the wheels.

Every hour on the hour, the short-wave radio brought updates of the war, courtesy of the British Broadcasting Corporation. None of the news reports mentioned the troop movement, which was a top secret maneuver at the time. Moving this many troops and this much equipment would have been impossible without an air umbrella. Air superiority had been established within days, and just like the Air Force promised, air supremacy had followed. Iraq was blind to developments on the ground. In reality, the Herculean logistical task of moving the entire Third Army to a starting line was under way. Seven Army divisions from VII Corps and XVIII Airborne Corps, plus two armored cavalry regiments and other units, were either on the move or getting ready to move. Norman Schwarzkopf later called this maneuver to the West his "Hail Mary play." It was a peculiar choice of words, though. In football, a Hail Mary is a prayer thrown up in desperation with the clock winding down by a team that was behind. In the ground phase of Desert Storm, the clock was just beginning.

The logistics wizards had set up refueling and rest stops in the middle of nowhere. Army Reserve and National Guard units had built places to eat, refuel and spend the night in cots under camouflaged tents. Some stops were named Yak, Unicorn, Vulture, Wombat and Exxon Valdez, where giant fuel bladders dispensed fuel to thirsty trucks and Humvees. In a nod to icons of a previous war, some places were called Bette Davis, Jane Russell and Greta Garbo. We stopped for food and fuel in a place set up by the 102nd Transportation Company from Brooklyn, New York. Beneath the flag of the Borough of Brooklyn was a hand-crafted sign that said: "More Than Just Gas. Hot Dogs. French Fries. Coffee. Latrines." The enormity of the movement reminded me of a line from the movie *Patton*. When surveying the convoys of trucks moving an army and all its supplies, the general marveled, "Compared to war, all other forms of human endeavor pale to insignificance."

The drive did have its drama. A truck caught fire and had to pull over, bringing the convoy to a halt. Of all the vehicles in the line of march, it had to be the ammo truck. One explanation was that sparks from the exhaust pipe on the deuce-and-a-half, the Army term for a two-and-a-half ton truck, ignited the canvas cover. The driver and his guard, however, said a white Nissan truck had been shadowing the convoy. The Arab driver gave a dirty look as he pulled alongside and sped off just before the fire erupted. There was no proof it was an act of terrorism, but looking back, you have to wonder. There was, after all, a segment of Islamic radicals in the kingdom who objected to Americans being in their country.

The ammo truck went up like a Roman candle. Streaks of orange light shot into the sky from the artillery and mortar shells, anti-tank rockets, .50 caliber machine gun rounds and illumination flares that exploded. Pieces of shrapnel whistled through the air, prompting dismounted troops from other vehicles, me included, to hit the dirt. The highway was blocked for an hour in both directions while an ordnance team checked the area for unexploded shells. The fire and explosions must have been visible for hundreds of miles. So much for secrecy. The destruction of the ammo truck underscored the first rule of Murphy's Laws of Combat. Whatever can go wrong, will.

As the convoy snaked forward, it was impossible not to notice that we shared the road with other Army units. Some trucks had the markings of the 101st Airborne, the 24th Mech, the 1st Cav and VII Corps. There were even French vehicles on the move. You can see forever in the desert, and from horizon to horizon, there was an unbroken line of stuff on the move.

A road sign appeared for the town of Hafr al-Batin and provided the first clue of where we were going. I had been here several times on Saudi-arranged trips. Then we turned west again onto Tapline Road, an arrow-straight, two-lane highway that paralleled the border between Saudi Arabia and Iraq. It got its name from an above-ground, abandoned oil pipeline than ran for most of its length. Traffic was so congested at the crossroads in Hafr al-Batin that it was later said that the most important soldier in the entire Kuwaiti Theater of Operations was the Military Policeman directing traffic. And anybody who survived the dangers of Tapline Road during the troop movement should have merited the Combat Infantryman's Badge.

Some time later, a highway marker announced the existence of a town called Rahfa. I had never heard of it. Having stopped for the night, I unrolled my sleeping bag and slept on the berm of Tapline Road. According to what I learned later, the convoy had motored a distance of 560 miles in two days. The end of the line was near.

CHAPTER 26
On The Doorstep

Thursday, January 24. The reason for investing all this time and effort was now at hand. We saddled up and left the pavement, heading into the forbidding desert toward the front. It would be too generous to call it a road. We followed tire tracks on pulverized sand to a lone point of reference — a scraggly bush that was the only visible form of life. Because the landscape was so barren, it was called The Tree, and it was here that we veered to the right and kept going north. Finally, maybe ten miles from Tapline Road, we reached the Tactical Operations Center of Tactical Assembly Area Hawk, the new home of the Second Brigade. A band of razor wire provided a perimeter, and two sentries manned the only entrance. A password was required. The sentries called out Jumper, and the major answered Cable. I had just gotten out of the vehicle to begin the foot slog through the sand to Colonel Rokosz's headquarters when a sentry yelled out: "Gas! Gas! Gas!"

Freezing in my tracks, and without taking another breath, I removed my Kevlar and placed it between my knees, took the gas mask out of its sheath, put it over my face and cleared it in nine seconds. It was just a drill. The purpose was to remind Army Combat Pool No. 1 that a war zone is a dangerous place. The assembly area was within range of Iraqi artillery, and some of those shells could contain chemical agents. Anything could happen up here at a moment's notice. Even drawing a breath of air was no longer taken for granted. Anytime somebody yelled a warning, or an alarm or horn sounded three times, it was mandatory to mask up. Going to war with the Airborne meant taking some of the same risks.

"I don't worry about getting shot. I can dodge a bullet, but I can't dodge gas," said one sentry, Specialist 4 Spencer Klemen, 19, of Honor Lake, Mississippi.

Colonel Rokosz ordered the gas drill to drive home the point of being alert at all times from now on. We were right on Iraq's doorstep. Off to the north was the border, visible in daylight because it consisted of the only apparent geological feature on this moonscape of wilderness. It was an escarpment, a ridge-like thumb of land that was as high as a football field is long. It looked like a mountain. The Iraqi defensive line didn't extend this far, but the Airborne would have to take that hill when the time came. The brigade already knew the Iraqi soldiers were out there.

"We're picking up windshield glints to the north from Iraqi vehicles," the colonel said. Failure to camouflage properly had given away their presence. Already standard on Army vehicles were pieces of burlap placed over the windshields. You could still see out, but there wouldn't be any reflections of sunlight to tip anybody off.

Where exactly are we?

"Put it this way, I don't smell the ocean," the colonel said coyly.

In truth, no other Army unit was this far north or this far west, but that was a secret.

How will you take the high ground?

"I'm banking on the ground stuff being as effective as the air technology," said the colonel, who had studied political science at Loyola University and had taught at West Point. "I have fast-movers (attack jets) on call any time we want it."

What's the plan?

"The objective now is to dig in and get everybody up here," he added. "It's time to earn our money."

Then we left headquarters, driving out to visit the scouts of the infantry battalions deployed on the northern perimeter closest to the escarpment. Disciplined and smart, scouts are chosen from the ranks as the best of the best. Lest they give away their positions by talking, they communicate with hand signals. Even whispers are rare because sound travels far in the desert. Radio silence was to be broken only in extreme emergencies. An update was given in hushed tones.

"There's nothing out there between Iraq and us but a lot of cold air and rocks," said Major Carl Horst, 35, of Seattle, operations officer for the 2nd Battalion.

Captain Mike Lerario of Damascus, Maryland, the commander of Delta

Company of the 2nd Battalion, said his soldiers were arrayed in the open desert to provide a line of defense for brigade headquarters.

"Our mission is to see and not be seen. We're like the old cavalry on the western frontier. We're a picket line of sorts to provide early warning," the captain said.

A war of nerves had begun for the Junkyard Dogs of Delta Company. "We know the Iraqis are there. We're keeping a low profile. If you want to stay alive, don't advertise," said First Sergeant James Southerly.

At his post, Staff Sergeant David Angerhofer, 37, of Milbank, South Dakota, said the alert status was high. "We're out in front of everybody. We're the eyes and ears of the battalion. It's an eerie feeling. You don't take anything for granted out here. It's stealth at its utmost," Angerhofer said.

Imagine that, stealth infantry. From now on, paratroopers were on a reverse time cycle. Like desert creatures, they holed up out of the sun during the day and operated in the dead quiet of the inky night. With their night vision goggles or the thermal sights of their antitank missiles, they could spot a man from three miles away. They had already mapped an Iraqi border post and the remains of an ancient frontier fort. The desert was so quiet that you could hear a man cough from 50 yards away. Lights and noise were kept to a minimum. Hot coffee was a bygone luxury. Building a fire was out of the question, even though it was cold, because an open flame could be spotted from miles away.

The previous night, temperatures had dropped to 34 degrees, which was more than twice as low as any temperature in Abqaig and almost 100 degrees colder than the high heat of August. It felt even frostier with frigid blasts of north wind swooping unchecked across the wasteland. Not wanting to lug around their sleeping bags, the scouts slept in parka liners. And lacking gloves, they wore green Army socks as mittens over their hands.

"Travel light, freeze at night. When I woke up, I couldn't feel my toes at all," said Specialist 4 Jason Rekers, 20, a scout from Pleasant Valley, Iowa.

We left the front to discover the paratroopers digging holes in the ground. The fighting positions served as places to live and as a defense against Iraqi incursions. The only sound interrupting the stillness was the scrape of shovels. Every few yards, infantrymen from lowly privates to officers, from trigger-pullers to the chaplain, scooped out sand. Infantrymen have been digging in for as long as there have been wars, and these paratroopers we're continuing the tradition.

"Normally, you can't get them to pick up a shovel. Now they're fighting over the goddamn thing," Colonel Rokosz said. "You should keep digging until somebody can't find you. It's a mental thing. It puts you in the right frame of mind."

Some troops filled sand bags to build bunkers. There is, of course, an Army manual on such things. The ideal bunker is dug to the depth of the armpit of the tallest man. Then four layers of sandbags are placed over roof beams for maximum protection. The bunkers would be improved daily if a board or scrap of wood could be found to reinforce it.

"If it will save my life, I'll be more than happy to fill sandbags," said Private First Class Bryan Richards, 20, of Victorville, California.

Private Gregory White, 20, of Los Angeles, didn't need anybody to tell him to dig his hidey-hole. In beginning his life as a mole, every shovel of sand could mean saving a limb.

"I'm going to dig until I can't dig no more," White said. "This shovelful means I might save an arm. That shovelful means I might save a leg. Each shovel could save a body part."

The question to ask is, how good do you want a shelter to be to if a round came in. The answer from the ranks was "dig 'em deep so we don't weep."

Even Army Combat Pool No. 1, assigned to live in the supply area of Tactical Assembly Area Hawk, dug in. Using aluminum bowls brought from Abgaig, we scraped out an L-shaped pit as a run-and-dive. In the event of incoming rounds, you run to the hole and dive in.

We had no tent, but CNN's Jim Clancy had the foresight to buy a piece of canvas in Rahfa. We propped it up with a pole and tied down the corners with sand bags. I set up my sleeping cot in a corner and nodded off. In all the time I had been in Saudi Arabia, it had rained exactly once. But wouldn't you know it? After months of unrelenting heat and cloudless skies, a cold rain fell that night. It wasn't a gentle rain either. This was wind-whipped, sideways rain, and it began to soak through my sleeping bag.

Fumbling in the dark, I gathered my gear and got permission from Major Ennis to sit in the Humvee. He accompanied me, and as the driving rain pelted the windshield, we passed the time talking. He probably thought I was ready to beat it back to the hotel in Dhahran. I reassured him that even though I was from New York City, I had grown up on a Pennsylvania farm at the end of a dirt road. Camping out was routine. In what used to be a coal mining region with company towns, I wasn't a stranger to outhouses either. I also had basic Army training to fall back on. He volunteered that he had specifically requested an Associated Press reporter for this assignment because it was the news agency with the biggest reach, and paratroopers wanted their story told. Anyway, we made it through to morning, and I wasn't alone in my misery. The weather had tested the troops.

"It was one of those nights you just try to survive, but guys adapt. The other side is going through the same thing we are," said Captain Brad Nelson, the brigade adjutant.

Hard-core infantrymen shrugged off the wet and the cold. Actually, the grunts with wings on their chests embraced it, because a grunt can hack it.

"It's more miserable for the Iraqis. They're fair weather soldiers. When it's cold, nasty and miserable, that's infantry weather. That's what we like. If it ain't raining, we ain't training," said Specialist 4 John Rowe, 27, of Red Bank, New Jersey. He was grinning as he spoke.

A chance to warm up was provided. In a supply tent that had a portable Coleman gas stove, I heated up a canteen cup of water to warm a spaghetti MRE for breakfast, then used the hot water to make a cup of instant coffee. Under the circumstances, it was quite a luxury.

Later, using the side mirror of the Humvee, I shaved with a disposable razor. Nicks and scrapes bloodied my face. With that field shave, I shed blood for my organization.

Probably out of pity, Major Ennis and Captain Esarey drove us back through the desert to Rahfa while arrangements were made to procure a tent for more reliable sleeping quarters. The town had a mosque, a shopping district, a gas station and a motel with a coffee shop. Believe me, no cup of coffee was more appreciated. Condensed canned milk was available too. It was much better than the powdered non-dairy creamers in the MRE packs. On the limited menu was pita bread with halava, a sweet confection made from sesame paste. I scarfed down as much as I could. Sharing the warmth of the cafe were some tough-looking Bedouins in heavy robes carrying loaded AK-47s. Were they Saudis or Iraqis, or both? Bedouins don't recognize borders.

The coffee and the sweet bread triggered a call of nature. Although there was a restroom in the back, it lacked toilet paper and a sit-down commode. Still, straddling a water trough and squatting was better than having to use the slit trench in the field. For wiping and flushing, a rubber hose provided water.

With rain falling all day, we rented rooms at the Rahfa Inn. Under normal circumstances, it would have been a fleabag joint. Now it was the Waldorf-Astoria. I can't say the mattress was without lumps, or that the blankets didn't smell like camel hide, but the room had a shower with hot water. Outside, a herd of goats occupied the courtyard. We were already joking about coming into town for a date with Baaa-bara or Shirrrr-ley, and the punch-line was, "Why did you choose the ugliest goat." In the morning, the call to prayer from the Rahfa mosque was a wake-up call. Captain Esarey was pulling guard duty, walking the hallway with pistol in hand.

In one of the stores I bought a portable electric razor and a pack of batteries. I also scored a pair of brown cotton gloves to warm my hands.

Life improved immensely by the time we returned to Tactical Assembly Area Hawk. From somewhere in the supply chain, two Bedouin tents had been requisitioned and erected. They stuck out like sore thumbs against the olive drab Army tents in the supply area, but at least they kept out the wind and the rain. A kerosene heater was obtained too. It gave off enough heat to ward off the chill, and it was great for heating water for coffee and or to warm up the MREs. I was still brushing my teeth out of my canteen cup, but I was no longer in danger of needing a blood transfusion by shaving with a disposable razor. Although the electric shaver didn't provide the closest shave, it kept the whiskers trimmed enough so that the rubber gas mask would seal on my skin.

On one side of my cot, I rigged my length of rope as a clothesline. The

Army sleeping bag was a lifesaver. It had a hood, and when it's zipped up, the only open space is a slit for the lips so you can breathe. It makes one look like a mummy.

We built a new and improved bunker too. Sand bags were provided, and with the help of Captain Esarey's entrenching tool, we spent a day filling them to reinforce the sides and the roof. The new shelter was passable. During one alert at 3:30 in the morning, eight of us squeezed inside and got through the hours without incident. Like Major Ennis kept saying, it just don't get no better than this.

CHAPTER 27
A Clearer Picture

Waiting for the ground war to start does not mean sitting around. While operating within artillery range of the Iraqis in the most desolate place on Earth, the Airborne is aggressively doing night combat patrols to prep the battlefield. I just got back from my first such experience, and it's a real education. Squads of infantry are going out beyond the forward observation posts to get a better picture of what's between them and the dwindling distance to the border, and they're laying down a telephone wire to establish secure communications. The unit that drew the line in the sand is now laying a line in the sand. The specifics of the ongoing mission can't appear in a pool report because it involves operational security, but I'm keeping the details in my notebook for later. A night patrol is kind of surreal. It was so dark at one point that I couldn't see my hand in front of my face. Some of my notes look like they were written in Arabic. Or Sumerian. Then the moon came up and bathed the sand in an eerie light. Light from the sun reflects off the dead surface of the moon, bouncing down in such strength it reflects off the desert floor. In the reflection of a reflection, you can see your shadow at night. With no man-made light visible in any direction, the cosmos becomes a blanket of stars and constellations.

Rules of engagement were spelled out in a briefing conducted by Major Ralph Delousa, 39, of Pemberton, New Jersey, the operations officer of the 1st Battalion. "This is no drill. This is for real. There are bad guys out there. Shoot to kill," Delousa told those going out. What followed was the sound of charging handles sliding back on cold steel to chamber bullets in infantrymen's rifles, a sound that gets a lot of attention. A final inspection was done before troops ventured out into the open.

"Did you oil your weapon today? Might have to use it tonight," Lieutenant Joseph Sacchetti, 28, of Philadelphia, the leader of a scout platoon, asked one of his troops.

Venturing outside the wire to get information is what the Army calls active reconnaissance. After months of being deployed, those going out on patrol welcome the chance to inch forward even if the painstaking work does not involve direct contact.

"We're taking it to them now," said Sergeant Pana Giannakakos, 27, of Chicago.

On patrol, soldiers press across No Man's Land to creep as close to the escarpment as they can. Protected by tank-killing missiles mounted on Humvees, squads on foot are uncoiling a telephone wire spooled in the back of a Humvee. They bury the wire as they go. A wire offers more secure communications than a radio for reports back to brigade headquarters, but there is a risk. If the wire is discovered, the Iraqis can trace it right back to Tactical Assembly Area Hawk. As an extra layer of precaution, infantrymen slather their faces with camouflage paint. Orders are to avoid contact, but if fired upon, they can return fire.

The night desert parka is the Army's best fashion idea since the invention of the field jacket. With its insulated lining, the parka was as good as it gets to protect from the night chill. Long underwear helps too.

To defeat the darkness, troops had night vision goggles and the infrared scopes of long-range weapons. Infrared scopes pick up heat signatures. The internal heat of an enemy soldier or a running engine shows up as a red blotch on a screen. Technology meant that the grunts owned the night. The scopes are so sensitive that the red dots of mice scurrying around on the desert floor could be seen from a distance of a thousand yards.

Specialist 4 George Johnson, 24, of Dallas, Texas, watched four Iraqis in his scope for four hours one night, but the orders were not to engage unless fired upon first.

"I wanted to fire them up, but we weren't supposed to give away our position. I want to get them before they get me. Just my luck they'll come back the next night and get me," Johnson said.

The patrols operate with strict noise and light discipline. Two armies are within shouting distance of each other, but there's nary a sound.

"We're already about as close as you can get without paying taxes on the other side," Captain Esarey said.

No response from the Iraqis yet.

We are totally cut off from the rest of the war, and from the world for that matter, except for the short-wave radio that picks up the BBC news updates every hour on the hour. It's like the old days when families would gather around the radio to get the news.

The highlights of a news conference given eight time zones away in Washington by Colin Powell, chairman of the Joint Chiefs of Staff, were just broadcast. Unlike the incremental escalation of Vietnam, he said this war would be fought with overwhelming force from the opening shot.

"Our strategy in going after this army is very, very simple. First, we're going to cut it off, and then we're going to kill it," Powell announced. "I'm not telegraphing anything. I just want everybody to know we have a tool box that's full of tools, and we brought them all to the party."

Powell also added that, unlike Vietnam, there would be no body counts to measure the progress of the war. That was received as good news by the Airborne. Body counts are a poor way of measuring progress.

Also in the news, Iraq has answered the bombing campaign by launching Scud missiles against Israel and Saudi Arabia. A weapon of pure terror, the Scud is ineffective against troops dispersed over wide areas in the desert, but if one hit a city, it would cause some damage and strike fear in the heart of the citizenry. Patriot missiles, a bullet designed to shoot down another bullet, were arrayed to intercept Iraq's most successful offensive weapon. Paratroopers prayed that Israel would stay out of the war. It must have worked. For the first time in its history, Israel relied on another country, the United States, for its security. And that security came with a price.

It was reported that Colonel David Eberly, the pilot I had met at the Al's Garage airfield, and his weapons systems officer, Major Thomas E. Griffith, had been shot down and were being held as prisoners of war. War becomes personal it affects somebody you know.

Eberly's F-15E Strike Eagle, on a mission to seek out Scuds in western Iraq, was rocketing along in the night sky. Man and machine operated as one, true masters of the air. Then the Iraqis launched two surface-to-air missiles. Eberly eluded the first one, but the second SAM found its target. Eberly ejected and fell to earth under his parachute. He almost made it to safety before a ground patrol captured him.

Captured pilots were being forced to read statements by their captors. One method to get Eberly to cooperate was to put a gun to his head while demanding that he confess to being a war criminal.

Eberly refused to give in. The Iraqi squeezed the trigger. There was a metallic click, but the weapon wasn't loaded. Eberly had given himself up for dead but lived to see it through to liberation.

"Once you go through that, it's downhill," Eberly said after the war.

In addition, the carrier *Saratoga* had casualties beyond Michael Scott Speicher, and each one seemed personal. Lieutenant Robert Wetzel and his navigator/bombardier, Lieutenant Jeffrey Norton Zaun, were conducting a strike against the H-3 airfield in western Iraq when ground fire struck their two-man A6E Intruder. A graduate of the Naval Academy, Zaun was beaten by his captors and forced to make a propaganda tape. The Iraqis also announced that American POWs would be used as human shields.

The *Saratoga* lost another plane three days after Wetzel and Zaun went down.

"That's the rules of war. We lose friends, good friends, and we still go forward and meet the objective, and we intend to win," said Chief Petty Officer Bill Young, chief of the Saratoga's flight deck.

There was also a report that Bob Simon and his CBS crew were taken prisoner. Trying to get around the restrictions of the pool system, they drove into Kuwait to film a news segment. They were captured, charged as spies and sent to a prison in Baghdad.

It's unwise to take unnecessary risks, even for reporters.

I'm on a C-130 out of Rahfa and bound for Dhahran, with our land vehicles. We're on our way back because the wife of CNN's Jim Clancy is about to deliver their child. A new CNN crew is being transferred in, and our land vehicles are along for the flight because we're going to drive back. The military can do anything. I got some good intel, however, while waiting for the flight as the Air Force crew measured gross vehicle weights to balance the load.

Rahfa is also the new home of an armored French force called the Dauget Division. The name translated to small deer, and the firepower of the unit, technically the 6th Light Armored Division, included tank guns mounted on wheeled vehicles and Gazelle helicopter gunships. The Second Brigade of the 82nd Airborne would be fighting alongside a division of soldiers from America's oldest military ally. Ever since World War II, conventional wisdom carried a low opinion of the French, but their soldiers looked first-rate. The French Foreign Legion is with us too. American paratroopers and French legionnaires could be fighting shoulder to shoulder. The Legion was an all-volunteer force too. One legionnaire who spoke English was a guy from Brooklyn — there's always a guy from Brooklyn — who joined the Foreign Legion to forget a lost love. I could relate to his pain and suffering. The French and the Americans were also doing what soldiers always do, trading goods with each other. The French would trade their pre-packaged rations for American centerfolds, and the paratroopers would trade their MREs for pictures of French porn stars.

Back in Dhahran, I studied the big map on the wall in the AP office to pinpoint the exact location of Rahfa. It was about 200 miles due south of Baghdad and closer to the Iraqi capital than to Kuwait City. Sizing up the distances and remembering what I had heard in conversations with soldiers, I thought we just might be going to Baghdad. Now that would be a mission.

That night, I had a dream that the brigade parachuted into Baghdad and apprehended Saddam Hussein at the Presidential Place. In the dream, I jumped too. To break the news to the rest of the world, I subverted the pool system by locating a pay phone and dictating a news bulletin to New York that would make all the bells ring.

A little knowledge is a dangerous thing.

CHAPTER 28
Pucker Factor

Wednesday, January 20. A crisis involving my sleeping bag was resolved without bloodshed, but it was a close call. The new guy from CNN, invited into the tent to get the lay of the land at Tactical Assembly Area Hawk, was sitting on my cot when he opened a ham slice MRE and spilled the juice on my bag. He might as well have doused it with a drum of toxic sludge. The Airborne officers were appalled. You can't fuck with a man's stuff out in the field, especially his sleeping bag. To remedy this egregious breach of field etiquette, he surrendered his newly issued bag that hadn't been slept in yet, and he got the one with the smelly MRE juice in return. Fair exchange. A man's mummy bag is his castle.

February 2. One of the fundamental duties of a solider is guard duty. No matter how many years it had been since basic training, I could still recite the general order: "I will guard everything within the limits of my post and quit my post only when properly relieved." Out here, those on guard duty were the first line of defense. So I put in a request, which Major Ennis granted, to pull guard duty with the troops at night in the desert. It was more than I bargained for.

At dusk, I was driven to the outpost of a five-man infantry squad positioned between brigade headquarters and the night patrols inching forward while laying the wire. Each man in the squad would stand guard for two hours while the others slept. Sergeant Kevin Barrett, a 23-year-old squad leader from Scranton, Pennsylvania, had the first watch and didn't mind the company as he peered north toward the escarpment.

Speaking in hushed tones, Barrett thought back to the day in August when the Second Brigade was called out to deploy. Troops had expected to be part of a readiness exercise after the brigade had assumed the role of being on call. Alerts in the middle of the night were as much a part of life as making a dozen training jumps a year or a completing a 25-mile road march at night in the rain. Barrett had been in the Army for six years and was following the footsteps of an uncle who had parachuted into combat with the 101st Airborne Division on D-Day in 1944. Barrett and his wife, Darethy, had recently purchased a three-bedroom ranch home in Fayetteville but hadn't moved into it yet. Their first wedding anniversary was September 6, and they were anticipating the birth of their first child. Barrett, who had attended all of his wife's visits to the doctor, had first heard the baby's heartbeat in March. When the phone rang informing him of an alert, Barrett figured it was a training drill.

"I kissed my wife and told her I'd be back in the morning," he said. "She'll never fall for that one again. I'll never forget the look on her face."

Six months of uncertainty later, he was swept up in a war, thousands of miles away from home, and unsure when he would return. He had never slept in the house he had bought. He had only seen his newborn son in a photograph, which he kept in his uniform pocket.

"I want to get out of here as soon as possible," Barrett whispered. "Get it over with and get out of here. I'd rather do it now than have my son have to worry about it. We're beyond the point of no return. There's only one way to go now. That's straight ahead. I wish we'd get the show on the road and get it over with. I'm tired of sitting here. I'm surprised they haven't hit us with artillery. They have to know we're here."

The desert at night can put a man in a reflective mood. And what did Sergeant Barrett reflect on?

"I just miss my wife. Getting off work and having her there to rub my back, cook my dinner. I know this hurt her when I had to leave. She wanted me to be there when the baby was born. I wanted to be there. A phone call in the middle of the night and I was gone. I worry about her constantly," Barrett said.

A chew of Red Man tobacco was one of his few luxuries, especially since the cans dried out quickly in the desert. He hadn't changed clothes or showered in two weeks. Home for him and his squad were the holes they dug. Their crapper was a wooden board placed across two sandbags.

Barrett had learned to search the night sky for spy satellites, fighter jets heading north and the contrails of B-52 bombers sent to soften up Iraqi positions. He pointed out a formation of three of the Stratofortresses on their way to a target.

"The more of those things I see going north, the better I feel," Barrett said. "Go get some."

Personal feelings aside, he was clear on the mission — to eliminate a madman before any more damage could be done.

"This guy is definitely insane. I think we'd be in for some real nasty times if he ever got his hands on some nuclear weapons," Barrett said. "He must know he's going to lose. I'd like to see him put out of the way. I'd like to see him turned over to the Israelis. I don't think the Iraqis realize the kind of beating they're going to get when the ground war starts. I don't have anything against the Iraqi soldiers. There's nothing stopping them from putting up their hands, but if they're going to be shooting at me, I'm going to be shooting back. I plan on making it home, and I plan on making it back with my whole team intact. I owe it to them. The only thing that really worries us is the gas threat. I hope to God he doesn't use gas. I keep my mask handy. I sleep with it right behind my head."

Barrett shared a piece of deer jerky sent to him by his father in Pennsylvania. He talked about how he loved to hunt and fish back home in Scranton. During the chilly watch, his muscles ached and his joints stiffened. At least the wind cut down on the flies. One develops a real appreciation for grunts by enduring some of the same challenges they face.

"It can be a long two hours when you're sitting here shivering. In the rain, you just want to crawl under a poncho, but you can't. The last half hour is the toughest. I can hear my sleeping bag calling my name," Barrett said.

His two-hour watch complete, Barrett woke up his relief. "Don't start nothing. I want to get some sleep," Barrett said.

Guard duty can be like war itself — long stretches of inactivity interrupted by a few moments of alarm. Sure enough, I had just hit the sack when explosions, gunfire and general commotion jolted me awake. Red tracers from machine guns and rifles pierced the darkness. Green tracers from the Iraqi weapons could also be seen. Son of a bitch, I go out on guard duty, and a firefight breaks out right in front of me. It could have been a couple of hundred yards away, or it could have been a mile. Distances in the desert were hard to judge. Two anti-tank missiles were fired. Inexplicably, they bounced off the sand and skipped into the sky, missing whatever Iraqi target they were aimed at. Flashes of light indicated that some machine gun rounds had bounced off an armored target, but other rounds were going harmlessly into the night sky as if someone was shooting at aircraft. In their first action, paratroopers were firing high. The sergeant on watch, Jeffrey McCall, 28, of Freeport, Illinois, chambered a round into his grenade launcher.

"Wake them all up. I figure they want to see this," McCall said.

Everybody in the squad got up to watch the show, but the shooting was over in a matter of minutes. It was impossible to tell what happened. Details were filled in at dawn. Elements of the 4th Battalion had been laying communications wire that night when an Iraqi patrol, comprised of maybe 25 soldiers in two vehicles, moved south. The opposing forces were about 250 yards apart when they noticed each other and opened fire. Battalion commander John Vines said his troops were setting up positions on some higher ground along a designated patrol route. Paratroopers opened up when they saw the Iraqis disperse into attack positions.

"They were clearly trying to set an ambush. We had to engage them to avoid being ambushed ourselves," Vines said. "When they put a force that size on this side of the border, I wouldn't say it was insignificant. Nothing smaller than a battalion could afford to send out that kind of force. They may have something over the border that they're very determined that we don't find out about, or it may be that he was trying to find out information about us. In my personal view, he may be trying to get a cheap victory and inflict some casualties on us."

The order to fire was given by 2nd Lieutenant Mitchell Rambin, 24, of Shreveport, Louisiana.

"We were lucky. You could see the muzzle flashes coming at you from AK-47s and rocket propelled grenades. The Iraqi vehicles drove off. Their soldiers fled on foot," Rambin said.

There were no casualties on either side, but I learned a new phrase. If somebody is shooting at you, the anal sphincter muscles contract to keep you from shitting your pants. It's called the pucker factor. My Old Man could have related to the phrase.

"The pucker factor will be a little bit tighter from now on, but we're ready," Rambin said.

The entire brigade went on full alert. There was suspected tank movement out front, which was probably the French reacting to the shooting. Another Iraqi patrol reportedly passed within 200 yards of a paratrooper patrol, but no contact was made.

At brigade headquarters, Colonel Rokosz figured it was only a matter of time before the two sides started shooting.

"It was inevitable we'd run into each other," the colonel said.

That night, I was typing up the story in the tent when word came over the short wave of a battle in Khafji, 300 miles to the west. It got a lot more attention than a firefight without casualties, and I wondered what I would have been doing if I were still in the pool with the Marines.

South the of Kuwaiti border, the Marines had set up a series of observation points located 12 miles apart, just to make sure the Iraqi army didn't respond as the bombs were falling on them. On the night of January 29, Observation Post 4 picked up movement to the north. Three columns of Iraqi tanks and armored vehicles were on the move, conducting a reconnaissance in force. Nearby, Spike Myerson, the Yale football player who was now a Marine lieutenant, heard the noise and checked the silhouettes against pictures of Iraqi armored vehicles and tanks. They weren't American. Two of the columns were stopped in their tracks by the Marines, but the third managed to occupy the Saudi Arabian town of Khafji.

In the initial confusion, eleven Marines were killed. It was later learned they were killed by their own forces. One Light Armored Vehicle opened fire on a second Marine LAV, killing ten. Another Marine vehicle was struck by a Maverick missile fired by an A-10 Thunderbolt jet.

In Khafji, meanwhile, the Iraqi 5th Mechanized Division had moved south to occupy the town. As fate would have it, two six-man reconnaissance teams from the 1st Marine Division were already in Khafji. They called artillery fire in on their own positions, and one of the Marines was hit by shrapnel. The wound qualified him for a Purple Heart.

A three-day battle kicked the Iraqis out of Khafji. Saudi and Qatari forces, aided by Marine artillery and air support, did the fighting on the ground. Khafji's streets were littered with booby traps and bodies and mangled Iraqi equipment.

During the battle, an Air Force AC-130 gun ship was shot down by an Iraqi surface-to-air missile, killing the 14 Americans on board. In addition, two Army heavy equipment transporters took a wrong turn and ended up in Khafji by mistake. One truck escaped, but those in the second truck were taken prisoner. Among them was Army Specialist 4 Melissa Rathburn-Nealy, 21, of Newaygo, Michigan. She suffered bullet and shrapnel wounds.

From Baghdad, Mother of Battles Radio claimed victory. "They fled in front of us like women and like shepherds roving aimlessly in the desert," said an Iraqi solider who was interviewed about the fighting. In truth, it had been a disaster for the Iraqi army. The engagement came at the price of 25 American dead and two soldiers taken prisoner.

On the short wave, the score of the Super Bowl was announced. The Giants beat Buffalo, 20-19, but no mention was made of Scott Norwood missing wide right on a last second field goal attempt that would have won the game for the Bills. Who cares anyway? It might be America's undeclared national holiday, but it's just a game. Even the Super Bowl takes a back seat to war.

Another report delivered on the short-wave radio involved the apparent defection of the Iraqi air force. Scores of its planes were bugging out and going to Iran, which was Iraq's archenemy in the region. The development was a head-scratcher. For all his bluster, Saddam Hussein wasn't doing well.

"This guy talks like Muhammad Ali and fights like the Bayonne Bleeder," Major Ennis said.

Getting pool reports back to the rear followed an established procedure. I would set the Combat Olivetti on the cardboard sleeve of an MRE box as a crude desk. When completed, the typed sheets would be handed to Major Ennis, who checked to make sure no military secrets were being compromised. Then Combat Pool No. 1 would drive back through the desert to Rahfa and turn east on Tapline Road to a place called Log Base Charlie, where the Army has set up a supply depot that doubled as a collection point for media stories. From there, the stories were flown back to Dhahran on cargo planes that used the paved road as a runway.

Trips to Log Base Charlie came with a fringe benefit. A roadside restaurant in Rahfa offered broasted chicken, which was a welcome change of pace from MREs. It was a chance to repay the public affairs officers by buying hot meals for them too.

The censorship rules, already onerous, tightened even more, however. By reading all the pool reports, intelligence officers serving with the Big Army in Riyadh had figured out the coming battle plan. From now on, I can no longer identify which unit I am with or that I'm located along the Iraqi border. A creative way around the new restrictions was found. The only airborne infantry unit on the line was the Second Brigade, so I refer to them in stories as paratroopers. The media back at the JIB would be able to figure that out, right? The old dateline I used for Combat Pool No. 1 was ALONG THE IRAQI BORDER. The new one is IN NORTHERN SAUDI ARABIA. Battles are fought in many forms.

CHAPTER 29
What They Carried

Saturday, February 9. My appreciation of soldiers is growing daily, especially after sitting up on night ambush on the coldest night yet. And by living among them, I chanced upon the first person in the 82nd Airborne who saw the storm coming. It was such a "eureka" moment that I typed the notes out on a separate sheet of paper. When I get back to the world and write this from the beginning, the first paragraph will start with Sergeant Dale Coggins, 24, of Rocky Mount, North Carolina, a squad leader in the Second Brigade. Pencils have their own definition of triumphs. Finding the beginning of a long story rated an asterisk.

The evening began with a briefing inside the wire at headquarters on the details of the ambush. Iraqi patrols had been observed coming into a shallow valley off the escarpment in an attempt to find out what was headed their way. In a cat-and-mouse exercise that opposing forces engage in prior to combat, the Airborne wanted the Iraqis to know as little as possible. This time, instead of just watching, troops had permission to open fire. Outside a command tent covered with camouflage netting, Major Carl Horst, operations officer of the 2nd Battalion, detailed the positions of a Command Post flanked by Checkpoints 4 and 5 on high ground overlooking the valley to a spot called Objective Mongoose. At each checkpoint would be infantry squads armed with rifles, machine guns, grenade launchers, wire-guided missiles and anti-personnel mines. Squads would have clear fields of fire and would be mutually supporting, meaning that any unlucky bastards probing south that night would be caught in a lethal crossfire. For those who have never seen the Airborne open up with all its weaponry, the volume of fire might just as well come from the Death Star. It's awesome in its power and sickening in the destruction it can bring. Anything that wandered into this kill sack would be toast.

Conditions for an ambush were perfect. The Iraqis operated by the light of the moon, which wouldn't be up until after midnight. The Airborne was equipped with night vision goggles and infrared sights that could pierce the darkness.

"It's darker than the inside of a camel's ass," Major Horst said.

Then he added wryly: "This whole place is the inside of a camel's ass."

The one drawback was the chill. With the blood red ball of the sun disappearing on the western horizon, the temperature dropped like a stone in a pond. It was cold enough to freeze the water in a canteen. In addition to my night desert parka and body armor, I had every piece of clothing on that I owned, including a wool sweater, insulated underwear, a knit cap under my Kevlar and cotton gloves. And I was still cold.

Before leaving the razor wire with his squad, Sergeant Coggins locked and loaded his rifle, then paused to answer a question about this lull between the air war and the invasion.

"I'm sick and tired of waiting. I'm prepared to go to war. The quickest way home is north," Coggins said. "I've got no argument with the Iraqi people. It's just one man who cost me. If there was a mission tonight to take out Saddam Hussein, I'd volunteer to go to Baghdad. I'd do it right now."

The steely resolve in his tone underscored how serious he was. His war had become personal because Coggins had exchanged wedding vows on the same day Saddam Hussein's army invaded Kuwait. He and his bride Donna were minutes away from boarding a Caribbean cruise ship docked in the port of Saint Thomas in the Virgin Islands. Tropical breezes, plentiful sunshine and the blissful days of a honeymoon awaited. All they had to do was walk up a passageway to put the real world in their rear view mirror for a week aboard a floating city.

With his sandy hair and chiseled features that could have come out of central casting as Hollywood's image of a paratrooper, Coggins abruptly changed plans. Every other tourist waiting to board that cruise ship shrugged, but Coggins was part of something bigger than himself. As a member of the brigade that had just gone on call, he was the military equivalent of a first responder who rushes toward a trouble spot when others are fleeing. Nobody told him to, but Coggins remained on shore. He had a gut-feeling something was going to happen and that his unit would be involved. Instead of honeymooning at sea for a week, Coggins and his bride opted to stay at a friend's beach house. No bride wants disruptions on her wedding day, but more than most, Donna understood. In the military, whole families shoulder the burden of a deployment. Her father was a retired sergeant major in the Special Forces and had served eight tours of duty in Vietnam. As a Green Beret, he fought that war with steadfast resolve long after public opinion had soured on a policy gone wrong, and he performed his duties right up to the point someone in higher authority ordered him to stop.

Coggins was flesh-and-blood proof that the butterfly effect in the chaos theory had been set in motion. The flapping of butterfly wings in one part of the world had touched off a chain of events leading up to a military clash. In hurricane territory, a storm first appears on weather radar after a hot blast of air huffs from the plains of Africa and gathers force over the warm waters of the Atlantic Ocean. Like war, a storm follows a path of its own and sweeps people up in it. A different kind of tempest, one that became known as Desert Storm, had swept Coggins and his comrades to the doorstep of Iraq to take the fight to the enemy.

"My bride and I have been apart for so long. I just want to get to know her again. The first four days were great. The last six months have been hell," Coggins said.

With that, he left the wire to hunker down in silence at his fighting position under a canopy of stars.

At one of the checkpoints, Sergeant John Kinkeed, 30, of Reading, California, was asked about the pucker factor while being out on night ambush. "The pucker factor starts when the bullets start whizzing. No use worrying about it. We'd all have ulcers by now," he said.

Sergeant Tim Luther, 26, of Fishersville, Virginia, said the alert level was higher now. "I've been sleeping with my boots on lately. I don't want to have a rude awakening," Luther said.

Making a sound or flashing a light was strictly forbidden.

"It's a tight trap. If they come through that valley tonight, they're in a lot of trouble," Lieutenant John Deedrick of Marietta, Georgia, said before manning his position. "The main thing is to remain calm and let the sensors do their job. The key word is patience. It's like being in a tree stand when you're hunting for deer. You're cold and miserable, but you just have to wait."

We sat out until the moon came up, expecting the guns to open up at any moment. No Iraqi patrols came down. The prey doesn't always cooperate when a trap is set. But those checkpoints were manned every night from then on.

Having exhausted my supply of clean clothes, I performed the mundane but necessary task of washing my dirty socks and underwear the way that sergeant had shown me at Champion Main. Non-potable water for the task was scrounged from a water buffalo parked in the supply area. Detergent was borrowed. The waterproof bag designed to hold a sleeping bag was filled and shaken vigorously. When the wash cycle was complete, I wrung out the contents and hung them on the wires that anchored the tent to the ground. Although the sun and the wind dried the wash, the items became encrusted with a thin layer of blowing sand. That meant shaking the clothes out to get rid of the grit. My shorts and socks were dirtier than before I washed them.

Ever since encountering that sergeant on the firing range who kept his wife's panties tucked inside his Kevlar, I was asking paratroopers what personal item they carried to war as a reminder of the world they had left or some good luck charm to get them through.

Steven Swanson, a first lieutenant, had an American flag in one breast pocket, pictures of his girlfriend in the other and an airsickness bag inside his Kevlar helmet.

"When it gets really bad, really cold, and you're really dirty, that flag gives me strength," he said.

And the airsickness bag?

"You never know where you're going to get back on the bird," Swanson said.

Private First Class Mathias Schubert, 20, of Hinesville, Georgia, toted his Bible as a companion. He was a crewman in a light Sheridan tank called Blitzkrieg.

"It's not a good luck charm. It's a my life," Schubert said. "If I'm defending my country, I'm defending God because the Constitution was founded under God. I don't want to go to war, but if I have to, I won't have any problem at that moment. The quickest route home is through Baghdad."

Staff Sergeant David Angerhoffer, 37, of Milbank, South Dakota, carried an inspirational message given to him by a Vietnam veteran. It read: "Freedom for those who fight for it has a special meaning the protected will never know."

Some items had practical use. Major Hank Keirsey, executive officer of the 2nd Battalion, had a beaver pelt inside his Kevlar. Keirsey's wife had sent it to him to warm his pate. He also some blaze-orange cloth that could be worn on the top of his combat helmet when the stuff hit the fan. It would alert Air Force pilots not to drop any bombs on a friendly trooper.

Lieutenant Terrance Rosales, 28, of Tacoma Park, Maryland, was already deployed to the desert when his child was born October 30. His talisman was a baby outfit and a lock of hair his wife had sent over with the news of the birth.

Some soldiers carried more than one item. Sergeant Gary Warsham, 28, of Fort Worth, Texas, had a teddy bear sent to him by his 4-year-old child and an anointed cloth from his Baptist church. His other keepsake was a rattlesnake tail liberated from a serpent he caught in the desert.

The item could be a war souvenir. One paratrooper kept a flattened Pepsi can with Arabic writing on it, just to prove he had been here.

Reminders of the opposite sex were favored by single young men. Specialist 4 Christopher Bolnar, 21, of Lexington, Kentucky, used to carry his girlfriend's crotchless perfumed panties. "I had to send them back. It was just too much," he said. Now he keeps pictures of Playboy centerfolds, which are illegal to have in the kingdom, but the religious police aren't this far north, and the mail system worked so well that current issues were available. "See this?" he said, pointing to the pink intricacies of Miss February's anatomy. "That's what I'm fighting for."

The business of war was never far from their thoughts. The most angelic face I'd seen on a paratrooper belonged to Specialist 4 James Alexander, 24, of Atlanta. But inside his Kevlar, he carried five aces of spades as death cards.

"I'm a killer, sir," he said. "We supposed to tuck the cards behind their ears."

For sheer attitude, my favorite was the calling card of Specialist 4 Richard Jones, 22, of Norfolk, Nebraska. It said: "I am an American paratrooper. If you are recovering my body, kiss my cold, dead ass."

Although each item had personal importance, special meaning was attached to the blue ribbon carried by Sergeant Darrin Ashley, 24, of Fayetteville, North Carolina. A squad leader in the 1st Platoon of Delta Company, he drew strength from the Congressional Medal of Honor awarded posthumously to his father during the Vietnam War. His mother hoped it would protect him.

Sergeant First Class Eugene Ashley Jr., on his third tour of duty, was killed February 7, 1968, in Quang Tri Province during the Tet Offensive. His name is etched in granite on the Vietnam Memorial and the wall of honor at the Airborne Museum in Fayetteville. A member of the 5th Special Forces Group (Airborne), SFC Ashley was the senior adviser of a hastily assembled force that set out to rescue brother soldiers at Camp Lang Vei. While directing air strikes and artillery support, he was hit by a rocket and by machine gun fire. Despite his wounds, he mounted a fifth and final assault on a hilltop where his comrades were pinned down. Some survivors of the camp did escape through the avenue created by Ashley. Ashley didn't make it, though. He drew his last breath saving others. His body was never recovered. His Medal of Honor citation noted his gallantry and intrepidity. He was 36 when he died. In his hometown of Wilmington, North Carolina, the high school bears his name.

"I was two years old at the time, so I never knew him," Darrin Ashley said. "My mom never talked about him that much. She hated talking about it, but she gave the medal to me because I would cherish it more than my four brothers. I joined the Airborne because I always wanted to be like my father. I can follow in his footsteps, but I can't fill his shoes. When I feel down, if I'm having problems, I just look at the medal and it motivates me. He was the kind of man who didn't give up. If he thought he could do something, he'd keep trying and keep trying. Drive on. If one of my guys was trapped, I'd try to get him out too. My father is my hero. I was proud of what my father did even if they didn't know what they were fighting for in Vietnam."

And what was he fighting for in the desert?

"We're fighting to protect the American way of life," Ashley said.

How did his mother feel about him being in the middle of all this, given what happened to her husband?

"My mom's behind me. She's behind this. She thinks it's right. There's a picture of my father on the wall of the JFK Special Forces Center in Fort Bragg. She's never gone to see it. Being a soldier is my job. It's why I came into the Army — to protect my country. I plan on going to Ranger school when I get back, then enter the Special Forces like he did," he said.

Sergeant Ashley had a wife and a little boy named Eric Eugene.

"I want him to choose his own life. If he does follow in my footsteps, I'd be happy," he said. "I just want to see my wife again."

What they carried meant the world to them.

I was zippered up like a mummy deep inside my sleeping bag one night, sound asleep but with my gas mask handy. An alarm sounded three sharps blasts, the warning for a chemical attack. "Gas! Gas! Gas!" someone yelled. Fearful of taking another breath, I unzipped my bag from the inside, fumbled for my mask, put it over my face and cleared it. There is nothing like the sensation of a cold rubber mask over your face at three o'clock on a chilly morning. A sensor that had been set up to detect poisonous gas had started all the commotion. The alarms spread, and I sat upright on my cot, staring straight ahead. After 30 minutes of tense waiting, the all-clear was sounded.

I hesitated before taking off the mask. How does anyone know it's OK? That first unmasked breath seemed chancy. Nobody even knew for sure if gas had been used. One possibility was that when the batteries in the chemical alarms get low, they work like a smoke detector and trigger the alarm. Whatever, even the involuntary act of breathing can't be taken for granted out here.

The Army doesn't travel with anything it doesn't need, but it prepares for everything, even casualties. The Second Brigade's supply tail included 250 body bags and a refrigerated van to serve as a temporary morgue. Any paratroopers killed in action would be placed in the morgue until they could be shipped to Frankfurt, Germany, and then on to the military mortuary in Dover, Delaware. Tucked away in one corner of Tactical Assembly Area Hawk was the 54th Graves Registration Company, based in Fort Lee, Virginia, home of the Army's Quartermaster Corps, the sustainer of armies. I did the math. Army planners were prepared for ten percent of the brigade to be killed in action.

The Graves Registration Company also had a supply of small olive-drab bags, known to soldiers as death bags. The tag said Parts Not Recoverable, Deceased Military Personnel, Personal Effects. The bags were for watches, rings, money and photographs of those who might be blown to smithereens or incinerated by a bomb blast. It's a time-honored tradition not to leave the dead behind, but it's not always possible to recover every body. Casualties would be identified by their dog tags, tattoos, scars or personal effects in their wallets — driver's license, Social Security number, credit cards, check books, pictures. They gave me one of the bags. It was a reminder of the risks.

"This is the most important job in the Army. We're the guys who send our soldiers home," said Specialist Aaron Houston. "We're the ones who get them out of here so their families can have them back again. All the parents and relatives don't accept the fact their son or daughter might be dead until they see the remains. If I'm able to send them home, I feel like I've done something for them and their families."

He planned to send each one back with a personal prayer.

"I ask the Lord to take of the soldiers on their journey home, the last leg," Houston said. "I also say a prayer each and every night that we don't have this war."

While working at the mortuary processing center in Dhahran earlier in the deployment, Houston handled the remains of 40 GIs and sailors killed in accidents before the bombs started dropping.

"We treat them as if they were unconscious. We're going to send them home in the best condition possible," Houston said.

His line of work comes with its own price. No matter how much time passes, the faces of the dead stay etched in his mind.

"They don't haunt me. I just remember who they are. I see their faces,"

Houston said. "It's better if you don't have personal feelings. You may just break down."

His colleagues had similar feelings. "Some things you see with your eyes get recorded in your brain and might stay there the rest of your life. I still remember the first guy I worked on. I remember his last name..." said Specialist 4 Carlos Toros, 37, of Puerto Rico.

While encamped in the desert, the Graves Registration Company found a practical, if not macabre, use for the body bags. They slept in them. A body bag protected them from the dust, and the extra wrapping helped keep them warm.

Because we had been out here so long, Log Base Charlie was more than a place to drop off pool reports. Like the paratroopers, I was starting to get mail and messages from the rear. One letter arrived in a blue AP envelope marked private and confidential. I figured it was the company brass thanking me for putting it all on the line to get this story. Instead, it was from the treasurer's office. The bean counters wanted me to account for the $10,000 advance I had taken out before I left New York, and to file my expense account. It was a new year, and they wanted to clear the books. Yeah, I'd get right on it, first chance I get.

Bureaucrats can find you anywhere. So can assignment editors. I also got a request from New York to write a story on mail. And because the ground war was still on hold after weeks of the air campaign, editors wanted a story on the day in the life of a combat unit. Can do.

CHAPTER 30
Bedouin Bob and The Nasty Boys

Thursday, February 14. Another trip to Dhahran is scheduled to switch out the CNN crew again. A family emergency had come up, and the guy with the ham slice sleeping bag had to return to the States. I'm staying behind. It might sound crazy to pass up a chance to get back to the world, sleep in a hotel bed with clean sheets and grab some laundered clothes, but I have stories to do. Besides, I didn't want to miss anything. An artillery strike has been ordered tonight, the first time the big guns would fire into Iraq. The calling card might provoke a response. I had come too far to miss the start of the ground war.

"See you when we get back, Bedouin Bob," Major Ennis said.

It was the first time I heard that name, and it feels like a field promotion from Pencil. The major had given me my *nom de guerre*. You have to be a grunt to have a war name.

A five-ton truck picked me up outside the tent for a supply run along a rutted trail of sand and rock. The driver was a reservist from a transportation company in New Jersey. People who in civilian life had been prison guards, school teachers and truck drivers were now serving the war effort at the front. The driver had been given a set of Airborne shoulder patches too. In the back of the truck was a commodity as vital in its own way as food and water. The cargo was red nylon sacks of hopes, dreams, smiles, fantasies, yearnings, news from home and everything else a letter might bring.

The mail run was the final leg of a delivery system. Mail by the ton arrived by plane in Dhahran, and the packages addressed to those in the Second Brigade were sorted before being trucked north in 18-wheelers to 82nd Airborne Division headquarters south of Rahfa. From there, the mail was sorted again for delivery to battalions and companies. To get the mail to paratroopers in Tactical Assembly Area Hawk, Army reservists from the 1015th Postal Unit of Michigan City, Indiana, sorted 10 to 15 tons of mail per day at a desert outpost.

"Just one letter can totally change a guy's attitude. It can make the difference between a good day and a bad day. It's just the idea that somebody back there cares," said Sergeant First Class Dennis Lawyer, 36, of Bloomington, Indiana, a U.S. Postal Service Employee who served in a reserve unit based at division headquarters.

It all happened behind the scenes, but nobody in Saudi Arabia worked longer hours every day than the reservists who made sure the troops got their mail. The payoff came when the mail truck arrived at a warming tent deep in the desert and within sight of the escarpment.

"We use a relay system. It's the same as the old Pony Express, except the mail handlers drive Humvees and wear Kevlar helmets," said Sergeant First Class James Ware, 37, of Charlotte, North Carolina, who supervised the distribution point for the Second Brigade.

Traditional mail call had gone the way of the steel pot helmet and bolt action rifle. No more does a gruff sergeant stand up and read off names while an appreciative voice answers, "Yo!" In Desert Storm, a supply sergeant carried the precious stack out to the shadow of the Iraqi border with the day's rations of food and hot water.

"Some guys tell me they'd rather get mail than eat," said Specialist Jimmy Perry, 22, of Pittsboro, North Carolina, the mail handler for his Airborne battalion.

Platoon sergeants gave bundles to the paratroopers while other men gathered around the truck and sifted through envelopes addressed "To Any Soldier."

Four letters arrived for Private First Class Scott Ramsey, 21, of Ripley, West Virginia. His buddies called him the Mail God because his hometown of 6,000 residents was whole-heartedly supporting him with mass mailings. His record haul for a single day was 30 pieces.

"Mail is the only thing that keeps you sane out here. It can make or break your day," said Ramsey as he opened an envelope. "That's what makes the difference, the people back home. We can fight battles. It's the people back home that win wars. When we first got here, I saw grown men crying over the mail. My hometown amazes me. I get so many letters. They told me they've put up yellow ribbons everywhere. The stores are handing out free flags."

Ramsey saved every letter. He shipped boxes of mail back home as a record of his war experience, and he hoped to answer every one after the war.

Mail from loved ones or total strangers delivered cookies, CARE packages, treats and appreciation. The overwhelming volume of stuff was mailed by school kids, church groups, civic clubs, radio stations and veterans organizations such as the Columbus, Ohio, chapter of the Vietnam Veterans of America.

"It makes you feel a little guilty about the soldiers in Vietnam, how roughly they got treated. People haven't forgotten us the way they were forgotten," said Specialist 4 Clayton Blackburn, 25, of Davenport, Iowa.

A letter can make grim duty seem tolerable, even if you're sitting in a fighting hole behind the trigger of a .50 caliber machine gun.

"Getting mail means you're still alive. People still remember you. You got a reason to want to get back home," said Sergeant Ruben Maisonet-Mejias, 38, of Rio Piedras, Puerto Rico.

Outside the warming tent, an Air Force attack jet could be seen making a run to the north. The sleek fighter dropped a bomb, and an orange ball of flame went up when it hit its target. Light travels faster than sound, so it took a few seconds for the shock wave and noise to make its way to the mail tent. The shock wave slapped my trousers against my leg.

"That's mail call for Haji," one paratrooper mused.

The next stop was the desert digs of Bravo Company of the 2nd Battalion of the Second Brigade. By the luck of the draw, I had reunited with The Nasty Boys who I had met at Abqaig.

"If you're crazy enough to be out here with us, I'm crazy enough to let you spend the day," said Captain Ed (Mac) McDaries, the Bravo Company commander.

When paratroopers are forced to wait, they call it race tracking. It's a reference to the oval patterns their planes fly over a drop zone when they have their chutes ready and adrenaline flowing but don't get a green light because of weather or high winds or some other delay. Bravo Company was in a mental state of race tracking. Hunkered down at the front, they had been out here for weeks awaiting orders to attack while the bombs were falling in Iraq and Kuwait.

"It's like the space shuttle. The countdown's been stopped before blast-off," said Private First Class Jerry Henderson, 20, of Caldwell, Idaho.

No one punches a time clock to punch in a war zone. Soldiers are on duty all the time. For my purposes, a typical 24-hour cycle for an infantry company began at dusk. As a crescent moon hung in the sky like a bright slice of melon, paratroopers attended to their tasks.

"Out here, night is when we go to work. We have heightened security at night. All our missions have been at night. It's a reverse cycle," said First Sergeant Michael O'Neil, 35, of Ripley, West Virginia. "We're as ready as anybody can ever be for war. We want to make sure we don't lose our edge. It's easy to become complacent if there ain't bullets coming at you every day."

At 8 o'clock that evening, Staff Sergeant Steven Ahlfield, 24, of Tucson, Arizona, was sighting in an infrared scope for his M16 rifle with the aid of his night vision goggles. The scope put a red dot from a laser beam on a target 100 yards away. If he held the dot steady, he couldn't miss whatever it was he'd be shooting at.

"It's right on. Got to get everything right before I go to sleep. I'd rather spend the extra time now," Ahlfield said.

An infantry company is a single organism made up of squads and platoons. The Nasty Boys think of themselves as rebels, misfits, hell-raisers, life-takers and heart-breakers. They pride themselves in being able to hump harder, faster and longer than other companies. When training at Fort Bragg, they sang cadence to Janet Jackson's song *Nasty* at the top of their lungs just to let everyone else know they were on the march.

"We get the job done, no matter what. They can count on us. We always come through," Ahlfield said.

At 11 o'clock, the artillery strike began. In the northern sky, tracers from a distant skirmish could be seen in the darkness. Clouds had rolled in and rain began to fall. The surreal thing was, with lightning flashing and thunder rumbling, I couldn't tell what was an artillery burst or an act of nature.

"The watch always goes faster when there's a show," said Lieutenant John Black, 24, of Williamsburg, Virginia, keeping his eye on the artillery bursts.

At 3 o'clock in the morning, Specialist 4 Darrin Janish, 21, of Apple Valley, Wisconsin, was awakened for guard duty. Entertaining a visitor, he stood watch from a fighting position dug into the dirt and surrounded by protective sand bags.

"Everybody's got a purpose in life. Mine is to sit in a hole," Janish said. "There's light at the end of the tunnel. Someday, this is going to end."

Just before daybreak, First Sergeant O'Neil shouted an alarm, "Get your asses up! There's Iraqis coming over the hill!" In reality, the Iraqis weren't coming, but his words were an effective wake-up call. Everybody in the company was up and moving.

Soldiers climbing out of their fighting holes looked like prairie dogs emerging from their burrows. Private First Class Matthew DeMeo, 20, of Aguilar, Colorado, grabbed an MRE for breakfast. "Chicken a la disgusting," he said. His rifle was locked and loaded.

After breakfast, troops cleaned the sand and morning mist off their weapons. Private First Class Anthony Johnson, 26, of Waco, Texas, ran a toothbrush and a coating of oil over his rifle barrel.

"I want to make sure she's there for me. She sleeps right there in the bag with me," Johnson said, referring to his weapon as a female companion.

As the sun appeared in the east, paratroopers checked their gas masks, brushed their teeth in canteen cups, shaved in cold water, cleaned their ammo and wrote letters home.

At 7:30 a.m., a paratrooper who had been on guard duty that night headed for his desert home — a poncho-covered hole with a blanket of burlap covering his sleeping bag. His squad leader told him to make sure he changed his socks. The first duty of an infantrymen is to take care of his feet. The trooper was Specialist 4 Daryl Smallwood, 21, of Gainesville, Georgia, the paratrooper who had hand-written a stack of death cards at Abqaig. He remembered me.

"I got in trouble for the death cards. The commanding general chewed my ass out," Smallwood said. "It's not your fault. You wrote what I told you."

He was different now. Hell, we were all different after being out here in the middle of nowhere for all this time. If the desert is a purgative, living on the enemy's doorstep made Smallwood see things in a different light. He was still willing to take the fight to the enemy, but he had no urge to put death cards on dead Iraqi soldiers. All he wanted to do now is make it home alive. Instead of creating death cards, he passed the time listening to his favorite George Jones gospel song, *Jesus, Hold My Hand.* His liked one particular verse: "I will be a soldier brave and true, And ever firmly take a stand. As I onward go and daily meet the foe, Blessed Jesus, hold my hand."

"Listening to that song gives me hope. I've got too much I want to do in life to die in a place like this," Smallwood said.

Even a Nasty Boy could find religion out here.

At 10:10 a.m., a mortar squad headed by Sergeant Darrin Jones was cleaning the 60 millimeter tube with steel wool, a toothbrush and cotton swabs. Members of the squad called themselves Mortar Maggots and referred to infantrymen as Bullet Stoppers, jokingly of course. The Mortar Maggots had honed their edge. All of this waiting had firmed up their resolve.

"We've been sitting here so long it's a psychological advantage. These guys are real hungry to go home. The only way we're going to go home is really do some damage," Jones said.

By noon, the giant heat tab known as the sun radiated enough warmth to defeat the desert chill. Sergeant David Kent, 27, of San Francisco, paused from his study of weapons to eat a ham slice MRE. He took a moment to share his thoughts about the Iraqi infantry.

"I honestly feel sorry for them. The majority of them are victims of circumstance. They may be my enemy, but I have more in common with them as infantrymen than anything else. We're all stuck out here in the desert facing each other, waiting for the fighting and the dying," Kent said.

Clusters of paratroopers gathered around to listen to the news on my short-wave radio.

"Waiting is boring. We wait around and see what doesn't happen today. My favorite word for this place is goodbye. It's a dump. A wasteland," said Sergeant Rich Gonzales, 24, of San Antonio, Texas.

At 2 p.m., Sergeant Tony Bell of Oxnard, California, conducted a drill for his squad members on how to place plastic handcuffs on prisoners of war.

"We're anticipating a lot of them. We expect a lot of them to surrender," Bell said.

At around 3 p.m., the wind shifted and was coming from the north. A sandstorm whipped up. Trillions of grains of sand, each one a tiny sharp dagger, pelted everybody and everything. Troopers donned their eye goggles and wrapped themselves in scarves, lowering themselves into their holes to seek shelter from the storm. No matter what else the 24-hour cycle held, part of it was always in the battle with the environment. Then the cycle started all over again. Another day in the KSA.

My ride arrived, and because of the driving sand, visibility was reduced to maybe twenty yards. We made it back, and with the wind howling like a lost soul, the canvas skin of the Bedouin tent bulged in and out. I buttoned up as best I could and sat on my bunk, alone, my back against the wind. A layer of dust crept inside and settled over everything.

I was about as far from civilization and New York City as you could get. Home was once the City That Doesn't Sleep. Now it's the Place Where Nothing Lives. The desert had sand-blasted away the past and left only the present. There really was nothing to do but think. Solitude is a writer's friend. Bedouin Bob was where he was supposed to be, in the company of The Nasty Boys and an Airborne brigade.

Whether they come from the big cities or small towns nobody's ever heard of, Airborne infantry have an earthy wisdom and gallows humor about them. They're professional soldiers, disciplined and willing to accept the risks, a bunch of colorful characters who represent a true cross-section of America. I just hope I'm up to the task of seeing this through with them.

CHAPTER 31
Apache Strike

Sunday, February 17. Maybe it was just as well no one told us how long we'd be out here. The air war started a month ago, and I've been on Iraq's doorstep for the better part of three weeks without knowing when the invasion would start. The real world is a distant memory. A human being can get used to anything, even living in the desert under the cloud of war.

Within the tactical assembly area, a squad of Airborne Military Police had carved out a baseball diamond. Home plate was a sand bag. The ball was a smooth, potato-sized stone bundled up in an olive drab sock and wrapped with black tape. The bat was a hickory ax handle. Rainouts were unheard of, but sandstorm delays are possible.

The coming battle causes mixed feelings. In their hearts, troops who are tired of waiting just want to get going so they could get the hell out of this wasteland. In their minds, however, they know that being patient means the Iraqi war machine gets weaker by the day. The more the Air Force bombs, the more of them will survive. It's impossible to say how many of their lives have been saved by pilots doing their jobs.

"The wait's been killing everybody, but the Army wants to minimize casualties. Waiting a little longer is worth lives. I'd rather wait a little and let the Air Force soften them up," said Specialist Steve Imus, 23, of Orange Park, Florida.

The troops that first landed in the kingdom back in August have been calling this Operation Desert Wait. The lull isn't made easier by the sameness of the desolate terrain, the cold nights and cold shaves, the disconnect from the rest of the Army and the real world. Impatience is understandable, but it beats the hazards of combat.

"Look at the faces around you and ask yourself if it's better to get home sooner if half the men aren't going to make it. It's more important that we take everybody back," said Lieutenant Buck Dellinger, 24, of Cherryville, North Carolina, the executive officer of an infantry rifle company.

The rigors of living in the desert have made the troops as tough as scorpions.

"Anything it takes, I'll do. All I want to do is go home in one piece," said Specialist 4 Chris Jusiewicz, 20, of Beverly, Massachusetts. He was in the company that guarded the colonel's headquarters.

Even those in the public affairs unit, like Specialist 4 Brannon Lamar of Columbia, South Carolina, learned the value of patience. "I couldn't tell you the day or the date, but I'm not getting shot at, so that's good," he said.

He also saw an opportunity for the parched landscape that was as flat as a K-Mart parking lot. "I've seen graveyards with more life. This place would make a great time share," he joked.

Monday, February 18. The brigade's Apache helicopters have been ordered to make their first strike into Iraq tonight. Maybe the light at the end of the tunnel is a Hellfire. On the flight line were combat-loaded flying machines that looked like giant angry insects. Three companies of the attack helicopters, plus some OH-58 Kiowa scout choppers and Blackhawks for command and control, were poised to strike 50 miles inside Iraq on a combat mission. The commanding officer, Lieutenant Colonel Bill Tucker, 40, of Roanoke, Alabama, gave a pre-launch briefing.

"The idea is to try to come in from where they don't think you're going to come in from," Tucker said. "It's the first time our unit has attacked Iraqi targets. They can't see us at night. We can see them. They can only hear us for a couple of seconds, and we're gone. The Apache is the Mercedes of helicopters."

Ground crews had written messages on the Hellfire missiles that give the Apache its primary killing power.

"I wish Saddam were here to see this. I'd laugh in his face," said Private First Class Robert Adams, 21, of Columbia, South Carolina. "I'd hate to be in his shoes. There's no place to hide. You can run, but you'll die tired."

Private First Class Thomas Nowacki, 21, of Detroit used colored chalk his mother had sent him to write on the Hellfires — *Camel Smoker, Eat This,*

Baghdad Express and the Hallmark-inspired greeting *When You Care Enough To Send The Very Best.*

When the moment came to launch, the turbine engines throttled up. With their blades cutting the air, the Apaches rose and thundered off into the inky black yonder under a blanket of stars. It was two o'clock in the morning.

This night had been chosen because it was the new moon. After the birds had gone, it was so dark I couldn't see my hand in front of my face. I stumbled around in the dark until I bumped into an armed sentry, who led me to a warming tent to wait for the pilots to return. Inside the tent, paratroopers passed the time talking about military history, such as Civil War campaigns or how Chief Joseph of the Nez Pierce Indians commanded the best light cavalry in the world. I found it curious that the hostile territory to the north is referred to as *Injun country*, and the Army's helicopters carry the names of Native American tribes. I crawled into a corner and dozed off.

The Apaches returned at dawn. One of those who participated in the raid was Major Lee Stuart, the executive officer of the aviation battalion. He was the Vietnam vet who talked before the bombing started about how soldiers, least of all, wanted war because they were the ones who bled in battle, and his quote in my pool report was widely disseminated.

"I wasn't going to talk to you back then, but I thought I'd give it one last shot. You wrote it down right," Stuart said. It was as if some wounds had healed.

He was still feeling the adrenaline rush as he walked in the sand. Here was a man who was at peace with himself after coming back from a combat mission in an environment where it was kill or be killed. During the assault, the Apaches knocked out two tanks, one armored vehicle, several trucks and number of bunkers. Return fire was sporadic. No damage was sustained by the helicopters, and there were no American casualties. The mission was a smashing success.

"The air smells good. The cold feels good. It's good be alive," said Stuart, wearing his flight suit and combat boots.

At the foxhole level, there is no spin on what war is like. Stuart gave an unvarnished version of what happens when highly trained men in the highest technology killing machines conduct a raid in the dark of night against an enemy that had no clue what was coming.

"We packed one right up his ass. We dealt him some serious punishment. We caught him totally by surprise," Stewart said. "The Air Force has been after them 24 hours a day. Now all of a sudden, somebody's coming out of the ground after him. They probably got the fear of God put into them. The Apaches rule the night."

Other pilots provided fresh details. Frustration that had been building for six months was released with the chance to do a mission.

"We went in fast and low. They didn't know where this stuff was coming from. It was a hunting party," said Captain Richard Daum, 27, of Fayetteville, North Carolina.

Captain Robert Tuggle, 31, a company commander from Columbus, Georgia, saw a Hellfire hit a tank, which turned into a burning hulk within seconds. He also saw Hellfires hit fuel tanks and a munitions dump, which set off secondary explosions.

"We popped the cherry last night. We got some real good hits. That thing lit up the battlefield," Tuggle said. "It sounds morbid to say it was fun, but it was like playing a video game. We caught them with their shorts down. They were in their sleeping bags. It was a turkey shoot. They were running around like a bunch of goobers. They didn't know which way to run."

Captain Stewart Hamilton, 34, of Kansas, the operations officer for the attack battalion, described the chaos and confusion delivered by a coordinated, devastating attack.

"We used the element of surprise. It was very violent. We did what we wanted to do the way we planned it. We were hand-delivering ordnance," Hamilton said. "The human being is a daytime creature. The Iraqi soldier's living cycle is so screwed up, he could hear us but couldn't see us. I think it scared the daylights out of him."

When the debriefing concluded, I made a request through channels to go on the next Apache mission. "Are you sure you want to do that?" asked combat officers who thought it might be too risky. But hey, during World War II, CBS newsman Edward R. Murrow flew bombing missions over Germany and described the details to his radio audience. I was here to experience what war was like for my readers. While there is no room for a passenger in an Apache, commanders said it might be possible to take me along in the command-and-control Blackhawk. They would let me know.

An invitation was extended to have an MRE dinner at brigade headquarters with Colonel Rokosz and Command Sergeant Major Slocum. I grabbed a diced turkey entree, my personal favorite, and made sure to wear my Kevlar and gas mask, just in case another gas alarm was on the agenda. The colonel and his right-hand man shared a two-man tent that had one prominent decoration, the guide-on for the 325th Parachute Infantry Regiment featuring battle streamers from the trenches of France in the First World War. Now the regiment would fight shoulder-to-shoulder with the French Dauget Division in the desert.

Rokosz showed some gun camera footage of the Apache raid, which went about as well as anyone could have imagined. In casual conversation over dinner, the colonel revealed that he worked crossword puzzles and played chess with Slocum to unwind. And instead of studying military manuals all the time, he lost himself in reading things like Stephen King's *It,* a sci-fi thriller about a monstrous entity that reanimates every so often to terrorize the innocent. The book could have passed as a war metaphor. Then he volunteered something that made my day.

"You're good for morale," Rokosz said.

How do you mean?

The colonel explained that stories from Combat Pool No. 1 were making their way back to Dhahran and eventually into newspapers in the States. Families and friends of paratroopers who hungered for news were reading anything they could get their hands on. Seeing a name and reading a quote meant that a soldier was still alive, which was no small relief. Then the families would write letters to the soldiers saying they felt better seeing the names in the news, and the soldiers felt better after hearing from home.

Good for morale? That's the same thing commanding officers said about

Ernie Pyle during World War II. Pyle's willingness to get down in the dirt with the grunts and write stories about their plight made soldiers feel better because somebody was seeing the war the way they lived it at the foxhole level. I was just doing my job. The challenges of covering this story were many, but even with operational security and a relay network stretching over vast distances, the colonel's remarks were the first validation that stories written down on a manual typewriter in the middle of nowhere were having an impact.

The dinner was symbolic. It was the colonel's way of saying the shit was about to hit the fan.

Wednesday, February 20. The Army provided a special treat. Inside a tent that served as a chow hall, a hot meal of roast beef and green beans was served, complete with a can of soda pop. It really boosted morale, and the enlisted man in charge of dinner was none other than Sergeant First Class Cameron (Hog Head) Woodson, the man with the ax handle I had written about at Abqaig.

He recognized me and pulled me out of the line. The item about his war club had made its way into one of the Detroit papers. Woodson's son had read it, and he wrote a letter saying that he was glad his father was OK.

"You fixed me up," Woodson said.

In appreciation, Woodson reached into a hidden box and gave me a couple of Snickers candy bars. Being on the good side of the cooks is an Army secret. Having two Snickers bars in the desolation of the desert made me feel like a kid in a candy store.

The hot meal was a five-star experience, even if the only way to wash for dinner was using a moist towelette. As we chowed down, I mentioned that we had been up here for so long that the supply train had caught up with us and was providing decent food. A paratrooper straightened me out.

"Uh, negative, sir. The Army serves hot food before we get sent into battle. It's like a last supper," he said.

There were more signs the time was at hand. Brannon Lamar, my buddy in the public affairs unit, sported a fresh haircut called a "high and tight." The sides of his head were basically shaved, leaving a Mohawk-type carpet on the top of his head. He had also written on his helmet "Haji Don't Surf," a play on a line from the movie *Apocalypse Now.*

Every soldier in the brigade had also been told to write out a last will and testament and to make sure beneficiaries were in order on the G.I. life insurance policies. Some wrote their blood types on their Kevlar and clothing to assist the medics in case they were wounded. The longer we were out here, the more we looked like them and talked like them. I wrote my blood type into my helmet too. Being in the company of soldiers at war is quite a learning experience.

CHAPTER 32
The L-Word

Thursday, February 21. Today would have qualified as a reprieve even if it had just meant taking shelter from the storm during the inexorable countdown to the invasion. The opportunity to get a room at the Rahfa Inn arose when the public affairs officers, after giving their best assurances that the war wouldn't start in their absence, were called to division headquarters to receive their final update. For 35 American dollars, I rented a room that at least offered a chance to get cleaned up and attend to some last-minute personal details. Then it turned out to be the kind of day one experiences maybe once in a lifetime. Love appeared like a mirage in the desert.

It's been a month since the air war started, but it seems like a lifetime has passed since we've been camped on Iraq's doorstep a lifetime ago. Back then, Rahfa was an oasis, a dusty way station for long-haul truckers and Bedouins traveling Tapline Road. The Airborne and the French were alone in the desert. Now it was teeming with American troops from other units. Anyone walking the streets could not have helped but notice the long line of soldiers queued up at the outdoor phone booths waiting to make calls. Their shoulder patches identified them as Screaming Eagles, members of the 101st Airborne. It made sense that the 82nd and 101st would be part of a joint operation, just like they were on the parachute drop into Normandy in the earliest hours of D-Day. A French journalist has found this place too. Unbound by the necessity of being on a media pool, he was aware of the French division's presence and was looking for intel on the mission. Secrets wouldn't last very much longer.

Though still rather rustic, a room at the Rahfa Inn at least offered a rare chance to be alone. Although there was no toilet seat on the commode, squatting on a porcelain rim was a much more civilized way to take a healthy dump than balancing oneself on a board placed over a slit trench. The shower was luxurious. It's amazing what hot running water from a shower nozzle and a little soap can do for a person's spirits, especially after sipping hot coffee and gulping down pita bread with halava served in the motel's diner. Washing off the grit and shampooing away helmet hair made for a clean start.

Only one state-controlled station was available on a black-and-white TV, but I hadn't watched the tube for weeks. A newsreader in an Arab headdress noted that King Fahd, the custodian of the two Holy Mosques, hoped that war might be averted through last-minute negotiations by peace envoys. There were also reports the Iraqis, still stubbornly clinging to Kuwait as their own, had booby-trapped something like 700 oil wells in a final act of defiance.

In addition to writing my own letters home, time allowed for keeping a promise made to a soldier. First Sergeant Jim Southerly of Delta Company, the Top Kick of The Junkyard Dogs, asked if I could get a letter out for a buddy. I said I'd be happy to mail it. He wanted me to write it. To his wife, no less. Geez, a last letter home was something only he could pen. But even though he jumped out of airplanes for a living and was prepared to lead his men into the Mother of Battles, he confessed that he had never been good at expressing his feelings. The request was impossible to ignore, and he gave me his home address.

On a sheet of notebook paper, the letter said: "The time is at hand for your husband to do his duty in the military operation that took him away from home many months ago. I am a journalist assigned to his unit, and I can't tell you any specifics for security reasons, but things beyond our control are about to play out. He wanted you to know that even if he couldn't write this himself, his final thoughts are of you and family. The time away from home and the desolation of the desert make one more appreciative of all the good things in life, and nothing is more important to him than you. Please know that he and his men are safe for now and are quietly but diligently performing the job their country has asked them to do. He will be in touch when he can. Knowing you received this will ease his mind in the days ahead. If he can't send you anything else, Jim sends his love."

I signed it and placed it in an air mail envelope. The last letter home is another of those unseen soldierly rituals. It's an insurance policy of sorts, a chance to express a final thought, just in case the worst happens. What it says is less important than why it is written. It unburdens the sender more than anything else. Lots of guys were writing letters home to wives, girlfriends, children, mothers and fathers. Not all of them were mailed. Some letters were written and tucked into shirt pockets or handed over to a buddy, to be mailed as a contingency after the fact, just in case.

Then a knock came at the door. Nobody outside the Airborne knew where I was. In the hallway was a non-commissioned officer from Special Forces, and I was just about to explain that I was authorized to be here.

"There's someone here to see you," the Green Beret said.

Before I could ask who, Sophia appeared from around a corner in the hallway.

"Are you going to invite me in, or do you have company?" she cooed.

What was she doing up here? Didn't she know it was dangerous? How did she find me in this hole in the wall? She explained that she persuaded a unit encamped on the south side of Tapline Road to let her tag along, and with some inside help from her military connections, she tracked me down.

A layer of desert dust covered her from her head to her boots, gritty confirmation that she had been out in the field for a time. We did what journalists do in these moments, filling each other in on what stories we had written and how things were going. Creative people working under stress find outlets for all the emotions they put subtly into their copy. Part of our attraction to each other was the common ground of sharing an appreciation for the human side of war. We also did what human beings do under such circumstances.

"You have to love these guys, don't you?" she said. "They always say sir or ma'am. And they accept what's thrown at them with such humor and willingness."

I had developed my own appreciation for what it takes to be a soldier, even though I never did write that story about the new generation of warriors being led by those who learned some powerful lessons in Vietnam. We also agreed that we weren't that much different from the troops — idealists doing their jobs in the worst of circumstances, putting the mission first, laying it all on the line, trying to operate with grace under pressure. I had never been more heavily invested in a story. Part of it was being in a foreign land, focused on only one thing for so many months. Part of it was living in the desolation of the desert, like being placed inside a sandy terrarium separated from the outside world. Plus, I had never joined the 82nd Airborne to get the story. Instead of just writing stories, I was living them — brushing my teeth in a canteen cup, living under the threat of artillery strikes and gas attacks, going out on night patrols, sitting up all night on guard duty, adapting to the realm of Bedouins and scorpions.

There was an awkward pause.

"I feel like I'm in a car without a steering wheel or brakes speeding out of control on a steep hill," she said. "I don't know where this is going or what will happen, but I want you to know I love you. And you better feel the same way."

She kissed me.

I hadn't shared that emotion with a woman in such a long, long time that I wondered if I would again. Saying it out loud under these circumstances was a way of making something right with a world on a collision course.

"I love you too."

Unbuttoning my shirt, she said, "I can't go another minute without taking a shower. Care to join me?"

Off came layers of clothing that fell into a pile. Who was I to pass up another shower? She stood under the nozzle, the grime rolling off her skin and flowing down the drain. Lathering her hair was, at the moment, better than being pampered at the fanciest salon in Rome. I scrubbed her back, taking my time to make sure I did a thorough job. We were both so lost in the moment that we didn't speak. Kisses and caresses did all the communicating.

We had barely toweled off before pulling down the bed spread on the lumpy mattress. She was in no mood to wait for her hair to dry.

Our hands wandered and probed and found familiar pleasure spots. If a person could be granted one last wish before the end of the world, spending an afternoon in bed with a sensuous woman was my best option at the time. We did it like there was no tomorrow.

"Now I know what you look like with a moustache," she said at one point after I kissed her inner thighs. Moaning, heavy breathing and audible sighs filled the room.

A couple of explosive orgasms later, she begged, "Now fuck my brains out."

Afterwards, with my head still spinning as she lay with her head under my arm, we shared a moment of sweet repose. I couldn't say how long any of this lasted, but the time together ended way too soon. Another knock came at the door. Her ride was here. She dressed quickly, but not in the same hurry as she did when disrobing. The brief interlude was overtaken by the reality of getting back to the business of covering the armed confrontation coming to a climax around us. Finding love in a war zone was as rare as finding an orchid in the desert. And just as fleeting.

After one last kiss and a breathy "I love you," she was out the door.

At the appointed time, I headed down to drop the letters into a box at the front desk and hooked up with Major Ennis and Captain Esarey for the drive back to the desert assembly area. This unexpected liaison would have been impossible without them having some hand in it.

When one of them asked me how my day went, I answered, "It don't get any better than this."

No other words were spoken. Brothers do things for each other.

CHAPTER 33
Line Of Departure

Friday, February 22. After a sound and uneventful sleep, I savored a canteen cup of instant coffee sweetened with canned milk to complete an MRE breakfast. Then came the order to saddle up with full gear. Maybe approval had come to go on the next Apache raid. But when the drive through the sand reached the fork in the road at The Tree, everything changed in an instant. G-Day, the start of the ground war, was at hand. A non-stop convoy of military trucks and equipment motored north on what had been designated a main supply route. It's one thing to see an army rolling along paved highways to reach an assembly point, but quite another to realize it was rumbling toward the starting line on a battlefield. No matter how much this moment was anticipated, this day of days hit like a punch to the gut.

All kinds of shit was in the unbroken column. Light armored vehicles, fuel tankers, tractor-trailers loaded with artillery shells and trucks laden with soldiers flashing the V for victory sign and shouting "Hoo-ah" were part of the procession. Hand-printed signs on some of the vehicles said War Pigs, No Sleep Til Baghdad and No Sleep Til Brooklyn.

A mixture of amazement and dread accompanied the sight of all that military might set in motion. The closest comparison I had was the feeling of sitting in the cockpit of a race car with its motor revving. The power was awesome, yet it could careen out of control if not managed properly, as if the power of war was subject to anyone's control.

"The clock is ticking. Our forces are moving into final attack positions for the ground assault," Major Ennis said as I scribbled furiously into my notebook and the reality sunk in.

The official word had come. The Second Brigade and the French division would cross the line of departure into Iraq tomorrow, a day ahead of the main ground invasion.

"Once you cross the line of departure, you are in battle. You are in the engagement. It's a day we hoped wouldn't have had to come, but the coalition has given diplomacy every chance to work, and up to this point, it has failed," Major Ennis continued.

The next move was back to Rahfa. The Airborne allowed for one final phone call home to tell the family something was up. It was a class gesture on their part, given that there had to be an element of trust in keeping the details secret. I was still mulling it over when we drove back to brigade headquarters to see Colonel Rokosz.

Outside the headquarters tent was the colonel's driver, Specialist 4 John Wilson of Parkersburg, West Virginia. We had gotten to know each other in the preceding weeks, and I asked him for his reaction. He said he had just written his last twelve letters home, including one to his mother. In the raw emotion of the moment, his eyes moistened and his voice cracked.

"I thanked my mom for raising me. Told her not to worry. I'll be home soon," Wilson said. "It's kickoff time. You never know if it's going to be the last goodbye or not. Once we cross that line, there's no looking back."

I made a mental note to thank my mom for raising me the first chance I got.

The colonel emerged from his tent with resolve in his eyes and the burden of command weighing on his shoulders.

"In sheer numbers, we're talking about an invasion on the scale of Normandy," he said.

Normandy? Six Army divisions and two armored cavalry regiments, two Marine Divisions, a British Division, the Saudis with their multi-national force, two Egyptian divisions and a Syrian division were poised to take part, all under an air umbrella of planes and helicopters. No Airborne drop was scheduled. The colonel did, however, bend down on one knee to draw lines in the sand with his right index finger, sketching out the mission of the Second Brigade and the French division.

"We're supposed to grab and hold a certain piece of terrain inside Iraq. It's a lodgment, or a toehold, to make sure the road is open," the colonel said. "There will be shit moving all afternoon."

The start line was the escarpment. In the weeks that the infantry had patrolled and inched forward, the Airborne had won a battle by advancing six miles forward and pushing the Iraqis off the high ground. All the grunt work in the preceding weeks had paid off.

Why had there been no response from the Iraqi army?

"We've already pushed them back," the colonel said. "We had all sorts of contingency plans for the escarpment. We were going to take it at night. We were going to bomb the fuck out of it. But it's possible we could go into Iraq and they don't even know we're there."

You must be eager to get going after all this time.

"I got no great desire to kill people. They're just poor schmucks who got caught in the middle of something," the colonel said. But he added a word of warning for Saddam Hussein: "He had better get out of Kuwait or we're going to annihilate his ass."

What was your message to the troops?

"I didn't have to give a big speech or say much. They know what's expected. We've trained a long time. They're as ready as we can make them. It's a very historic moment. Let's go do it," he said.

What's going through your mind?

"After six months of all we've been through, if we left this place without doing what we came for, I'd have a hard time staying in the Army. There's so much commitment to do what we're here for," he said.

Under the plan, the 4th Battalion would lead the assault, with the 1st and 2nd Battalions right behind, all of them supported by artillery, helicopters and air power. The command post would be right behind the 4th Battalion.

What's the difference between this army and the experience of Vietnam?

"It's night and day. If we're going in, we're going to do it right," Rokosz said. "Twenty years ago at the end of Vietnam, the Army was at its worst. That was a hard time. The ranks were filled with guys who didn't want to be there or guys who were given the choice of joining the Army or going to jail. Before, when you had a troublemaker, he was the leader. Now, you get a troublemaker and he's the oddball."

Leaving headquarters and the safety of the wire, we drove north to find the 4th Battalion had already broken camp. It would be the first to cross the line of departure. In the battle with the desert, during which they missed birthdays and anniversaries and holidays, they had been toughened into scorpions. In lieu of a combat jump, infantry squads would take the fight to the enemy aboard five-ton trucks driven into battle by the reservists from New Jersey and Arkansas.

Battalion commander John Vines said everything was good to go.

"I have never seen morale as high as it is today. Time to get the show on the road. It's one step closer to home. One step closer to seeing the wife and kids," Vines said.

Any message for the troops?

"I told them it ain't going to be like Panama," Vines said.

Did you write something special in your last letter home?

"I always think the letter I just wrote will be my last," he said.

To get reaction from the sergeants and privates going into war, I walked along the convoy of trucks. Each one contained 25 paratroopers, their weapons ready, their eyes focused, their jaws set. If anyone ever wants to feel really small, try looking up at truckloads of Airborne infantry who are about to go into battle. I can't say I envied them, but I admired them. They weren't choir boys, but nobody would want a choir boy to fight a war. Like their forefathers before them, they were a determined bunch, ready to take on a tyrant in the Mother of Battles. Not a man wavered. It was more like they had to be reined in, at least temporarily. The road north had already been unofficially designated the Highway to Hell, and by the look of it, the AC/DC version described it best. *No stop signs, speed limits....I'm on my way to the Promised Land.*

This was no time to be asking stupid questions, but I did anyway. It was my job. The most innocuous thing I could think of to break the ice was, "Anyone from Pennsylvania?"

Sergeant William Hutchison, 22, said he was from Wexford, a northern suburb of Pittsburgh. "It's the beginning of the end. We know when this is all over, we're going home," Hutchison said.

Sergeant Brian Henderson, 26, was from Titusville, home of the first commercial oil well, in northwestern Pennsylvania. Toting a Bart Simpson doll his two children had sent him as a good luck charm, Henderson said: "Time to get the show on the road. It's one step closer to home, one step closer to seeing the wife and kids. It's the only way home that I know."

The silence broken, other troopers volunteered their sentiments.

"We're like a jack-in-the-box. You crank it up and crank it up and crank it up, then it pops. That's us, a coiled spring," said Staff Sergeant Kenneth Guyer, 29, a platoon leader from Syracuse, New York. Just before the Normandy invasion, an infantryman in England described the American army as a coiled spring about to be turned loose on Germany.

The war was no longer about liberating Kuwait or the politics of restoring the status quo in the Middle East. It was about survival, about not wanting to let down the paratrooper on the left or on the right. It was also payback time for Saddam Hussein, the mouthy bully responsible for their asses being in the Sand Box all this time.

"Everybody's got a score to settle. One man changed so many lives forever. We just want to go in there, go home and get our lives back on track," said Sergeant Michael Spellman, 21, of San Diego, California.

"We're going to kick ass and take names," added Private Gary Faison, 19, of North Carolina.

"It's one day closer to going home and drinking some cold ones," said Specialist 4 Glenn Ashley, 27, of Plattsburgh, New York.

The order came to move out. With some soldiers waving American flags, the column of trucks crept toward the escarpment. From a worm's eye view, the line of troop carriers stretched from horizon to horizon. Foxholes that men had lived in for months were abandoned to be filled in by shifting sands and to be reclaimed by the desert. A discarded Nerf football was stuck in the dirt, the only physical evidence that three companies of Airborne infantry had been holed up here for five weeks. Kickoff was at hand.

Back at the tent, personal chores required attention. Six main meals of MREs were set aside to be slipped inside my shirt, with a plastic fork tucked inside a shirt pocket. Canteens were filled. Extra water bottles were loaded onto the Humvee. Sand bags from our bomb shelter were emptied, and the bags were tied in a bundle to be taken along. They were too valuable to be left behind, and we might need them where we were going.

Captain Esarey placed a folded American flag into the Humvee.

"Lots of guys are making peace with themselves tonight," he said.

As night fell, I wandered outside the tent and gazed up at the firmament. It was like seeing the cosmos for the first time. *How many times can a man look up before he sees the sky?* The grandeur, magnitude and the magnificence of all the stars and galaxies reaffirmed the existence of a Supreme Being. Here I was, one person in an army of hundreds of thousands, a grain of sand in the desert, one desert on a planet in a solar system inside a galaxy that contained billions of stars in a universe made of up billions of galaxies. I never felt so small. I also wondered, if there is intelligent life out there, what must they think of us, that the way we settle disputes is to kill each other in battle. They're really going to do this. Yet on the eve of war, a peace I had never before known blanketed me.

That night, the ambush that had been set for so many nights had been sprung at Objective Mongoose. Riding in a civilian vehicle, four heavily armed Iraqis had ventured across the border on an ill-timed scouting mission. The Junkyard Dogs of Delta Company in the 2nd Battalion, led by First Sergeant Jim Southerly, lit them up with an anti-tank missile, killing three and seriously wounding the fourth. The wounded soldier was found under the vehicle, badly burned and missing most of an arm. The killing had started. If it had occurred the night we were on ambush, it would have been a major story. Now it had been reduced to a footnote. How many more would die in the invasion?

In the morning, after burning what we didn't need, Combat Pool No. 1 squeezed into two Humvees and left Tactical Assembly Area Hawk for the last time. Sleeping cots were left behind. They were excess baggage now. From somewhere in the supply depot, Captain Esarey found a carton of Starburst Fruit Chews and put them in the back of the truck. As we drove away, the Bedouin tent became smaller and smaller until it disappeared over the southern horizon.

At 11 o'clock in the morning, 17 hours before the main ground assault, we drove up and over the escarpment into Iraq. It was so quiet I could hear the rubber tires turning over the rocks. Even though three battalions of Airborne infantry had preceded us, I half expected us to hit a land mine at any moment or take incoming fire. Like standing up to a schoolyard bully, crossing that line of departure was the toughest thing I ever did or ever would do. The predominant thought was, "Grit your teeth and get it over with." Somebody had to write it down. We cleared the border just before noon. Of all the roads I had been on to get me to this point, this one was unique. This was the gateway to war.

At the spot separating Saudi Arabia from Iraq, a sergeant had erected a handmade sign. "Airborne all the way, Gold Falcons made the way, LTC J.R. Vines leads the way, Hey, Saddam, we're coming your way. Welcome Devil and Panther Paratroopers to Falcon Country. Your host, SFC Perez." There was also a marker from Fort Bragg that said, "Ardennes Street," the home address of the 82nd Airborne.

Out of nowhere, a paved road appeared. The asphalt in the wilderness was ostensibly put there for Muslims making the pilgrimage to Mecca. For the Airborne, it led due north into Iraq, straight toward Baghdad. A small building that served as a post for border guards had been abandoned. Whoever was here hurriedly left behind combat helmets, papers and other gear. Within yards of the structure was a huge crater, the calling card of a bomb dropped by the Air Force. It had to be 15 feet deep and 30 feet across. From the bottom of the crater, it was impossible to see over the top. No wonder the Iraqis bugged out. The concussion alone would have scared the bejabbers out of them.

Staff Sergeant Roger Cox, 22, of Shelby, North Carolina, had scored the first souvenirs of the war. Three Iraqi combat helmets had been discarded and were there for the taking.

Major Mark Siemer, 38, of Sparta, New Jersey, gave the first situation report. "We had no resistance as we crossed the border. We were not supposed to be this far west. Night recon painted a good picture for us," said Siemer, the brigade's logistics officer.

But this was no time to take anything for granted. The quickest way to die on a battlefield is to let your guard down.

"Nothing is easy. Anytime you move forward, you move forward with concern. There's always the possibility of something else being there. You always have butterflies when there's enemy ahead. Lots of adrenaline is flowing," Siemer said. "There is a sense of relief, though. We didn't have to lose anybody."

Once inside Iraq, the first thing everybody did was to mark the territory by urinating on it. Infantrymen emulated Churchill pissing into the Rhine. The Airborne owned this territory now. I even added my own stream to the occasion.

Major Ennis found a discarded Iraqi shovel and put it in the Humvee. We might be able to use it later. He also spoke of the surreal notion of invading without a shot being fired. If somebody had invaded Texas, there surely would be a response. Why hadn't the Iraqis fired on us?

"It was anticlimactic because we were unopposed," he said. "It's still sort of like being in a Grade B western. Here we are on the open plain, and we haven't seen the bad guys yet. But they're out there."

The border post, designated Objective Falcon, was now secured. We continued north for a while to secure the toehold before stopping for the night. The guns would surely open up tomorrow. The silence was as deafening in its own way as an artillery blast.

CHAPTER 34
Hasty Epiphany

Saturday night, February 23. Under normal circumstances, and if what I reported did not jeopardize my own life or the lives of anyone around me, I would have been filing news bulletins that said the 82nd Airborne had invaded Iraq in advance of the ground war the world had been anticipating for so long. As it was, all I could do was peck out a pool report on my Combat Olivetti portable typewriter about the events of the day. The story wouldn't even leave our area of operations until eight o'clock the next morning, four hours after the main assault was scheduled to begin. A military helicopter was supposed to pick up the pouch and fly it to Log Base Charlie, where the next available flight back to Dhahran would deliver it to the reporters in the Joint Information Bureau. With that in mind, I took a calculated risk of using the dateline Rahfa for the first time. The dateline could have been FROM THE FAR SIDE OF THE MOON, for all it mattered, but if the war had started, the secrecy of our location in Saudi Arabia was no longer an issue. We were in Iraq now. Major Ennis let it through.

From the inside of my shirt, I pulled out an MRE of escalloped potatoes and ham. Unheated, it tasted like rubber erasers mixed in with wallpaper paste, but I picked it for a reason. Ham is forbidden in Muslim countries, and even if Iraq had a secular government, I was fighting the war the only way I could — by being rebellious. Up yours, the second coming of Nebuchadnezzar.

Time allowed for some last-minute reporting. The Airborne was too disciplined to park in a column or bunch up in a pack, which would have invited mass casualties if the Iraqis fired their artillery. I had to walk about 50 paces through the sand to the nearest Humvee, curious to know what a soldier does the night before a war. At his post, locked and loaded, was Staff Sergeant John Sanders, 25, of Oxford, Alabama. A squad leader in Alpha Company of the 2nd Battalion, he was reading his Bible. Sanders said his little brother was in the Marines, and he was thinking of him, but if your whole universe is what you can see from your position, it was hard to comprehend that brothers separated by 300 miles of desert were part of the same invasion.

"We've been waiting almost seven months now. We couldn't care less if peace was declared or if we went all the way to Baghdad. We want it to be over," Sanders said. "I am at war with anybody who stays in their hole and shoots at me. I pray the Iraqis give up."

For spiritual solace, his Bible was opened to Psalm 91, also known as The Soldier's Psalm. An Old Testament verse, the song of the warrior/poet David was just as relevant for a sergeant in the 82nd Airborne who, in the last great war of the bloody 20th Century, put his fate in the hands of a higher power:

You will not fear the terror of the night, nor the arrow that flies by day, nor the pestilence that stalks in darkness, nor the destruction that wastes at noonday. A thousand may fall at your side, ten thousand at your right hand; but it will not come near you. You will only look with your eyes and see the recompense of the wicked. Because you have made the Lord your refuge, the Most high your habitation, no evil shall befall you, no scourge come near your tent. For he will give his angels charge of you to guard you in all your ways. On their hands they will bear you up, lest you dash your foot against a stone...

On the walk back to the Humvee, I chanced upon Private Edward Corcoran, 21, who carried a squad automatic weapon for Alpha Company. He had the lowest rank a soldier could have after completing basic training and jump school, and he had recently arrived in country to join the fight. For shelter, he was digging a fighting position that would serve as his place to sleep, just like his drill sergeant had taught him in basic training.

"I don't know what war's going to be like, so I'm doing what I was trained to do," Corcoran said. "I'll try to get some sleep. I have guard duty later."

Back at my Humvee, Major Ennis underscored the gravity of the moment.

"No lights tonight, and no talking," he whispered, "but if you have to, you can whimper softly to yourself."

He had a way of putting things in perspective.

"It's been a long time since somebody lined up half a million guys on one side and half a million guys on the other side and went at it in battle," Major Ennis continued. "There ain't a guy on this side or a guy on that side who thinks he's going to die tomorrow. Some of them are wrong."

The order came to start taking the nerve gas pills again. What happened next can only be described as an out-of-body experience. We had invaded a hostile country whose leader had equipped his army with chemical weapons and nerve gas. Our Humvee, like every vehicle in the invasion, was marked with a symbol designating it as part of the coalition. Maybe the inverted "V" would stop some trigger-happy comrade from shooting us by mistake. A panel of blaze orange fabric adorned the Humvee roof to alert the Air Force it was a friendly vehicle. On the back of my Kevlar were two reflective strips that marked me as part of the force, discouraging anyone behind me from shooting me in the back. Out there somewhere was the Grim Reaper, and he was trolling for souls.

An inner voice told me to fetch the contraband Iraqi shovel. In starting to dig, I discovered why the Arab word for rock is Iraq. This patch of desert was mostly rock with some sand, the opposite of Saudi Arabia. Remembering my Army training, I dug a hole six feet long, three feet wide, and 18 inches deep, with all the shoveled dirt stacked along the length to the north. It provided shelter from the wind and was the only thing available to block any shrapnel from an incoming round. If a shell hits directly, however, there's no chance of survival. But all they have to do is shovel the wall of dirt on top of you because you have dug your own grave. It was never more apparent that a great adventure carries with it a great risk, and that war is serious business.

I settled into my mummy bag, fully clothed and sleeping with my boots on, looking up at the night sky again. A moment of clarity sank in. It was my epiphany about the realities of war, not unlike the epiphany of Paul and the road to Damascus, which by the way was only one country over. The light comes on, and you can suddenly see. If I tell someone that war makes you a different person, and they ask me how, I can only refer to this night. Crawl into a grave you have dug for yourself and it's like all the molecules in your body are rearranged. Under the circumstances, I realized there was a good chance I could be killed. So good, in fact, that just like that, I accepted my own death. Once you accept the fact you're already dead, you can do your job and take whatever comes without having to worry about it. The amazing thing was how quickly and easily the feeling washed over me. With the only sound being the beating of my own heart, I made peace with myself too.

A personal conversation with the Creator followed. The Almighty had a lot of things to look over at the moment, but a quick word was in order. I thought about the mistakes I had made in life or, given the benefit of hindsight, the things I would have handled differently. I forgave myself because I was young, and I had honestly tried to learn from them. I offered a silent goodbye to my mom, my brothers and my sisters. I also said goodbye to my estranged wife and my two daughters, praying that they would all be OK if I didn't make it back and hoping they understood I was doing what I was born to do. What the experience does is make one realize what matters most in life, and family is most important. Leaving never crossed my mind. But if I got out of this, I might consider a less risky line of work.

The feeling is what one would feel looking down from a mountain peak. Everything else seemed insignificant. Just as soldiers get rid of all their excess baggage before going to war, they rid themselves of emotional baggage too. In the moment, I forgave the New York woman who had ripped my heart out. I didn't want to carry any hatred into the next life. It didn't matter anymore, and I let it go. To my surprise, the moment of forgiveness was the moment healing began. After searching for it all over the world, I found inner peace on the eve of war. The desert had sanded away the mortal shell I had outgrown. By lightening my own load, I finally understood what Michael Herr said in his book about Vietnam: "You don't cover a war. It covers you." The old me was buried in that hole. A new me climbed out of it in the morning.

Time to sleep. Nobody appreciates sleep more than a soldier.

CHAPTER 35
Highway To Hell

Sunday, February 24. Wake-up was two o'clock in the morning, zero dark stupid, two hours before the attack. Hurry up and wait. Lacking hot water, I had my first field coffee. Take a packet of freeze-dried instant coffee from an MRE pack, toss the crystals into the mouth and swish it around with a swig of cold canteen water before swallowing. It tastes like shit, but it packs a caffeine jolt. As a precaution against a chemical attack, orders came to don the Mission Oriented Protective Posture gear. The activated charcoal in the suit leaves a residue of dark grime over whatever it covers. So much for clean clothes. We all looked like aliens, but the suit helped defeat the cold. Not far behind my hasty was a five-ton truck bristling with infantry at the ready. It's not too much of a stretch to think of them aboard an amphibious landing craft about to assault a beach.

"History is being made right here. It's something I thought I'd never do myself. It's something I can tell my grandkids," said Private First Class Reginald Carter, 24, of Atlanta, Georgia.

At H-Hour, we moved out on the Highway To Hell. From the trail of MRE wrappers left in our wake, the adrenaline rush of war must whet the appetite. A response, any kind of response, was anticipated at any moment. None came, which was an eerie rather than comforting feeling. Maybe they were drawing us in. According to Murphy's Laws of Combat, when the attack is going really well, you've walked into an ambush.

Some miles into the journey, the column halted. The French launched a reconnaissance drone to get a picture of what was ahead. Artillery pieces and multiple launch rocket systems were unlimbered and readied to fire as soon as the drone returned with intel on targets.

Off to the side of the road was a Mercedes-Benz truck abandoned in the sand. A dead Iraqi soldier was inside the cab. Not wanting to be morbid, I refused to look at first. But when the drone took longer than expected to return, I relented and walked over. The front of the truck was shot up with rockets or chain gun rounds. The dead man was slumped over in the middle of the seat. Bullet holes exited his back. Grains of sand salted his dirty, matted black hair. He never knew who or what had killed him, and he was in no position to answer silent questions.

Who are you? Where are you from? Were you married? Did you have kids? Will your family ever know what happened to you? Do you know what you died for? How do you feel about war? How many more of you, and us, will end up dead?

The drone returned. At 8:55 a.m., a 155-millimeter howitzer called The Saddamizer belched fire and sent the first round down range. The concussion from the firing of the shell slapped the pants against my leg. More cannons joined in, their crews pulling the lanyards with grim purpose. Then hissing missiles from the multiple launch rocket systems filled the sky. Trailing white smoke, the rockets rode a rainbow arc to their destination in the north. A few moments after the rockets disappeared into the distance, a muffled rumble could be heard as the 644 bomblets in each rocket exploded onto what was out there. The targets were beyond visual range. In the desert, even the ground war was long distance and impersonal.

Private First Class Jason Genereaux, 19, of Cincinnati, Ohio, shouted an emotional outburst from the truck behind me. "We know where that's going. Yee-hah! Hoo-ah! Blow 'em a new asshole. Fuck Iraq!" he said.

The column drove on but stopped again at a swale where the ground sloped off and then rose again in the distance. A recoilless rifle was aimed straight at us, but no crew could be seen. Infantrymen dismounted to take up fighting positions. Everyone was locked and loaded. Then came our first encounter with the world's fourth largest Army in the Mother of Battles. Off in the distance, with the weapons of a brigade of riflemen zeroed in on them, two sullen figures with their hands raised walked toward our line. Reaching the vehicles, two Iraqi soldiers surrendered and lay face down in the sand to be searched. One didn't even have boots. He wore sandals, and his black socks had holes in them. They were pathetic looking wretches.

All around us were bunkers and fighting positions that the Iraqis had dug and fortified with rocks. These bunkers were concealed by the terrain but had been abandoned. If the soldiers who built them had stayed and fought, it would have taken a lot of firepower to root them all out. The sand would have been saturated with blood.

We drove on until noon, when an attack was prepared against a series of rocky ridges where Iraqi radar scanners and transmission towers had been erected to detect and report the presence of any invaders. The area had been designated Objective Rochambeau, in honor of Lieutenant General Comte de Rochambeau, commander of French forces in America during the Revolutionary War. Rochambeau had marched from New York with seven infantry regiments, an artillery brigade and some light cavalry — about 7,000 troops in all — to assist George Washington in the surrounding Lord Cornwallis and his British army during the climactic battle at Yorktown. Without French help, there may never have been a United States.

Objective Rochambeau was defended by a brigade of the Iraqi 45th Division, which had fought in the war against Iran. The assault began with an ear-splitting barrage of cannons. Artillerymen put their fingers in their ears as lanyards were pulled. An artillery shell need not score a direct hit. If one lands in the general vicinity of a position, it can still kill or put the fear of God into those on the receiving end. No fire was returned.

At the area where the big shells landed, a couple of Russian-made T-55 tanks were abandoned on the ridges. Radar stations were blown to smithereens. Airborne combat engineers jumped down from the tailgates of their trucks and set about blowing up the bunkers the Iraqis had dug to defend the radar site. Whatever force the Iraqis had assembled fled without a fight.

"I'd rather see guys walk away than not. They don't want to fight here," said Lieutenant Fred Drummon, of Hastings, Nebraska, an officer in the 307th Engineer Battalion.

Combat engineers had a field day. Using fuses with 45-second delays, they set explosive charges inside the bunkers. The cry would go up, "Fire in the hole!" During one such sequence, I hugged the ground, trying to be invisible. Then an explosion went off. Thick, putrid black smoke wafted into the air from the bowels of a blown-up bunker. I got a good whiff of it, too. It smelled like Satan's breath.

Everywhere on the desert floor were AK-47 assault rifles that, according to the jokes, had never been fired and only dropped once. The engineers destroyed mortars, grenade launchers and wooden boxes. So many combat boots and uniforms littered the ground that it looked like the Iraqis disrobed and ran right out of their shoes.

Major Bob Pinson provided an upbeat situational report.

"We're not here to kill Iraqis. We're here to liberate Kuwait," Pinson said. "I think we took them by surprise. It's got to be a psychological blow that we've been able to penetrate this deep this fast. I don't know of a cut finger at this point on our side. It's been a tremendous success."

With no hint of resistance, the Mother of Battles was a dud thus far.

"I think it's going to be a piece of cake," Pinson said. "We've got the best soldiers the world has. By cutting his supplies this deep, we've cut off his ability to transport. Without supplies, he's going to wither on the vine. If you can't feed soldiers and fuel vehicles, everything comes to a grinding halt."

More engineers moved methodically across the battlefield to destroy any Iraqi equipment with charges of Composition 4 explosives. One pound of C4 could wipe out a bunker. With each explosion, the engineers would yell "Fuck Iraq!" or "Hoo-ah!" and then run to the next target.

Staff Sergeant Kenneth Nobles, 29, of Meridian, Mississippi, a member of Bravo Company in the 307th Engineers, said a booby trap had been found on an abandoned tank. Grappling hooks had disabled the threat, but overall, the attack was one-sided.

"This is nothing. I figured it would be harder," Nobles said. "They're scared. They're giving up. I've been in the Army four years. I finally get to earn my paycheck. We love it. But it ain't over yet."

A shout went up reminding everyone to drink their water, lest they become dehydrated. Oh, and take another pill.

Private First Class Hector Soto, 18, of Anaheim, California, said he had blown up seven or eight bunkers, three or four ammo dumps and two artillery pieces. "It's going really smooth. The artillery scared them out of their holes, and they came toward us. We searched them, tagged them, told them to wait for an escort," Soto said.

Sergeant Arthur Hiscox, 21, of Downer's Grove, Illinois, and a member of the 4th Battalion of the Second Brigade, said all the Iraqis he encountered surrendered. They had no stomach for combat.

"They were scared, big time. They were freaking out. We got too much firepower. I got 15 prisoners in one batch," Hiscox said.

In fact, so many Iraqi soldiers had surrendered that the numbers slowed the advance.

"We're kind of overwhelmed by all the POWs. The biggest hazard now is being trampled by Iraqis trying to give up. We took 450 over there, 150 over there. I mean, hundreds of them at a time," said Major Carl Horst, operations officer for the 2nd Battalion.

From their area of the battlefield, where artillery fire was constant and convoys were everywhere, The Nasty Boys engaged an Iraqi battalion, which promptly surrendered. One Iraqi soldier named Thomas spoke some English and said, "Bush good, Saddam bad." They had been reduced to one slice of bread per day, and they wolfed down the MREs the Americans gave them. As they were loaded onto trucks to be taken to a staging area for POWs, some shook hands and wished The Nasty Boys well.

As the attack moved forward in the afternoon, an A-10 Thunderbolt could be seen flying like a bird of prey in a figure-eight loop on the northern horizon. On the ground was a company of Iraqi tanks. The Air Force jet dove, opening fire with the Gatling gun in its nose. Seven rotating barrels spit rounds out at the rate of 4,000 per minute. It sounded like an angry chain saw. "Br-r-r-r-ack." The rounds were made of depleted uranium, which would penetrate steel and cause enough friction to set fire to anything inside the tank — fuel, ammunition, human flesh. The A-10 took out one tank, then another, then another. Quite a show.

As the attack jet reaped its grim harvest, a column of Iraqi soldiers appeared on the northern horizon. Marching in a formation, hundreds of them advanced toward the Airborne ranks, waving, smiling, flashing peace symbols or holding safe passage cards. There were no guards herding them. Their weapons discarded, they just wanted to surrender.

"Look at that! When was the last time the world saw an army giving up like that? The First World War?" Captain Clint Esarey said. "There's no shame in that. Their government abused them. It's the best way. They'll be treated well. They'll live to see their families."

Military Police swung into action when the Iraqi soldiers reached our position. A prisoner's hands would be bound with plastic restraints, but POW after POW said again and again, "Thank you, thank you." It was as if they had been rescued.

So many prisoners gave up that the MPs ran out of plastic cuffs. With Airborne infantrymen on the perimeter providing cover, Iraqi soldiers were ordered to sit in the sand with their hands on their heads. Then one by one, they lay spread eagle on the ground to be searched.

One bearded prisoner wearing a bewildered gaze did as ordered. An MP told him to empty his pockets, and from his shirt, the guy pulled out pictures of his family and his false teeth. He was a beaten man. Not only had he given up, his dignity was gone. His most personal belongings had been handed over to his foe. Then the American soldier who searched him handed back his photographs and his teeth. A different kind of look, one of disbelieving gratitude, appeared on the POW's face. He looked like he wanted to shed tears of joy.

More and more prisoners were searched. After all the buildup and sacrifice, one MP said somewhat ruefully that he had expected a battle. "I came here to fight a war, not run a fucking processing station," he muttered.

But Lieutenant Mark Shepard, 29, of Lewisburg, Ohio, attached to Headquarters Company of the 4th Battalion, welcomed the sight. "No better way to fight a war. The infantry's just throwing up their arms. You can only bomb a man so much before he starts asking why am I fighting," Shepard said.

As the day wound down, brigade commander Ron Rokosz provided a situation report. First and foremost, there had not been a single Airborne casualty.

"We have had not one man scratched," the relieved colonel said. "There's no way I would have thought we could have ever done it, not in a million years. To take that much territory, that much equipment, that many prisoners, without having to lose anyone, it's amazing."

How many POWs total?

"There are thousands of prisoners. You'd come over the ridges and they'd be out of their bunkers, all over the place. Very, very few small arms were fired. We did fire some anti-tank rockets. After a while, though, we didn't even call in artillery prep. As soon as we got within sight, boom! the white flags went up. We expected to hit a brigade at Rochambeau. That's where we thought we were going to have to fight. Every guy I saw surrendered. I saw nobody fight back," the colonel said.

It had not gone unnoticed that the Iraqis had prepared a layered defense.

"If they would have stayed in their holes, if they would have fought back, the result would have been the same, but it would have been a long day," the colonel said. "Their officers ran away, which tells me they've got a big-time morale problem. These soldiers don't want to fight. We could have gone a lot farther, except we had so many prisoners. It's the most incredible thing I have ever seen. They just came out of their holes and waved white flags. If the same thing happening here happens in Kuwait, it's going to be a short war."

Just before sunset, the column stopped. We all thought we'd just keep rolling forward, but the French didn't want to move at night.

The weather was changing. A line of high clouds foretelling a weather front moved in from the northwest. The wind kicked up sand. Then it started raining.

I propped up my Combat Olivetti on the cardboard sleeve of an MRE and typed up a story on the day's events. A helicopter from the XVIII Airborne Corps was supposed to pick up the pouch in the morning, but the helicopter hadn't shown as expected after we cleared the escarpment either. Then I dug another hasty grave, this one a little deeper, and covered up under a poncho to ward off the cold rain. A sensation in my nasal passages told me a sickness of some kind was coming on. Or maybe it was something from the black fumes that came out of the destroyed bunkers that was making me sick. Or maybe it was a side-effect of the pills. At any rate, something wasn't right. It would be a chilly, wet, nasty, miserable night. Infantry weather.

CHAPTER 36
Death From Above

Monday, February 25. Boom! Boom! Boom! It was an artillery strike, but thank heavens, it was outgoing. Still, there's nothing like waking up to the bark of firing cannons. Zipped up tight in my sleeping bag, I swear I jumped four feet off the ground and spun around in mid-air. It was 5:30 a.m. As soon as the guns fired, 14 waiting Iraqi soldiers appeared out of the wet sand and turned themselves in. Another field coffee helped washed down a diced turkey MRE for breakfast. The helicopter tasked with picking up the pool reports was supposed to arrive at eight o'clock, but it never showed. After an hour's wait, Captain Esarey took the media pouch and drove south in his Humvee. I'll say this about the Airborne. It went to every length to get the story back. Whether it made it back to the hotel or not was out of their hands. But because the brigade resumed its march at daybreak and had a big head start, we saddled up with the intent of catching up.

"Let's ride to the sound of the rustling white flags," Major Ennis said.

As the rain continued to fall, my condition deteriorated. But it's not like you can call in sick with a fever and a cough during a war. I stopped taking the pills. We drove and drove and drove, passed the burned out hulk of an Iraqi truck and other detritus of a broken army. At one point, there was an Iraqi truck on the side of the road, its motor still running. The left rear had been jacked up, and it looked as if the occupants were in the act of changing a tire before they fled on foot and took shelter in a drain pipe. Kind of spooky to stumble across an idling enemy vehicle. They were close.

How long we were on the road was tough to say, but we pulled over when explosions could be seen in the distance. Leaving the Humvee on the side of the road, we walked out into the desert. Hundreds of paper leaflets littered the sand. Each one was a message to Iraqi soldiers that they would be granted good treatment and live to see their families again if they surrendered.

To the north, a pair of A-10 tank-killing Thunderbolts circled in the air and then attacked a line of eight Iraqi tanks arrayed on a skirmish line facing our advance. One jet would dive, the Gatling gun in its nose firing, and seconds later an Iraqi tank belched flames. Then his wingman repeated the maneuver, torching another tank.

Colonel Rokosz and Command Sergeant Major Slocum drove up and walked out to watch with us. Another enemy tank, then another, then another, was consumed by fire. It was quite a show, until an agitated French officer drove up to our vantage point.

My college French was a bit rusty, but by the tone in his voice, he basically said: "Would you mind pulling your derrieres back? We called in this air strike, and there's nothing but open air between you and those burning tanks."

Damn, Army Combat Pool No. 1 had passed everybody else up. We were the FLOT (forward line of troops). My mission had been to get as close to war as I could, and this was as close as it gets. We pulled back until the attack jets completed their work, then drove up to inspect the damage.

Flames licked at the metal hulks of the destroyed tanks. Ammo cooking off inside the wrecks went pop, pop, pop. They were Soviet relics, not the top-of-the-line models, and a cursory inspection showed that rust spots on their exteriors had been painted over. The T-55s were not only antiquated but poorly maintained. Still, a tank was a tank, and if the crews had stayed with the machines and fired off a few rounds, it might have been a different story.

Behind the burning hulks was a series of abandoned bunkers, filled with foot lockers and personal gear. More stuff for the engineers to destroy.

"Every hole we went in had rifles and equipment. That's tons of stuff we'd have to tote around," Colonel Rokosz said. "If we can't take it with us, we destroy it in place. You don't leave anything behind on a battlefield the enemy can use."

He also said his troops were more confident than ever. "Yesterday showed them that they could survive. I'll never forget that," Rokosz said.

Inside the bunkers were cans of tomatoes, stale bread and moldy fruit next to cooking utensils and some bed mats. Discarded helmet liners and uniforms littered the ground. Foot lockers had been shredded by bombs, and pictures from magazines fluttered on the breeze. Every army has pin-up girls, and the Iraqis sought solace in pictures of women to hang in their bunkers. Their models weren't as revealing or appealing as the pictures of Claudia Schiffer and the other models the Airborne had, but the photographs reminded somebody of someone.

Then came compelling evidence that the war was over. Just inside the entrance of one bunker was a pile of human excrement. The Iraqi soldier who dumped it there was so afraid to leave the shelter that he stopped venturing outside for calls of nature. It's a desperate way for soldiers to live. You don't shit where you eat and sleep.

Resuming the march, we drove to what was a support area for Iraqi vehicles. Armored personnel carriers and ten wrecked trucks sat empty. On the side of the road were ten Iraqi soldiers.

Unarmed and unattended, these wretches milled about like they were waiting at a bus stop. They surrendered to Combat Pool No. 1. We offered them food, water and Starburst Fruit Chews. We left them there to be picked up and trucked south to a POW camp set up outside Rahfa. The rules for the media prohibited the taking of pictures or interviewing captured soldiers, but a Pencil armed with nothing more dangerous than a notebook could claim he took prisoners.

We stopped for the night again a short time later.

At our camp, Staff Sergeant Wayne Cofer, 27, of Martinsville, Virginia, a scout in the 4th Battalion, sat on a cardboard box and reflected on the events of the last two days.

"All this is better than bloodshed. It beats getting shot at," Cofer said. "But if they were going to fight it this way, why couldn't they have settled this over the phone?"

My sickness worsened. I could barely function. The weather was atrocious. I dug another hole to sleep in.

The short-wave radio delivered welcome news during the night. Mother of Battles Radio was quoted as saying the Iraqi army is pulling out of Kuwait. But the Republican Guard, the elite formation targeted for annihilation, has yet to be destroyed. The fighting isn't over yet.

"Otherwise it's a half victory. We didn't come over here to spend seven months and billions of dollars for a half victory," Major Ennis said.

According to Murphy's Laws of Combat, anything you do in a war zone can get you killed, including doing nothing. In two days at the tip of the bayonet, an unarmed civilian inside Iraq on the forward line of troops could be unscathed while watching the Air Force take out enemy tanks. But 500 or so miles to the rear in Saudi Arabia, reservists who hadn't even received a mission yet could be blown up by a Scud missile.

It happened to the 14th Quartermaster Detachment of the U.S. Army Reserve, a 69-member water purification unit based in Greensburg, Pennsylvania. On January 13, 1991, days before the air campaign started against Iraq, the members of the unit received a phone call and heard the words "Roaring Bull," which was their code to report to active duty at the reserve center. They said goodbye to family and friends. Then, escorted by state police cars and local fire engines who bid them Godspeed, they began a three-day drive to Fort Lee, Virginia, to receive refresher courses in their training. The unit's primary mission was to produce drinkable water by using the process of Reverse Osmosis Water Purification. Planners had figured that if the war dragged on, water for troops or civilians in the Kuwait campaign might be needed. And the 14th Quartermasters, the modern-day Gunga Din, was equipped to provide it.

The unit arrived in Dhahran on February 18, four weeks after the bombing started and one week before the ground assault. Its members were housed with other reservists in an old, corrugated tin warehouse situated along a four-lane highway near a little shopping center that housed a doughnut place and a photo shop. The warehouse was about three miles from the Dhahran airfield that coalition planes were using to pummel Iraq.

On February 25, the 14th Quartermaster Detachment expected to receive orders the next day of where it might be going and what it might be doing. After all, the Iraqis had blown up the desalinization plant in Kuwait City, and drinking water was needed. As they awaited their orders, some soldiers did laundry or walked outside to the shower tent. Some wrote letters home. On a Monday night, eight of them played Trivial Pursuit on their sleeping cots.

Iraq had already launched 45 Scud missiles at the coalition and 42 against Israel. A relic of the Cold War, Scuds were Russian-made cousins of the vengeance weapons introduced by Germany in World War II. The liquid-fueled ballistic missile had a single stage and a single warhead. It could be fired from fixed sites or mobile missile launchers. During its war with Iran, the Iraqis had launched 350 of them, killing 2,000 Iranians and wounding another 6,000, not to mention scaring the wits out of whole populations. The Scud had a crude guidance system and was notoriously inaccurate. An unsophisticated gyroscope kept the missile on track, but once the rocket motor shut down after running out of fuel in 80 seconds, the entire assembly coasted in the general direction of its target. The longer the distance of a Scud's flight, the higher its inaccuracy. Some Scuds looked more like hot water tanks than missiles, and plywood fins were cobbled to their sides to stabilize them in flight. The weapon was largely ineffective against troops in the field, which were widely dispersed rather than being concentrated. But urban areas in Israel and Saudi Arabia were unnerved if a Scud bore down on them. Of all the weapons in the Iraqi arsenal, Scuds had the biggest impact.

Then came one of the last Scud launches of the war. A 41-foot long missile, powered by kerosene fuel and an oxidizer, lifted from its launch pad from inside Iraq. In little over a minute, it was screaming along at 3,600 miles per hour in the general direction of Dhahran, its 350-pound warhead primed to explode on whatever it hit.

Military briefers in Riyadh had given the impression that the coalition was protected by an air umbrella of Patriot missiles. Video released to the media showed Patriot missiles intercepting warheads in flight, a bullet destroying another bullet. Ground radar would lock onto an incoming Scud, then relay signals to a Patriot control station to provide information on speed, trajectory and predicted course. When the February 25 Scud was launched at Dhahran, two Patriot batteries could have intercepted it. But one was shut down for maintenance, and the other was not functioning properly because it had been operating for four days straight. If a battery operated continuously, an error would develop in the computerized tracking system. Operators were aware of the glitch, and a program to correct it had arrived in the war zone. It was due to be installed the next day. Priority for fixing the program had gone to batteries closer to Iraq. The upshot was that as the Scud approached Dhahran, no Patriot was launched to intercept. And fatefully, this Scud held together. Anything that can go wrong, will.

Sometime in mid-evening, a warning siren wailed. But sirens had been wailing for days in and around Dhahran. Troops got used to hearing them. Besides, the first 40 hours and 28 minutes of the ground war had brought over-whelmingly good news. Then at 8:32 p.m., the warhead crashed through the metal roof of the warehouse with a wrenching sound. In the blink of an eye, an ear-splitting explosion sent out shock waves. A hellish orange blast consumed the building.

Staff Sergeant David Campbell, 41, of the Pittsburgh suburb of Bethel Park, was reclining on his cot after doing his laundry. He had served a tour in Vietnam without receiving a scratch, but one week into his tour in Desert Storm, he was hit by the blast.

"They couldn't hit that building again if they tried. It was just fate, a fluke shot." Campbell said.

He suffered four broken ribs, a collapsed lung, a broken left arm and two burst ear drums. A piece of shrapnel the size of a license plate embedded in his left leg.

"In a split second, I remember the roof blowing in and the wall separating. It felt like somebody smacking you in the head with a baseball bat. I guess I flew like a rag doll like everybody else," Campbell said.

Sergeant Lester Bennett, a 40-year-old Johnstown banker and a father of three children, was on his way to take a shower. His trip was interrupted by the fireball. A jagged, searing hot piece of shrapnel ripped into his leg. Both of his ear drums were perforated.

"It was over in the time it takes to turn off a light switch. I felt the heat. It was difficult to breathe because the explosion sucked all the air of out of place," Bennett said. "It was just chaos and confusion."

Ken Bier of Blairsville, Pennsylvania, was napping on his cot and awoke to a scene from Dante's Inferno.

"I remember being under some rubble and I crawled out," Bier said. "I walked out to the parking lot to get a fire extinguisher. I must have been in shock because I still didn't know what I was seeing. It looked like a giant sculpture — all this twisted metal, the glow from the flames. I finally realized, 'Geez, that's the building.' You'd go crazy trying to figure it out or wonder why it happened the way it did. You just have to accept the fact that it happened."

In all, 28 soldiers lost their lives, and 99 were wounded. Of the dead, 13 of them, including two women, were from the 14th Quartermaster Detachment. Of the eight people playing Trivial Pursuit, six perished. Another 43 members of the unit were wounded. More than 80 percent of their complement lay dead or wounded, the worst casualty rate for any unit in Desert Storm. The explosion in that warehouse accounted for nearly one-fourth of all the U.S. combat casualties for the entire war.

The dead ranged in age from 20 to 44. In the real world, they were mail-truck mechanics, environmental engineers, lumberyard supervisors, forklift operators, secretaries and college students. They came from small Pennsylvania towns like Penn Hills, Hickory, NuMine, Monongahela, Monessen, Rochester Mills, Armagh, Latrobe and Unity.

The youngest to die was Sergeant Frank Walls of Hawthorne, Clarion County. Having served two years of active duty in the Army, he joined the reserves and was a freshman at the Kittanning Campus of Indiana University of Pennsylvania.

The oldest was Sergeant John Boxler of Johnstown. A Little League coach and volunteer fireman, he joined the Army Reserve to make extra money. He had brought his telescope to Saudi Arabia to study the stars, and he smuggled out bread crumbs from the chow hall to feed the local birds. He left behind two teen-aged children, a grieving wife and a heart-broken mother.

Specialist Christine Mayes, a 22-year-old student at Indiana University of Pennsylvania, got engaged the day she left for the Gulf. She gave the ring back to her fiance for safekeeping until she returned. The ring was buried with her when her body came home.

Specialist Beverly Clark, 23, who had enrolled at Indiana University of Pennsylvania to begin elementary education classes, had a premonition before she left Pennsylvania to serve in the war. Her words have haunted her mother ever since. "Mom, I'm not coming back," she had said. When she came home to southwestern Pennsylvania, it was in a coffin.

CHAPTER 37
Objectives Secured

Tuesday, February 26. The helicopter designated to pick up the pool reports failed to show again. Captain Esarey hopped in his Humvee and drove the pouch back toward Log Base Charlie. It was impossible to know what, if anything, made it back, but I kept doing my job. Expectations were for the advance to continue, but we were in for a prolonged delay. The first thought was there must have been a fight up ahead, but as it turned out, gridlock set in because the 24th Division's supply train was crossing in front of our column. A traffic jam had occurred on the one road available in the desert. Hacking and wheezing from a wicked cough, I was feverish and chilled all at the same time. I must have looked as bad as I felt because I heard somebody say, "You look like shit." Major Ennis took a side trip through the armada of vehicles and found the nearest medic. The medic could treat a sucking chest wound or put a tourniquet around a bleeding artery, but he was a little short of medications for whatever ailed me. For a fever, nausea, persistent cough and flu-like symptoms, he gave me some throat lozenges.

When the traffic started flowing, the drive continued up the Highway To Hell, which was Hell only for Iraqis. The terrain changed from open desert to something extraordinary. Blades of green grass dotted the landscape. The grass was too thin to be considered a lawn, but the dun-colored sand had a layer of green. We even came upon a cultivated field. Farmers chopping at the soil with their hoes tended their tomatoes and onions. The remarkable thing was that the men and women never even looked up. The American army had invaded their country. A column of military vehicles that stretched from horizon to horizon motored along the road. But they just kept farming. We didn't stop to chat, but they had the look of people who had been beaten down for so long that it didn't matter what foreign power was overrunning their land this time. They certainly weren't rising up or greeting us as liberators either. Anyone who thought they could ever build a democracy in this country must've killed a whole lot of brain cells.

A short time later, we reached the outskirts of the village of As-Salman. Designated as Objective White, it had an airfield and was a launch point for Scud missiles. It also was the headquarters of Iraq's 45th Division, or Talkla Division. French forces had already surrounded and taken the town. Using loud speakers, French troops warned that As-Salman would be wiped off the map if the Iraqis failed to surrender. The Iraqis fled. But as the French rolled in to occupy the place, two French soldiers were killed and 10 were wounded by land mines or unexploded ordnance. Danger can pop out of the ground from anywhere on a battlefield.

The Second Brigade rolled in without incident. Paratroopers found discarded Iraqi uniforms, abandoned guns and a field hospital set up in a school. Some buildings were adorned with 10-foot high portraits of a smiling Saddam Hussein. All of the buildings were unoccupied. The objective had been secured.

"If this war ended right now, it would be the greatest feeling of my life," Colonel Rokosz said. "I never thought we could do what we've done without having to lose anybody."

The word on the short-wave radio was that the Iraqis were fleeing Kuwait.

"If he is withdrawing from Kuwait right now, it's a rout," Rokosz said.

Command Sergeant Major Steve Slocum, speaking on the record for the first time, said that the village was deserted when the infantry rolled in.

"There wasn't anybody left in town except for a few dogs. It's just mud huts and empty streets," Slocum said. "Nobody believed we could have done this without a single casualty. Everybody is feeling great right now."

All around us was the detritus of a defeated army that had bugged out. Military uniforms, combat helmets, berets, stretchers, posters, maps, books and stacks of mortar rounds were left behind in the buildings.

Captain Keith Bax, 28, of the 1st Special Operations Command said the town was taken by a psychological operations team rather than bullets.

"It's like a ghost town," said Bax, a resident of St. Petersburg, Florida. "We've been going house to house. We found one 12-year-old boy with an AK-47 given to him by a fleeing Iraqi soldier. I think the Iraqis wanted us to capture them. They ran out of food and were freezing. They never got a chance to fight. They knew we were coming. They were outmaneuvered. We know they were still here two days ago. They disappeared between now and then."

Captain Dom Caraccilo, 29, Seneca Falls, New York, commander of Headquarters and Headquarters Company for the Second Brigade, said paratroopers found pots of food still cooking on portable stoves. The Iraqis fled or surrendered before they could eat their last meal.

"The ones who gave up were saying, 'Thank God you're here. Thank God I'm alive. We were waiting for days.' When the bombing started, they all ran north or they turned themselves in. There were so many, you couldn't keep track. You'd be five kilometers away and guys were raising their hands," said Caraccilo, a 1984 graduate of West Point.

And he really got a kick out of one piece of intelligence gleaned from Iraqi prisoners. "They were told that the 82nd Airborne was coming, and to be in the 82nd Airborne, you had to be a convicted murderer or have killed one of your parents," Caraccilo chuckled.

The taking of As-Salman wouldn't make any headlines, however. Newscasts picked up on the short-wave said that the Kuwaiti flag flew once again in the central square of Kuwait City, and that U.S. Special Forces had parachuted in to re-take the American Embassy.

The part of the mission that linked the Second Brigade to the French division had been accomplished. Paratroopers bid *au revoir* to the French, and the brigade consolidated with the First and Third Brigades. For the first time since World War II, the 82nd Airborne was fighting as a unified division.

Their orders were to move into the Euphrates Valley and to fight as dismounted infantry in the city Basra, if necessary. Instead of driving on due north as it had been, the division wheeled to the east. Captured Iraqi flags flew from the Humvees. A monster sandstorm kicked up late in the afternoon.

After the Airborne moved out of As-Salman, a separate unit of combat engineers moved in to clear the airfield of unexploded ordnance. The strip was needed for planes bringing supplies, and the runway was made unusable by explosives dropped from American planes.

Through howling wind and blowing sand, the engineers gathered up the bombs and stacked them in a single pile. Then something went terribly wrong. There was an explosion. Seven combat engineers perished.

"We were all best friends. Brothers. One guy was going to be the best man in my wedding. Another one's wife was about to give birth. I can't believe it," Specialist Daniel Bartz, 21, of Sheboygan, Michigan, was quoted as saying in a pool report.

Nobody knew what set off the blast. It may have been the blowing wind knocked over the stack, setting off the explosion.

"You can go to school after school and learn about these things, and they'll teach you exactly how each explosive is supposed to act and react. Then you go out and try it and it'll do something different. You have to really respect this stuff," said Sergeant Mike Panaranto, 36, of Terre Haute, Indiana.

What happened to the Iraqi army that was supposed to be fighting the Mother Of Battles? Answers could be gleaned from the war journal of an Iraqi lieutenant stationed in As-Salman.

The officer was full of fight when the war started. But after weeks of the air war, Apache strikes and artillery bombardments, his spirit degraded. Here is what he wrote in a journal now archived at Mississippi State University:

Tuesday, January 15 — The army is in a state of total alert to prepare itself against allied and American aggression expected against our well-loved territory. I am very worried for my parents because I know what these conditions represent for them. But God is good. We wish the war had not happened, but it has, so combat would be welcome.

Thursday, January 17 — "Say this: all that happens is what God has decided for us." (A verse from the Qur'an.) This morning at 2:45 a.m., I heard military aircraft. A few seconds later, the guard came in and told me in a voice tinged with caution, fear and consternation, "Lieutenant, lieutenant, there may be bombing." I dressed quickly and then realized that the American and Atlantic attack against our country was starting and that the war had begun. This is war, with all that the word implies. Afterwards, the enemy planes began their intensive bombing on the airfield that we have been assigned to defend, at As-Salman.

Friday, January 18 — Heavy enemy bombing continues. The bombing and raids kept up all last night.

Sunday, January 20 — The bombing and enemy raids began very early today. Air-to-ground missiles began to explode at 3:30 this morning. I am very worried for my relatives.

O God! Protect. O God! Save us all.

Monday, January 21 — Our military communiqués say that the enemy has bombed most of the regions and provinces of Iraq with planes and missiles. I am constantly gripped by anxiety.

Tuesday, January 22 — I went to the brigade bunker to move troops to another place because of the raids and heavy bombing at the emplacement. When I got there, I found four bombs. The situation was very difficult because we had to pass close by them. But God protects. What an awful sight. One of the soldiers (disturbed) one of the bombs and suddenly it exploded and the soldier disappeared and I saw (two pieces) of his flesh on the second story of the bunker. Allah akbar. What a terrible thing to see.

Wednesday, January 23 — Threatening weather. Time drags. We wait and watch. I am very afraid for my brothers...The planes came back to bomb again. They were close and we could see them. "If only I had wings."

Thursday, January 24 — The raids began early...and have continued heavily without a let-up. I heard news that Basra has been bombed heavily. May God have come to help my relatives. I am very worried about them. Where are they now? God only knows. Ahhhhhhhhh!

Saturday, January 26 — Enemy air strikes continue, and I'm very worried, depressed and bored. I think about my children.

Sunday, January 27 — The air strikes began this morning...My mind and my heart are with my relatives, and only my body is with the army. I very much need to see my relatives. I had a dream yesterday and it was not a good omen at all.

Monday, January 28 — The enemy air raids continue and I am in a (shelter). The top of it is only tent canvas. God protect us all. After sunset, a flock of sheep came up to us. Apparently the owner of the flock had been killed in the air raids. The enemy with his modern planes has launched air strikes on a shepherd. Maybe the enemy took the sheep for nuclear or chemical or petroleum sheep. For shame.

Tuesday, January 29 — This evening, after a series of enemy air strikes and watching their in-flight refueling over our territory, I decided to go to the tank battalion that belongs to the armored brigade. All the food I had was a little gruel and tea.

Wednesday, January 30 — The air strikes began heavily today and I am still alive. I could be killed at any moment. I am more afraid for my relatives than I am afraid to die. The air raids are nothing new to me, but I am very worried.

Saturday, February 2 — I was awakened this morning by the noise of an enemy air raid. I ran and hid in the nearby trench. I had breakfast and afterwards something indescribable happened. Two enemy planes came toward us and began firing at us, in turn, with missiles, machine guns and rockets. I was almost killed. Death was a yard away from me. The missiles, machine guns and rockets didn't let up. One of the rockets hit and pierced our shelter, which was penetrated by shrapnel. Over and over we said, "Allah, Allah, Allah." One tank burned and three other tanks belonging to the 3rd Company, which we were with, were destroyed. That was a very bad experience. Time passed and we waited to die. The munitions dump of the 68th Tank Battalion exploded. A cannon shell fell on one of the soldiers' positions, but thank God, no one was there. The soldiers were somewhere else. The attack lasted about 15 minutes, but it seemed like a year to me. I read chapters in the Qur'an. How hard it is to be killed by someone you don't know, you've never seen and can't confront. He is in the sky and you're on the ground. Our ground resistance is magnificent. After the air raid, I gave great thanks to God and joined some soldiers to ask how each of them was. While I was doing that, another air strike began.

Sunday, February 3 — Few air raids today. The pain I've been having all the past 6 months has returned. I am sad. In the last 5 days, I've eaten only a few dates and boiled lentils. What have we done to God to endure that? I have no news of my relatives. How can I, since I don't know what is happening to me. What will become of me? What is happening to them? I don't know. I don't know. God protect them. How I miss my children. P.S. While I was writing these lines, another air raid occurred.

Monday, February 4 — Few air raids today. I stayed alone in the shelter. Worried about the bombing. Worried about hunger. Worried about water.

Tuesday, February 5 — I woke up this morning to the sound of enemy air raids. I quickly put on my uniform and ran to the trench. I had my helmet on. Thank God, the raid ended. In the afternoon, I went to wash up inside an armored troop carrier. I washed quickly because these vehicles are usually targets for aircraft.

Wednesday, February 6 — I awakened to the noise of air raids. I dressed quickly and put on my helmet. Afterwards, I had breakfast. Then there was another air attack. I ran to the trench...the planes dropped a lot of bombs before returning to Saudi Arabia. We were covered with dirt. We were buried alive. God is good.

Thursday, February 7 — Not many air strikes on us. I thought of my relatives. My illness is getting worse and I feel tired. The planes come and go, and the shelter holds many a comrade.

Saturday, February 9 — The air raids began, and with them began my descent into the grave.

Monday, February 11 — Enemy planes have come back and bombed heavily. We went to the trenches, or rather, the graves. I was very upset when I heard that people born in 1973 are being drafted. That means that my brother will have to go into the army. He is naive. He'll make a fool of himself. He's too picky about his food. Where will he find room for that in the army? And especially this army! How I wish I were with him so I could help him.

Tuesday, February 12 — I have been here for more than 35 days because leaves were canceled. I am bored and sad. This morning, I learned that 26 soldiers from our division were condemned to death for deserting the front. They were apprehended near Samawa and executed at 2nd Division headquarters. Two of them were from the 68th Tank Battalion that we were with. They were unlucky. Their shame is very great. God is good. God protects.

Thursday, February 14 — I woke up at 8 this morning and said my prayers.

I couldn't make my ablutions with water before praying, so I had to use the sand that had fallen on me and covered me from head to foot in an enemy air raid that had been going on continuously since midnight. The planes launched missiles at our positions and at the tanks that were with us, believing that the tanks were missile-launching sites. Smoke and dust rose into the sky mingled with the smell of powder. None of us thought we could get out of this bombardment safely. I stood because I couldn't get into the trench on account of my illness. But, thank God, I wasn't hit.

Saturday, February 16 — I feel so fatigued that I can't breathe, and I think I am going to faint at any moment from my illness. The only thing that you can find everywhere in the world is air, and yet I can't breathe it. I can't breathe, eat, drink or talk. I have been here for 39 days and have not yet gone on leave. The planes came and bombed battalion headquarters. Most of the positions were destroyed and three soldiers were killed.

Sunday, February 17 — My illness is getting worse. I am short of breath. I hurt. I have begun taking medicine. I don't know what it is for, but the main thing is to take it because I know the medicine can't cause me any more pain than I am already enduring. The air raids have started up again.

It was the journal's last entry. Nobody knows what happened to the lieutenant.

CHAPTER 38
Mine Field

Wednesday, February 27. We've reached the Euphrates Valley, but it looks like the same old desert. No welcome mats are out. The division is primed and ready to go to Basra. It doesn't like we're going to Baghdad. Fuck. In the language of the military alphabet, this operation is Tango Uniform. Tits Up, the way a corpse is laid out in a coffin.

An update was provided by the commanding officer of the First Brigade, Colonel Jack P. Nix Jr., 43, a 21-year veteran of the Army and a Georgia Tech graduate. He had two mustard splats on his Airborne wings — one for a combat jump in Grenada, and one for the combat jump into Panama. From the point of view of those who had invested so much sweat equity during their months in the desert, the operation hadn't been quick or easy.

"For a short war, this son of a bitch has seemed like an eternity. It has seemed like forever," Nix said.

He theorized that the Iraqi army had disintegrated because its soldiers lacked a cause.

"I don't think they believed in Saddam and what he was espousing. To live out in these holes for weeks upon weeks and have bombs falling over you, you gotta have something to believe in," Nix said.

Some troops were geared up emotionally for Armageddon and were prepared to go all the way to Iraq's capital city. Now there was something of a letdown because close quarter combat never materialized. All the shots fired were mostly long range and in one direction. Logistics, maneuver and air support over the vast distances of the desert negated the necessity of close-in fighting.

"Some guys feel that if they sat over here for seven months, they ought to get part of the action. I know guys are saying, 'Boy, I wished I would have seen more war.' But down deep they're saying, 'I'm glad I didn't.' They know some of them would have been killed or severely wounded," Nix said. "There's a lot of kids who really grew up over here. They learned a lot about themselves. You don't take life and life's good things for granted."

What about the resurrection of the all-volunteer American army after the ashes of Vietnam?

Nix said the outcome had been twenty years in the making.

"It took all of the Seventies to recover. In the Eighties, it became OK to be a serviceman again. We turned it around," the colonel said. "We were getting the dregs of society for a time, but the quality of the soldiers we have today is second to none. I don't think Americans like being losers. I think they were tired of having sand kicked in their faces by third world countries."

In the ranks, soldiers had their own take on what the last five days, and the last seven months, have been like. Most of them took the long view.

"We were the deterrent to aggression. We drew the line in the sand," said Staff Sergeant Bob Kelly, 25, of Goodwater, Alabama.

What about the troopers who wanted to see more action?

"Some guys aren't too damned smart. I don't feel left out. I'm not too thrilled at being shot at. People who want more war scare me," Kelly said.

Sergeant Armando Romero, 32, of Barstow, California, had a sense of relief.

"Nobody had any desire to destroy the Iraqi soldiers. We could have totally taken them off the face of the earth," Romero said. "I hope it ends soon. I don't want no bullets shot at me, and I don't want to shoot at anybody else if I don't have to."

Private First Class Paul Jurgensen, 20, of Hicksonville, Long Island, had mixed feelings.

"On the one hand, you wonder why did they even bring us over here if we're not going to see any action. But I just want to go home alive. Everybody feels left out some, but being left out is a lot better than going home injured or dead," Jurgensen said.

Private First Class Scott Hickman, 20, of Louisville, Kentucky, was cleaning his gas mask in the desert and didn't seem to mind the lack of firefights.

"I'd be ecstatic if it ended today. Saddam Hussein can talk the talk, but he don't walk the walk. I don't think he realized what he was getting himself into," Hickman said.

First Sergeant Gregory Duhon of Eunice, Louisiana, said the Iraqis never had a chance.

"I'm surprised they held on as long as they did," he said. "Besides, it's like the rest of the United States declared war on Rhode Island."

That night, the short-wave carried accounts of Norman Schwarzkopf conducting the Mother of All Briefings from the hotel ballroom in Riyadh. The Iraqi army had been destroyed, and the gate was closed, he said. In reality, however, there were a couple of back roads being taken by Iraqi forces fleeing north. At least one Republican Guard division, and parts of others, had yet to be touched. Schwarzkopf also said there were never any plans to go to Baghdad, but if there were, he had the force to do it. The briefing served as Schwarzkopf's victory speech.

Thursday, February 28. The voice of Major Ennis broke the pre-dawn silence.

"Hey, Bedouin Bob. Wake up and turn on the radio. The war's over," he said.

Crawling out of my bag, I muttered to myself. If the war is over, why am I getting up? Then I fumbled through my gear and turned on the five o'clock newscast. From the White House, President George Bush declared a cessation of offensive operations. The objective of evicting the Iraqi army from Kuwait had been achieved. The shooting would stop in three hours, which would make it a 100-hour ground war. The end came just like the start — announcements by the president broadcast over a short wave radio while in the company of the 82nd Airborne.

I kept waiting to hear that Iraq had surrendered, but there was no mention of it. Saddam Hussein hadn't capitulated. We just decided to stop. It seemed like an awfully large loose end. If it takes two sides to wage a war, how can it end with just one side saying it was over. But the military is under civilian control. When the man says go, you go. When the man says stop, you stop. Still, it just didn't seem like a very definitive end.

All adventures have a natural let down, I suppose. If war penetrates every fiber of your being, if it becomes part of your life day after day after day, you hardly know how to react when somebody orders a halt. Well, nobody asked me when it started either.

I had a three-hour window to get reaction, write a final pool report and drive to some map coordinates in the desert, which had been designated as a pickup point for the helicopter to carry the news pouch back to the rear.

Reaction was decidedly mixed. Point of view depended on the age of the paratrooper and whether he had experienced combat before.

The closest trooper was Private First Class Robert Enculion, 20, of Elmyra, New York. When told offensive operations had ceased, he didn't believe it.

"Over? I hope it's not over. I haven't even fired a shot. I wanted to empty my magazines three or four times. I want to get into the war. It's been too easy," Enculion said.

Nobody celebrated or fired weapons exuberantly into the air. There was no outward display of emotion.

"Very disappointed. It's kind of a let down," said Specialist 4 Timothy Marques, 21, of Depue, Illinois. "There was a lot of frustration built up because we stayed out here so long. We wanted to take it out on somebody."

Corporal Baxter Morrison, 22, of Fayetteville, North Carolina, was more philosophical. He was aboard the first flight out of Fort Bragg, that Trans-America DC-10 that landed in Dhahran at 4:30 p.m. on August 8. He had painted his face with camouflage before landing while he and his comrades drew the original line in the sand. Because he spoke French, he had served as a liaison between the Second Brigade and the forces from France, but the mission turned out to be more of a five-day truck ride than a combat assault. Training was tougher than the actual mission.

"I was part of a whole. I did my part. I contributed to the liberation of Kuwait. I'm going home alive," Morrison said. "It's like studying for a test and never getting to take the final exam. I got in my seat. They gave me the paper. I got an A. Even though I didn't fire my weapon, I did my part. We completed the mission. We did the job."

Major Ennis spoke for the division.

"We stood up to a tyrant. No telling what he might have done if he was allowed to keep Kuwait. I consider Saddam's defeat a triumph of good over evil," he said.

A deeper purpose had been achieved as well.

"I think this war has healed the wounds of Vietnam. Our country really came together spiritually. I think America has fallen back in love with its military. Our military is at the highest peak it's been since World War II. I just hope the politicians don't dismantle it," the major said.

Captain Esarey empathized with troops who had geared themselves up to fight the Mother of Battles but faced a foe that refused to stand and fight.

"There's definitely a letdown for some soldiers," he said. "They thought that by going into combat they would find glory. They'll find out the American public is so proud of them, they'll get everything they wanted just by going home. They did their jobs. Now it's up to the American public to do its job and welcome them back."

Ah, home. The news meant that soldiers would be returning to the world of beer and pizza and fresh salads.

"The mother of all parties is about to begin," said Specialist Brannon Lamar, 21, of Augusta, Georgia.

Although "Haji Don't Surf" was still written on his Kevlar, he had a new perspective.

"When I saw the way our guys handled those POWs, without mistreating them or mowing them down, I wanted to say how proud I was to be a U.S. soldier. Maybe we are the good guys," he said.

Interviews done and the story cleared, we piled into the Humvee and drove to a point in the desert where the helicopter was supposed to land. Once again, it never showed.

A cluster of Iraqi mud huts could be seen in the distance. I wondered if booze was legal in Iraq and if the village might have a liquor store. If the end of a war isn't cause for a drink, what is? But the answer never came. I was walking in the desert about 50 yards from the Humvee when I heard an explosion. Using a walking stick, Captain Esarey had picked up something in the sand and flung it. When the object landed, it exploded.

"Hey Clint, how did you make it do that?" I asked.

With a sober look on his face, he replied: "We're in a minefield. Retrace your steps back to the truck."

I looked back at my boot prints. Taking the first step was the toughest. Yeah, I knew I had walked out, but maybe something had been disturbed and would explode on the way back. If I triggered an explosion, a blast could turn me into pink mist, the infantry's term for the blood that falls back to Earth after some unlucky bastard steps on a mine and gets blown to smithereens. It was the damnedest feeling. I took the first step, and every time I stepped again, I thought it would be my last. Fifty yards may seem like nothing, but it was the longest walk I ever took. Now I understood the cliché. War is long stretches of routine punctuated by a few seconds of terror.

"This is fucking great," I muttered under my breath. "The war's over. The Mother of Battles never happened. We're not going to Baghdad. And now I might step on something that will kill me. That's just fucking great."

Having experienced the pucker factor, I made it back to the truck with a huge sigh of relief. In the meantime, other media pools behind us had been told to drive to the same coordinates. We tried to warn them off by waving. They thought we were waving hello. They drove right up in our tire tracks.

Nobody moved as the combat engineers raced forward to take care of those nasty things in the sand. Using tiny red warning flags attached to sticks, the engineers marked the positions of each device. As it turned out, they weren't land mines but unexploded bomblets dropped by American planes. No matter. They were dangerous. In no time, a forest of red flags grew out of the desert. Then the engineers began setting charges and blowing them up in place. Someone would yell, "Fire in the hole!" I hit the deck, listened for the ka-boom, then heard whistling metal flying through the air.

We gave up waiting for the chopper. To get the dispatches into the pipeline, Combat Pool No. 1 would drive back to a support area and find a transport headed for Dhahran. Reaction to the end of the war, after all, was big news. At this point, however, I no longer trusted the open ground we were riding on. As a precaution, I took off my Kevlar and sat on it.

When other media asked why, I said in my best *Apocalypse Now* voice: "Because I don't want to get my balls blown off."

They laughed. Then they sat on their helmets too.

Across the open, rocky desert, we drove and drove and drove. After being jostled and jangled for several hours, I finally yelled for Captain Esarey to stop.

Maybe it was because I was sick. Maybe it was because the war was over and the letdown had set in and the adrenaline was wearing off. Maybe it was getting up before dawn. Maybe because I thought I was going to die in that minefield. Maybe because the chopper never showed once during the entire war. Maybe it was the rough ride. For whatever reason, I jumped out and flung my helmet against the Humvee's tailgate as hard as I could.

"I was out here for all this time, and that's all there is? Mother-fucking war..."

The helmet dented the tailgate and landed in the sand. Major Ennis and Captain Esarey nodded knowingly.

"We know exactly how you feel, Bedouin Bob."

Ancient poets such as Livy expressed it in more lyrical terms when he wrote about war in the days of the old Roman Empire: "The outcome corresponds less to expectations in war than in any other cause whatsoever."

Sanity restored, the trek continued. Some hours later, we found an aviation unit and boarded a Blackhawk helicopter that flew us to Log Base Charlie. Taped to the ceiling were centerfolds of naked women showing pink.

"That's what I'm fighting for," said the grinning crew chief who had put them there.

Night had fallen by the time we got to the log base. There weren't any more planes flying back to Dhahran that day, but there was a military fax machine. My story was put through first. Confirmation came that the last story I filed from Army Combat Pool No. 1 went through and was received at the JIB in Dhahran. Then the fax machine died. Nobody else got their stuff out. They were now as pissed off as I had been.

In the darkness, the helicopter flew us back into the field, sometimes flying under high tension wires. A feeling of dread gripped me again, or maybe it was the fear that I had postponed over the last five days. I was convinced we'd crash and burn, and that I'd die some meaningless death in the middle of nowhere. I stared at the floor, never once looking at the centerfolds and eye candy decorating the helicopter's interior.

Nothing happened, though. We landed without incident to sleep in the dirt again.

CHAPTER 39
The Left Hook

A position on the edge of a battlefield situated in a sea of sand offers as much perspective of what went down as being on a sleeping cot when the jets roared overhead at the start of the air campaign. It's like being disconnected from what is happening elsewhere, even if there was a vague awareness that the frontal assault by the Marines led to the liberation of Kuwait City, that air power had destroyed Iraqi columns trying to flee on the Highway of Death and that Army units had cut off Iraqi forces trying to skedaddle back to Baghdad. Iraqis had surrendered by the tens of thousands, and the impression was conveyed that the war had been quick, clean and easy. The least amount of attention had been paid to the main attack by Army tanks, which in reality encountered the fiercest engagements.

The first mention of the main attack came a day after the cessation of offensive operations by Colonel Keith Kellogg, the 82nd Airborne Division's chief of staff. On the hood of a Humvee, he sketched out how attacks in the East and the West isolated the Iraqi army while the armored divisions of VII Corps rumbled north and then into the flank of the Republican Guard. The maneuver is known to history as the Left Hook.

"It was an enormous envelopment. It was a tremendous feat of arms," Kellogg said. "We took out all his early warning. He never knew we were there. All of his forces were facing south. Nobody was facing West."

Kellogg also gave an overview of the all-volunteer military.

"America will be very proud of its Army. In my 24 years, it is without question the finest Army I've ever seen fielded," Kellogg said.

Years later, still driven to fill in the blanks, I visited the U.S. Army War College in Carlisle, Pennsylvania, and sheepishly told a helpful librarian that I was with Army troops in Desert Storm but didn't know what happened.

"Neither do they," she replied. "It's the nature of war."

The sheer scale of the battle was hard to fathom. According to the manuscripts, maps and microfilm, the battlefield was roughly the length and width of Pennsylvania. Someone in Pittsburgh would have no clue of what was taking place in Philadelphia or of the main effort happening around Harrisburg. Imagine a giant scorpion holding down its prey with its claws while plunging its venomous tail into the center. What Alexander, what Caesar, what Napoleon could have done with such a force.

By itself, VII Corps consisted of 145,000 soldiers, 1,500 tanks, 1,500 Bradley Fighting Vehicles, 669 artillery pieces and 220 attack helicopters, all moving in a coordinated effort guided by the Global Positioning System. The logistics boggled the mind. For each day of combat, the armored corps consumed 6.5 million gallons of fuel, 3.3 million gallons of water and 6,075 tons of ammunition.

"It was probably the most powerful armored corps on the move in history," said Major General Ronald Griffith, commander of the 1st Armored Division.

After two days of maneuvering, the leading wall of tanks reached the Republican Guard late in the afternoon on February 26. Because a monstrous sandstorm cut visibility to less than 1,000 yards, Apache attack helicopters were grounded. Ground troops were on their own. Rumbling in from the western desert at 20 miles per hour was the 3,800-man 2nd Armored Cavalry Regiment. With three squadrons abreast, and three troops in each squadron, the cavalry was supposed to locate the Tawakalna Division, a name that means "Go With God," and hold it in place. Larger, more powerful formations would then roll in to engage. But the battle plan goes out the window the moment the first shot is fired.

At three o'clock in the afternoon, Eagle Troop realized it had reached the Iraqi flank when it took machine gun fire from some cinder block buildings. Return fire destroyed the position as the troop moved forward, its tanks moving out in front of nine Bradley Fighting Vehicles that had been serving as scouts. From his tank, and with four tanks on each of his flanks, troop commander Captain H.R. McMaster ordered: "Follow my lead."

The M1A1 Abrams main battle tank is powered by twin 1,500-horsepower turbine engines. It's the closest thing to flying anyone could do in a 72-ton killing machine. The four soldiers who live in its belly work as one to fire the tank's main gun, a 120-millimeter cannon. The gun shoots two types of rounds — the high energy, anti-tank (HEAT) round and the Sabot, or silver bullet, which is a yard-long dart made of depleted uranium.

Loaded in the gun of the first tank was the high energy, anti-tank (HEAT) round. An even more effective way to kill a tank is the Sabot, or silver bullet, a yard-long dart made of depleted uranium that was in good supply in the ammo compartment. While the dart doesn't explode, it impacts with the kinetic energy of a race car slamming into a wall at 200 miles an hour, except the energy is concentrated into a spot the size of a golf ball. The friction of the dart slicing through steel creates what the military calls a pyrophoric event. Shards of uranium ignite in molten sparks, and because uranium burns hotter than steel, the sparks set fire to anything — armor plating, ammo, fuel, human flesh. The tank can spot targets even in sandstorms through thermal sights that pick up the heat signatures of enemy vehicles. Laser beams measure the precise distance to a target, with the information relayed to a fire control computer. The tank's Achilles heel was its fuel consumption. In combat, the Abrams consumed four gallons of fuel per mile. In a fight, it could go for four hours before refueling.

McMaster's tank, designated Eagle 66, was driven by Specialist Christopher Hedenskog, who reclined in his seat as he steered the machine. The gunner, Staff Sergeant Craig Koch, moved the turret back and forth while hunting for targets through his thermal imaging sights. The loader, Specialist Jeffrey Taylor, had the job of making sure the tank was on the right heading. Everyone wore protective, charcoal-lined overgarments in case of a chemical attack. Then at 4:16 p.m., as McMaster's tank crested a slight rise, Koch spotted eight hot spots on his thermal screens and yelled: "Tanks! Direct front!" They were Russian-made T-72s, the best in the Iraqi arsenal, dug into fighting positions hidden by sand berms. The range finder flashed 1,420 meters to the first target.

McMaster gave the order to fire.

In a tank battle, the gun that shoots first usually wins. The gunner centered the red dot of his sights on a target and sent the round down range. The projectile struck a spot four inches above the turret ring on an Iraqi tank. Four pounds of explosive ignited, and a 3,000-degree jet of burning metal shot inside. In an eye-blink, a 15-ton turret spun 20 feet through the air like a steel Frisbee. Black smoke poured from the wreckage.

Under a practiced sequence, the loader opened the steel door of the ammo compartment. He hit a release button, and a Sabot popped forward. The loader cradled the 54-pound projectile, twirled it like a baton and slammed it into the breech. The fire control computer adjusted the barrel, taking into account the variables of cross winds and tank speed. The range finder read 600 meters. Just as the Iraqi tank was turning its turret to engage, the gunner fired. A second tank erupted in flames.

Although a pair of Iraqi tanks shot back, the rounds fell short and to either side of McMaster's tank. The gunner in Eagle 66 aligned the sights on a third target, a tank just 400 meters away. Another round left the barrel. The sound of it leaving the gun and the explosion of the intended target were as one.

In just seven seconds, three tanks had been taken out with three shots.

The eight tanks to the left and right of McMaster came on line and joined the fight. Within 10 seconds, five more enemy tanks became burning wreckage. Each crew worked to the rhythm of a four-count procedure intended to identify a target, confirm that a round is loaded, trigger the firing mechanism and announce the round is heading down range. It goes like this: "Target. Up. Fire. On the way." The sequence was repeated again and again.

In 23 minutes, Eagle Troop had destroyed an enemy force four times its size without taking any casualties. Burning were 30 enemy tanks, 20 armored personnel carriers and 30 trucks. Fires reflected off the heavy low clouds, casting an eerie glow over a horrendous scene. Artillery had joined the fight and destroyed 35 trucks, fuel dumps, stockpiles of ammunition and bunkers. Secondary explosions added to the cacophony. Enemy dead, most of them dismounted infantry mowed down by machine guns, littered the battlefield. Time becomes compressed on a battlefield. After the engagement, when commanders walked through to piece together the sequence, it took two and a half hours to review everything that had happened in those 23 minutes of fury.

The fight happened about 30 miles west of the Kuwait border. It was called the Battle of 73 Easting, named after an imaginary line drawn on a map.

Just to the north of McMaster's position, the 150 soldiers of Ghost Troop also engaged the Tawakalna Division. During a six-hour fight, an account was preserved of what an armored battle feels like. Private First Class Jason Kick, 18, from Pembroke, Georgia, carried a tape recorder as he drove his Bradley due east. He planned on sending the tape home to his mom at war's end.

When his Bradley eliminated its first Iraqi armored personnel carrier, Kick said: "All I can say is better them than me. That sounds cruel, but it's true."

With a ferocious wind blowing, a blizzard of sand confronted the cavalrymen. By late afternoon, Ghost Troop took up a position on a ridge overlooking a dry river bed at and parallel to the 73 Easting. Enemy troops and vehicles were dug in. Then all hell broke loose.

"We've pulled up on line now. 4:42 p.m. We're engaged in a pretty decent firefight right now. This is chaos here. This is total chaos," Kick said. "I see smoke on the horizon. That means we killed something. What it is, I don't know...I just spotted the biggest damn explosion at about 12 o'clock. I don't know what the hell it was."

A nearby Bradley encountered a problem. It's anti-tank missile launcher was inoperative, and its 25 millimeter cannon had jammed. While the crew attempted a fix, a round from an Iraqi vehicle hit the Bradley's turret. Inside was Sergeant Nels A. Moller, 23, of Paul, Idaho. He was killed instantly.

"One just got one of our guys...Sergeant Moller was killed. Time about 5:49," Kick said. "Can't let this...can't let this affect us or get us down at all. Or we're gonna die. And he wouldn't want that. He don't want that. But I'm scared."

At 6:04, Kick spoke again. He used the military jargon of victor for vehicle:

"This is chaos. Total chaos...Got nine dead victors to our front. Enemy victors. And got more coming," Kick said.

Visibility was down to 50 yards, but thermal sights could pick out targets out to a half mile. Two Iraqi tanks were headed right at Kick's Bradley, and his gunner opened up.

"Boom. Hit. Hit and kill. That's revenge for Sergeant Moller. You sonuvabitching Iraqis. God, I hate them. Sergeant Moller was a good guy.

That's four Iraqi victors killed for this track alone," Kick said.

Over a 360-degree panorama, burning hulks turned the desert floor into a scene from Dante's Inferno. Ghost Troop found itself at the northern end of a valley that the Iraqis had designated as their escape route. Tanks, vehicles and soldiers of the Tawakalna Division and other formations were running for their lives straight into the guns of the cavalrymen.

First Lieutenant Keith Garwick, 25, a West Point graduate from Fresno, California, said Iraqi vehicles would be shot up, and then Iraqi infantry would dismount and keep coming, only to be mowed down by American guns. As the leader of a platoon that included Moller's Bradley, Garwick later told Vince Crawley of the newspaper *Stars and Stripes* that a grisly sequence happened over and over and over.

"A certain part of you just dies. Somebody trying to kill you so desperately for so many hours, and coming so close. We just couldn't understand it. I still don't understand it...Those guys were insane. They wouldn't stop. They kept dying and dying and dying. They never quit. They never quit. If the rest of their army had fought as hard as the Tawakalna fought, we would have been in trouble," Garwick said.

At one point, Garwick tried to radio for artillery support, but the network was so thick with conversations he couldn't get through. He then dashed from his Bradley to ask for emergency fire support from an artillery spotter riding in a nearby vehicle. After calling in the fire mission, he and the spotter scrambled under the Bradley as death rained down around them.

"We just sat there crying, just shaken, until we could get back from underneath the Bradley. The air bursts were coming right on top, ricocheting around us. We were in a corner of hell. I don't know how we made it out of there. I don't," Garwick said.

The batteries of the 6th Battalion, 41st Field Artillery Regiment, fired more than 1,600 rounds in seven hours. Artillery, the King of Battle, saved Ghost Troop from being overrun. It was impossible to say how many Iraqi soldiers died before they stopped trying to get through.

"At the time, none of us understood what was happening...That morning, I was so excited to have killed a Republican Guard. And the end of the battle, if

I never saw another Republican Guard in my life, I'd be happy. I couldn't wait to see combat. What a fool I was. Why did they fight? Why did they fight?" Garwick said.

Someone made a wooden cross and stuck it in the sand for Moller. He died with his hand on the trigger, looking for targets.

To the north of Ghost Troop, the 3rd Armored Division was being led by its own eyes and ears — Alpha Troop, 4th Squadron, 7th Cavalry Regiment, commanded by Captain Gerald Davie. Davie was in a Bradley, with six of the armored vehicles on each of his flanks. With visibility still less than 1,000 yards in the relentless sandstorm, Alpha Troop drove straight into a defensive line manned by the Tawakalna Division. Iraqi infantry fired rocket-propelled grenades, and Iraqi tanks opened up.

"At that point, we were really just fighting for our lives," Davie said.

One Bradley took a direct hit from an Iraqi tank. The gunner, Staff Sergeant Kenneth Gentry, was mortally wounded. Two other Bradleys rushed in and tried in vain to save his life.

"We were 10 times too close to the enemy than we would choose to be. Actually, we were in what would be called their kill sack, right where they wanted us to be," Davie said.

The situation deteriorated rapidly. American tanks coming up behind Alpha Troop joined the fight and began firing at the Iraqi tanks. But in the confusion, some rounds from Abrams tanks also hit Alpha Troop's Bradleys. Davie's troop found itself in a lethal cross-fire. At one point in the two-hour melee, with ammunition and fuel running low, Alpha Troop had no choice but to pull back. Two of the troop's soldiers had been killed, and 12 were wounded. A dozen Bradleys had been damaged. During Desert Storm, Alpha Troop's engagement was the only one in which an American force had to back up to regroup.

The main attack by the Army's armored corps continued on February 27. Daylight revealed a brimstone scene of biblical destruction. The tankers of the 1st Armored Division were in hot pursuit of the Republican Guard and expected to catch up with them this day. But first there was a reminder of the carnage the artillery had wreaked from miles away.

One soldier who preserved the episode in his journal was Sergeant First Class Patrick Douglas, a maintenance sergeant in the 1st Field Artillery Regiment, which had been assigned to the 1st Armored Division. He didn't know who he was writing for, but he wanted to keep a record. Having taken his nerve gas pills and donned his protective garments to guard against a chemical attack, Sergeant Douglas described the scene.

"We went through our kill zone. It looked like the land of the dead. Burning and twisted vehicles everywhere. Some fully loaded with ammo, so they were exploding. One truck was literally in a million pieces. I saw an engine out in the open, still burning. Lots of POWs....So this is war. I'm not scared of it," he wrote.

The most powerful array of tanks and mechanized firepower unleashed since World War II thrust eastward across southern Iraq in search of what remained of the Republican Guard. From south to north, a thundering line of tanks from four armored divisions extended over a distance of about 100 miles long. The largest tank engagement of Desert Storm was at hand.

At the northern edge of the line, the 1st Armored Division moved out at dawn with three brigades abreast. Under a dark and brooding sky, with a wet wind sweeping across the heavy sand, the division's Second Brigade, or Iron Brigade, surged along under the command of Colonel Montgomery Cunningham Meigs. A West Point graduate, Meigs was the great- great- great-grand-nephew and namesake of the man who served as the Union Army's Quartermaster General during the Civil War, and the man who created Arlington National Cemetery on the Virginia plantation of Robert E. Lee. Meigs had four tank battalions abreast forming a six-mile wide wall of mechanized death. The brigade entered a shallow valley and climbed up the far side at about 11:30 a.m. This low rise, which ran north to south for seven miles, became known as Medina Ridge because parts of the Medina Division and the Adnan Division, both Republican Guard formations, were dug in on the far slope.

The Iraqi vehicles glowed as hot spots in the American targeting scopes. In the first hour of shooting, one Iraqi tank disintegrated into flames every 60 seconds. With the skill mastered during countless hours on the practice ranges, four soldiers acting as one team fired as fast as the main guns could be loaded. Target. Up. Fire. On the way. Again and again. With the weather having improved, Apache helicopters joined the fray. From three miles behind the forward line of battle, Hellfire missiles left their racks and obliterated targets. Air Force jets swooped in to join the frenzy. From miles in the rear, artillery put a punctuation mark on the deadly scene.

"All 24 guns in the battalion are standing almost toe-to-toe, in a big lazy W formation. It is incredible," Sergeant Douglas wrote in his journal. "F-16 fighter jets come in and we get close air support for the first time. The Air Force flyboys are always trying to get all the glory. An A-10 tank killer begins circling the air in front of us, firing on targets. An enemy ammo dump behind us explodes. Tracers and fireballs explode. A lot of noise, smoke and confusion. We are really kicking some ass now...A multiple launch rocket system fires to the east, its rockets going almost straight up, which means its targets are not far away. The missiles come straight down in front of us again. The rain finally stops and the sun comes out."

In two hours, the Battle of Medina Ridge had cost the Iraqis 186 tanks and 127 armored vehicles, with jets and helicopters accounting for at least 38 of the kills. On the American side, one tank was knocked out and three damaged. Inside his Bradley, Specialist Clarence Cash was hit by a missile square in chest. It was the division's only death during the battle.

In a fight, soldiers are too focused on staying alive to absorb the butchery of war. But after the guns fell silent, Major Mark P. Hertling, operations officer the 1st Squadron, 1st Cavalry Regiment of the 1st Armored Division, took a closer look from ground level. He wrote down his thoughts in a journal that he was keeping for his son.

"This was a long-range war. When tanks and Bradleys met the enemy, they could engage from 2,000 to 3,500 meters. One Iraqi soldier, when asked when he knew U.S. tanks were approaching, said he knew when the tanks to the left of him then to the right of him exploded. He didn't even see what hit them," Hertling said.

"An interesting twist for those of us who fight. We didn't really see the people we were killing. We only saw equipment blow up. But for me, that has changed over the last few days, and it become very personal," he added.

Hertling had asked his crew to pull over so he could examine a destroyed Iraqi tank.

"I got off the Bradley and stared at the faces of that tank crew for a while. I saw different expressions on each face. All I could think of as I looked at these three Iraqi tank crewman was what a terrible waste this was; how war is an evil thing," Hertling wrote. "These three Iraqi tankers may have sons just like me, but their sons would never see their fathers again. Their wives would mourn their deaths. They would miss all of life's best because a political leader told them to fight for something that centered on power and status, rather than on dignity and freedom."

One last piece of business remained for the armored corps. In one more day, the tanks would complete their charge to the Gulf and finish off whatever was left of the Iraqi army. Whole battalions worth of Iraqi equipment and guns were abandoned on the battlefield, but the Republican Guard's Hammurabi Division was still out there.

Only one man could have stopped it. President George Bush decided that Iraq's army had had enough, announcing that offensive operations would cease 100 hours after the main ground assault had started. The final battle had been called off. If some Iraqi units and tanks escaped, so be it. The mission of evicting the Iraqi army from Kuwait had already been accomplished, and the view from Washington was that continuing the battle would amount to slaughter. On board with the president's decision was Colin Powell, chairman of the Joint Chiefs of Staff, who believed that there still is chivalry in war.

Confusion arose over what Bush's order meant, however. Some units stopped in their tracks. Others continued to move and fire until the order to cease offensive operations took effect. Every unit was authorized to shoot back if fired upon. A clean transformation from all-out war to peace was impossible.

The 1st Field Artillery Regiment received and carried out fire missions in the wee hours of February 28. At 5:30 in the morning, six targets were radioed in, and the 24 big guns in Sergeant Douglas's battalion gave the remnants of the Medina Division a wakeup call of exploding artillery bursts. From the time the war started, Douglas hadn't taken off his boots. He reminded himself to do so, but at present he was pulling the lanyard of an artillery piece. Here's how his war ended:

"Holy fuck! My hands are shaking. We fired 48 rounds in 45 minutes from each gun. Each round weighs over 120 pounds and the ones we fired were especially nasty ones. Dual purpose improved conventional munitions, each round explodes, 88 grenades fall and explode, each grenade capable of taking out a bunker. We set this desert on fire," Douglas wrote. "The tankers radioed back that we didn't leave them anything to shoot at. Even officers helped out, humping ammo, cutting charges. I guess we've all got some blood on our hands now."

Another fire mission was radioed in at 7:50 a.m., but ten minutes later, just as soldiers prepared for the final blow, the order came to stop.

"Clear all weapons. Cease-fire ordered by President Bush. No way. WHY? WHY? WHY? Everybody's pissed and angry. We had them in our sights and now they are getting away," Sergeant Douglas wrote. "We are deep in enemy territory, and we are giving them time to regroup. Now we are sitting ducks for them. I can't believe this is happening. Nobody is happy; we are all getting scared now. We are just sitting here. Two enemy tanks open up on our tanks. I knew this would happen. I guess they don't know about the cease-fire. Our tanks return fire, destroying them."

Combat troops weren't the only ones with mixed feelings when the fighting stopped. After he had announced the suspension of offensive operations, President Bush wrote in his diary: "Still no feeling of euphoria. I think I know why it is. After my speech last night, Baghdad radio started broadcasting that we've been forced to capitulate. I see on the television that public opinion in Jordan and in the streets of Baghdad is that they have won. It is such a canard, but it's what concerns me. It hasn't been a clean end — there is no battleship Missouri surrender. This is what's missing to make this akin to WWII, to separate Kuwait from Korea and Vietnam."

Yeah, well, his army may have given up in waves, but Saddam Hussein never surrendered. Gods don't back down.

After some time spent pondering things, and with the light of 700 oil well fires in Kuwait glimmering under a blackened sky, Sergeant Douglas concluded his writings.

"Last night the oil fire spread and I counted 13 separate blazes from 20km away. They must be huge," he wrote. "Time to think and reflect. A lot of back-slapping and comradeship among everybody. We are really proud of the job we've done. We didn't want to let the people back home down. No casualties in our battalion, even though we were (one kilometer) from the front lines many times, tucked right behind the tanks, watching them fire their main guns and coaxial machine guns into bunkers. Stories floated in from other units. A group of Iraqis refused to come out of a bunker, so a bulldozer was called in and they were buried alive."

His last sentence was: "250 miles into enemy territory in under 100 hours; what a rush, man, what a trip."

CHAPTER 40
Full Circle

Friday, March 1. A new day dawned. There is no war to chase, except for the distinct possibility that the ceasefire, or whatever it's being called, might be temporary. When war becomes part of every fiber of your being over a period of time, there's a sense of disorientation when it's gone. I haven't shaken the feeling that I had waited and waited to see some big attraction, and just when my turn came, somebody shut it down. The out-of-body experience may be over, but it feels like all the molecules in my body have been rearranged. It's funny what a night's sleep can bring, though. Being able to emerge alive from a hasty grave is no small reward either. I had accepted my own death and survived, and surviving in the middle of all this insanity was noble enough. For the first time, I relaxed enough to take pictures of the sun coming up. With the darkness lifted, the giant heat tab appeared on the eastern horizon to light the world again. In a state of whimsy, I borrowed an M-16 rifle and picked up the American flag, posing for a photograph with the rising sun in the background. Another feeling emerged. I can say out loud that I was proud to have been in the company of paratroopers and proud to have once been a soldier. This quest began by wondering what difference one man could make, and it ended with an appreciation of the difference it could make in one man.

Still as woozy as a debilitated camel, I found an empty jar that once held instant coffee and filled it with Iraqi sand. The jar's label was printed in Arabic, perfect for bringing back my keepsake. Part of Iraq would always be with me, just as part of me would always be in Iraq.

Just because somebody pulls the plug on an operation doesn't mean the switch is turned off. I'd have the rest of my life to realize that war stays with you forever. Although I was physically unscarred, war left an indelible, invisible mark. The one-thousand yard stare is made of such stuff.

If there had been any sound, it would have been the hissing of the air whooshing out of the balloon as if a paratrooper's knife had stabbed it. Vietnam was a prolonged slog. This one ended within days.

A dark layer of activated charcoal from the protective suit covered my clothes and skin. Sand and grit infiltrated every bodily crevice. A fire was started, something that would have been unthinkable a day earlier. It was an appropriate sacrificial pit to burn the underwear I had been wearing. I had been saving my last clean ones just for this occasion. Water was heated in a canteen cup for instant coffee. A hot sip on a cold morning does wonders to lift the mood.

A courier found me at my foxhole and said I was wanted on the phone at field headquarters. A phone call? Out here in the middle of nowhere? Off I went, and on the line was George Esper, who had taken over as the AP bureau chief in Dhahran. Esper covered the Vietnam War for ten years, staying at his post even after Saigon fell, and had mastered the art of reaching combat units in the field by working the military phone lines. The connection was weak and had a triple echo, but from what I could understand, a story was in the works about what each unit did during the ground war. Esper wanted four paragraphs on the 82nd Airborne's mission, and he needed it now. Four paragraphs? Was everything that I had gone through worth four measly paragraphs?

Back at my foxhole, I typed up a story, noting how an Airborne brigade assembled north of Rahfa, slipped into Iraq a day ahead of the main assault and drove on to As-Salman and beyond, handling thousands of prisoners of war without having sustained a single combat casualty. Death was in front and behind, but not one member of the Second Brigade was killed or wounded in the battle. The Graves Registration body bags weren't needed. During a drive more than one hundred miles into Iraq, barely a shot had been fired back.

There was no time to put the summary into the pool system and have it flown back to Dhahran. The only practical way of shipping it was via a military fax machine, which was available now that the shooting had stopped. But when we tried to transmit, the fax malfunctioned and conked out. The summary never was transmitted. I'd have to write it when I got back, just as I had thought all along. And in a symbolic gesture, I held a mock execution for the Combat Olivetti.

There was talk the Airborne would participate in a victory parade in Kuwait City, but the battlefield was still so dangerous that the march never took place. Word did come that units would be sent home according to the order in which they arrived in the kingdom, which meant the Airborne would be one of the first to depart. Already thinking ahead, I put in an official request to accompany them on the flight home. They said they'd get back to me. The media pools were being disbanded. It was time to leave the battlefield.

The first leg back to Dhahran meant driving across the desert and then down the Highway to Hell, also designated as Main Supply Route Texas, to the escarpment and across the frontier back to Rahfa. While the trip had taken five days during the war, we did the reverse in a matter of hours. The abandoned fighting positions and the destroyed radar stations on the ridges at Rochambeau had been picked clean of souvenirs. We went back through the same door we entered, but everything seemed different. No, wait. I was different.

The Saudi soldiers now mulling around in Rahfa looked so untouched, so unaffected, so clean. An inner rage still smoldered. If anybody said anything to me, just one word, I was ready to pounce. Nobody did, and I mugged for a couple of pictures instead. Tapline Road took us to Log Base Charlie, where a flight was arranged aboard a C-130 cargo plane for a short hop to the airfield at King Khalid Military City.

The 24th Mechanized Division asked for photographers, but no Pencils, to venture north to record the aftermath of a clash it got into after the cessation of offensive operations.

From what I learned later, the division's tanks had thundered 190 miles into the Euphrates Valley, then wheeled east with the intent of joining the Left Hook into the flank of the Iraqi army. One of its units had assaulted an Iraqi airfield at Talil, where part of the property overlapped the archeological remains of the ancient city of Ur, once the capital of Sumeria, the birthplace of the written word and thought to be the home of Abraham, the patriarch of the religions of Judaism, Christianity and Islam. Not only had the 24th Division had won high praise from U.S. commanders in Riyadh, even the beaten Iraqis marveled as its fighting ability. "You were like the wind. You come, blow and go away. You cannot shoot the wind," one Iraqi commander said.

The division was driving down Highway 8 when the order came to halt, but when an Army helicopter went down in front of its forward line, the division moved up to secure the area. Although orders were not to fire unless fired upon, a Catch 22 was created. The 24th moved east with orders to avoid contact, but by moving east, it was impossible to avoid contact with an Iraqi force that happened to be heading west in search of an escape route. The bumper-to-bumper column of vehicles belonged to the Hammurabi Division of the Republican Guard.

About 40 Iraqi vehicles were spotted moving into the 24th Division's security zone from the east. They were either trying to escape along Highway 8 or had missed the turn onto a causeway across Lake Hammar, a large swampy region south of the junction between the Tigris and Euphrates Rivers. An unlucky Iraqi soldier fired a rocket-propelled grenade, and another Iraqi vehicle moved into position to fire an anti-tank missile. Charlie Company of the 2nd Battalion fired back. In 10 minutes, six T-72 tanks, two lesser tanks, four armored personnel carriers and two other vehicles were shot up. American artillery fired to good effect. Attack helicopters joined the fray. Iraqi tanks and armored personnel carriers littered the desert. There was no question the Iraqis fired first, but what happened next was a metaphor for the fog of war.

About 40 minutes after the firing had stopped, Barry McCaffery, commanding general of the 24th Division, concluded the Iraqi column posed a threat to his forces. The Iraqis hadn't yet announced they had agreed to a cease fire. If they turned to fight, McCaffery didn't want to be caught flat-footed. He ordered a company of Apache attack helicopters to assault the vehicles on the causeway, which had been recently repaired after it was knocked out during the air campaign. One helicopter fired at the head of the column and hit an ammo truck. Ammunition cooked off for hours. More helicopters attacked the stationary column as Iraqis ran for their lives to the safety of the marshes.

Meanwhile, the 24th Division positioned two infantry battalions in blocking positions to prohibit any Iraqi force from approaching its lines. Another force, the 4th Battalion of the 64th Armored Regiment, maneuvered around the Iraqi column and opened fire. All hell broke loose.

The shooting lasted for five hours in an engagement area ten miles long and six miles wide. Sealed off by artillery and Apaches, the Iraqis were trapped in a kill sack. Among the Iraqi losses were 81 tanks, 95 armored personnel carriers, five artillery tubes, eleven missile launchers and 23 trucks. One American tank was damaged because it was too close to a burning Iraqi tank, but there were no U.S. casualties. Afterwards, an anonymous letter was sent to Army investigators, contending that McCaffery's orders to fire upon a retreating column amounted to war crimes. An Army investigation exonerated the general. But in May of 2000, journalist Seymour Hersh, writing for the New Yorker magazine, called it a massacre. Among those quoted by Hersh was James H. Johnson Jr., commander of the 82nd Airborne Division, who said: "There was no need to be shooting anybody. They couldn't surrender fast enough. The war was over."

The engagement was variously called the Battle of the Causeway or the Battle of the Junkyard, because so many Iraqi vehicles were destroyed. Another name for it was the Battle of Rumaila, a patch of ground on the border between Iraq and Kuwait. Rumaila sat atop an enormous reservoir of oil that was shaped like a giant banana. The underground cache of crude was primarily in southern Iraq but brushed up against the western border of Kuwait. Both countries were eager to tap its riches. To extract their share, the Kuwaitis drilled down and at a western angle. Saddam Hussein openly challenged the technique of slant drilling and cited Rumaila as one reason he invaded Kuwait in the first place. The place of the war's origins had become the site of the last engagement after Desert Storm was supposed to be over.

Saturday, March 2. The no-frills waiting room off the airstrip at King Khalid Military City, a.k.a. Emerald City, is filled with soldiers waiting for a military flight back to Dhahran. I have been separated from the Airborne and feel like I'm in a trance. Desert dust still covers my parka, but my bootprints in the sand have probably vanished by now.

Boarding call was announced. Like the 33 other passengers who took their seats aboard the military transport, I was buckled in and ready to roll. Then crewmen loaded the final traveler, the body of a dead U.S. soldier locked inside a metal coffin. The box was clamped down right in front of me. Try as I might to ignore it, or wish in vain that I was seated somewhere else, I couldn't help but stare.

Who are you? How did you die? Was it a bullet, a land mine, friendly fire? Do you have a wife and kids back in the States that will never see you again? Do you think this war was too short? Do you feel left out? Was it worth the price you paid?

Another moment of clarity hit home. You look for it, and look for it, and look for it, then when you find out what war is really about, you wish you had never heard of it. How could I stress over not going all the way to Baghdad, or fret over not being witness to some climactic battle, when I was going home alive and this poor soul was going back in a box? War is a seductive mistress. You fall in love with it, but when you see it up close, it's an ugly bitch of death, destruction and danger. I asked for forgiveness and began the process of making peace with it. The occupant of the coffin would have gladly traded places with me. After riding in a plane with an American soldier killed on the same battlefield I was on, how could I ever have a bad day again? Every day from now on would be gravy.

That surreal flight landed in Dhahran about an hour before midnight. A military van provided transportation back to the hotel. It had been transformed too. In the ornate lobby was the wreckage of a Scud missile that had been shot out of the sky. Nearby, a hand-written sign warned journalists not to bring back live ammo from the field because somebody showed up with a live grenade as a souvenir. Like what kind of Cherry would do something that stupid?

First stop was the AP office to see if they needed anything. Nope, said David Crary, the editor on duty. All the stories for the Sunday news cycle had been filed, including the one about what all the individual units did during the ground war. Then he said something that made my heart sink.

"We thought you got lost out there," Crary said.

Lost? Actually, I was found. But did he mean I was out there all that time as nothing more than a voice in the desert? Had any of the pool reports even made it back? Even if they had, everything was under operational security anyway. He suggested I write it up when I got back to New York.

After getting the key to Room 132, I stood under the shower and let the hot water run for an hour. Hacking and coughing, and still feeling groggy, I never did feel clean. My emotional baggage streamed down the drain in tandem with the beads of water.

Just as my head hit a real pillow and I tried to get used to a real mattress, a knock came at the door. It was Sophia.

CHAPTER 41
One More Hill To Climb

The Do Not Disturb sign stayed on my door for 48 hours. My memory of it is hazy, but Sophia says we've done it nine times in two days, a personal record. The only breaks were for chicken soup and meals delivered through room service. I do remember her saying at one point: "Gee, if you can't do it this often all the time, I'll begin to think something is wrong in the relationship." She had already gotten a media credential from the new Kuwaiti desk in the Joint Information Bureau, the first step in going up north to pursue some follow-up stories and to see the burning oil wells. She asked me to join her. "We can cover the story by day and sleep under the stars at night, rubbing our bodies together to start a fire," she said. I went through the process of getting a Kuwait credential but said it would depend on whether I flew home with the 82nd Airborne.

Coverage of the March 3 cease-fire ceremony in the Iraqi town of Safwan was left to others. For all I knew, it was a formality to end a war that ended with a lopsided victory by the U.S.-led coalition. But wars are easier to get into than they are to end.

Given the benefit of hindsight, the selection of Safwan was problematic. Thought was originally given to having the ceremony on *USS Missouri*, the battleship that had shelled Iraqi forces during the war and which was the floating armory used to accept Japan's formal surrender at the conclusion of World War II. The Saudis balked at the choice, however, because a ceremony aboard a U.S. warship would make it seem like the war had been solely an American affair. Besides, it would take days to make preparations to get all the parties together and transport them to the ship. Other sites were considered and rejected, mostly for security reasons, before Safwan was chosen. Located three miles north of the border with Kuwait, the town sat at a road junction. The one running east to west led to Basra from the Gulf port city of Umm Qasr, said to be the site of Alexander The Great's landing in Mesopotamia in 325 B.C. The road running north to south had been used by the Iraqi army in its invasion of Iraq. And from the hills around Safwan, Iraq had launched Scud missiles at Dhahran. There was one glaring hitch, however. Although situation maps in Riyadh showed Safwan was in American hands, it was still occupied by an Iraqi force. U.S. helicopters had flown over Safwan and reported no military activity, but there were no American boots on the ground, and unless you put some boots on it, you don't own it.

To secure Safwan, elements of the 1st Infantry Division saddled up again after being ordered to stop offensive operations. The Second Brigade, or Dagger Brigade, drove ten miles north to confront the Iraqi commander whose tanks occupied the hills surrounding the town.

"If you don't leave, we will kill you," Colonel Tony Moreno, commander of the Second Brigade, told the Iraqis.

They left, but the process had caused a delay of a full day.

The two-hour ceremony began at 11:30 a.m. inside a 12-foot high tent, but only after everyone on both sides was searched for weapons. Norman Schwarzkopf and Saudi Arabia's Khalid bin Sultan, the co-commanders of coalition forces, sat at a simple rectangular wooden table. In the tent with them were generals representing Britain, France, Italy, Canada, Kuwait, Egypt, Syria and other members of the coalition. Representing Iraq were Lieutenant General Sultan Hashim Ahmad, the deputy chief of staff of the Ministry of Defense, and Lieutenant General Salah Abud Mahmud, commander of an Iraqi corps that had been wiped out as a fighting force. The White House said that they were of sufficient rank to speak on behalf of Iraq.

The Iraqi delegation never signed a document ending hostilities. No such document was ever drawn up. Surrender was never mentioned. There was no talk of dethroning Saddam Hussein. The two Iraqi generals merely gave their word they would abide by United Nations Resolution 686, which had been adopted the previous day. It called for a cease fire, the release of prisoners under the direction of the Red Cross and the return of the remains of the dead. Iraq agreed to free 41 prisoners of war from the coalition side, including 17 Americans, but no accounting was made about the remains of Scott Speicher, the Navy pilot shot down on the first day of the air war. The number of Iraqi POWs was about 80,000.

The only point of contention was raised by General Khalid, who asked for an accounting of Kuwaiti civilians who had been taken to Iraq during the war. Assurances were made that anyone who had come to Iraq since the invasion of Kuwait would be free to approach the Red Cross and leave if they wanted.

Then the Iraqis brought up a separate matter. Because their roads and bridges had been obliterated during the air campaign, they asked permission to fly their helicopters inside Iraq. In making the request, they said officials of their government required transportation, and in some cases, the helicopters providing transportation would be gunships. Schwarzkopf had insisted that he was not prepared to give the Iraqis anything after such a convincing victory on the battlefield, but he approved the request.

"From our side, we will not attack any helicopters inside Iraq," Schwarzkopf said.

In reality, however, Iraq used some of those helicopter gunships to suppress rebellions by the Shiites and Kurds. Schwarzkopf later said he got "snookered."

To conclude the ceremony, the delegations saluted and shook hands. Then Schwarzkopf mingled with the soldiers of the 1st Infantry Division. He shook hands, signed autographs and mugged for photographs before the flight back to Riyadh.

"For the first time, I had a sense, not of triumph, not of glory, but of relief... It really is over," Schwarzkopf later wrote in his autobiography.

Before he left Safwan, General Khalid answered questions from the media. When asked if peace had been achieved, Khalid answered in the affirmative and removed his Kevlar.

"I take off my war helmet and put on my peacetime cap," Khalid said.

Only much, much later did the Saudi prince say that some loose ends bothered him. He wasn't consulted about the Iraqi request to use helicopters, and he felt that the matter of Kuwaiti civilians held by the Iraqis was unresolved. He remained silent at the time because he didn't want to disagree publicly with Schwarzkopf. Later, in his book *Desert Warrior*, the commander of the Joint

Forces said Safwan was a failure.

"I had a sense of anticlimax," Khalid wrote. "No document of any sort had been signed by the Iraqis, let alone a document of surrender. Very little of substance had been achieved — save by the Iraqis in securing the freedom to fly their gunships. It was a strangely fluid and uncertain way to bring to a close a war, which on the battlefield had been so decisive. It was as if, watching a great movie in a theater, one gears oneself up expectantly for a grand finale, only to be let down by a feeble, unconvincing ending. Safwan, I felt, was a mistake."

In Washington, President Bush declared: "By God, we've kicked the Vietnam syndrome once and for all." Defining that syndrome is open to interpretation. I took it to mean that if given a just and doable mission supported by the world and our allies, if military planners and not politicians prosecute the battles, if the American public supports the effort, if the foe wears uniforms and fights on a battlefield, if we get in and get out without getting bogged down in the quicksand of trouble spots, if our warriors are given every resource they need to fight, if the Air Force and the Navy and the Marines and the Army fight in a coordinated effort that accomplishes the mission with speed and decisiveness, the grief will be minimal.

In Baghdad, Saddam Hussein declared victory for having survived and having remained in power. For him, the war was merely the opening phase of the Mother of Battles.

March 6. Major Ennis appeared at the hotel to say my request to fly back to Fort Bragg had been approved. He said to pack one bag and be ready, discreetly, by four o'clock the next afternoon. Those in charge of the AP office thought it was an excellent idea that would produce a meaningful homecoming story, but it also meant I wouldn't be going to Kuwait. All my non-essentials were packed in a box to be shipped home separately as commercial freight. All the outstanding bills for my hotel room and rental car were turned over to the accountants. In my safety deposit box was $2,000 in cash from my initial advance, and I put that in my wallet for the return journey.

In the morning, I walked Sophia to a bus bound for Kuwait and said goodbye. It's the life of a journalist to follow the stories assigned to them. A messy scene was avoided. She went her way. I was going mine. Wartime romance, fanned by the unique forces that exist only when people are thrown together in times of intense drama, had no chance of making the transition to the real world anyway. We stayed in touch for a time, but it was never the same. How could it be? The war had changed us both.

When Major Ennis came to get me, we exited the hotel via the back steps. I barely had time for one last look over my shoulder at what had been home. A short drive later to an assembly area near the airport, hundreds of paratroopers were waiting to be processed out. I was the only one in civilian clothes.

"Who's the pogue?" one of them said.

Among those headed home was Lieutenant Colonel John Vines, commander of the 4th Battalion. Having been first into the kingdom and into Iraq, the battalion would be among the first units sent home. He talked about the experience.

"A lot of guys have a different perspective on life now," Vines said. "I told the men it wasn't going to be like Panama, and I was right. The Panamanians fought."

He laughed at his own joke before turning serious again.

"The predominant feeling is one of relief, but you can't forget about the good soldiers who aren't coming home. There is always a price," Vines said.

We then spent some time in a dormitory-style building known as Khobar Towers, which was originally built as winter quarters for Bedouins. I stretched out on the cold floor, listening to the chatter.

Major John Little, the division's transportation officer, lent me a sleep shirt for warmth. "It's going to be like a tornado going through Bragg. I'd walk home if I had to," Little said.

The conversation wasn't about celebration. Most paratroopers hadn't fired their weapons, which was all right with them, and most of the combat in their sector occurred over long distances. Mostly, they talked about how much they appreciated the freedoms of being an American, about never taking for granted the things that mattered most because those things can be taken away so fast.

"We actually felt sorry for the Iraqi soldiers. They were just up against it. There was only one evil guy," said Sergeant First Class Gary Hammond, 38, of Fayetteville. "People back home are going to ask, 'Did you jump into Kuwait?' And I'll say, 'Well, I really can't talk about it. It's classified. It brings back too many memories... Of MREs.' " He laughed at the thought.

Things had come full circle for Master Sergeant David Leary, 35, the non-commissioned officer in charge of coordinating airplane transportation for the 82nd Airborne. A part of the Panama operation who was presented a Bronze Star by Dick Cheney, he had also been on the first plane to Saudi Arabia, arriving with camouflage paint on his face, locked and loaded. Now he was eager to resume his life.

"My wife left the Christmas tree up. I just want to go back and relax," Leary said. "Truthfully, the war has changed me in lots of ways. It's unfortunate it had to come to this. I feel sorry for the soldiers that were killed. Think of the lives that were wasted because of this one man. I never thought one person could be so stubborn."

How had he changed?

"You pray a little bit more. You think back about your life, the screw-ups you've made, things you should have handled differently. It's given me a better perspective," he said.

I could relate.

"My worst nightmare as a soldier was a long war," Leary continued. "I've got so many plans I don't know what to do first. I got a tee time for Sunday. Well, first we have to account for everything we brought over and turn in our gear. That's the way the 82nd is. We're always ready for war. I didn't fire a bullet, but I couldn't have been more prepared. We believe in the team effort. Nobody wanted to kill."

Sergeant First Class Sal Elguera, 33, of San Diego said it felt like part of him was still out in the desert.

"I don't think I can sleep in a soft bed. I'm used to sleeping on the ground. When I get home, I might take off the covers and pillows and sleep on the floor," Elguera laughed. As an afterthought, he added: "You know, if we wanted to, we could have killed them all." There was relief in his voice that it wasn't necessary.

Word finally came to board trucks to an out-processing station. I was jammed in among the rucksacks. Written in chalk on the tailgate was, "Kuwait is Free. Let's Go Home!" A formation was called at four o'clock in the afternoon. We had to stand in line to go through a customs checkpoint. A sign said live ammo was prohibited.

At the airport, Sergeant Major Charles Terrian, 39, of Fayetteville, was in charge of getting us on the plane.

"I feel like Dorothy in the Wizard of Oz. There's no place like home. There's no place like home. I wish we could click our heels together and just get there," he said.

Terrian said what he missed most was his toddler son, who he called his shadow. For him, this homecoming was twenty years in the making.

"I think of this as my coming home from Vietnam. The people are making up for it. To me, it healed a lot of wounds. At least now I can go back home and wear my uniform proudly. Coming home from Vietnam, I took it off," Terrian said.

The officer with the highest rank on the flight was Brigadier General Bernie Timmons, 48, of McLean, Virginia. As the assistant division commander, he had been on the first plane over. A veteran of two tours in Vietnam, he expressed a feeling of tremendous satisfaction in leading his paratroopers home.

"We were President Bush's line in the sand. In August, 3,000 paratroopers were here by themselves. Those were some uncertain moments," Timmons said.

What was going through his mind?

"This war will be remembered not so much for the intensity of combat, which was relatively lopsided, but for the professional excellence of the U.S. military. This time, the president turned the fight over to the military. We have validated what we said we were going to do. We rebuilt the Army and proved our soldiers have no equal. Think of all those prisoners we took. Everybody thought we were going to kill them. They expected a bullet in the head."

Had the war changed him?

"It can change a man very quickly. These men came here because they wanted to do their duty. They came of age in terms of what an army does in the field day in and day out. It is very, very dangerous stuff. They appreciated the burden of responsibility. They all grew up," Timmons said.

I called the office to dictate a story and had barely hung up when up went a cheer of "Hoo-ah!" Boarding time had arrived. Soldiers formed double lines to climb the steps into the passenger compartment of a 372-seat Northwest Airlines L1011. Civilian flight attendants wore yellow ribbons and big smiles. Kevlar, rucksacks and rifles were stored in overhead compartments. The plane was fully loaded at 10:15, but it didn't leave the gate until 38 minutes after midnight.

"It's always the way it is. Like when we're training, just when you think you can't stand it anymore, there's always another hill to climb or another mile to go," Major Ennis said.

The plane taxied for two miles to reach the head of the runway. From the flight deck came the announcement that we would be flying over the Red Sea on an eight-hour leg to an air base in Germany. Including layovers, the trip back to Fort Bragg would take 26 hours.

The jumbo jet gathered pace as it rumbled down the runway. Wheels up at one o'clock. Whoops and cheers filled the air. Paratroopers pumped their fists or gave a big thumbs up. "That's it. Goodbye, Saudi Arabia," someone yelled.

The 22 members of the flight crew did their best to make it a special occasion. Each of the crew had volunteered for this flight. They had pinned American flags on their uniforms, and they planned to wear the flags until every soldier deployed during the war came home.

"We begged to get these trips," said flight attendant Ann Sapa of Boston. "When we were bringing troops over before the war started, we promised them when we dropped them off that we'd be back to pick them up. I wish we could do more. I wish we could have had a party all the way home."

No booze was served. It didn't matter.

"We just want to show our men and women we are extremely proud of what they did," said Jerry Cymove of Oklahoma City, a member of the flight crew. "They're heroes to me. I just did not want Vietnam repeated."

The chief flight attendant was Dennis Tepler, of St. Paul, Minnesota. During Vietnam, his brother had flown missions aboard a B-52. Over the plane's intercom, he paid tribute to the paratroopers, and more than one had a lump in his throat.

"Thank you. Each and every one of you, thank you for upholding the American values of justice and peace. You have our utmost respect and gratitude. God bless you all," Tepler said.

We landed at dawn, local time, at Ramstein Air Force Base in Frankfurt, Germany. The hangar was adorned with giant banners and patriotic tributes. "Welcome Back. We're Proud of You," one said. A four-hour wait was required for servicing the plane and bringing aboard a fresh flight crew for the hop across the pond. The Red Cross supplied razors and toothbrushes. AT&T had set up a bank of phones to call home for free. After all the troops made their calls, I phoned the AP office in New York with an update. Then I stared at the wall a lot.

Finally, we were back in the air. A familiar face occupied one of the seats. He was Keith Nobles, the combat engineer who had blown up bunkers on the first day of the war.

"Hey, I remember you. You were out there with us," he said.

What was he thinking about now?

"Sex, sex, sex and more sex. Put this in your story. Paratrooper survives war but dies from over sex," Nobles laughed.

I could relate to that too.

A flight across an ocean later, an announcement came from the flight deck. "In case anyone is interested, that coastline you see is Maine. You're back in the States," he said.

The first glimpse of America in seven months came from the window of a jet. There were toothy grins, misty eyes and lumps in the throat at the site of frozen lakes and a snowy landscape.

"Yesssssss!" someone yelled. "Anyone want to jump?"

Instead of flying right down the coast to North Carolina, we landed at JFK Airport, where I had departed for the war five months earlier. All I had to do was walk off the plane, and I'd have a short cab ride to my apartment, but I was determined to go all the way. These guys took me to war and brought me home, and the way home was through Fort Bragg. But first, a surprise reception awaited.

With sirens blaring, four New York City fire engines turned on their hoses as a salute. Police cars with lights flashing provided an escort to the gate. The Airborne got off the plane to receive an unabashed outpouring of patriotism. A military band played *New York, New York*. Mayor David Dinkins had come to personally welcome home the troops. America loves winners. The country was exorcising the demons of how the home front acted when troops returned from Vietnam.

"It makes you feel like the days we sweated it out in the desert wondering what our future would be are all worthwhile. This makes it all worth it," said Major John Little.

Staff Sergeant Dennis Wood, 27, Savannah, Georgia, found it a bit overwhelming. He had fired the first artillery round into Iraq in support of the Second Brigade, and now he was being greeted as a hero at home. "This is our reward. It puts an end to it," he beamed.

Someone noted it was March 8, seven months to the day that the Second Brigade began moving troops to Saudi Arabia. That was a lifetime ago. Soda pop and pizza were set out for the troops. Mayor Dinkins autographed their Kevlar.

"This is what I joined the Army for," said Private First Class Todd Meyer, 21, of Huntington Beach, California. "We're making history. Hopefully, this will tell other nations not to mess around with us anymore."

Major Ennis was interviewed by a local reporter. Asked what he was going to do first, he smiled: "I'm going to put a lip-lock on my wife."

I broke away to dictate an update to my news desk from an unused bank of pay phones in the gate area. Before I could dial, an Army warrant officer who played clarinet in the welcoming band started giving me a raft of shit.

"The phones are for the soldiers," he lectured.

Flaring up was the same rage that made me to throw my Kevlar against the Humvee tailgate on the battlefield inside Iraq. I know what I wanted to tell him. *Look, you mother-fucking pogue. I just spent the last five months of my life taking orders from people about what I could and couldn't do. I went to war with these guys to tell their story. Crossed the line of departure into an enemy's country. Dug my own grave. Swallowed nerve gas pills and wore a chemical suit. Got sick as a fucking dog. Found myself in a minefield after the war was over. And you're going to tell me I can't use a public pay phone in New York City in the United States of America? My brother got spit on after he got his ass shot up in Vietnam, and you're trying to spit on me now. Say one more word, you cherry-ass REMF, and I will rip off your head and shit down your neck!"*

In reality, and using as civil a tone as I could muster, I showed him my media credentials and explained that I was with the 82nd Airborne during the war. The phone I held was unused because all of the troops had called home during our stop in Germany. As soon as I dial my office, the nation and the world will know that the 82nd Airborne has come home to a hero's welcome.

He backed off, and I did my job. When I rejoined the group to board the plane for the flight to Bragg, the paratroopers were amused.

"Tell him, Bedouin Bob," Major Ennis said. "You have more time in a foxhole than he has behind that clarinet."

Why telling this story was so hard was beyond me, but white-hot rage must make a flight seem shorter. In no time, we were flying over the familiar pine trees and sandhills of North Carolina. Under gray skies, the plane came to a stop on the tarmac at Pope Airfield, just off the Green Ramp leading into Fort Bragg.

There wasn't a mad dash to the doors. No one departed the plane and ran into the waiting arms of loved ones, not in the spit-and-polish 82nd Airborne. When paratroopers descended the steps, they formed up, four abreast. With General Timmons leading them, they marched in formation toward a reviewing stand and a set of bleachers. I didn't know where to stand, so I tagged along off to the side, walking out of step.

When the troop formation stopped, the paratroopers stood ramrod straight at attention. *All the way, sir!* Timmons saluted them and issued his final order of Desert Storm: "Dismissed!"

Mission accomplished, the paratroopers were free to seek out the friends and family who had gathered to greet their conquering heroes. Tearful reunions came in clusters. It was a red, white and blue reception augmented by yellow ribbons. I had never seen happier people in my life. This is what a welcome home should be like for any warrior in any war.

Sunday, March 10. I woke up in a Fayetteville hotel room, trying to figure out where the fuck I was. The last thing I remember was sipping a Heineken, my first beer in months, at the NCO Club. I had slept in my clothes. I had no memory of checking in.

Major Ennis swung by. He and his family invited me to services at the Snyder Memorial Baptist Church. In the church lobby, yellows stars were put up for each member of the congregation who had deployed. At one point in the service, returning paratroopers were asked to stand and be recognized. Major Ennis and his brothers in arms were applauded. The congregants sang in their honor, "Stand up, stand up for Jesus, ye soldiers of the cross." They also sang the major's favorite hymn, *Count Your Blessings.*

"I wish every soldier gets the same kind of reception. I want the last soldier to come home to get as good a reception as the first," Major Ennis said.

The Reverend Sandy Saunders spoke from the pulpit.

"We pray for the loved ones who won't be coming back, for those killed in defense of that small little country, Kuwait. There is joy in our hearts for those returning. There is sadness in theirs. We will not forget," the reverend said.

As circumstances would have it, Fayetteville had scheduled a parade that day.

"It started out as a show of support, but the war ended so fast it's become a victory celebration for us," said Mayor J.L. Dawkins.

He called it the biggest moment in American history since World War II.

"We felt these men and women deserved our total support. We asked them to do a job, and they did a fantastic job. They wouldn't let us win in Korea. They wouldn't let us win in Vietnam," Dawkins said. "But we must not forget those who paid the ultimate price. We have to keep those families in our prayers. There's no greater sacrifice a human being can make than to lay down his life for our country."

The parade started at one o'clock. A smattering of snow flakes drifted on the wind. In overcoat weather, paratroopers fresh from the desert rode like celebrities in convertibles as the crowds cheered.

Not far from a parade honoring returning heroes, however, a solemn ceremony was held in another part of Fayetteville. While the 82nd Airborne had been mercifully spared any loss of life in combat, other units based at Fort Bragg buried their dead. Among them was Sergeant First Class Russell Griffin Smith Jr., 44, a member of Alpha Company, 37th Battalion, 20th Engineer Brigade (Combat) (Airborne). It was the unit I had spent Christmas Day with, and I wondered if I had met him. Griffin was one of the engineers killed clearing unexploded ordnance at the As-Salman airstrip. I had chewed some of the same dirt as him. Now, far from the rock and sand of Iraq where he was killed, he was laid to rest in the sandy loam of North Carolina.

Surrounded by chilly mourners in overcoats, Smith's wife, Patricia, sat in a wheelchair. Next to her was his mother, Louise Breton of Fall River, Massachusetts. His four children sat on metal folding chairs. An honor guard of seven white-gloved riflemen, wearing their distinctive Airborne berets and spit-shined jump boots, fired three volleys each for a 21-gun salute.

In the lengthening shadows, Sergeant First Class Eric E. Sever, a bugler from the 82nd Airborne Division band, played *Taps* as teardrops streamed down cheeks. Then the American flag was removed from the gunmetal gray casket and folded with precise military movements. It was presented to Smith's widow with the thanks of a grateful nation. Four family members placed a red rose on Smith's casket. After a 30-minute ceremony, the mourners filed silently away to their cars.

American casualties had been light — fewer than 150 killed in action and about the same number killed in accidents. For those who perished, however, the war was the end of the world.

CHAPTER 42
Dead On Arrival

Monday, March 11. No discharge papers had been signed. No formal dismissal from Fort Bragg was arranged. I just checked out of the hotel and caught a commercial flight home. A notice into the investigation of my death was tacked to my apartment door. Consolidated Edison, the giant New York power company, left a letter saying it had asked the landlord to open the apartment to see if I had passed away because no electricity had been used for five months. Everything had been shut off, including the refrigerator, and I had been off the power grid. It happens more than people think in New York City. So many people live alone that the only clue that they're gone is absence of activity on the electric bill, and the power company suspected that I had checked out. Not that a ticker-tape parade had been anticipated, but this morbid welcome reception produced a laugh. If only they had known how close to the truth they were. At least somebody had missed me. The office has been alerted that I'm coming in tomorrow. The last journal entry is nigh. I'll be glad to end it.

Given that I was ten days removed from the battlefield and hadn't ridden the subway in five months, the morning commute was an exercise in culture shock. Walking to the station, I looked up at a construction site to see "82nd Airborne - All The Way" written in chalk on the top steel beam. My neighborhood had supported the troops I was with. Squeezing onto the train was an adventure. I just wasn't used to being underground or being surrounded by many people in such tight quarters. The subway odors told me I was back home. But in addition to feeling claustrophobic, I was hyper alert, looking around for land mines, sniper nests and possible ambush sites. Strap-hangers scanned newspapers or looked down at the floor. I kept a tight grip on my pack containing my notebooks and the jar of dirt, trying to adjust to wearing a necktie for the first time in forever.

Fresh from the middle of nowhere, I was back at the crossroads of the universe. Millions of people scurried to go to work. At the office, my desk was adorned with yellow ribbons and balloons. Faces I hadn't seen in a while drifted back with all kinds of questions. They had known me as Bobby Deadline. Now I was Bedouin Bob.

How was it? Were you ever in danger? Where did you sleep? What did you eat?

"There were only about five or six times when I thought I might die. I dug my own grave and slept in a foxhole. I was actually at the very front of the battle one day, watching A-10s taking out tanks. I was taking these nerve gas pills and putting on a gas mask when the alarms sounded. I captured some Iraqi POWs. If you think MREs are bad, let me tell you what a field coffee tastes like. And I ended up in a minefield…"

Then the executive editor, the guy who had sent me to cover the war, motioned me into his office. Seated in a chair in front of his desk, I struggled to put into words what I had just gone through. "I got on a ground combat pool just like you asked me to and was with the 82nd Airborne. We were inside Iraq a day before the invasion. The only way to file stories from the desert was on a portable typewriter, but I was under operational security anyway and couldn't tell what was really going on —"

He cut me off.

"I have to bring you down from the mountain," he said.

I thought he was putting me on. I hadn't been around the caustic humor of a news room in a while.

"Mountain?" I replied. "I wasn't on a mountain. I was in the desert. I still have sand in my shoes. Really, the main thing was I couldn't say what was happening or exactly where I was, and even the pool reports that made it back didn't have any context —"

He interrupted me again.

"What? That? I was in a war. I was in a real war."

Boom! He had just killed my story without even listening to the post-action account. War teaches you to be alert for anything and to keep your head on a swivel. This blindside hit was so unexpected because it came from the guy who told me to keep a journal. Unsure how to react, I tried one last time. The biggest challenges for a reporter had been getting access to the troops and dealing with a military bureaucracy that censored the news. The things I went through weren't on TV or mentioned at the briefings, and there were things that happened that I didn't even know about. Now that I was back in the realm of freedom of the press, the inside story of the war could be told. How can you say it wasn't a real war unless you hear what it was like?

"Look, if you think I'm full of shit, you can tell me I'm full of shit," he said.

"You're full of shit," I answered.

With that, he got up and slammed the office door. Then he sat back down and did all the talking. How in the hell was this possible, I kept asking myself? After everything I had been through, after all the risks I took and the sacrifices I made to bird-dog the story, he dismissed it out of hand. An editor's job is to separate the wheat from the chaff and then print the chaff, but this was ridiculous. He might as well have spit on me too. One hallmark of insanity is the absence of reason, and reason just crashed and burned. After about an hour's worth of futility, he said he had work to do and suggested I should get back to work too. It's one of Murphy's Laws. If you have a personality conflict with someone who sits atop the chain of command, he has the personality and you have the conflict.

In a double daze as I walked back to my desk, my supervisor noticed the homecoming hadn't gone well. I tried to tell her about the disconnect of being on a combat pool in the desert without being able to write what was really happening. It was like being trapped inside a bubble. A story isn't a story unless it's told.

The news cycle, however, had moved on. Desert Storm was yesterday's news.

"Quit re-living the war, Bob" she said.

"It's not about re-living the war," I replied. "It's about a story I never got to tell."

Everything was so unequivocal during the war. Now it was as muddled up by editorial decisions as it was by politics. The Vietnam Syndrome was supposed to be kicked once and for all, but there's always the five percent that don't get the word. AP correspondent Mark Kellogg was killed at the Little Bighorn before he could write about Custer's last engagement. Ernie Pyle was killed in one of the last battles of World War II before he could write his final chapter. Is it more merciful to be killed by the last bullet of the last war instead of dealing with a blockheaded boss? Cripes, I felt more like Gomer Pyle than Ernie Pyle. If they were going to do it this way, why didn't they cover the war over the phone?

The yellow ribbons at my desk were torn down pitched in the nearest garbage can. I was going to trash my journal too, but something stopped me. My life-changing adventure may not have meant anything to the people who sent me off to do it, but nobody could take it away from me either. How would anybody know what it took to win the war if nobody ever heard about Abqaig, Rahfa or As-Salman? Who would know or remember the names of those who fought? It was my story now, and my responsibility to write.

EPILOGUE
Just A Thing

The paddle-wheeler Mississippi Queen, a symbol of a bygone era, churned its way up the Ohio River at the leisurely pace of eight miles per hour. Being on the water was a balm for all those days in the Sand Box. Viewed from a rocking chair on the front deck of a boat, the forested hillsides and the warble of songbirds made for a soothing scene of an America at peace. Fresh green salads served at dinner were a special treat. So was sipping a cocktail that hadn't been smuggled. The vacation was as good a way as any to pick up my life as best I could.

On the stretch of river between Cincinnati and Pittsburgh, the boat made a port of call on an island that was part of West Virginia. In a booth among the tourists attractions and souvenir stands, a woman in a pioneer costume sold Desert Storm teddy bears made in the distinctive camouflage pattern of chocolate chips. While buying one, I volunteered that I had just returned from the war. She replied her son was over there too. He was Private First Class Scott Ramsey of Ripley, West Virginia, the "Mail God" from the Second Brigade of the 82nd Airborne who I had quoted in a war story. What a coincidence to have met a paratrooper on foreign sands and his mother peddling souvenirs on an island in an American river.

When I got back from the cruise, I phoned Scott Ramsey at Fort Bragg. He was already training for whatever mission might require the services of America's 9-1-1 response team. During the conversation, I asked him how he had processed Desert Storm.

"We have a saying in the Airborne. It's just a thing," Ripley said.

And there it was. It was just a thing. Don't mean nothing. A five-day truck ride. We'd have the rest of our lives to sort it out. All we could do was ante up, kick in and drive on.

For a story on Memorial Day of 1991, I spent some time in and around the southwestern Pennsylvania town of Greensburg, 30 miles east of Pittsburgh. Cities in other parts of the country were celebrating with ticker-tape parades.

The home of the 14th Quartermaster Detachment, struck by that Scud missile in Dhahran, was draped in black crepe.

The Scud had torn a gaping hole in Connie Clark's world in the tiny community of Armagh. She baked a birthday cake for her daughter, Beverly, who would have turned 24 on May 21 had she not died in the blast. It was a devastating loss for a mother who had put up yellow ribbons when her daughter deployed.

"I tore down all my ribbons. I just grabbed them and threw them in the garbage. The yellow ribbons didn't do anything for me," Mrs. Clark said. "She thought it was her duty to go, but my little soldier didn't come home."

In time, a gymnasium at Fort Lee, Virginia, was dedicated in honor of Specialist 4 Beverly Sue Clark. A training area at the U.S. Army Quartermaster Center and School at Fort Lee was also dedicated to the 14th Quartermaster Detachment. Members of the Clark family raised over $100,000 to endow a scholarship in her name at Indiana University of Pennsylvania.

At the armory in Greensburg that served as the unit's headquarters, a monument of black granite and bronze was erected, facing east, toward Saudi Arabia. Thirteen hemlock trees, the state tree of Pennsylvania, were planted in honor of those killed. Part of the money raised for the monument came from Vietnam veterans who thundered to the armory on their Harley-Davidson motorcycles to drop off their donations.

Under their tattered guide-on, the surviving members of the unit had returned home to a hero's welcome.

"For years, the world has known we give it our coal, our steel and our football players. Now it knows we also give it heroes," Westmoreland County commissioner Ted Simon said at a memorial service.

The survivors, however, struggled with the word.

"People call you a hero, but basically we didn't do anything. We were wasting time in a warehouse," said Lester Bennett, the banker from Johnstown who was a sergeant in the unit. "We didn't even have a mission. I think it was a foolish waste of life. A lot of us believed we had no reason to be there. We had no equipment, no mission. Why were we there? That Scud was like an attack on our entire community. Thirteen pieces of me died over there."

David Campbell also wrestled with the aftermath.

"I wasn't a hero. A hero is someone who rescues somebody from a burning building. I was just lying on my bunk," Campbell said. "But I darned sure don't want to forget the ones who lost their lives."

On White House stationery, President George Bush penned a letter to the families. "Your loved ones did not die in vain," the president wrote. "Selfless and willing to serve in the struggle against tyranny, they helped to lead not just Kuwait but the world into a new path of peace and freedom — a path paved with respect for the rule of law and for the unalienable rights of all mankind."

The grief that tore at the hearts of the community underscored that war, even the shortest one in American history, exacts a price. The family of Sergeant John T. Boxler, 44, of Johnstown was left with a void it could never fill.

"He's gone. You just keep looking for him to come home, and then you realize he's not. You just have to take it as it is," said his mother, Lydia Boxler, 70.

Boxler's children had no reason to attend the victory parade in his hometown of Johnstown.

"They felt they didn't have anything to be victorious about. It's not fair, but what can you do. Nothing's going to change the outcome. Nothing's going to bring him back," said Boxler's wife, Elaine.

Shirley Burton lost her only child, Specialist John Boliver. Boliver's wife and two children, aged two and one, lost their husband and father.

"It was like I was punched in the face. I will never, ever be called mom again. They should never have sent an only child to war. I have nightmares about it every night," Shirley Burton said.

Diane Radocaj, leader of the unit's Family Support Group, said there would be no such thing as closure.

"Everybody says the war is over. For us it isn't. It's something we're never going to get over. We're never going to have back the loved ones we lost," she said.

The war left its mark in other ways and in other places.

Within months of returning home, some who had deployed reported feeling ill. There were numerous, seemingly unrelated symptoms — fatigue, muscle pain, inability to concentrate, post traumatic stress, skin rashes and sexual dysfunction. Suspected causes included depleted uranium munitions, sarin gas, fumes from burning oil wells and combat stress. The constellation of disorders collectively became known as Gulf War Syndrome. One government study could not confirm or rule out the possibility that the pyridostigmine bromide pills were the cause. In trying to protect us from a nerve gas attack, they might have made us sick. Call it Murphy's Law of Unintended Consequences. About a quarter of a million of the 700,000 Americans who served in the war were afflicted. There are no unwounded soldiers in war.

In his autobiography Norman Schwarzkopf defended the decision to end the war without going to Baghdad. He said the coalition that had liberated Kuwait would have ruptured if America had gone on to Baghdad, and besides, there weren't any Jeffersonian statesmen in Iraq capable of creating a democracy.

"Had we taken all of Iraq, we would have been like the dinosaur in the tar pit — we would still be there, and we, not the United Nations, would be bearing the costs of that occupation. This is a burden I am sure the beleaguered American taxpayer would not have been happy to take on," Schwarzkopf wrote. "Emotionally, I would have loved to have gone to Baghdad and grabbed Saddam Hussein, but this was not an emotional decision, it was a strategic decision, and strategically, we were smart enough to win the war and win the peace."

Secretary of Defense Dick Cheney also rationalized the decision to leave Saddam Hussein in power but in check.

"And the question in my mind is how many additional American casualties is Saddam worth? And the answer is not very damned many. So I think we got it right, both when we decided to expel him from Kuwait, but also when the president made the decision that we'd achieved our objectives and we were not going to get bogged down in the problems of trying to take over and govern Iraq," Cheney said at a 1992 speech to the Discovery Institute in Seattle.

"All of a sudden you've got a battle you're fighting in a major built-up city, a lot of civilians are around, significant limitations on our ability to use our most effective technologies and techniques. Once we had him rounded up and gotten rid of his government, then the question is what do you put in its place? You know, you then have accepted the responsibility for governing Iraq," Cheney added.

"Now what kind of government are you going to establish? Is it going to be a Kurdish government, or a Shi'ia government, or a Sunni government, or maybe a government based on the old Ba'athist Party, or some mixture thereof? You will have, I think by that time, lost the support of the Arab coalition that was so crucial to our operations over there," Cheney said. "I would guess if we had gone in there, we would still have forces in Baghdad today, we'd be running the country. We would not be able to get everybody out and bring everybody home."

Desert Storm also proved that the failings in Vietnam were the result of flawed policy and not on the shoulders of those who were asked to fight. Robert McNamara, the secretary of defense who oversaw the escalation of that war, wrote a 1995 book called *In Retrospect: The Tragedy and Lessons of Vietnam.* "We were wrong, terribly wrong," he wrote. But his admission was too late for the 58,000 American dead whose names are etched on The Vietnam Veterans Memorial Wall. McNamara also said that real power is knowing when not to use it, and that some problems do not have military solutions.

H.R. McMaster, the cavalry officer whose troop devastated a Republican Guard formation at the Battle of 73 Easting, wrote the 1997 book *Dereliction of Duty*, which became required reading for military brass. McMaster faulted military leaders, particularly the Joint Chiefs of Staff, for failing to communicate their reservations over what President Lyndon Johnson and Robert McNamara were asking them to do by going to war.

"The war in Vietnam was not lost in the field, nor was it lost on the front pages of The New York Times or the college campuses. It was lost in Washington, D.C.," McMaster said. "The military engaged in a mutually deceitful relationship, in that they did not question a strategy that they knew to be fundamentally flawed and instead went along with the game."

Maybe we had finally learned our lessons. War is the most serious endeavor a nation can undertake. It's about killing and dying and blowing things up, and then caring for those harmed by it. Whatever glory there is in war belongs to those in the arena who serve with honor under hostile circumstances. America should be forever grateful that, from its infancy to the complications of the modern world, it can count on the 82nd Airborne and the U.S. military as a whole to defend it. American troops have no equal when they are properly led and are given a mission that is worthy of their sacrifice. For their sake, at the very least, war should only be fought when absolutely necessary and for the clearest of reasons. If war is unavoidable, it should be waged with overwhelming force to get it over with as quickly as possible. Anything less is a crime.

Wisdom could be found in the words of Lieutenant General Chuck Horner, the Air Force officer who commanded the Instant Thunder air operation during Desert Storm.

"They call it the Nintendo war. It loses sight of the fact that there's great suffering and death in war," said Horner, who wrote a book with Tom Clancy called *Every Man A Tiger.* "War doesn't work. The way to halt suffering is to get war over with as quickly and decisively as you possibly can. If you're going to enter into this adventure where you take human life, you have a moral obligation to get it over with as quickly as possible."

Meanwhile, I kept my foxhole promises, leaving the AP and New York to take a job with the Pittsburgh Post-Gazette. I ended up working in the sports department. At least when I got on a plane, I had a reasonable idea of what was waiting on the other end, and nobody was going to die, except maybe me.

On the tenth anniversary of the war, I wrote a letter to James Johnson, the now-retired general who led the 82nd Airborne into Saudi Arabia and Iraq. I don't know how to explain it, but I felt some sort of unbreakable bond with the unit. The only people who could relate to what I had been through were the paratroopers I was assigned to cover. The letter resulted in an invitation to attend a training exercise at Fort Bragg.

On Tuesday, October 3, 2000, a military plane loaded with paratroopers and observers approached a practice drop zone as part of a joint readiness training exercise. Some of the jumpers slept during the short flight. Others, flush with adrenaline, grinned and flashed thumbs up. John R. Vines, a battalion commander in Desert Storm, was now a two-star general who had just assumed command of the 82nd Airborne Division. When the word came for

Airborne personnel to stand up and hook up their rip cords
Vines was the first to stand in the door of a perfectly good airpl
120 knots about 1,200 feet off the ground. And when the green lig
Vines was the first paratrooper to put his knees in the breeze and fall
sky beneath the shrouds of his parachute.

The training jump showcased the Airborne's readiness for future missi
After landing and shedding their harnesses, troops formed up on the groun
for a mock assault that night on a fortified position. The Airborne was not im-
mune from the downsizing and cutbacks following Desert Storm. Its arsenal
no longer included a company of light tanks. It no longer had Apache attack
helicopters but relied on smaller OH-58 Kiowa gunships that carried less po-
tent weaponry. Some of the barracks were in disrepair and had leaky roofs, but
maintenance money had dried up. Nevertheless, the division was still on call
to go anywhere in the world within 18 hours of notification to take the fight to
any aggressor who threatened America or its vital interests.

When the order came to open fire against the mock target, two machine
guns set up in a classic crossfire position began spitting out rounds. From both
flanks came the sound of whispering death, the hissing rockets from the Kiowa
helicopters. Two A-10 Thunderbolts rolled in overhead, adding the unmistakable burp of their nose guns to the cacophony, as a platoon-sized force on the
ground assaulted a position that had been reduced to a smoldering ruin. The
show of choreographed force was at once beautiful, awesome, overwhelming,
deadly, hideous and stomach-turning.

"The 82nd Airborne has never failed the American people and never will,"
General Vines said at a briefing during the exercise. "It can draw a line in the
sand or bloody someone's nose. We can fight our way in from the sky, which
is something no other division can do. Our very existence is a deterrent to
aggression."

I recalled a line from George Orwell, who once wrote that we sleep safely
in our beds because rough men stand ready in the night to visit violence on
those who would do us harm. And I honestly thought that never again would
we be plagued by the toxic combination of arrogance of power and ignorance
of the consequences.

o a static line,
ane flying at
ht flashed,
from the
ns.

nection to the Airborne arrived in the inbox of
Jerry Henderson, who came across my name
ing research online. He asked if I was the
h the 82nd Airborne Division and had au-
a day in the life of an infantry company
ot that story had appeared in a newspaper, and
the Army, framed it and hung it on the wall of his of-
stablished contact, he invited me to a reunion of members of
Company, 2nd Battalion, 325th Parachute Infantry Regiment of the 82nd
Airborne Division. Twenty years after they had put their lives on the line for
each other in the First Iraq War, this band of brothers gathered again at the Fayetteville, North Carolina, home of First Sergeant Michael O'Neil. Although
we had only spent 24 hours together, that story from an independent witness
documented their service in the Sand Box. Over food and drink, we swapped
memories. When my turn came to speak, I said I hate war, but I love those who
volunteer to take the fight to the enemy. A toast was made to the most colorful
characters and the best soldiers I ever had the privilege to meet. A thousand
years from now, if the human race survives, historians will say that the 82nd
Airborne in particular and the U.S. military as a whole are the rightful succes-
sors to the legions of Rome as the most powerful fighting force ever. *Hoo-ah!*

Those men pitched in to create a plaque that certifies Bedouin Bob as an
honorary member of The Nasty Boys. It is my most cherished award.

All I wanted to do was live the rest of my life in peace, savoring every moment I spent with my granddaughters. Then came September 11, 2001. Yes,
it was absolutely necessary to bring to justice those responsible for attacking
America. But Osama bin Laden eluded capture in Afghanistan, and it was left
to another president to hunt him down, while the focus shifted to Saddam
Hussein, who had nothing to do with the terrorists who turned civilian jetliners
into guided weapons.

After promising myself that I would never get angry again, a white-hot
rage reignited during the course of the Second Iraq War when the search for

Saddam Hussein's weapons of mass destruction ended without any being found. The stated reason for returning to Iraq did not exist.

The Iraq Study Group, chaired by Karl Rove, built a case for regime change by creating the narrative that contended Saddam, the tyrant who talked like Mohammad Ali but fought like the Bayonne Bleeder, had a stockpile of weapons that threatened the United States. National Security Advisor Condoleeza Rice uttered a phrase that would be repeated again and again: "We don't want the smoking gun to be a mushroom cloud." Colin Powell, as secretary of state, went before the United Nations to say there was "solid evidence" that such weapons existed. Vice President Dick Cheney and Secretary of Defense Donald Rumsfeld joined the chorus.

Their folly was unmasked not by long-haired Hippy freaks, but by military officers more suited to carrying out orders than speaking up against the flawed decisions of their civilian masters. Joseph Hoar, a retired four-star Marine general who succeeded Norman Schwarzkopf as leader of Central Command, sounded a warning as the case was being made to return to Iraq: "When I was a young officer, my government miscalculated the nature of the war in Southeast Asia, and we paid the price. We're about to do that again in Iraq," Hoar told Congress.

Anthony Zinni, a retired Marine general who also once headed U.S. Central Command, co-authored a 2004 book called *Battle Ready* with Tom Clancy and noted: "In the lead up to the Iraq War and its later conduct, I saw at a minimum, true dereliction, negligence and irresponsibility, (and) at worse, lying, incompetence and corruption."

Another critic was John Batiste, a die-hard Republican who was senior military assistant to Deputy Defense Secretary Paul Wolfowitz in the Bush administration. Both of Batiste's grandfathers had served in the military, and his father was a career infantry officer. A West Point graduate, Batiste had commanded Army formations from platoons to divisions, including commanding the 1st Infantry Division in Operation Iraqi Freedom. But five months after he retired, he made a gut-wrenching decision that he called crossing his own line of departure. In a speech to the Rochester Rotary Club on April 4, 2006, Batiste said the Bush administration's decisions had in reality placed the nation in peril with a flawed policy and a bad war plan. "We got this war terribly wrong," Batiste said.

Haunting echoes of the past came in the words of William E. Odom, a retired three-star general who once served as head of Army intelligence and was former director of the National Security Agency under Ronald Reagan. A West Point graduate with a Ph.D. from Columbia, he taught at Yale University. In a February 11, 2007, op-ed piece in The Washington Post, Odom wrote that the Bush administration's policy was "based on illusions, not realities. There never has been any right way to invade and transform Iraq." The notion of creating a democracy in Iraq defied logic, Odom said, pointing out that the war had the unintended consequences of strengthening Iran and opening Iraq's doors to al-Qaeda, which did not have a presence in Iraq until Saddam was toppled. He predicted that Iraq would splinter into areas controlled by Sunni, Shiites and Kurds. And he saw ominous parallels to Vietnam, given that phony intelligence from the Tonkin Golf got America into a disastrous war in Vietnam, and phony intelligence about weapons of mass destruction got America into a war in Iraq.

In a speech at Brown University for the Watson Institute of International studies, Odom said, "The Iraq war may turn out to be the greatest strategic disaster in American history."

The most damning summation came from Greg Newbold, a three-star Marine general and former director of operations for the Joint Chiefs of Staff. He retired four months before the Iraq invasion because the rationale for war made no sense and because of his opposition "to those who had used 9/11's tragedy to hijack our security policy." But he didn't speak out publicly until he published an April 10, 2006, essay in Time magazine.

Newbold cited successive policy failures — the distortion of intelligence in the run-up to the war, not enough resources to secure Iraq, the decision to disband the Iraqi military and the initial denial that an insurgency had taken root.

"My sincere view is that commitment of our forces to this fight was done with a casualness and swagger that are the special province of those who have never had to execute these missions — or bury the results," Newbold said.

He was all for destroying al-Qaeda and giving the military a mission that was "as honorable as their sacrifice." But that was not what he saw.

"A fundamentally flawed plan was executed for an invented war, while pursuing the real enemy, Al Qaeda, became a secondary effort," Newbold said. "The cost of flawed leadership continues to be paid in blood."

Newbold regretted that he had not spoken out earlier. But he also said Congress should be held accountable as well as the news media, which acted more like a lapdog than a watchdog in failing to heed those who contested the Bush administration's strategy.

"We must never again stand by quietly while those ignorant of and casual about war lead us into another one and then mismanage the conduct of it," he said.

Newbold referenced the song *Won't Get Fooled Again* by the Vietnam-era rock group The Who.

"We have been fooled again," Newbold said.

Accordingly, in a piece clearly marked opinion and intended for the Forum section of the Pittsburgh Post-Gazette, I put my anger into words. I felt misled in every sense of the word by the Bush administration, and as a Vietnam-era veteran who had witnessed war in Desert Storm, I didn't like being misled. My inspiration was Henry David Thoreau, author of the essay *On Civil Disobedience,* who wrote that citizens in a democracy have a responsibility to speak out if they feel that something is wrong, lest they be complicit to the crime. Silence is consent. If Islamic militants who kill in the name of God wanted war, I say give them more than they could handle. But the politicians who took us to war talked like John Wayne and fought like Wayne's World. Decision-makers who should have learned lessons from the quagmire of Vietnam were now responsible for a debacle in Iraq.

The architects of the war blamed an intelligence failure. Roger that. There was definitely an intelligence failure. Like Dwight Eisenhower once said, "Wars are stupid, and they start stupidly." No war that is predicated on a false premise can have a good outcome. And the all-volunteer military, which found itself embroiled in a religious civil war, was being bled as it tried to build a nation out of chaos. Still, no matter what anyone tried to do to clean up this mess, they'd be better off trying to build a time machine that would have negated the fighting of an unnecessary war. For the second time in my life, the country I was brought up in fell apart and died. The Vietnam Syndrome had mutated into the Iraq Syndrome.

Two editors cleared the piece for publication, then sought clearance from the paper's top brass. The executive editor killed it. He said he didn't want his reporters writing opinion, which was bullshit because any number of reporters at the paper wrote opinion pieces from time to time. I had done so myself. If journalists can't express their views in something clearly marked opinion, who can?

"Do you have something against Thoreau? Or the First Amendment?" I asked him.

He said that a number of prominent Democrats had voted for the war.

"Lots of people voted for the Gulf of Tonkin Resolution too, before it was learned that a second attack on a U.S. warship never happened. In the chain of command, the one who gives the orders is the one to be held accountable."

My argument fell on deaf ears. The power exercised by an executive editor is not open to challenge. He was the same boss who told me after I had been bought out following a 46-year career in reporting and writing: "You didn't fail journalism. Journalism failed you."

No shit.

I would have liked to forget the whole mess, to "Chuck it in the Fuck-It Bucket, and drive on," as they say in the Airborne. And this was before anyone realized that the Second Iraq War created the conditions for the birth of the Islamic State, an off-shoot of al-Qaeda that aimed to establish an independent caliphate through a grisly campaign of terror and blood.

By the time of the 2016 presidential election cycle, the folly of going back to Iraq had been laid bare. Democratic presidential nominee

Hillary Clinton said her Senate vote in support of the war had been a mistake. Bernie Sanders, a Democrat who had voted against the war, called it "one of the biggest foreign policy mistakes in modern history." And Donald Trump, the Republican presidential nominee, chimed in: "The war in Iraq was a big, fat mistake. Going into Iraq may have been the worst decision…any president has made in the history of this country."

From where I sit, it wasn't a mistake. It was a crime. More than 4,000 of my brothers and sisters, including more than 100 members of the 82nd Airborne, were killed in that war. More than 32,000 were wounded. Others served multiple tours to do what they thought was right, and I have no problem whatsoever separating the warrior from the war. The national treasury was drained of trillions of dollars. Instead of building a democracy, we became entangled in a region where war was raged since the beginning of time in the cradle of conflict.

Who am I to stand up and call out the commander-in-chief and his crew for misleading the country into a foreign policy FUBAR? Well, who do you have to be?

Whatever. Surrender is not in my creed. The only way to drive on was to have the last word. My generation grew up never trusting anybody over 30, and now I don't trust anybody who hasn't crossed a line of departure. Even if I am a voice in the desert, even if nobody cares to listen, even if others have viewpoints different from mine, I did what I set out to do. I wrote.

BIBLIOGRAPHY

Personal Perspectives on the Gulf War. Arlington, VA: Assoc of U.S. Army, 1993. 106 p. DS79.74P47. Anthology of letters, diaries, etc.

Atkinson, Rick. Crusade: The Untold Story of the Persian Gulf War. Houghton Mifflin Company, Boston - New York. 559 p.

Caraccilo, Dominic J. The Ready Brigade of the 82nd Airborne in Desert Storm: A Combat Memoir. Jefferson, NC: McFarland, 1993. 211 p. #05-82-1993.

Carhart, Tom. Iron Soldiers. NY: Pocket, 1994. 325 p. #05-1AR-1994. 1st Armored Division.

Clancy, Tom with Horner, Chuck. Every Man A Tiger. NY: G.P. Putnam's Sons, 1999.

Clancy, Tom with Franks, Fred. Into The Storm: On The Ground in Iraq. NY: Berkley Books, 1997. 562 p.

Gingrich, John R. Battle For Safwan, Iraq. Student paper, AWC, Apr 1992. 44 p. Arch. 1 March 91 action of 2d Bde, 1st ID.

Khalid, Bin Sultan. Desert Warrior: A Personal View of the Gulf War by the Joint Forces Commander. NY: Harper, 1995. 495 p. DS79.74B56.

Kindsvatter, Peter S. VII Corps in the Gulf War: Ground Offensive. Military Review (Feb 1992).

Krause, Michael D. The Battle of 73 Easting, 26 Feb 1991: A Historical Introduction to a Simulation. Study, CMH & Def Adv Rsrch Projects Agency, Aug 1991. 61 p. DS79.72K72.

Moore, Molly. A Woman at War: Storming Kuwait with the U.S. Marines. NY: Scribner's, 1993. 336 p. DS79.74M66.

Scales, Robert H. Certain Victory: The U.S. Army in the Gulf War. VA: Brassey's Inc., 1993. 435 p.

Schwarzkopf, H. Norman, & Petre, Peter. It Doesn't Take A Hero. NY: Bantam, 1992. 525 p. E840.5S39A3.

Swain, Richard M. Lucky War: Third Army in Desert Storm. Ft Leavenworth: CGSC, 1994. 369 p. #03-3-1994.

ACKNOWLEDGMENTS

Special thanks to brigade commander Ron Rokosz and the Army's 82nd Airborne Division for allowing me to experience war at the foxhole level during Operation Desert Storm, and for bringing me home. Without a handshake of trust, this life-changing episode would never have happened. *Airborne All The Way*. Special thanks, too, to the team at Tactical 16 for giving voice to veterans. It's not a story unless it's told.

CREDITS AND CONTRIBUTORS

Publishing: Tactical 16, LLC
CEO, Tactical 16: Erik Shaw
President, Tactical 16: Jeremy Farnes
Cover Design: Kristen Shaw

ABOUT THE AUTHOR
Robert J. Dvorchak

Robert J. Dvorchak was a war correspondent assigned to Army Combat Pool No. 1 and the 82nd Airborne Division during Desert Storm. A former national writer based in New York City for The Associated Press, he worked as a journalist for more than 40 years and has authored five books, including *Battle For Korea*. He is also a U.S. Army veteran whose father served in the Navy during World War II and whose oldest brother served with the 11th Armored Cavalry Regiment during Vietnam. Inducted into the inaugural class of the Uniontown (Pa.) High School Hall of Fame, he has received several national, state and local writing awards. Now 67 and living in Pittsburgh, he is also married with two daughters and five granddaughters.

ABOUT THE PUBLISHER
Tactical 16, LLC

Tactical 16 is a Veteran owned and operated publishing company based in the beautiful mountain city of Colorado Springs, Colorado. What started as an idea among like-minded people has grown into reality.

Tactical 16 believes strongly in the healing power of writing, and provides opportunities for Veterans, Police, Firefighters, and EMTs to share their stories; striving to provide accessible and affordable publishing solutions that get the works of true American Heroes out to the world. We strive to make the writing and publication process as enjoyable and stress-free as possible.

As part of the process of healing and helping true American Heroes, we are honored to hear stories from all Veterans, Police Officers, Firefighters, EMTs and their spouses. Regardless of whether it's carrying a badge, fighting in a war zone or family at home keeping everything going, we know many have a story to tell.

At Tactical 16, we truly stand behind our mission to be "The Premier Publishing Resource for Guardians of Freedom."

We are a proud supporter of Our Country and its People, without which we would not be able to make Tactical 16 a reality.

How did Tactical 16 get its name? There are two parts to the name, "Tactical" and "16". Each has a different meaning. Tactical refers to the Armed Forces, Police, Fire, and Rescue communities or any group who loves, believes in, and supports Our Country. The "16" is the number of acres of the World Trade Center complex that was destroyed on that harrowing day of September 11, 2001. That day will be forever ingrained in the memories of many generations of Americans. But that day is also a reminder of the resolve of this Country's People and the courage, dedication, honor, and integrity of our Armed Forces, Police, Fire, and Rescue communities. Without Americans willing to risk their lives to defend and protect Our Country, we would not have the opportunities we have before us today.

Thanks to **Steel City Vets** for sponsoring this project.

Steel City Vets, Pittsburgh's first Post 9/11 Veterans support organization focusing on connecting Veterans, serves the over 50,000 Veterans of Afghanistan and Iraq that reside in the Greater Pittsburgh and South Western PA region. Through social activities, SCV aims to be a resource for Veterans through their transition from the military to civilian life.

Steel City Vets is a Veteran founded and run non-profit. For more information please visit their website at steelcityvets.org and connect with them on Facebook by visiting facebook.com/steelcityvets.

www.steelcityvets.org

CPSIA information can be obtained
at www.ICGtesting.com
Printed in the USA
BVOW10s0904180617

487187BV00017BA/804/P